The AMERICAN
HERITAGE
History of the
Making
of the Nation

1783-1860

The AMERICAN HERITAGE
History of the
Making
of the Nation

By the Editors of
AMERICAN HERITAGE
The Magazine of History

Editor in Charge
Ralph K. Andrist

Narrative
Francis Russell

Pictorial Commentary
Rex Lardner

AMERICAN HERITAGE/
BONANZA BOOKS
New York

EDITOR
Ralph K. Andrist

ART DIRECTOR
John J. Conley

COPY EDITOR
Joan Wilkinson

PICTURE EDITOR
Linda Silvestri Sykes

ASSISTANT EDITORS
Rex Lardner
Lynne Parsons
Susan Baker

EDITORIAL ASSISTANT
Margaret Christ

EUROPEAN BUREAU
Gertrudis Feliu, *Chief*
Mary Jenkins

PICTURE CREDITS. PAGE 1: NEW YORK HIS-
TORICAL SOCIETY; PAGES 2–3: MUSEUM OF
THE CITY OF NEW YORK; PAGES 4–5: *Dean's
Universal Penman*, 1808, LIBRARY OF
CONGRESS

This 1987 edition is published by
Bonanza Books, distributed by Crown
Publishers, Inc., 225 Park Avenue South,
New York, New York 10003, by arrange-
ment with American Heritage, a division
of Forbes Inc.

Manufactured in Hong Kong

Library of Congress Cataloging-in-
Publication Data

The American heritage history of the
  making of the nation.

  Includes index.
  1. United States—History—1783–1865.
I. Andrist, Ralph K. II. American
heritage.
E301.A495 1987   973   87-11620

ISBN 0-517-63167-9

h g f e d c b a

To commemorate the nation's past, Erastus Salisbury Field painted his Historical Monument of the American Republic, *a dazzling representation of the important figures and events from the colonial period up to his own time. Field hoped that one day the towering edifice—steam railway and all—would be constructed.*

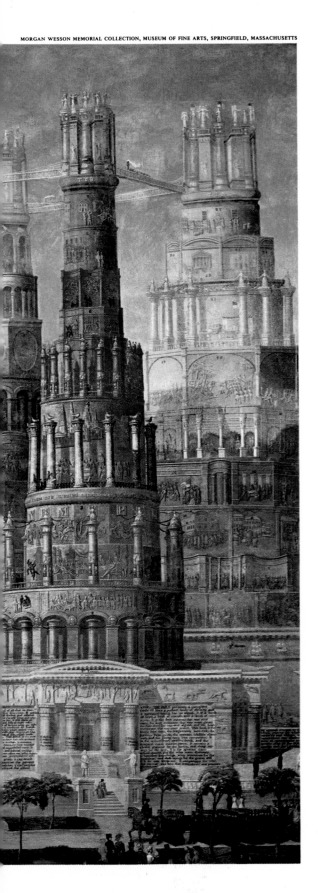

Introduction

Much of history is recorded in the epitaphs of nations that have perished because of their internal weaknesses and schisms. For when a people become more preoccupied with narrow self-interest and family quarrels than with their national good, they fall easy prey to the enemy outside their gates or crumble under the stresses and strains within.

For a time it appeared that the young American Republic would also be numbered among the states that had not been able to surmount their fatal divisive tendencies. As author Francis Russell brings his account on the following pages to a close, seven Southern states have seceded and others are about to take the same disastrous step, a man chosen by only a minority of the voters is on his way to be sworn in as President, and a beleaguered Army garrison in Fort Sumter is preparing to resist an expected attack. If this book had been published at that time, its editors would probably not have been thought unduly pessimistic if they had entitled it *The Death of a Nation*.

Yet the republic survived—and survives today. When its supreme ordeal came in 1861, it had developed inner strength and sinew stronger than the forces working to sunder it, strong enough to let it endure a sanguinary Civil War, strong enough so that its unity would never again be threatened. What enabled a young nation to prevail over cleavages caused by slavery, by sectional antagonisms, by economic rivalries? In part it was the wisdom—with some intuition—of the Founding Fathers in creating a Constitution that defined workably the intricate relationships among citizen, state, and federal government. In part it was an instinctive feeling that the freedom Americans had won together was indivisible. And in part it was a complex of shared experiences: frontiers pushed forward, roads and canals built, redoubts stormed, industries established. This was the glue that in time bound the country together. How it came about in three-quarters of a century is the story related on the following pages.

The Editors

The New Nation

The ramshackle toll bridge across the Schuylkill at Gray's Garden outside Philadelphia was owned by the brothers G. and R. Gray, and in honor of its passage by the first President of the United States the brothers had concealed the rickety sides with cedar branches and erected a laurel arch at either end. A row of banners fluttered along the bridge's north side—one for each of the eleven states that had ratified the Constitution—while the flag of the American Union stood alone midway on the south side. Flags lined the approach. One proclaimed "The New Era"; another displayed an enormous liberty cap with the familiar, if scarcely appropriate, warning "Don't Tread on Me"; still others expressed the wish that Commerce might flourish, or displayed the rising sun of empire.

Not unaware of the publicity value of patriotism, the brothers Gray had spared neither money nor ingenuity, even arranging to have a small girl perch on the near arch and drop a laurel wreath on General Washington's brow when he passed beneath her. Fortunately both for her reputation for accuracy and the General's equanimity, the brothers developed second thoughts. As Washington, on his splendid white horse, rode under the arch, the child merely lowered the wreath until it hung just above his head. Austerely elegant in buff and blue, unobservant of the suspended laurels, the President-elect clattered across the uneven planks and onto the Philadelphia road. It was the morning of April 20, 1789, bright and springlike.

Four days before, Washington had left Mount Vernon by coach for his New York inauguration. He was accompanied by a former aide, Colonel David Humphreys, and by the secretary of Congress, Irish-born Charles Thomson, who had brought him the formal notification of his unanimous election as the first President of the United States. To the retired General, only recently recovered from a severe attack of rheumatism, Thomson's arrival was more expected than welcome. During the years of the Revolution, through all the exigencies and frustrations of command, Washington had quietly fixed his mind on a future day when he could lay aside his sword and return to Mount Vernon. That estate on the Potomac had been his pride and

With patriotic toasts and parades, the glory of independence is celebrated by citizens of early Philadelphia on a Fourth of July holiday. The painting is by J. L. Krimmel, an artist of the time.

9

constant preoccupation ever since, as a young man, he had first leased it from the widow of his half brother Lawrence. At her death in 1761, he became its owner. Even as a tenant he had made extensive alterations. After General Braddock's death in the wilderness disaster in 1755, he, as the general's only surviving aide-de-camp, had gone to Boston to see Governor Shirley, whose son Edward, Braddock's secretary, had also fallen in the campaign. At the governor's mansion in Roxbury he had paid his respects to his dead friend's father. Yet neither military affairs nor formal grief had prevented his noticing the wooden rustication and the ornate cupola of Shirley Place, features that he later incorporated into Mount Vernon.

Though Washington had vast holdings in the Ohio Valley, it never occurred to him to move westward after the Revolution. An eighteenth-century gentleman in dress and bearing, he would have found the frontier lacking in the order so cherished by the age of reason. Republican he was, as befitted the age, yet his ambition was to model his Potomac estate on those of the English gentry. To that end he planted, transplanted, laid out his formal gardens, plotted his Serpentine Road, even for authenticity imported a manager from the no-longer mother country. As squire of Mount Vernon he rose at first light, read his mail, and at seven ate a big breakfast. Then followed six hours in the saddle, supervising his acres. Dinner came at two. Most of his afternoons were devoted to correspondence. After supper there were family gatherings, whist, or sometimes the General busied himself with the latest book sent him from London. And always there was time for a run with the French hounds "on a good scenting morning" in the autumn.

For all the importunities of guests and relatives, here among his green acres he was at last able to make a reality of his long-held dream. If his country could thenceforth get along without him, so much the better for himself and Mount Vernon. But the foundering coalition of the thirteen states could not. Whether the Union with its newly adopted Constitution and its new Congress would endure or fall apart seemed to depend on General Washington. An English merchant returning home after a visit to America wrote him that "it is the general opinion of the friends to the new government that if you decline being at the head of it, it never can or will take effect."

Washington was indeed the father figure, more re-

vered and honored than loved familiarly, a republican with the dignity of a monarch, standing above shifting opinions and party strife, a symbol for *all* Americans. Many people have followed the Pied Piper lure of a seeming father figure to their ruin, but Washington was truly what he seemed—the embodiment of selfless duty. Since his duty was so apparent, he must and would accept the unanimous offer of the electors to become the first President.

He would infinitely have preferred tending his acres for the span that the Great Watchmaker had allotted him to directing the uncertain destiny of the emergent nation. Even financially he felt the pinch, for he was land-poor, and the lavishness of Mount Vernon's hospitality strained his resources. On agreeing to accept the electors' offer, he borrowed five hundred pounds to discharge his debts and then had to borrow a hundred more for his expenses to New York. Before setting out on his journey, he wrote to his bluff old companion-in-arms General Henry Knox: ". . . in confidence I tell you, with the *world* it would obtain little credit, that my movements to the chair of government will be accompanied by feelings not unlike those of a culprit who is going to the place of his execution; so unwilling am I, in the evening of a life nearly consumed in public cares, to quit a peaceful abode for an ocean of difficulties, without that competency of political skill, abilities and inclination which is necessary to manage the helm. I am sensible that I am embarking by the voice of the people, and a good name of my own, on this voyage; but what returns will be made by them, Heaven alone can foretell. Integrity and firmness are all I can promise."

What happened as the coachman cracked his whip and the coach drew away from Mount Vernon, what the men said to one another, were not recorded, but Washington in his diary noted his own depression. He found its converse in the jubilant mood of his countrymen waiting to greet him along the way. For the future of the Union with its new Constitution and Congress seemed assured with the old commander in chief at the helm. At Wise's Tavern in Alexandria, in the first of a succession of such festivities, the mayor and leading citizens gave him a dinner at which thirteen toasts were drunk and he was extolled as the "best of men and most beloved fellow-citizen." Some of the more enthusiastic toast drinkers even crossed the Potomac with him on ferryboats sent from Georgetown.

Washington tried to cover the maximum distance in a

day, starting every morning at sunrise and traveling until evening, and he soon found the zeal of his escorts a hindrance to a speedy journey. He spent the first night at Spurrier's Tavern, a little over twelve miles from Baltimore, where the city's volunteer artillery welcomed him the next day with a roar of cannon. After a supper with some of his former officers at the Fountain Inn, he listened to more complimentary addresses, which were becoming repetitious. At ten he was in bed, and by half past five was once more in his coach. An unsensational two-day journey through a thinly settled countryside brought him to Wilmington just after sunset. The next morning Wilmington's burgesses and Common Council made their formal address to him, which he had managed to see informally beforehand in order to prepare a reply. Another escort of eager hampering gentlemen

rode beside his departing coach.

At the Pennsylvania boundary waited a new guard of honor, composed of members of the Pennsylvania assembly and the City Troop of Horse, smart in white breeches, high-topped boots, and round black hats bound with silver. Washington left his coach to mount the white stallion that they had brought for him. The party breakfasted at Chester at the early hour of seven. After making a brief speech, Washington rode on at the head of an ever-lengthening column—whose brightest luminary was General Arthur St. Clair—until he came to the laurel arches of Gray's Garden.

The dusty main road from the bridge was lined with people. Washington, in his blue coat, passed with grave grace, bowing constantly to the shouts and handclaps of the spectators. As he neared the city, cannon boomed,

Columbian Magazine, 1789

The usually plain Gray's Ferry (actually a floating bridge) took on a festive appearance with its leafy decorations and banners honoring the President-elect as he crossed the Schuylkill on his journey to New York City.

11

church bells rang, and the ships anchored in the Delaware ran up all their flags. Twenty thousand applauding Philadelphians stood by to watch him ride down Market and Second streets to City Tavern. There leading citizens had arranged a great dinner for him to which "all the clergy and respectable strangers in the city" were invited. Fourteen toasts were drunk, while Washington "as usual, captivated every heart."

Seventy-five miles still lay ahead, a distance that could be covered in two and a half days if the weather held out and there were not too many speeches along the way. Before Washington left Philadelphia the next morning under an overcast sky, he had to listen to five more addresses. He did manage, however, to persuade the City Troop not to escort him to Trenton. A light rain began to fall as the coach moved across the placid Delaware countryside, where the Continental Army had once marched so painfully. Just before Trenton, at the bridge over the Assunpink Creek, where Washington had faced the British on a desperate afternoon twelve years before, a group of women and girls with flowers in their hair waited to sing an ode in his honor. Behind them the bridge was masked by an arch of greenery against which hung a banner with the date of Trenton's liberation and the words "The Defender of the Mothers will also Defend the Daughters." The female voices concluded their ode:

Strew, ye fair, his way with flowers—
Strew your Hero's way with flowers.

As the last couplet echoed, little girls with baskets of flowers pushed forward to scatter blossoms in the General's path. Bowing deeply and obviously moved, Washington thanked them for the great honor done him. In the evening, after a public dinner, he found time to write—in the third person—thanking the young ladies for the "affecting moment" at the bridge. The next morning he was off again at sunrise with a Trenton escort that rode with him the eight miles to Princeton, where he had breakfast. He was met at almost every town by the mayor and a group of leading citizens, and the inevitable address followed to the accompaniment of cannon and church bells. At Elizabeth Town Point, where he was to embark for New York, the whole population seemed to have gathered at the water front. Before the brief harbor voyage on the ceremonial barge awaiting him, the General reviewed a detachment of militiamen drawn up on the dock.

That barge, prepared and paid for by forty-six prominent New Yorkers, had a forty-seven-foot keel, a mast and a sail, and places for a crew of thirteen oarsmen. New York pilots had vied for the honor of rowing in the new President. They, with the coxswain, wore white smocks and fringed black caps. After admiring the barge, Washington embarked, followed by a joint committee of Congress and dignitaries of the city government of New York. Not until midday did the barge pull away from the pier, the artillery firing salutes from the shore while the troops on the water front stood at self-conscious attention. With sail and oar in a following wind the presidential party moved swiftly across Newark Bay and past Staten Island.

Approaching Upper Bay, the oarsmen changed their stroke. In that larger reach of water a sloop under full sail bore down on them, and as she closed, Washington heard the familiar melody "God Save the King" sung to new words honoring him. From a smaller boat a male chorus rendered an ode in harmony, and one of the seagoing choir managed to hand the coxswain some printed copies. To complete the festive progress, porpoises began playing around the barge's prow. As the brisk wind whipped the barge forward, the southern tip of New York grew clearer, and soon the masses lining the water front from the fort to the end of Wall Street became distinguishable as individuals.

Old enmities forgotten, a British packet at anchor south of Governor's Island fired a salute of thirteen guns, which was answered almost at once by an American battery. Not to be outdone, a nearby Spanish vessel broke out the flags of a score of countries and dispatched a fifteen-gun salute. Among the ever-growing flotilla in the wake of the barge was the schooner *Columbia*, commanded by the Revolutionary poet Philip Freneau and laden with a cargo of African monkeys.

In New York all work had stopped. Everyone whose legs could carry him was at the water front to see General Washington's barge arrive at Murray's Wharf, at the foot of Wall Street. Three huzzas were given with vigor as the cannon of the Battery fired their welcoming salute. The barge docked at about half past two. So great was the ensuing din that even the pealing bells were drowned out. Washington, in his wig and three-cornered hat, looking as stylized as a rococo porcelain figure, walked down the gangplank with slow, stately steps and up a flight of carpeted stairs, its rails hung in crimson velvet. He was met by Governor George

Although done much later, this primitive painting by J. Califano of Washington's welcome at Trenton is based on contemporary drawings and descriptions of the event.

Clinton and a crowd of officials. A self-important officer commanding the guard of honor saluted the General and announced that he awaited orders. Washington thanked him, then, turning to the crowd, added: ". . . after this is over, I hope you will give yourself no further trouble, as the affection of my fellow-citizens is all the guard I want."

So dense was the throng at Murray's Wharf that the planned parade could not get started. When at last the guard had forced a narrow way to the waiting coach, it took Washington a half hour to move the ten-minute distance from the dock to Franklin House, his assigned residence. Not even Franklin House—previously used by the president of Congress and now refurbished for the President of the United States—offered him sanctuary from importunate well-wishers. He had not time to change his clothes before Governor Clinton's coach was back at the door to take him to the inescapable honor banquet. Before the toast-ridden dinner ended, rain was again falling, but even that did not dampen the fireworks display that the weary General was forced to applaud before gaining the refuge of his Franklin House bedroom.

The next morning Washington assured a joint committee of Congress that any arrangements made for his induction into office would be acceptable. Congress promptly voted to inaugurate him on April 30. During the intervening six days he was so overwhelmed with visitors at Franklin House that Mount Vernon in retrospect seemed a hermitage. "I was unable to attend to any business whatsoever," he admitted later. Meanwhile Congress was debating a proper title for the incoming President. John Adams, with a non-Puritan affection for dynastic trappings, favored "His Most Benign Highness." The Senate preferred "His Highness, the President of the United States of America, and Protector of the Rights of the Same." Fortunately for posterity, the representatives, goaded by the sharp tongue of the Pennsylvania frontier democrat William Maclay, determined on having nothing more than was set down in the Constitution: "President of the United States." Washington wanted no title at all.

Inauguration Day was announced at sunrise by thirteen guns of the Battery. Washington dressed with unusual care in a new suit of brown American-made broadcloth that had been woven at Hartford and that was set off by metal buttons stamped with the American eagle. His hair was powdered, and he wore the customary white silk stockings and silver shoe buckles. Although the joint committee of Congress would not arrive before noon to escort him to Federal Hall, crowds began to gather hours earlier in front of Franklin House, festive in the April sunshine, their holiday mood made more solemn by the measured ringing of church bells. At the committee's arrival, militiamen lined up in the roadway and forced the crowd back. Washington entered the ornate coach-and-four provided for him by Congress, his hat in his hand, a dress sword in a steel scabbard at his side, and his inaugural speech tucked into a special inner pocket of his new suit. Preceded by dragoons, artillerymen, and grenadiers in all the gay contrasts of their dress uniforms, the presidential coach, with a coachman on the box and a lackey on one of the horses, moved through the banner-decked and cheering streets to Federal Hall on Wall Street, where the two houses of Congress awaited their President.

Congress was already assembled in the Senate Chamber, a square classical room draped in crimson damask, its ceiling decorated with a sun and stars. Vice President John Adams stepped forward to welcome Washington formally on his arrival while legislators and their guests rose from the semicircle of seats. To Adams' formal question as to whether he would take the oath, Washington replied that he was ready to proceed. The Vice President conducted him across the room and through a triple doorway to a porticoed balcony overlooking Wall Street. On the balcony stood an armchair and a red-draped table on which lay a velvet cushion holding the large Bible belonging to St. John's Masonic Lodge of New York. There, in the open air, with two of his old generals and a few other guests standing by him, Washington took the oath of office.

New York's Chancellor Robert R. Livingston administered the oath, which Washington repeated, his hand on the Bible: "I do solemnly swear that I will faithfully execute the office of President of the United States and will, to the best of my ability, preserve, protect, and defend the Constitution of the United States." "I swear, so help me God," Washington added in his grave voice; he then bent forward and kissed the book. With a broad gesture toward the crowd, Livingston shouted: "Long live George Washington, President of the United States!" In a surging roar the crowd took up the cry, cheer after cheer billowing through the streets, with one repeated identifiable phrase: "God bless our President." The new flag was raised above Federal Hall's cu-

This engraving of Washington's inauguration on the balcony of Federal Hall in New York is from a drawing by Peter Lacour.

pola, and as it fluttered brightly from the staff, the guns of the Battery responded in salute while the cannon of anchored ships boomed and church bells pealed.

Amidst the congratulatory din Washington stood quietly in his brown suit of American cloth, bowing acknowledgment, the recognized embodiment of the new nation. Those cheering in the streets as well as those gathered in the hall felt the uncertainty about the future replaced by confidence through his presence. Already they were calling him the Father of his Country. By the grace of Washington, Americans were assured that the new nation would endure.

During six years following that October afternoon in 1781 when Lord Cornwallis' redcoats had stacked arms and marched out in surrender between the drawn-up ranks of French and Americans, the nation still had

15

not decided whether the United States would be united or merely states. Although British troops had continued to occupy Charleston and Savannah for another year, although Sir Guy Carleton with his regulars and Hessians and Tories had sheltered behind the Royal Navy in New York for more than two years, although the actual peace treaty had not been signed by the Americans until September, 1783, the War of the Revolution, for all practical purposes, had come to an end with Cornwallis' surrender at Yorktown. At that surrender British bands had played the popular tune "The World Turned Upside Down" with a sardonic humor that was in many ways as applicable to the victors as to the defeated. For wars have a way of turning upside down the things for which they have supposedly been fought. The high goals become dim, the high-flown phrases tattered, and peace brings its own divisive disillusionment.

In six years of fighting, the paper money of the Continental Congress had depreciated to the point that it finally became worthless, and its memory would live on in the phrase "Not worth a Continental" for the next hundred years. War profiteers, merchants, and self-seeking contractors had made their fortunes while the soldiers who had fought the war remained often neither paid nor fed. Large numbers of the educated and wealthy had fled the country as loyalists. New rich had in many cases replaced old Tories, as a disenchanted relative of General Joseph Warren observed. Walking the streets of Boston immediately after the war, he noted that "fellows who would have cleaned my shoes five years ago now ride on chariots."

A surly and unpaid Continental Army still remained under arms, a potential threat to any civilian government. Fifteen months after Yorktown, in January, 1783, a deputation of Army officers presented the Army's grievances to Congress, with the underlying threat of rebellion if its demands were not heeded. In June, 1783, several hundred disgruntled and well-liquored soldiers surrounded the Statehouse in Philadelphia, where Congress was meeting, cursed, threatened, and occasionally thrust bayonets through the windows until the terrified congressmen fled the city for Princeton, leaving the new nation without even a capital.

Revolutions, when they are not blind acts of desperation, are the work of determined minorities. For most people are inert by habit, preferring the ways they have grown up in, uneasy at the thought of abandoning familiar loyalties. "I am a poor quiet man, a native of the place and a loyal subject of the king, God bless him," said Rip Van Winkle on awaking from his twenty-year slumber through the Revolution. So most rural Americans probably felt in the years before 1771. Certainly, despite all provocations, only a minority then envisaged dissolving the bonds between them and their ancestral homeland. As the minutemen and the redcoats were exchanging volleys at Concord Bridge, Benjamin Franklin, in mid-Atlantic returning home from London, still had not entirely given up his belief in a united self-

In this painting—The American Star— Baltimore artist Frederick Kemmelmeyer symbolized the reverence in which Americans held the hero and savior of their country.

governing America within the British Empire, a combination that he felt would become the most powerful political unit in the world. As for Washington, even after the Battle of Bunker Hill, when he took command of the Continental Army at Cambridge, he was still not sure that the war was to be one of independence. The First Continental Congress, meeting in September, 1774, protested its loyalty to King George despite all its differences with the mother country. The following spring the Second Continental Congress found conservatives like John Dickinson and John Jay, who favored "Negociations for Peace," still in the majority, although the strength of those demanding independence, like Samuel Adams and Patrick Henry, was growing. Conservative Gouverneur Morris, dismayed at Samuel Adams' activist anti-British Sons of Liberty, declared that if the disputes with England continued, the better people would eventually be ruled by a riotous mob.

If a public opinion poll had been taken at the time of the Revolution, it would have shown about one-quarter of the population adamantly republican and determined on independence. Another quarter would have been made up of loyalists. The remaining half would have been the neutrals, more concerned about their own immediate affairs than about the outcome of the war (except when it was fought in their vicinity) and wanting above all—like most common men before and since—to be let alone.

Of the wellborn and the well to do in the colonies probably more than half were at the beginning loyalists—royal officials and officeholders, many lawyers, doctors, Anglican clergy, those generally with a vested interest in stability. North and South, the bigger merchants tended to take the English side. It is estimated that as late as 1776 half the population of New York remained loyalists. Among the most violent in their allegiance were the Carolina back-country rednecks.

Of the discontented middle classes and smaller merchants of the seaports most were patriots. Of the colonial aristocracy the planters were the most influential group that backed the Revolution. Although there were exceptions, like Virginia's loyalist William Byrd III, most planters had chafed at the British tie. They harbored many grievances against the trade restrictions of the English commercial system. They were heavily indebted as well to London merchant houses. Philosophically they were republicans of the age of reason, formed by Locke and Montesquieu and Hume;

for them the doctrine of the divine right of kings was meaningless. As rationalists, their ideal was of an aristocratic republic in the classic model, authoritative but restrained, ruled by an educated elite. Equally committed to the Revolution—but otherwise opposed to the republicans—were the doctrinaire democrats, the federalists, who wanted no powerful unified republic controlled by an elite but a loose federation of sovereign states where the common man would find his political voice through the state legislatures. The rationalists believed in a republic and feared a democracy. The federalists believed in a democracy and feared a republic. Nor would the Constitution resolve this fundamental rivalry, which would continue through the decades of the national era to the bitter confrontation of the Civil War.

The period of the Confederation is one of the most disputed in American history. The nineteenth-century historian John Fiske spoke for the prevailing view of his day when he portrayed the Confederacy era as a time of commercial and economic chaos in which an incompetent central government, lacking both power and ideas, sank into anarchic futility. In his interpretation, the country—mired in depression, its commerce stagnant, its merchants bankrupt, and its shops idle—was rescued only by the miracle of the Constitution. Although later historians have demonstrated the shallowness of Fiske's conclusions, the popular impression still remains of the Confederation as a dismal interlude between two triumphs. Those who lived through that period, who experienced it in all its daily immediacy, from month to month and year to year, would have been surprised to learn what they were supposed to have lived through. For in spite of a depression and money crises and some popular unrest, the prevailing mood was of optimistic planning for the future.

The Articles of Confederation—America's first constitution—were deliberately weak, for those who had established them were wary of control after their experience with English rule. John Dickinson, who drew up the first draft of the Articles in 1776, believed in a strong central government and his constitution would have given Congress wide powers in fixing state boundaries and in administering Western lands. These lands had long been controversial. New York, Connecticut, North and South Carolina, Georgia, and Virginia all claimed that under their colonial charters and grants their boundaries extended to the Mississippi. Virginia claimed the huge area northwest of the Ohio River. New York demanded the region between the Great Lakes and the Ohio River by virtue of a treaty with the Iroquois. The states with definite western limits, like Pennsylvania and Maryland, in turn bitterly resisted Virginia's claims to lands extending indefinitely into the West. Georgia and South Carolina wanted no part of any provision to give the "free inhabitants of each state all of the privileges and immunities of citizens" but demanded—as did Maryland—that these privileges and immunities be restricted to whites. States with large populations, led by Virginia, objected to the proviso limiting each state to one vote in Congress. So turbulent was the opposition that Congress dropped the Articles and did not take them up until the following year. The federalists then insisted on an amendment that "each state retains its sovereignty, freedom and independence." Congress could exercise only those powers delegated by the states, which retained ultimate power.

By February, 1779, every state except Maryland had ratified the amended Articles. The Maryland legislature demanded first that control of the Western lands be given to Congress "for the good of the whole," with the significant exception of the claims granted to land companies before the Declaration of Independence. Since Governor Thomas Johnson of Maryland, Robert Morris, and Benjamin Franklin had large interests in those claims, the good of the whole also included their good. But the Virginians were willing to give up their claims to the lands northwest of the Ohio only if Congress declared void all earlier deeds received from the Indians. A bitter wrangle followed. Delegates from the landless states insisted that Congress make no such promise. Looking beyond the immediate disputes, a group of agrarian-minded Virginians, led by Thomas Jefferson, finally persuaded their fellow Virginians to yield the old claims, attaching only the condition that all Indian deeds disposing of Virginia's western lands be declared void before the lands passed to Congress. New York had already agreed to restrict its western boundaries. Maryland, unable to object further, finally ratified in March, 1781, and the Confederation became fact.

The great drawback of the Confederation was its lack of an independent income. But to remedy this by a duty of 5 per cent on goods brought into the United States was more than the individual and sovereign states were prepared to allow. Let Congress estimate its needs and make requisitions; the states would levy their own taxes and support the Confederation with desultory grants. State legislatures preferred taking over that part of the national debt owed their citizens to leaving the responsibility for a national debt to a central government with authority to levy taxes on no-longer sovereign states.

Equally convinced that a public debt meant central authority, though far happier at the thought, was Superintendent of Finance Robert Morris, the deft manipulator of funds and credit who from 1781 to 1784 directed much of the economic life of the nation and brought system into the chaos of Revolutionary financing. He, Alexander Hamilton, Secretary for Foreign Affairs John Jay, Gouverneur Morris, George Washington, and James Madison formed the group within the Confederation that advocated a powerful central government as the only means of maintaining national honor and prestige. Opposed to them were the ardent Revolutionary leaders like Samuel Adams, Patrick Henry, Superintendent Morris' enemy Richard Henry Lee, George Clinton, James Warren, and Elbridge Gerry, who felt that the greatest gain of the Revolution had been the shaking off of central authority and insisted that the states could best be governed without an authoritarian central government. The political history of the Confederation revolves around the struggle of these two groups to shape the character of the fragile Union.

The war's end left that Union with problems almost as staggering as the war itself. What should be done with the ex-soldier? What should foreign relations be with friend and foe? Should commerce be free with all nations or limited only to trade among the states? How should the war debt be paid? What kind of taxes should there be? Where was Congress to find the money necessary to function? Yet for all the difficulties, the destruction, the stagnation of commerce, the kiting of paper currencies, war, with its insatiable, unproductive demands, had stimulated the economy. Manufacturers as well as artisans had managed to thrive in providing supplies for the Army. And peace brought compensating advantages along with its problems. The minority Anglican Church was disestablished. The criminal codes from the old country were revised and made more humane—although English common law still remained the basis of the American legal system. Laws of primogeniture and entail, however, were abolished. The vast confiscated lands of the Tories were usually subdivided. Several Northern states had ended slavery, and others were providing for gradual emancipation.

In 1777 Continentals encamped at Ballston Spa (near Sara-
toga Springs, New York) purportedly found the mineral
waters more to their taste than whiskey. By 1794, when this
sketch was made, the spa had become a popular resort.

In Paris, Franklin—with his fur cap and stringy hair, artfully simple and adored as always by the French—headed the American peace commission; he and John Jay met the British representatives in September, 1782, and were joined by John Adams in late October. Adams thought that the boundaries agreed to two months later by both sides were of the "greatest moderation." Actually, over the backstage maneuverings of France and Spain—who for all their professed friendship would have confined the emergent nation to the east of the Appalachians—the American commissioners had quadrupled the area of their new country by extending its Western boundary to the Mississippi.

By the Peace of Paris, signed the following fall, England formally recognized American independence while leaving the boundaries of a large forest area between Maine and Nova Scotia still vague. The Americans agreed that "no lawful impediment" would be placed in the way of British creditors collecting prewar debts owed them in America. Congress would recommend to the states the restoration of confiscated property, and persecution of the loyalists would stop. The British in turn agreed to surrender the military and trading posts that they still held along the Great Lakes frontier. Both sides lagged in carrying out their agreements. Although the states gradually repealed laws that were in conflict with the Treaty of Paris, the radical Revolutionary leaders and the people at large were violently opposed to any compensation for the loyalists. The British, secure in their forts at Oswego, Niagara, Detroit, and Michilimackinac, were in no hurry to make a withdrawal, particularly since Canadian fur traders had begged them to stay at least three more years.

Even before the signing of the peace treaty, British merchant ships loaded with luxury goods were docking at American ports. Eager British merchants circularized their former customers, offering credit and easy terms. In spite of the repudiation of the Continental currency, hard money was plentiful, for the British and French armies, in paying for their supplies in gold and silver, had left much specie behind. As after most wars, the pent-up demand for "foreign superfluities" was enormous and the cash was ready for laces, velvets, silver, wines, even pianos. Mechanics took to wearing silk stockings and farmers' daughters bought satin Sunday dresses. Inflated and supported by credit, the buying spree of the seaports grew like a bubble and spread inland. And like all such bubbles it eventually burst. By 1785 so much specie had returned to Europe that in the ensuing money shortage luxury goods gathered dust in warehouses while merchants on both sides of the Atlantic faced ruin. Although farm prices remained above prewar levels, scarce money, heavy taxes, and stringent debt collections led to agrarian distress that culminated in disorders like Shays' Rebellion.

Yet, in spite of the 1785 depression and the hardships of New England farmers, the years of the Confederation were not the time of stagnation and decay described by Fiske. Banks were founded, factories planned, new businesses launched. Americans formed societies for digging canals, building bridges, and improving roads. Britain closed the West Indian trade to America, but independence meant that American products could be carried anywhere else. Although England still absorbed most of America's trade, the whole world was a market and a source of supply. American ships sailed the seven seas. American commerce expanded rapidly. Moreover, new commodities were being exported. The tonnage of American vessels increased. Rhode Island underwent a huge boom in imports, exports, and shipping. Virginia planters were receiving twice as much for their tobacco crops as in the best prewar years—until the bottom temporarily fell out of the tobacco market in 1785. In the Carolinas, in Georgia, the expansion was immense and uninterrupted, and annual exports more than doubled. New York, Philadelphia, and Boston exceeded

their prewar mercantile opulence. American ships sailed as far as China. During February of 1784, even as financial clouds were beginning to gather around him, Robert Morris sent his 360-ton *Empress of China* to Canton in the biggest and boldest commercial venture yet undertaken by an American merchant. American ships were returning to port not only with cargoes but with men. For with its independence America became for many Europeans—as it would remain—a dream fulfillment. Immigrants arrived in swelling numbers from Scotland, Ireland, and Germany; and when they could cross the ocean in no other way, they came as indentured servants.

On his eightieth birthday, in January, 1786, when the Confederation was all but collapsing politically, Benjamin Franklin could write: " . . . America never was in higher prosperity, her produce abundant and bearing a good price, her working people all employed and well paid, and all property in lands and houses of more than treble the value it bore before the war; and, our commerce being no longer the monopoly of British merchants, we are furnished with all the foreign commodities we need, at much more reasonable rates than heretofore. So that we have no doubt of being able to discharge more speedily the debt incurred by the war, than was at first supposed."

National feeling in the tentative new nation grew more slowly and more by chance than it came to seem in retrospect. A frontier country with a brief history and shallow roots gains a sense of unity only with time and shared experiences. After 1783 there was not even a "tyrant" to unite against. The colonists grew aware that they were no longer Englishmen before they became aware of anything else. First they had developed a local pride with an indifference and even a hostility to other settlements. In 1769 and for a number of years afterward Connecticut and Pennsylvania settlers had skirmished over the possession of the Wyoming Valley in northwest Pennsylvania in what became known as the Yankee-Pennamite Wars. During the Revolution, New Jersey militiamen, defying Washington, refused to swear any oath of allegiance except to New Jersey. After the war, farmers from New Hampshire had so little sense of nationality that they did not even want a state, let alone a national, government.

War was the bitter solvent that did the most to erode both state and local loyalties. The Massachusetts, New Hampshire, and Connecticut militiamen who captured

Louisbourg in 1745 were proud of themselves as New Englanders and beginning to become aware of themselves as Americans. During the French and Indian War the colonists' sense of unity was sharpened by a common danger and a common enemy, while the colonial militiamen reacted as one to the condescending British officers in their elegant uniforms.

With the coming of the Revolution, New England boys who had never been more than a dozen miles from their own rocky farms found themselves marching with the Continental Army through lush unfamiliar countryside with orange-brown rivers. Southerners endured the harsh winters of the North, New Yorkers bivouacked in holly groves, and Virginians stared across the blueness of Lake Champlain. Unknown regions became transiently familiar, and the soldiers could not help but feel that for all its diversity this land they marched and fought over was one land. The delegates to the Continental Congress, in gathering for a common task, became aware of each other as men, and sensed the common interests that underlay regional differences.

Practical necessity did much to foster the new nationalism. At the war's beginning the colonists marched under flags as various as their militia units; no one emblem represented all the colonies. There were the state flags; the New England Flag; the Bunker Hill Flag; the Grand Union, or Continental, Flag with the British jack still in the canton, under which Washington had taken command of the Continental Army; the Gadsden Flag with its rattlesnake and "Don't Tread on Me" motto; the Pine Tree Flag with its appeal to God; the Bennington Flag; the Texel Flag with its red, white, and blue stripes, supposedly designed by Benjamin Franklin; the many regimental flags. A rallying symbol was needed, and Congress, on June 14, 1777, adopted the Stars and Stripes as the flag "of the thirteen United States."

Two decades before the Revolution, Benjamin Franklin, as "Deputy Postmaster and Manager of all his Majesty's Provinces and Dominions on the Continent of North America," had reorganized the infant postal service, establishing Philadelphia as the center of a network that disregarded state lines and linked all the colonies from Maine to Georgia. Soon there were seventy-five post offices with as many branches. For its day the service was efficient. Several times a week the couriers rode to New York, and a Philadelphia merchant could write to Boston and expect an answer within three weeks. After the Revolution the postal service became unavoidably the responsibility of the new national government. During the Confederation, Congress made little effort to expand the service, but after the adoption of the Constitution, the government—uncertain of the loyalty of the settlers beyond the Alleghenies and realizing the political advantages of better communications—cut rates and pushed the service as fast as possible into the Western regions.

Though the Congress of the Confederation was primarily a policy-making body responsible not to the people but to the state legislatures, inevitably it developed a functioning bureaucracy. This bureaucratic accretion had been opposed by the more radical members of Congress, who had kept their distrust of executive power and maintained that Congress, through its committees, could and should run all government departments. Nevertheless by 1781 the overburdened committee system gave way to single executives in charge of war, foreign affairs, and finance, and in 1782 of the post office. Bumbling General Benjamin Lincoln became the first secretary of war. The first secretary for foreign affairs was the wealthy and conservative New Yorker Robert Livingston, who was soon succeeded by John Jay, when the latter returned from his Paris peace mission with Jefferson. The aristocratic Jay, as brilliant as he was pompous, soon became embroiled with Congress on the question of American claims to use of the Mississippi.

Louis XVI is extolled as America's liberator
on this French medallion, which bears portraits
not only of the French monarch but also
of Franklin in a fur cap and George "Waginston."

21

The frigate Alliance *flew an early version of the Stars and Stripes, above, in 1779. The New England Liberty Tree Flag, below, featured a stylized oak. Commodore Esek Hopkins' 1775 flagship bore the Gadsden Flag, bottom.*

ABOVE: CHICAGO HISTORICAL SOCIETY; BELOW: FREEDOMS FOUNDATION, VALLEY FORGE; BOTTOM: UNITED STATES NAVAL ACADEMY MUSEUM

Jay, flattered by the urbane Spanish minister Diego de Gardoqui, favored surrendering such claims for a period of twenty-five to thirty years in exchange for Spain's offer of trade concessions. Such a deal would have been of immediate advantage to Eastern merchants in allowing them to exchange American products for hard cash, but it would have wiped out most Western land claims. Congress, under pressure of popular opinion, instructed Jay to make no such concession.

As the first superintendent of finance, Robert Morris, one of the richest men in the country, was the figure round whom rallied those determined to create a powerful central government—and by force if necessary. Speaking for those opposed to Morris, William Lee called him the most dangerous man in America and accused him of having been bankrupt at the beginning of the Revolution and, at its end, of having left the country bankrupt while amassing a huge fortune for himself.

Operating at a quieter and more permanent level than these controversial figures were the men who formed the nucleus of a future civil service. There was Joseph Nourse of Virginia, who became the register of the Treasury in 1779, kept books, prepared reports, and remained at his post for fifty years. There was the preeminent civil servant of the Confederation, Charles Thomson, secretary of the First Continental Congress, who carried on correspondence with state governments, signed and sealed the official copies of ordinances, commissions, and treaties, and even served for a time as president of Congress.

The beginnings of officialdom during the Confederation were small—Jay's staff consisted merely of an undersecretary, a doorkeeper, a messenger, clerks, and three interpreters—but its continuity began to shape the outline of the emergent nation. Even more significant for the future of the country were the two great land ordinances, that of 1785 and the Northwest Ordinance of 1787, by which the government of the Confederation took over the control and disposition of Western lands. After 1783 the settlers pushing westward had begun to demand their independence, with freedom to secede from the old states and to form new ones. Speculators had been insisting on validation of their land titles. By the Ordinance of 1785 Congress laid down regulations for the survey, sale, and government of the land in the West and for making treaties with the Indians.

Jefferson, the believer in agrarian democracy, was largely responsible for this first colonial policy of the

United States. In 1784 he proposed that the West be divided into fourteen regions, with names he invented, like Cherronesus, Polypotamia, Michigania, and others. Whenever the number of inhabitants in any one of these territories reached twenty thousand, the people were to form their own government and could send a nonvoting delegate to Congress. When the population of the territory equaled that of the free citizens of the smallest of the thirteen states, the territory, on agreeing to assume its share of the federal debt and to maintain a republican form of government, was to be admitted to the Union as an equal partner. The plan was never approved by Congress, but it formed the basis of the Northwest Ordinance of 1787.

The Ordinance of 1785 divided the public lands into townships six miles square. These in turn were subdivided into thirty-six sections a mile square, with one section reserved for public schools, and four for future national use. Land was to be sold at auction for a gold dollar an acre, in lots no smaller than a square mile. Payment could also be made in soldiers' land bounty certificates and in national debt certificates, many of which had been bought up by speculators at ten cents on the dollar.

In 1784 North Carolina had turned over its western, or Tennessee, territory to Congress, with the provision that all speculative titles in the ceded area be validated. Militia companies in the region convened to form the new state of Franklin; in the following year the Franklin legislature met and the Indian-fighter John Sevier became the first governor. The Ordinance of 1785, with its provisions for territorial self-government, threatened the land speculators who claimed millions of acres within Franklin, and the speculation-minded North Carolina legislature proceeded to revoke the cession.

For all his woodsman's ways and his frontier nickname, Nolichucky Jack, Sevier's heart was with the speculators, and he did his best to act for them while keeping popular support in his rebel state until he was able to maneuver Franklin back into North Carolina. Settlers in the Kentucky territory of Virginia were eager to form their own state, but the speculators were influential enough there to delay statehood until the end of the Confederation and the advent of the greater security of the new Constitution.

To the more conservative members of Congress the democratic self-governing provisions of the 1785 Ordinance were not only distasteful but alarming. As president of Congress, Richard Henry Lee, for all his states' rights stance, was dismayed at the squatters and other riffraff flooding westward. It would be necessary, he wrote Washington, "for the security of property among uninformed, and perhaps licentious people, as the greater part of those who go there are, that a strong toned government should exist, and the rights of property be clearly defined." Clearly defined they became by the Northwest Ordinance of 1787. This more restrained and restraining ordinance divided the Northwest into not more than five or fewer than three districts over each of which Congress was to appoint a governor, a secretary, and three judges. Whenever a district grew to five thousand male inhabitants, the voters—those who owned fifty acres or more—could choose an assembly. Any laws passed by the assembly could be vetoed by the governor. As soon as a district reached sixty thousand free inhabitants, it could write a constitution and establish its own government. Slavery was prohibited in the Northwest Territory.

Sale of land took precedence over settlers in both ordinances. Nevertheless, the ordinances were a departure in history, a colonial policy that regarded new territories not as colonies to be exploited but as an extension of the nation itself. In the years to come these ordinances would remain the basis for the sale and governing of Western lands and would justify those who had believed that the national domain alone could pay the nation's foreign and domestic debt.

The practical exigencies of politics and commerce quietly speeded the development of a sense of American nationality after the Revolution. More manifest influences were the ideas of the age of reason embodied in the Declaration of Independence: the novel belief in progress, in natural rights, in the underlying reasonableness of man, nature, and God. Scholars and artists tend to be more sensitive to the time-spirit than more practical men, and as early as 1771 the poet-sailor Freneau was predicting in the "Rising Glory of America"

A New Jerusalem, sent down from Heaven
Shall grace our happy land.

In 1778 a New York clergyman, John Rogers, told his congregation that since God had "put all the blessings of liberty, civil and religious, within our reach, perhaps there was never a nation that had the fair opportunity of becoming the happiest people on earth, that we have now."

Yet even if the War of the Revolution had never been fought and the Declaration of Independence never written, if the thirteen colonies had fulfilled Franklin's dream of forming a dominion within the British Empire, the development of an American consciousness and an American type would still have been inevitable with the deeper influences of time and space at work. The new environment was bound to produce alterations in manners, habits, attitudes, even speech and accent. Just as later English colonists were to become Canadians, Australians, New Zealanders, and South Africans, so Americans were bound to rise from the soil of the New World, somewhat different perhaps in a Dominion of the United States, but still Americans. The Revolution only accelerated an irreversible process.

By the end of the war, new names and heroes had emerged: Washington unsheathing his sword under the elm at Cambridge; Colonel Prescott and his men facing the red line of grenadiers at Bunker Hill; John Paul Jones impudently carrying the sea war to the mother country; Montgomery dying in the snow before Quebec; Nathan Hale's brave end and, by antithesis, the treachery of Benedict Arnold; Francis Marion, "the Swamp Fox"; the soldiers who withstood the winter ordeal of Valley Forge; Lafayette and Von Steuben. Only Franklin endured out of that colonial past when Sir William Johnson, surrounded by his Iroquois at Johnson Hall, was thought by many to be the greatest man in the colonies, and when Boston went into mourning for William Shirley, the most popular of Massachusetts' royal governors. Dead less than a decade, Johnson and Shirley already seemed of another age, their heirs fled, their estates confiscated, their names dim. Even street and place names had changed. In Boston, King Street had become State Street and Queen became Court, although Hanover Street residents refused to abandon their "perpetual reminder of a detested house."

National feeling expanded visibly among the old soldiers in the Society of the Cincinnati, an association of former Revolutionary officers and the first nationwide private organization. Founded casually in 1783 by retired General Henry Knox, the society in its mild and enlarged way was a counterpart of the European orders of chivalry. Membership was restricted to officers and—in descent—to their eldest sons. Washington, who in recruiting his officers had given instructions to "take none but gentlemen," became the society's first president.

To Knox's and Washington's surprise the Society of the Cincinnati was soon under attack as an attempt to set up a hereditary aristocracy. Franklin considered the hereditary descent clause absurd; others denounced the entire society as an upper-class pressure group preparing the way for a military oligarchy. In spite of the denunciations, Washington continued as the society's president, but he requested its members to strike out anything in the rules that had a political tendency and to discontinue the hereditary qualifications. However, the hereditary clause remained—and survives today.

During the Confederation various learned societies had sprung up, modeled after the American Philosophical Society in Philadelphia, made famous by Franklin. There were attempts to found similar societies in New York, Massachusetts, Connecticut, and Virginia, but the only one to endure was the American Academy of Arts and Sciences, organized in Boston by John Adams and James Bowdoin. The Boston society—by encouraging the studies of antiquity, natural history, medicine, mathematics, astronomy, meteorology, agriculture, commerce, and the arts—did much to stimulate a national intellectual unity. Bowdoin, a scientist as well as a politician, became its first president.

Intellectual unity was fostered more generally by the increased demand for education at all levels. John Adams wanted instruction for "every class and rank of people, down to the lowest and poorest." In the one

The map of the Northwest Territory at the left was drawn by John Fitch—inventor, adventurer, and speculator—from surveys made by his land company in 1783 and 1785. Above, Fort Franklin, overlooking French Creek just south of Lake Erie, served in the 1780's as a frontier outpost against possible Indian attacks.

hundred and forty years before the Revolution nine colleges had been established in the colonies. From the Revolution to the century's end at least sixteen colleges were founded, some of them short-lived, but including Georgia, North Carolina, Vermont, St. John's, Georgetown, Williams, Bowdoin, and Middlebury. In 1782 a medical institution was established at Harvard. Dr. Benjamin Rush, former surgeon general of the Middle Department of the Continental Army and a signer of the Declaration of Independence, urged a national university specializing in politics and economics, and even suggested that federal office be limited to graduates of such a university, who would be imbued with "federal and republican ideals."

Higher education would for generations be the privilege of a minority. Far more important in shaping the mass of Americans to a new conception of their nationality was Noah Webster, who felt Americans needed their own system of language as well as of government. No firebrand, Webster spent the years of the Revolution at Yale, claiming draft exemption as a student. While there, he planned an American speller, a grammar, and a reader. During the colonial period American textbooks had been merely reprints of English ones. Webster planned to free Americans from English texts. In the preface to his 1783 speller he wrote: "For America in her infancy to adopt the present maxims of the old world, would be to stamp the wrinkles of decrepit age upon the bloom of youth and to plant the seeds of decay in a vigorous constitution. American glory begins to dawn at a favourable period and under flattering circumstances." He hailed the writings and speeches of the Revolutionary statesmen as "not inferior in any respect to the orations of Cicero and Demosthenes."

During the Confederation, as the nation's boundaries expanded, as the ordinances opened the territory to the west of the Alleghenies, Americans grew increasingly curious about the land they lived in and they turned to authors ready to satisfy that curiosity. There were many books awaiting. Jedidiah Morse, pastor of a church near Boston, published his *Geography Made Easy* in 1784, the same year that John Filson completed a book on Kentucky and Thomas Hutchins produced *An Historical Narrative and Topographical Description of Louisiana and West Florida.*

If the Confederacy had endured, it might have left the United States like the Swiss Confederation, a loose government that would by pragmatic necessity have evolved in time into something more centralized. More likely it would have split in three to form New England, Middle, and Southern Confederations. In its eight-year life span the Confederation had some solid accomplishments to its credit. It settled the peace treaty with England and established the great land ordinances. It set up a functioning civil service. By the sale of land and collections from debtors, by Treasury warrants and through grants from the states, it paid off much of the domestic national debt. It lived through and beyond the postwar depression. It brought to most of the federalists the realization that the government must be granted additional powers to survive. Above all it nurtured the idea of a nation as an entity.

Yet, whatever it may or may not have done, the Confederation failed to create the necessary aura of respect. There was not even the focal point of a national capital, for Congress, after having been driven ignominiously from Philadelphia, had wandered from Princeton to Annapolis to Trenton and finally to New York. Congressmen-elect tended to consider their home affairs more important than cross-country journeys on horseback to a Congress that might not even be able to muster a quorum. Men looked with contempt on the shifting national government. "A shadow without substance," Washington called it, and told John Jay that he did not think the nation could endure unless the Confederation had the power over the states that the states had over their own inhabitants.

There was talk of giving up the Union altogether as the states went their independent ways. Shays' Rebellion in Massachusetts was the event that brought the wobbly Confederation to a crisis. As a rebellion, it was scarcely more than a few winter skirmishes between irate farmers and reluctant militiamen, but its challenge to authority brought Washington back to public life and indirectly forced thirteen bickering and contrary governments to consider "a more perfect union."

Shays' was in essence a debtors' revolt. With the states left to their own currency devices, seven had experimented with the hazards of paper money. Most extreme was the experiment in Rhode Island—the state

became known to the hard-money-minded as Rogue's Island—where the legislature was so prodigal of paper money that debtors were seen pursuing their reluctant creditors with handfuls of the dubious currency.

In Massachusetts things were different. No debtors could control a legislature where the vote was even more rigidly restricted to property holders than under the old royal charter. Farmers in the west of the state, faced with hard times and unable to pay in specie taxes that sometimes ran to one-third of their nonspecie income, found themselves haled before courts, their property and livestock put up for sale and they themselves sometimes confined in debtors' prisons. These seam-faced rustics, who had fought at Bunker Hill and Saratoga and Yorktown, had not fought for the security of wealthy Boston merchants. They demanded an easing of taxes, a reduction of formal legal costs, and, beyond that, cheap money. Even more ominous to the merchants in their brick Boston town houses were the murmurings by malcontents that all debts should be canceled and all property divided up.

Since the hardscrabble farmers found no relief from the property-minded legislature, they banded together, finding their almost accidental leader in Daniel Shays, a western dirt farmer and a former captain in the Continental Army. Calling themselves regulators, wearing hemlock sprigs in their hats, and shouting, "Hurrah for Daniel Shays!" the armed bands riding through the Berkshires in the autumn of 1786 threatened judges,

Symbolism, much of it somewhat obscure, runs rampant in this border design from a Society of the Cincinnati membership certificate. Although widely criticized, the society raised money for victims of the Revolution and tried to promote cooperation between the states.

sheriffs, and creditors and blocked the sitting of any court that "should attempt to take property by distress." For a while the weathered men with the hemlock badges seemed to control the interior of the state. "A despicable, degenerate mob," Governor James Bowdoin called them, in words worthy of a royal governor, and he asked the legislature to pass a riot act.

Shays, in his old buff and blue uniform, made an attempt, with a thousand of his followers, to capture the United States arsenal at Springfield in the bitter winter of 1787, but when four of his men were shot, the rest fled for home. Meanwhile Governor Bowdoin had sent out, under General Benjamin Lincoln, a force of four thousand militiamen, who overwhelmed the unregulated regulators in a snowstorm, capturing a hundred and fifty and scattering the rest. Even though the rebellion spread for a time into New Hampshire, it was relatively bloodless. Yankee farmers and militiamen showed great reluctance to fire on one another, and although some of the captured leaders were condemned to death, the sentences were never carried out.

Nevertheless the fear waves from Shays' Rebellion spread far beyond Massachusetts. Jefferson, from the serene distance of Paris, observed that "a little rebellion now and then is a good thing," but those at home felt otherwise. Noah Webster was so upset that he decided a limited monarchy was preferable to republicanism on the rampage. Washington at Mount Vernon wrote to Henry Lee that he was "mortified beyond expression when [he viewed] the clouds that have spread over the brightest morn that ever dawned upon any country." His conviction that the government was simply too frail to function grew.

Early in 1786 the Virginia legislature—stimulated by its agreement with Maryland over the joint use of the Potomac River and Chesapeake Bay—had passed a resolution calling on all the states to send delegates to a general convention in Annapolis for the purpose of regulating interstate commerce. Summer wilted the freshness of the spring idea. By the time the Annapolis Convention met on September 11, only twelve delegates from five states—New York, New Jersey, Pennsylvania, Delaware, and Virginia—had been willing to brave the heat, the bad roads, and the bedbug-ridden inns.

On the very day they met, Shays's regulators rode into Concord, only eighteen miles from Boston, to keep the court there from holding session. Although few delegates showed up at Annapolis, those who did included

James Madison and Governor Edmund Randolph from Virginia, John Dickinson from Delaware, and Alexander Hamilton from New York. They could do no more than meet to adjourn, but they did take advantage of the opportunity to propose a subsequent convention, to be held in Philadelphia in the spring, that would go beyond regulating commerce and would revise the Confederacy itself. Hamilton was appointed to prepare a report asking the five states to name delegates and requesting the other eight states to do likewise.

To make that nebulous convention a fact, Hamilton would, for the next eight months, exert all his polemic brilliance, his lawyer's skills, his persuasive charm, and his adroitness. For the great spokesman for American conservatism had long become convinced that the "futile and senseless Confederation" ought to be replaced by a central government controlling "all but the mere municipal laws of each state." He was convinced that the thirteen states, if left to their sovereign selves, would go the destructive way of the Greek city-states.

The hearthstone loyalty of Americans to their states was scarcely comprehensible to Hamilton, born on the island of Nevis in the West Indies, thirteen hundred miles from New York. He himself was illegitimate; his father, the ne'er-do-well son of a Scots laird, deserted his mother, the estranged St. Croix wife of a German merchant. In spite of his birth stain, in spite of poverty and a broken home, Hamilton was of the fortunate few who seem to have success stamped on their cradles. From the time he was a child, his mind absorbed learning almost without effort. When his mother died in 1768, he, at the age of thirteen or fifteen—the exact year of his birth is not known—went to work for the wealthy trader Nicholas Cruger in St. Croix. A slight red-haired boy whose feet still dangled from the clerk's stool where he sat inscribing ledgers, he felt no sense of deprivation in being shut up in a countinghouse but rather an engrossing curiosity about the dockside world of business. He learned to fathom markets, prices, and cargoes, the export of sugar, the import of almost everything else. Hardly more than a boy, he became Cruger's right-hand man, making bold recommendations, deciding when to buy and sell for foreign clients, going on missions. He might have evolved into Cruger's partner if the hurricane of 1772 had not blown him into history. A letter that he wrote describing this disaster, printed over his objections in the island newspaper, made his impressive youthful brilliance noted in the small com-

America was growing rapidly, but even its cities had a small-town look. This is the Manhattan end of the Brooklyn Ferry, painted not long after New York was the Capital.

munity and even brought him to the attention of the governor. A group, headed by his old tutor and his employer, subscribed funds to send him to continental America to further his education.

At seventeen he arrived in New York and after some preliminary instruction enrolled at King's College—later Columbia. Slender, fine-featured, with an easy air of self-assurance, equally at home in French and English, graceful in speech, manners, and even the way he wore clothes, he kept a calculated energy and an incisive intelligence beneath his urbane exterior.

Though by inclination an aristocrat and by temperament a royalist, Hamilton was never tempted to the king's cause. At first he would have been content with dominion status within the British Empire. But when that hope faded he joined conservatives like Dickinson and the Morrises in their efforts to keep the Revolution from taking a radical direction. He himself would have preferred a Declaration of Independence that found self-evident the right to Life, Liberty, and Property. His most profound and durable conviction, reinforced by Locke, was that America formed an economic whole and that Providence, the very order of nature, had de-

creed a great and powerful nation on this continent. That the government in London could not or would not see this, was justification enough for breaking the old ties.

Hamilton was twenty-one when he left college and militia training to join the Continental Army. As a captain of a New York artillery company, he fought at the Battle of Harlem Heights, was with Washington during the retreat to Pennsylvania, and took part in the surprise attacks on Trenton and Princeton. Even the aloof commander in chief was impressed by the young captain and invited him to join his staff. Careful to pick none but gentlemen for what he called his family, Washington made Hamilton his aide, with the rank of lieutenant colonel. Soon the aide became Washington's confidential secretary; he prepared reports, dispatched orders, and corresponded voluminously with Congress and with the other commanders. He did manage to escape desk duty long enough to fight with courage at Monmouth and to participate in the siege of Yorktown.

He married well and he married for love, both requirements being equally essential to him. Nor did his rich, gouty, aristocratic father-in-law, General Philip

29

At Princeton in 1777 the brilliance of Captain Alexander Hamilton so impressed Washington that he appointed Hamilton his aide. This painting is by William Mercer, the son of a general mortally wounded in the battle.

Schuyler, raise the issue of his dubious birth. With his combination of astuteness and charm, Hamilton had a way of bending events and people to his will. A minority, nevertheless, remained impervious to his talents. Jefferson never liked him, and John Adams called him "the bastard brat of a Scotch pedlar."

In his self-acquired aristocratic person, Hamilton came to personify the rising opposition to the Confederation. The world, he maintained, was divided into the "rich and the well born, and the mass of the people." Most sharply remembered for his offhand remark that the people "is a great Beast," his more fundamental feeling was that the people were like a beast of burden that would in the end plod to the right destination if only provided with a firm checkrein. He believed that business leaders, merchants, the educated "generality of considerate men," should have a "distinct and permanent share in the government" in order to give it stability and continuity and to protect it against the "imprudence of democracy." After serving a term in Congress and trying in vain with Madison and James Wilson to persuade the states to grant Congress the power to tax and to raise revenue, he could find no more good in the Confederation. Replacement rather than reform became his goal. He and his fellow nationalists were lucky that Shays' Rebellion came during the Annapolis Convention, persuading the convention conservatives by example that only a strong and stable central government could protect them from even worse disasters. Without the goad of that rebellion, the Philadelphia Convention might never have found the resolution to adopt the Constitution. During the interval between the two conventions Hamilton had himself been elected to the New York legislature, where he spoke so eloquently—over Governor George Clinton's deaf ears—in favor of the proposed convention that the congressmen meeting in New York stopped in to listen to him. Congress itself, in language far stronger than that of the Annapolis Convention, was persuaded to issue a call for the Philadelphia meeting.

Ostensibly the document drafted by Hamilton at Annapolis—and toned down by Randolph—merely proposed to revise and amend the Articles of Confederation. But what Hamilton and his associates really planned for Philadelphia was the total revision of the existing government, an act of incalculable portent for the future shape and course of the nation.

31

The Constitution

The coldest of winters had given way to the wettest of springs as the delegates from the twelve states—Rhode Island having defiantly abstained—made their way through the mire to the "Fœderal" convention that would retrospectively become known as the Constitutional Convention. Only fifty-five of the seventy-four selected undertook the damp journey across the bedraggled landscape to Philadelphia. They drifted in on their own schedules, and though the convention's opening day was May 14, 1787, the last delegate did not arrive until August 6.

Benjamin Franklin, Doctor of Laws of the University of Edinburgh and president of the Executive Council of Pennsylvania and the most elderly of the delegates, was fortunate in not having to leave his home just off Market Street, where he had built a new dining room, large enough for twenty-four, to entertain visiting delegates. Philadelphia's one-legged Gouverneur Morris—the Tall Boy, they called him—was equally fortunate in not having to travel, although his wooden leg was said to be no disadvantage in pursuing the ladies. Pennsylvania's eight formed the largest group, including besides Franklin and the two Morrises, Gouverneur and Robert, the rusty narrow-shouldered figure of James Wilson. John Dickinson, representing Delaware, was convinced that a limited monarchy was the best form of government but had decided regretfully that it was out of the question for America.

The shy, soft-voiced, and scholarly Madison had in his systematic way arrived from Virginia eleven days early. He had spent the winter poring over bundles of books that Jefferson had sent him from Paris: volumes by Voltaire, Diderot, Neçker, and others; histories, books on political theory and the law of nations. In contrast to the black-clad classical figure of "Jemmy" Madison, with his queued hair carefully arranged to minimize his baldness, his colleague the unpredictably doctrinaire Edmund Randolph wore his dark hair loose and unpowdered in the romantic style. With them came George Mason, Washington's fox-hunting planter-neighbor, owner of thousands of acres and several hundred slaves, republican, abolitionist, and author of Virginia's Bill of Rights. Patrick Henry, suspicious of the anti-Confederation bias of the con-

Confidence in Washington as the dedicated unifier of the nation was expressed in this detailed work of 1789—for display in schoolrooms and parlors. Wearing civilian dress, the President is surrounded by the coats of arms of the thirteen original states and the federal government.

33

vention, had refused to come at all, saying that he "smelled a rat." In Massachusetts Sam Adams, with an equally keen nose, had not even been given the chance to refuse.

Although Madison may have had a new Constitution already formed in his head, although Hamilton may have seen the Philadelphia gathering as the ripened chance to demolish a ramshackle structure of government, the majority of the arriving delegates had no conscious intention of exceeding their instructions of meeting "for the sole and express purpose of revising the Articles of the Confederation." Some, like William Blount of North Carolina, doubted if even that was possible. Blount felt that "ultimately and not many years [hence, we shall] just be separate and distinct governments perfectly independent of each other."

Towering above all the other delegates, Virginia's General Washington stood out not only in physical presence and in reputation but in the legend that had already begun to blur his natural outlines. He had arrived in the city in his coach the day before the convention opened, escorted by the City Troop and an honor guard of his old senior officers. Passersby had cheered as he had passed. The bells of Christ Church had pealed their welcome. Artillery had boomed. Six years after Yorktown the hero was a hero still.

During the period of the convention the General was to stay in the solid mansion of Robert Morris, although before he left he would begin to suspect that the foundations were not as solid as they appeared. For despite Morris' reputation as a financial wizard, the path of land speculations had already begun to take the turning that would lead him in the end to the Prune Street Debtors' Prison.

It was eleven days after the opening of the convention before the minimum requirement of seven state delegations could be mustered. The delegates met in the East Room of Philadelphia's brick Statehouse, the room in which the Continental Congress had held its sessions and the Declaration of Independence had been signed. A restrained, formal room, forty feet square and painted a cool blue-gray, it had high, wide windows on two sides. Delegates sat three or four together at tables covered with green baize. Against the paneled east wall, on a dais between two fireplaces, was the presiding officer's chair, a sunburst carved on its back. Robert Morris, speaking in place of Franklin, who was kept home by age and bad weather, proposed Washington as the

convention's president. Approval was unanimous, and Washington was formally escorted to the chair, where he would sit for four months in quiet dignity.

The first three days were spent adopting the rules, including one to keep proceedings secret. Of the forty-two delegates from eleven states present by the end of May, seventeen beside Washington had been officers in the Continental Army, and four of these had served on his staff. Another thirteen had been militia officers. Eight had been members of one or both of the Continental Congresses of 1774 and 1775. Twenty-one were college graduates. Twenty-nine had been lawyers or judges. Nearly all had held political office. Among them there were nine relentlessly determined to manipulate this gathering to their purpose of creating a great nation. They were: Hamilton; Madison; the two Morrises; Franklin (to the extent his health permitted); the rustic but wily ex-shoemaker and former Yale treasurer, Roger Sherman, and the skilled, if stingy, Oliver Ellsworth, both from Connecticut; Rufus King of Massachusetts, Yankee-shrewd by nature and wealthy by marriage; and the arrogant planter from Charleston, "Dictator John" Rutledge.

After the rules had been laid down, "Mr. Randolph," as Madison noted, "then opened the main business." Resonantly, persuasively, the Virginia governor introduced the plan carefully prepared by Madison and his delegation and known as the Virginia Resolves. Presented as a basis for discussion, the plan did not alarm the delegates unduly even though—with no regard for the Confederation—it boldly proposed a national executive, a national judiciary, and a national legislature of two houses. Through the long discussions in the weeks to follow, the delegates, almost unaware, grew used to the idea of a consolidated government.

The Virginia plan proposed a legislature consisting of a lower house elected by the people, an upper house elected by the lower, and an executive elected by both houses. A government of three parts seemed acceptable to everyone, but the words "national" and "supreme" did not. Did these terms imply the end of state governments? Randolph—a supporter of state sovereignty—said they did not, and Morris explained, "When the powers of the national government clash with the states, only then must the states yield." When Randolph had finished, the convention formed itself into a committee of the whole—an old English parliamentary device by which the delegates could debate and vote

34

without recording or binding themselves. Symbolic of this change, Washington stepped down from his sunrayed chair to join the rest of the Virginia delegates.

Spring dampness gave way to searing heat as the delegates haphazardly took up the fifteen resolves, discussed them, wrangled over them. Should an upper house be elected by a lower house, by a national executive, by the people, by the state legislatures? Dickinson wanted the upper house to consist of men distinguished in rank and property, and this at least was unanimously agreed on. Should a lower house be elected by the people? Charles Pinckney of South Carolina preferred its election by the state legislatures, since "the people were less fit judges." Madison felt that the people ought to elect at least one branch. The people were, of course, those with property qualifications for voting. Beyond that lay mob rule, Shays triumphant.

Franklin favored a one-house legislature, like Pennsylvania's, but did not put it to a motion. Suffering from gout and the stone, he came only erratically, carried in a sedan chair by four prisoners borrowed from the Walnut Street jail. The sedan chair he had had brought from France as the only transportation his aged, ailing body could endure. Washington appeared with scrupulous regularity, walking to the Statehouse each morning from Morris' home in his blue coat and cocked hat. Other delegates were less conscientious. Rarely were more than thirty present, often fewer.

By midday, with the windows shut, the hall would grow stifling. The Northerners, in their woolen clothes, minded the heat most. Yet if the long windows were opened, the air soon swarmed with flies. Although a nation's destiny was being decided there, it was a languid scene: a handful of men around green tables, bluebottle flies droning above the ebb and flow of voices.

Virginia's seventh resolve called for a "national executive," whose form was not specified. Randolph, fearing "one-man power," suggested three individuals: one each from the South, the North, and the Middle States. James Wilson, of Pennsylvania, his steel spectacles hooked to his wig, made a countermotion in his furry Scots accent for "a single vigorous executive." To the dismayed Randolph such unilateral power was "the foetus of monarchy." Mason thought it would pave the way for a hereditary ruler. Even Dr. Franklin had his doubts, for—as he remarked—though the first man at the helm would be a good one, who could say what manner of leader might come after?

The ominous question on which the convention would almost shatter was that of representation. Were the states to be represented by equal votes as in the Confederation or in proportion to their population? If in proportion, how could the small states protect themselves from the large? Embittered discussion dragged on until the shrewd Sherman suggested a compromise. Let each state's members in the lower house be in proportion to the number of free inhabitants in the state. But let each state have one and only one vote in the upper house. There was a further objection from the Southern states. Slaves might be property, but for tally purposes they wanted them counted as inhabitants. This time the legal-minded Wilson evolved the compromise—the number of congressmen from each state to be proportioned to the whole number of free citizens plus three-fifths of all remaining persons.

For four weeks the Virginia Resolves were discussed and amended. The opposition then took the floor in the diminutive person of New Jersey's William Paterson. He maintained that the duty of the convention was to revise, correct, and enlarge the Articles of Confederation and that the delegates had no authority even to discuss the Virginia Resolves. Instead he offered his own plan: a single-chamber legislature with limited power derived from the states; a plural executive branch.

While convention delegates were debating elsewhere in Philadelphia in 1787, a minor tragedy on Lombard Street was captured by C. W. Peale in this rare etching. A verse underneath told of the girl's dropping "the pye from Bake-house," to the amusement of sooty chimney-sweeps.

The venerable traditions of England's two legislative bodies—the House of Lords, above, and the House of Commons, below—strongly influenced the thinking of the Founding Fathers in their creation of a new government.

Madison at once attacked the plan as powerless to prevent more Shays' Rebellions. Before it could even be voted on, Hamilton offered his own alternative. Haughty, his blue eyes darkened with angry zeal, he proposed a single executive and an upper house of senators, both elected for life; state governors appointed by the national government; a lower house elected by the people every three years. He was certainly astute enough to realize that such an authoritarian plan would never be adopted, and probably hoped to subtly make the Virginia plan look tame by comparison.

If such was Hamilton's intention, he was indeed successful, for the Virginia plan remained the framework for the evolving Constitution. On June 20 Washington resumed his chair as the delegates met in full convention. Once more the great and bitter debate—the issue of small states versus large—echoed: Should representation be by population or by state? The feeling grew that the convention itself was foundering. Franklin, for all his deism, suggested resorting to formal prayer—a piety to which Hamilton objected as a signal to outsiders that the convention was in deep trouble and which in any case was ruled out by the lack of any means to pay a chaplain. Finally on July 16 the worn-down delegates settled on the great compromise, essentially the one offered by Sherman. Each state would have two senators; the state's population would determine the number of congressmen.

What went on day after day in those sweaty secret sessions was a tantalizing mystery to the public. There were whispers that the new America would emerge as a monarchy, one persistent rumor being that the second son of George III, the Bishop of Osnaburgh, would be invited to ascend an American throne.

The proceedings grew increasingly tedious. It took sixty ballots to decide on a method of selecting a President. First the delegates voted to have the President appointed by the national legislature, then by electors chosen by the state legislatures. The Virginia plan left unspecified the term of the Executive. Motions were offered for a six-year, an eleven-year, a fifteen-year, and finally a seven-year, term—later changed to four years.

At last, on July 26, the exhausted convention appointed a five-man Committee of Detail to draw up a tentative constitution and adjourned until August 6. The committee members meanwhile worked at smoothing the convention's various resolutions into a first draft of a constitution, which they submitted on August 6. It would, however, take five more weeks of intensive and often savage debate before the delegates could agree to give the document to the Committee of Style and Arrangement for final polishing.

Before the polishing could take place, the question of slavery had to be settled, a question second only to representation in its intransigency. As a gesture of conciliation, the Northerners agreed that for the purpose of representation and taxes five slaves would be equivalent to three whites and that the import tax on a slave would not exceed ten dollars. The Southerners then agreed that importation of slaves could cease after 1808.

There were lesser matters to settle: a definition of treason; the seat and extent of the taxing power; the ratio of congressmen to population in the various states; whether there should be religious qualifications for office, or sumptuary laws regulating dress and furnishings; the method of amending the Constitution; the number of states necessary to ratify in order to put the Constitution into force; and whether the states should ratify by conventions or through their legislatures.

On September 8 the convention handed over to the Committee of Style twenty-three resolves that had been debated, fought over, voted upon, many times rewritten, and at last reduced to the passivity of paper. The committee, which met for four days, consisted of Hamilton, Madison, Gouverneur Morris, Rufus King, and the new president of Columbia College, Dr. William Samuel Johnson. Morris, entrusted to do the writing, reduced the twenty-three articles to seven. "We the People of the United States," he began, by that striking phrase avoiding any mention of states that might opt to remain outside the Union. "We the People of the United States, in Order to form a more perfect Union, establish Justice, insure domestic Tranquility, provide for the common defence, promote the general Welfare, and secure the Blessings of Liberty to ourselves and our Posterity, do ordain and establish this Constitution for the United States of America."

There were still a few days of debate, but at last the work was completed. Forty-two delegates were present on the final day, September 17. Dr. Franklin rejoiced in the brisk, fresh air as he arrived in his sedan chair. The doctor admitted with disarming urbanity that there were parts of the new Constitution of which he did not approve. Nevertheless he was astonished to find it did as well as it did, and he felt that America's enemies would be astonished too by what they had achieved.

Soberly the delegates filed forward by states to sign the parchment. Franklin had to be helped forward, and as he penned his name, tears ran down his seamed cheeks. Hamilton was anxious that every delegate sign, but Randolph, Elbridge Gerry of Massachusetts, and Mason still refused. Franklin, glancing at the rayed sun just above Washington's head, remembered that during the summer he had often wondered whether it was rising or setting. Now he knew that the sun was rising.

The issues that had been argued, fought over, and decided in secret in the blue-gray Philadelphia hall now had to be argued all over again openly in the thirteen states. Never before had American newspapers devoted so much space to any one subject as they did to the new Constitution. Gerry and Randolph and Mason published their objections. Hamilton came to the defense in the eloquently reasoned *The Federalist* papers, which appeared as eighty-five separate essays in New York's newspapers. Of these Hamilton himself wrote two-thirds, the ailing Jay five, and Madison the rest. Although too quietly intellectual to cause a great stir at the time, *The Federalist* papers were destined to be numbered among the seminal documents of American history.

The old Congress of the Confederation, meeting in New York, was quick to recommend that the states call ratifying conventions while blandly avoiding the word "Constitution." Ten of the members attending its final meeting had been delegates at Philadelphia and—in the transmutation of names not unfamiliar to politics—they became known as Federalists while the old federalist opposition took the name Antifederalist.

It was clear that the battle for ratification was going to be uphill work. Nine states would have to agree before the Constitution could become effective, but if just one of the big states—Pennsylvania, Massachusetts, New York, or Virginia—chose to remain outside, that would, practically speaking, be the end of the Union. Men still distrusted the idea of a strong government, a strong congress, and a standing army. Yet the Antifederalists had no alternative plan to offer, and in taverns, shops, and on street corners the most convincing argument of the Federalists was that the Constitution must be a good thing since Washington and Franklin had approved it.

Delaware, by unanimous vote, was the first state to ratify the Constitution. At the Pennsylvania convention Wilson pleaded day after day for ratification, tirelessly,

adroitly, and at last successfully. An outdoor rally at Carlisle celebrated the Federalist victory with bonfires and speeches. Unreconciled, a mob of Antifeds rushed in with clubs, beating Wilson half to death.

New Jersey and Georgia followed Pennsylvania with little doubt or hesitation. Massachusetts, where the rural resentments that had engendered Shays' Rebellion still smoldered, was another matter. Of the huge convention of three hundred and fifty-five that met in January in the Brattle Street Church—the Statehouse was too small—the majority of the delegates were Antifederalists and twenty-nine had ridden with Shays. But Boston Federalists actively and suavely cultivated the city's artisans and mechanics, with such success that the old Sons of Liberty became vociferous supporters of the new Constitution. Sam Adams found himself made mute by the defection of his old street supporters.

John Hancock, though governor of the state and president of the convention, retreated with an attack of gout to his Beacon Street mansion until he could determine which way the wind would blow. Meanwhile, Federalists whispered to him that if—as seemed likely —Virginia failed to ratify, then George Washington would not be available for the Presidency. And who in that case would be more eligible than John Hancock? When the governor finally did appear at the convention, carried to his seat, his feet swathed in bandages, he had swung over to the side of the Constitution.

Winning other vacillating delegates with promises to support amendments in the nature of a Bill of Rights, the Federalists carried the convention by 19 votes. In contrast to Pennsylvania, the losers accepted their defeat gamely. As bells rang and cannon roared, the delegates trooped to Faneuil Hall, where Feds and Antifeds drank toasts of conciliation until, according to a Boston paper, "all appeared to be willing to bury the hatchet of animosity and smoke the calumet of union and love."

Virginia and New York were now the key states. In Virginia, Richard Henry Lee, who, like Patrick Henry, had refused to serve as a delegate in Philadelphia, denounced the Constitution with bitterness. He was joined in his opposition by Henry, Mason, and the young James Monroe. At the belated June state convention Henry—stooped, spectacled, an old man at fifty-two—became once more the impassioned orator. Twisting his brown wig two or three times around his head at tense moments, he appealed by turns to prejudices of

In this painting by Thomas Rossiter, Washington presides over the final official act of the convention delegates—signing the Constitution they created. Rossiter invoked artistic license in placing the tapestry with its sunburst behind Washington; actually the wall was paneled.

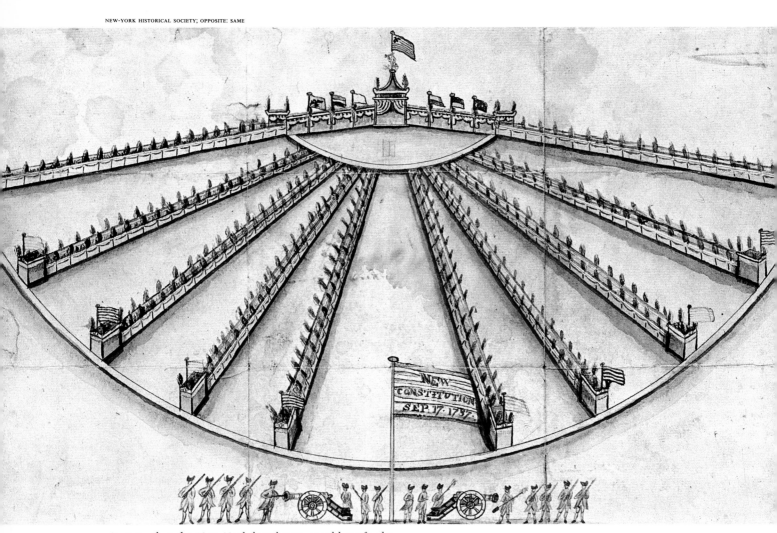

*Certain that the New York legislature would ratify the
Constitution, citizens in New York City celebrated three
days early. Above is the official banquet pavilion,
where, after the parades, 6,000 feasted and heard speeches.*

the poor, the wealthy, the slaveholders, the debtors, the
republicans, those fearing an established church. So
compelling was his warning voice that one spectator involuntarily felt his wrists to be sure the fetters were not
already there. For all Henry's hypnotic persuasiveness,
his followers were still not strong enough to prevail
against Washington, Madison, John Marshall, and the
wavering Randolph, and the convention ratified the
Constitution by a vote of 89 to 79.

It was in New York—that most Antifederalist of
states—that the odds were heaviest against the Constitution, the opposition being led by the popular and
perennial Governor George Clinton. New York's con-

vention met in Poughkeepsie on June 17 with Clinton
presiding. When the delegates first assembled, only
nineteen out of sixty-five could be counted for the Constitution. Alexander Hamilton's great parliamentary triumph was in building up his forces during six weeks of
debate to turn this hostile majority into a majority of
three for ratification.

At the height of the debate the encouraging word
came that New Hampshire had ratified as the ninth
state, thus dissolving the old Confederation and making
a reality of the new Constitution. The news a short time
later of Virginia's adherence brought further doubt and
confusion to the less dogmatic Antifeds. Melancton

Smith, Clinton's floor lieutenant and Hamilton's chief opponent, was finally persuaded to change his mind for the sake of a greater unity, believing that the radical defects he still saw in the Constitution could be corrected with amendments—he suggested thirty-two. North Carolina and Rhode Island, stubbornly isolated, did not come into the Union until after the first federal election.

Even before New York's surprising turnabout, Philadelphians had staged a ratification celebration that began on July 4 with the pealing of the Christ Church bells and a cannon salute from the ship *Rising Sun*, anchored off Market Street, continued with a symbolic parade of all the trades and tradesmen, and ended with a "plentiful cold collation."

New York's celebration on July 23 was as much in honor of Hamilton as of the Constitution. The commercial city was ready to welcome ratification with the panoply of full victory. A mammoth parade began at a signal from thirteen guns fired from the feature of the parade, the Federalist ship *Hamilton*, with a crew of thirty—a twenty-seven-foot copy of a frigate of thirty-two guns, full-rigged, drawn through the streets by ten horses. Down cheering Broadway the *Hamilton* moved, along Great Dock Street, Hanover Square, and Queen Street, followed by mechanics and tradesmen with their floats and their banners and by apprentices of every trade: hatters, wigmakers, nailers, carpenters, shipwrights, cobblers, blacksmiths.

The first election to the new Congress in the autumn of 1788 was for the most part a quiet, almost anticlimactic event. A mood of unity spread through the country, a feeling of a crisis overcome, an act completed. All the states except Virginia and New York (with North Carolina and Rhode Island still outside the Union) chose friends of the Constitution as their representatives. That first Congress contained thirty Federalists and less than a dozen Antifederalists.

The Constitution stipulated that each state should appoint presidential electors equal in number to the total of the state's senators and representatives; the electors were then to meet in their respective states and each vote for two persons. The person having the greatest number of votes—providing it was a majority—would be President, the person with the second largest number, Vice President. Since the Constitution did not specify the method of selection, in five states the legislatures chose the electors, in three others they were elected by popular vote, while Massachusetts and New

Hampshire devised a complicated combination of both systems. New York, North Carolina, and Rhode Island remained unrepresented.

To choose anyone but Washington as the first President would have been unthinkable. No such sense of inevitability hovered over the Vice Presidency. With considerable reluctance Hamilton, as the nominal head of the Federalists, supported the roly-poly New Englander John Adams—whom he referred to as the Duke of Braintree. Adams, having served as peace commissioner and then as United States envoy to Great Britain, had just returned after ten years abroad. Since Hamilton needed the support of the New England Federalists, he agreed to accept Adams, at the same time doing his best in secret to whittle down Adams' vote and to diminish his political influence. Washington received all 69 electoral votes; Adams only 34.

Conscious of himself as a symbol and realizing that his initial acts and deportment as President would set a precedent for generations to come, Washington felt he walked "an untrodden ground." Shortly after his inauguration he asked Hamilton's advice on presidential etiquette. Hamilton suggested that the President hold one formal reception, or levee, a week, conversing with invited guests on "indifferent subjects" and after half an hour withdrawing. His public entertainments should be limited to a few ceremonies on national holidays. The President should meet official persons at small private dinners. Only secretaries of departments,

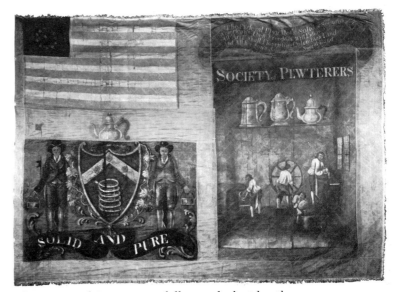

The Society of Pewterers joyfully marched with tailors, brewers, upholsterers, and other craftsmen in the federal procession of 1788 in New York. The society's silk banner, above, featured its coat of arms, an optimistic verse, a national ensign, and pewterers at their trade.

ambassadors, and senators should have direct access to him. He should return no visits.

Washington for the most part followed Hamilton's austere advice, although he accepted Adams' suggestion that he hold two weekly levees. He was adamant in his restraint. He would accept no private invitation, not even to funerals. His public receptions he limited to three: Martha Washington's Christmas Eve entertainment, his own New Year's Day reception, and the President's birthday.

Washington did not find his Cherry Street house either as large or as handsome as he thought an official residence should be, and shortly after assuming office he moved to a mansion on Broadway that had been vacated by the French minister. Fourteen white servants and seven slaves brought from Virginia made up his household staff. The Washingtons entertained with frequent and elaborate dinners. The President's wife—called by courtesy Lady Washington—held her own levees every Friday evening.

The President drove through New York in his coach, drawn by six cream-colored horses and accompanied by four servants and two gentlemen outriders. When he chose to go on horseback, he rode a white horse with a leopard-skin housing and a saddlecloth bound in gold. Dissenters—there were a few—might mutter about a republican court, but the President was meticulous in observing the exact boundaries of his office.

At the beginning of his term Washington looked forward to a harmonious four years. With Hamilton in the Treasury cooperating with Madison, Majority Leader of the House of Representatives, the dust of party strife seemed laid. Yet for Congress as well as for the President the new government was an unprecedented step that demanded precedents. The Constitution was a

Convention sessions were enlivened by the views of these four outspoken delegates: Elbridge Gerry of Massachusetts, above, wanted the President elected by state governors; both Luther Martin of Maryland and William Paterson of New Jersey (top and bottom, left) feared for the rights of the small states, while Pennsylvania's Gouverneur Morris (far left) favored rule by aristocrats.

compromise between varied interests, between those who believed in the voice of the people and those who feared the roar of the mob, between the autocracy of an all-powerful central government and the anarchy of independent states. How would that painfully evolved paper unity work in practice?

The first Congress, meeting in New York's remodeled City Hall, was late in arriving and slow in organizing itself. Its most pressing problem was that of raising revenue, but its most insistent was the Antifederalists' agitation for a Bill of Rights. Hamilton had taken the position that the new federal government had only those powers granted to it by the states. "Why declare that things shall not be done," he asked, "which there is no power to do?" But something more than logic was required to meet the requests of five states for a Bill of Rights and the demands of four others for various amendments to the Constitution. Fearful of the growing insistence on another Constitutional Convention, Madison had methodically gone through the states' various demands, selecting the eighty most popular and

practicable, and then, by combining and eliminating repetition, had reduced them to seventeen. These were further reduced by Congress in joint session to twelve. The first two, concerning the number and salaries of congressmen, were never ratified, but the remaining ten—known as the Bill of Rights—went to the states for ratification and in December, 1791, became part of the Constitution, the guarantee that the individual would be protected from the arbitrary use of power.

The new government badly needed to raise money, and the most reliable source of revenue seemed to be a tariff. Madison devised a measure that maneuvered skillfully between Northerners demanding protection for their nascent industries and Southern planters, who wanted a low tariff for revenue only. Most imported articles were to be taxed at 5 per cent, but there would be specific duties up to 50 per cent on steel, ships, cordage, tobacco, salt, indigo, and cloth, and foreign ships were to pay tonnage, a duty of so much per ton, upon entry into an American port.

In the long run the organization of the Supreme Court and of the first Cabinet would be more important than the Tariff of 1789. Jay, resplendent in varicolored silk robes, took his place on the bench as the first Chief Justice of the Supreme Court. Wilson had had his heart set on the post but had to be content with becoming one of the five associate justices. Randolph, as a reward for his return to the federal fold, received the new office of Attorney General. In the other government offices Knox, as Secretary of War, continued in the post he had held during the Confederation. Hamilton achieved his wish in becoming Secretary of the Treasury—a position second in importance only to that of the President. Thomas Jefferson, home on leave as United States minister to France, was named Secretary of State. Washington had had a high opinion of Jefferson ever since the two men had served in the Virginia House of Burgesses. But more than friendship and admiration were involved. Jefferson's services were essential for his knowledge of the portentous events in France.

There remained to Congress the problems of how to deal with the national debt inherited from the Confederation and what to do about the proposed Federal City. The Confederation had acted like an improvident housekeeper, running up bills with no concern about repayment; it had not even paid interest on the money it had borrowed. States had followed the national example. Unbacked certificates given to ex-soldiers for their services and to merchants and farmers for supplies sold or requisitioned during the war, had dropped to one-quarter or one-eighth of their value during the Confederation years. A rejuvenated government brought back the possibility of their being redeemed, at par or at a discount. Speculation in the seesawing Continental Loan Office certificates became a national pastime among the more prosperous merchants and bankers and even spread abroad to the financially alert Dutch. Most of the original small holders—the farmers, merchants, and ex-soldiers—had long since disposed of their certificates at a fraction of face value.

The foreign debts—French and Dutch—that the new government had inherited amounted to twelve million dollars, while the domestic debt ran to more than forty million dollars, including thirteen million dollars arrears of interest. Adding the war debts of the states to these sums gave a grand debt total of eighty-one million dollars. "What are we to do with this heavy debt?" Washington asked Robert Morris, and Morris replied that Alexander Hamilton was the only man in the United States who could tell him.

Hamilton devised his Report on Public Credit, his formula for rescuing the nation's credit and establishing its solvency, from European models, particularly from the example of the British Exchequer, and added his own brilliant improvisations. No sooner was it known that he was preparing to present his report to Congress than speculators flocked like starlings to New York's Federal Hall to try to pick up advance information. Other hardier speculators headed for the Carolinas and Georgia to buy up state certificates from the unwary and the uninformed. Speculation fever was in the air.

In January, 1790, the report of the Secretary of the Treasury was read before Congress. It argued that the new government had both the need and the power to protect its credit. Such credit was necessary for the reputation of the United States. Debts owed to foreigners, the Secretary said, should be paid precisely according to the terms of the original contract. The domestic debt was a more complicated matter, for the question rose as to whether the present holders of certificates— most of them speculators—should be paid the full face value of their securities or whether an arrangement should be made to reimburse the farmers, merchants, and soldiers who had been the original owners. While sympathetic to the latters' claims that hard times and taxes had forced them to sell the certificates at a fraction

*Major Pierre L'Enfant, the French architect who later de-
signed Washington, D.C., remodeled City Hall in New
York to accommodate the branches of the national government in its first Capital. This is the chamber of the
House of Representatives in Federal Hall, as the building was
renamed, where the Bill of Rights was presented in 1789.*

of their value, Hamilton insisted that the government could take no other course than to reimburse the present holders. Speculators they might be, but they had bought at the market value from those who had sold for what had seemed to them good cause. The government had made the certificates assignable. To alter the terms would be a breach of contract that would undermine public confidence.

As for the state debts, whatever the resulting inequities—for some states had paid off most of their obligations while others had not even met the interest—Hamilton felt that the debts had been contracted in a common cause and that the government, if it was to be truly a national government, had no choice but to take them over.

To obtain the money to pay off the several debts, Hamilton proposed to fund them. For one thing, he believed that a properly financed public debt formed the cement of union. Moreover, he knew that the new government would not receive sufficient revenue to pay the old debts. In his funding operation he planned to have the creditors convert their old securities into new securities. The necessary interest—plus six hundred thousand dollars to run the government—would be raised by increasing import duties and by taxing carriages, licenses to practice law, playing cards, sales at auctions, wines, spirits, tea, and coffee.

Debate on Hamilton's proposals occupied almost the whole six months of the second session. Few disputed that the debt owed to foreigners should scrupulously be paid. But there was bitter debate on whether the speculators or the original holders of domestic government

In the nation's early years artisans and workmen were in such demand that wages were high, capital wooed labor, and most labor organizations were formed for social and fraternal purposes. Above is a membership certificate (1791) of the New York Mechanick Society—a benevolent association for various types of manually skilled workers.

ecurities should be reimbursed. Congressmen appealed for the "gallant veteran" with his "tender wife and children," who out of need had been forced to part with his certificates for a pittance. Hamilton, adamant in his convictions, was comforted by the knowledge that he controlled sufficient votes to override the opposition.

In the matter of assuming the states' debts he had no such comfort, and with Madison leading the Southern opposition, the House of Representatives voted 31 to 29 against the measure. Realizing that his only chance for passage lay in compromise, Hamilton sought out the newly disembarked Thomas Jefferson, so soon to be his bitter enemy. Although he differed politically with Hamilton, Jefferson maintained a more objective view of the credit report than did his fellow Virginians, and he was able to listen with some detachment when, in a curious meeting in front of the presidential mansion, Hamilton asked his aid in averting a national crisis. The next day, at a dinner at which Madison was also present, Jefferson set forth the terms he could offer: he would obtain enough votes for passage of the Funding-Assumption Bill, a bitter pill for the Southern states, if Hamilton in turn would yield to the Southern demand for a "midway" Capital on the Potomac, an equally bitter pill for New Yorkers.

With Jefferson's backstage assistance the proposals of Hamilton's report were accepted by Congress. With Hamilton's help a bill was passed transferring the Capital to Philadelphia at the close of the session and at the end of ten years moving it to the ten-mile-square "Grand Columbian Federal City" that would be built on the banks of the Potomac. "We may as well have a set of gamblers for rulers," the Boston *Gazette* remarked in disgust. Jefferson soon came to feel regretfully that he had been tricked into favoring stockjobbers and speculators, and a year later told Washington that "of all the errors of my political life, this has occasioned me the deepest regret."

At the close of the session Washington took the road south, stopping briefly in Philadelphia, where the municipal corporation had engaged Robert Morris' house as the President's future official residence. Although the handsomest mansion in the city, Washington found it inadequate for the "commodious accommodation" of his family, and after directing various alterations, left for Mount Vernon, where he arrived early in September. As he sat on his terrace watching the changing leaves, he could reflect that fortune had been with him.

The theories of the Philadelphia Convention had become reality. The funding of the national debt and the assumption of the state debts had been accomplished, and the seat of the government had been settled. A shortage of grain in Europe had brought ships to buy up the bountiful American harvest at high prices. As Washington had observed with satisfaction before leaving New York, ". . . population increases, land is cleared, commerce extended . . . and Heaven smiles upon us with favorable seasons and abundant crops."

A few weeks after the rather uneventful congressional elections, Washington returned to Philadelphia. The Morris house was livable, though all its alterations were not completed. But he was disturbed to discover that a Pennsylvania law provided for the freeing of adult slaves six months after their owner had become a resident of the state, and though he felt that the law did not apply to him, he prepared to send his black servants back to Virginia lest someone "entice" them or they become "insolent." His brief address at the opening session of Congress concerned finance and Indian affairs. He recommended that the federal debt be reduced as fast as possible and revealed that he had sent Pennsylvania's General Josiah Harmar to clear the Northwest of troublesome Indian raids—not realizing as he spoke that the incompetent and alcoholic Harmar had already been defeated at the Maumee River by a coalition of tribes led by Little Turtle.

Much of what the United States was to become a century and a half later was inherent in Hamilton's grand design. For him industrialization was the key to the future of the still-agricultural country if only the central government could be strong enough and energetic enough to foster such a development. He foresaw a Union impervious to sectional jealousies, in which Southern raw materials would supply Northern factories to the benefit of all Americans—planters, farmers, mechanics, shipowners, merchants, and manufacturers.

The first step in his grand design, establishing the nation's credit, still left the United States without a central bank and without an adequate currency. To remedy this double lack he proposed a Bank of the United States, on the model of the Bank of England, to issue notes—payable upon demand in gold and silver—legal tender for all sums owed the government, which would become the country's principal currency. The government would own a quarter of the bank's stock and the rest would be offered to the investing public. Although

Congress approved and the President signed the measure, the opposition to Hamilton hardened. Madison, Jefferson, and Randolph insisted that nowhere in the Constitution could there be found any authorization for such a bank.

Whatever the theory, the practical effect of Hamilton's measures was immediate. By 1792 the war debt was being liquidated, government securities were stabilized at close to their face value, and hoarded wealth came out in the open, while foreign capital poured into the country as confidence in the government's credit grew. With the functioning of a national revenue system, the power of the federal government was decisively asserted over the states. Hamilton's blueprint for the power state is set forth in his Report on Manufactures, which he submitted to Congress in December, 1791. In this document he called for protective tariffs, bounties for the improvement of old and the establishment of new industries, awards for inventions, and exemption from duty of essential raw materials. Though much of his report was at the time rejected, he foresaw the industrial civilization of the future.

To Jefferson Hamilton—whom he considered a mon-

archist at heart—was rapidly becoming as repugnant as his views. Their rivalry within Washington's Cabinet was the genesis of that party system that Washington and the other signers of the Constitution had hoped to avoid. Even before Washington's first administration was over, the lines were drawn that would turn Jefferson and his Antifederalists into Republicans, in opposition to Hamilton and the Federalists.

Paradoxically Hamilton, the prophet of the twentieth century, remained rooted in the eighteenth century. Believing with Burke in tradition, in continuity, in a government by a responsible elite, he felt that a complete democracy could lead only to the rule of the demagogue. For him the French Revolution was freedom run wild. Jefferson saw the French Revolution as a new dawn. To him, inclined to the romantic nineteenth-century belief in the wisdom of the common man, the farmer with his hoe and his hundred acres was the ideal citizen. An industrial revolution with factories belching smoke was the worst thing that could happen to America. Farming was a God-ordained way of life; the best government, a minimal one.

Born into the lesser Virginia gentry, Jefferson had none of Hamilton's early hardships to overcome. In 1760, at the age of seventeen, he had entered the College of William and Mary in the capital of Williamsburg. Beyond his studies, his were the accomplishments of the young Virginia gentleman of the period—dancing, fencing, riding, and his favorite amusement, playing the fiddle. He danced at the Raleigh Tavern, visited at plantation houses and at the Governor's Palace, fell in love, and yet managed to spend most of his waking hours at his books. Learning would remain a passion with him. He read Cicero and Vergil in the originals; Newton, Locke, and Bacon formed his philosophy.

After two years he left William and Mary to study law under the noted lawyer George Wythe. Five years more he remained in the capital, leading a genial scholar's life. A familiar at the governor's table and among the burgesses, he knew everyone of any importance in Virginia. In 1769 he was elected to the House of Burgesses, where he would serve for the next fifteen years. Two years later he married a wealthy and well-connected young widow, Martha Wayles Skelton, and took her to the hilltop mansion Monticello, which he had designed and built himself.

In his young manhood he was of the same rufous complexion as Hamilton, but he had a jutting chin,

Thaddeus Kosciusko, a highly skilled Polish engineer who served as an officer in the Continental Army, drew this medallion portrait of Thomas Jefferson. The chaplet symbolizes Jefferson's deep absorption in the classics.

awkwardly large hands and feet, and a face flecked with freckles, and lacked his rival's grace. His health was nevertheless abounding, his teeth white and whole in a country already noted for early tooth decay. Out of an innate shyness—his enemies called it shiftiness—he could never bring himself to look anyone in the eye. Lacking the oratorical panache of a Patrick Henry, he preferred to express himself on paper. In taste and learning he had no equal in Virginia.

When the Second Continental Congress selected him, John Adams, Franklin, Roger Sherman, and Robert Livingston to compose a Declaration of Independence, Jefferson was left to do the actual writing. Conscious of his moment in history, he secluded himself in a Philadelphia rented room, where, bent over his portable writing desk, he nimbly framed the long-considered and unforgettable phrases in which his pen would substitute for the divine right of kings the inherent right of the governed.

He was governor of Virginia during the stern war years 1779–81, a period in which the state was ravaged by Benedict Arnold's raiders. In 1784 he sailed from Boston to replace John Jay, Franklin, and Adams at the peace treaty negotiations. He remained to replace Franklin as minister to France. In spite of the turmoil of politics, Jefferson found time in the five years he spent in France to constantly send back information about practical affairs—news about French inventions and discoveries, tips on winegrowing and agriculture, samples of seeds and plants. On returning to America and taking up his post as Secretary of State, as the tension with Hamilton grew, Jefferson gave Philip Freneau a sinecure in the government and persuaded him to start up a Republican paper, the *National Gazette*, to counteract the "poison" of John Fenno's earlier-established Federalist *Gazette of the United States*. Freneau, his poetry run dry, could still command a flood of invective, and he attacked Hamilton as a monarchist and a toady of aristocrats while proclaiming that "another revolution must and will be brought about in favor of the people." Fenno returned the fire, calling Jefferson a disunionist and a victim of the "French disease"— meaning the philosophy of the French Revolution.

The struggle between the two Cabinet members was at last out in the open; it was a power struggle as well as one of ideas, with each man seeing himself as the President's successor. Washington appealed to Hamilton and Jefferson to compose or at least compromise their

Not far down the avenue from Bruton Parish Church in Williamsburg, Virginia, stand the buildings of William and Mary College, among whose noted alumni were Thomas Jefferson, James Monroe, and Edmund Randolph.

differences, for such deep personal animosities could no longer be overcome. But even as Hamiltonian Federalists and Jeffersonian Republicans closed their ranks, both sides realized the need for Washington's stabilizing father figure. Washington's own most durable wish was to leave public life forever at the end of his term and retire to Mount Vernon, and he had already asked Madison to outline a valedictory address for him. Hamilton and Knox tried to persuade him to change his mind, Madison told him that his retirement would be a shock to the people, and Jefferson wrote that "North and South will hang together if they have you to hang on." Reluctantly, with his old compelling sense of duty, in his sixty-first year he put aside his cherished Mount Vernon dream to stand once more as the candidate of all the people.

His re-election was unopposed, a mere formality that brought out scarcely 10 per cent of the eligible votes. The Republican opposition vented its spite on John Adams, accusing that crusty New Englander of surrounding himself with luxury and of being a monarchist. Virginia and New York politicians tried to elbow him aside by uniting on Governor Clinton, but Adams mustered enough Federalist support to win re-election by 77 votes to Clinton's 50.

Washington's admitted aim was to keep the Presidency above politics, to preserve harmony with other nations and accord among his countrymen. At the beginning of his second term he could look with satisfaction on an expanding, prosperous Union. Vermont had ratified the Constitution two years before—after spending fourteen years as a quasi-independent republic—

becoming the first new state to join the original thirteen. Kentucky followed, its settlers having long been restive under Richmond's remote control.

Yet for all Washington's hopeful intentions, party storms and foreign clouds were already shadowing the sky as he took the oath of office for the second time. The British still stubbornly occupied their military and trading posts—including Detroit—within American territory adjoining Canada. The Spaniards had kept the Mississippi closed since 1784 and were stirring up the

The French Revolution took an especially violent turn in 1792, and in January of the following year the deposed king, Louis XVI, was executed (below). His wife, Marie Antoinette, was guillotined some months later. While the terrorism repelled many Americans, the majority favored the overthrow of autocratic rule in France.

Indians on the Southwest border of the United States. France had been proclaimed a republic, and Louis XVI had been guillotined. Jefferson thought the execution a salutary warning to corrupt rulers, while the more extreme Republicans appeared gleefully on the street in liberty caps. Washington, remembering the white uniforms of the French grenadiers at Yorktown, could find no satisfaction in the death of the simple-minded friend of America.

In the 1792 elections the emergent Republicans had won a majority of nine seats in the House of Representatives. The new party—an incongruous amalgam of great planters fearful of a strong government that might interfere with slavery, of large and small farmers opposed to the "avaricious Spirit of Commerce and Commercial Man," of those who followed Jefferson in believing in reason and progress, of doctrinaire republicans of the stamp of the old Sons of Liberty—proclaimed its devotion to republican institutions, to the welfare of the masses, and to the approaching nineteenth century, which Republicans saw as the age of the common man.

The Federalists, their backs resolutely turned on the new century, and with a frankness that would be their undoing, continued to assert that upper-class Americans had both a duty and a right to rule their social and economic inferiors. But the merchants, lawyers, bankers, speculators, and landowners who composed the Federalist elite lacked a magnetic rallying point. After the ringing words of the Declaration of Independence, ordinary men were less inclined to accept their betters at their own valuation, and the ballot box was expanding. Already Vermont had universal manhood suffrage.

Scarcely had Washington's second term begun when France declared war on England, Russia, Spain, and the Netherlands. The dominating problem of the administration became the relation of the United States to Revolutionary France. Washington, after his comrade-in-arms Lafayette had been proscribed by the increasingly radical regime, joined the Federalists in their basic distrust of the Revolution and their dismay at the excesses of the Terror. Jefferson felt that despite the excesses, liberty everywhere was bound up with the French Republic, and he declared he would rather have half the world devastated than see liberty fail. For the man in the city street, nursing his class grievances, the Revolution became as popular as it had become unpopular with the man in the countinghouse.

The issue grew sharp with the arrival in Charleston of the minister plenipotentiary of the French Republic, the cocky, self-assertive Edmond Charles Genêt. Genêt docked in a ship that bore a liberty cap on its masthead, glowing with the conviction that the two republics should stand as brothers-in-arms against all the monarchies of the world. He was authorized to commission as many as three hundred privateers to be fitted out in American ports. Making his way north with the dogmatic arrogancy of a young Revolutionary, he was hailed by city crowds and was tendered banquets along the way at which enthusiastic Republicans sang the "Marseillaise."

What Genêt demanded from the sister republic was a winking neutrality, in which French-chartered privateers preying on British shipping could bring their prizes to American ports for sale and salvage. Let the United States now return the aid that the French had given the Americans eleven years before!

Washington, determined to keep his country neutral in the power struggle overseas, issued a Proclamation of Neutrality. Jefferson at once protested that this was unconstitutional. Hamilton replied that the 1778 treaties with the French royal government had been voided and disapproved of Washington's even receiving Genêt. Washington did receive the French minister but with a cold formality that outraged Genêt, who considered American neutrality an affront. He was further incensed by the glimpse of a bust of Louis XVI in the President's parlor.

Genêt's attitude was more that of a commander than a minister. He demanded the immediate liquidation of the French debt to provide arms for the French forces. He supplied funds to the alcoholic George Rogers Clark and distributed commissions to raise a volunteer army for an expedition against Louisiana and Florida. His commissioned privateers brought captured British merchantmen into American ports to be sold by French consuls. When Washington finally prohibited privateers from fitting out in the United States or from enlisting American crews, Genêt turned defiant. Disregarding Washington, he refitted the captured British vessel *Little Sarah* in Philadelphia and sent her on her privateering ways as *La Petite Démocrate*.

When the government took steps against him, he threatened to go directly to the people. Finally his actions became so insolent that public opinion turned against him, and even Jefferson found it impossible to tolerate him. Before Washington could ask formally for his recall, the Jacobins overthrew the Girondists in Paris and orders came for Genêt to return to France to stand trial for his "criminal maneuvers." Convinced that he would be returning to the guillotine, the deflated Revolutionary was forced to appeal to Washington, who magnanimously granted him sanctuary.

Neither French nor English showed hesitation in confiscating American cargoes bound for what they defined as enemy ports, but the British, to the dismay of their Federalist friends, outdid themselves in blatant highhandedness. On secret orders in council the Royal Navy seized more than two hundred and fifty unarmed and unsuspecting American vessels carrying supplies to the French West Indies. Republicans roared for action. Madison and others demanded retaliatory measures against British ships and merchandise. By the spring of 1794 another war with England seemed near, and Hamilton and the antiwar Federalist senators persuaded Washington to send Jay as an emissary to London.

Jay, to his relief, found the British government under Grenville surprisingly conciliatory. Flattered by the cordiality of his reception by the British aristocracy, he even bent so far as to praise George III's "justice and benevolence." Grenville, anxious to settle differences with the Americans, relaxed British prohibitions on American trade with France and offered a most-favored-nation status to the United States, with the British West Indies open to American ships. He also agreed to surrender the disputed frontier posts and to allow joint commissions to settle questions of debts and boundaries. Jay in turn renounced his country's theoretical freedom of the seas where it interfered with Great Britain's struggle against France, and agreed to bar American ports to privateers.

On Jay's return, with the treaty in his pocket, he was assailed as a lickspittle by the more chauvinist Republicans, who accused him of having sold out to England. The Federalist-weighted Senate passed Jay's Treaty by a two-thirds majority with one vote to spare.

Contrary to dire Republican predictions the treaty worked out well. Despite obstacles raised by such lovers of France as Monroe, American envoy in Paris, it confirmed American neutrality while bolstering trade. In the next five years American exports to the British Empire would increase by 300 per cent. Yet the uproar against the treaty did not die down. Republicans found a political platform in the accusation that the Federalists had abandoned American rights, and even Washington, in his defense of the treaty, was brought into the maelstrom of politics.

Although the Father of his Country had chosen to see himself above party and faction, his buff and blue person was no longer inviolate. His second term found him assailed openly and with increasing virulence as the spokesman of the rich and the abettor of monarchy. There were even mean rumors that the Commander in Chief had secretly attempted to betray the Revolution. Washington blamed the French-oriented Democratic Societies for much of the diatribe against him, and at one Cabinet meeting said he would rather be in his grave than endure such abuse. His suppression of the disgruntled Pennsylvania farmers objecting to the excise tax on liquors—the so-called Whisky Rebellion— though bloodless, had left further long-smoldering resentments. Before he left office Washington would hear himself cursed in public. In the wake of Genêt's agitation a mob surrounded the Morris house in Philadelphia, screaming insults at the President, demanding war against England, and crying the praises of the French and all virtuous republicans.

Longing for Mount Vernon's placid acres, weary of the burdens of office, surfeited with politics, and deeply hurt by the venomous attacks on him, Washington determined that his second term would be his last. Once he had made his decision he began his Farewell Address—using as the framework the valedictory address Madison had prepared for him four years earlier and sending the completed draft to Hamilton for suggested revisions. In the summer of 1796 he allowed the final version to be published. Federalist though he was, he was a Federalist with a difference, for—as is clear in the Farewell Address—he never lost his faith and trust in the people. In his last formal statement of his Presidency he shed any Federalist trappings to stand forth as the symbol of a united country. That unity was his basic theme; it was challenged, in his belief, only by the harmful "Spirit of Party." Begging Americans to put aside old rancors, Washington warned them to maintain a true neutrality toward all nations. Then, in phrases that would echo for future generations—often with deliberate distortion—he urged his countrymen to have as little "political connection as possible with foreign nations," for Europe's interests are not ours and "our true policy [is] to steer clear of permanent alliances with any portion of the foreign world."

With a mannered grace of phrasing that would die with his century, the Father of his Country ended his farewell: "I anticipate with pleasing expectations that retreat, in which I promise myself to realize without alloy the sweet enjoyment of partaking, in the midst of my fellow citizens, the benign influence of good laws under a free Government, the ever favorite object of my heart and the happy reward . . . of our mutual cares, labors and dangers."

Even before Washington had published his formal farewell, the two great adversaries in his Cabinet had resigned. With the Proclamation of Neutrality, Hamilton's opinions, even in the conduct of the State Department, were beginning to take precedence over Jefferson's. Jefferson had not intended to remain Secretary of State for more than four years, and his conflicts with Hamilton and this rebuff sharpened his intention to leave. He handed in his resignation in July, 1793, and formally retired to Monticello in January. In his

'HE farewell previous to the *WESTERN EXPEDITION*.

At the urging of Alexander Hamilton, Washington called up a sizable militia force to quell the Whisky Rebellion, an insurrection of Pennsylvania farmers who violently objected to a federal tax on the beverage. Here a member of the 12,000-man army bids farewell to his sweetheart.

tempered view—it was not always tempered—Hamilton was "a singular character. Of acute understanding, disinterested, honest, & honorable in all private transactions . . . yet so bewitched and perverted by British example, as to be under thoro' conviction that corruption was essential to the government of a nation."

Hamilton in turn saw Jefferson as "tinctured with fanaticism . . . too much in earnest in his democracy . . . crafty and persevering in his objects . . . not scrupulous about the means of success . . . a contemptible hypocrite. . . . [But] there is no fair reason to suppose him capable of being corrupted." The Secretary of the Treasury left office in January, 1795, to return to his law practice. Yet, as a private citizen in New York, he remained the dynamic center of the Federalist party. Cabinet members, legislators, and ministers from abroad turned to him for advice. Washington consulted him on every major issue of foreign policy, and his successor in the Treasury, Oliver Wolcott, remained his subordinate.

Washington's retirement was viewed by the Federalists with fear, by the Republicans with hope. Jefferson and Adams, the accepted candidates of their parties, were at the same time old friends. Hamilton was privately as dubious about Adams as he had been eight years before.

Adams, long viewed as the President's successor, knew that he could never draw men to him like a Washington, or even like his rabble-rousing second cousin, Sam Adams, could, but he was enough of a self-righteous old Puritan not to care. Officially a Federalist, he was fundamentally an independent. Jefferson said of him that he viewed all parties and all men with a measure of contempt. Plump, round-bellied, intense, he carried himself with the self-importance frequent among men of small stature. Unfairly accused of being a monarchist, he did believe in a strong executive, which in periods of stress might become an office of life tenure or even hereditary. Unlike Jefferson, he felt that natural rights were overlaid with base impulses, and saw men guided as much by customs and prejudices as by reason. Without some control over the transitory popular will, orderly government would prove impossible. There were for Adams two kinds of people: the simplemen and the gentlemen. The simplemen, or the common men, were the mechanics, artisans, farmers, and small merchants. Opposed to them were the gentlemen, not the men of wealth and property in Hamilton's sense,

53

Because Jay's Treaty failed to define disputed bound-
aries, the British fur post of Grand Portage on the north
shore of Lake Superior did not officially become
American until the border with Canada was fixed in 1842.

but "all those who have received a liberal education."
Lest the simplemen voters be debauched by demagogues, Adams would have chosen gentlemen for senators, to serve for life. Republicans were to find his
views a tempting target.

John Adams owed his rise in polite society to his
mother, an upper-class Boylston, whereas the Adamses
had been in their four generations farmers and rustics in
the village of Braintree, ten miles south of Boston.
Young Adams had farmed, he had gone to Harvard, he
had graduated and taught school in Worcester, and afterward he had turned to the study of law. In 1758, at
the age of twenty-three, he was admitted to the Boston
bar and seven years later made himself known as one of
the Whig leaders in the agitation against the Stamp Act.

At the time of the so-called Boston Massacre of 1770,
when a squad of redcoats, who were goaded beyond en-
durance, opened fire on a threatening mob, Adams,
with characteristic disregard of inflamed public opinion, undertook the successful defense of the soldiers,
who were charged with murder. He was a member of
the two Continental Congresses and one of the leaders
singled out by George III as a fomenter of rebellion.
Congress appointed him, with Franklin and Lee, commissioner to the French government, and in 1778 he
left for Europe with his ten-year-old son, John Quincy.
Except during one brief interlude, he spent the next
decade abroad, through the later years of the Revolution and the whole period of the Confederation. With
Franklin—whom he considered a profligate—and Jay

54

he negotiated the peace treaty with Great Britain and the later commercial treaties with other European powers. For a time he acted as minister to the Netherlands, but his heart's wish was to be the first American minister to the Court of St. James's.

For all his pride as a New Englander, Adams never lost his affection for the mother country. Unlike Jefferson, who confessed that he yearned for the day when he could drink tea with French generals in London, Adams felt the tug of his English roots.

After some maneuvering he did manage to achieve his wish, and George III received as minister from the new nation the man he had once proscribed. Oddly enough the men resembled each other—chubby, short, choleric. The king, though ill at ease at their first meet-

ing, did his best to be cordial. "I am very glad the choice has fallen upon you to be their minister," he told Adams. "I will be very frank with you. I was the last to consent to the separation; but the separation having been made, and having become inevitable, I have always said, as I say now, that I would be the first to meet the friendship of the United States as an independent power." The king's courtesy, nevertheless, had its limits, for when Adams later brought the visiting Jefferson to court, George turned his back on the man who had so traduced him in the Declaration of Independence.

During Adams' two terms as Vice President the Federalists had come to take it for granted that he would be their candidate to succeed Washington. As his running mate they picked Thomas Pinckney, a soldier, lawyer, and diplomat who had negotiated a popular treaty with Spain. According to the terms of the Constitution, the candidate receiving the most electoral votes became President and the one with the next highest number, Vice President. Hamilton publicly urged all the Federalist electors to support Adams and Pinckney with the "great object of excluding Jefferson." Privately he planned to draw away enough electors from Adams to insure Pinckney's election.

The Republicans had picked as their candidate for Vice President the lawyer, political boss, and former senator from New York, Aaron Burr—or, more accurately, he had picked them. For this short hawk-nosed aristocrat with the asymmetric face was a skilled manipulator, an adventurer, and a libertine, with an instinct for political intrigue and a passion for speculation. He could claim high intellectual descent, for his father had been the second president of the College of New Jersey—now Princeton—and his mother, a daughter of Jonathan Edwards. He was early orphaned, early troublesome. At the outbreak of the Revolution he had left his law books to join the American Army. As a captain and still under twenty, he had marched with Arnold to Quebec, and after the repulsed attack on the frozen citadel, was reputed to have carried General Montgomery's body back in his arms. For a time he had served on Washington's staff, but the two men proved antagonistic, and he was transferred to the staff of General Israel Putnam. He served with some distinction in the fighting on Long Island and during the evacuation of New York. Commissioned a lieutenant colonel in 1777 and given command of a line regiment, he became known both for daring and discipline.

Quitting the Army in 1779, partly out of chagrin at his failure to win faster promotion, partly because of ill health, he resumed his law studies and married a British officer's widow, ten years his senior and with five children. For all his other faults he remained a devoted husband while she lived, although always in debt, always overlavish in his ways. He revived the moribund Society of St. Tammany for his own political ends, and from a transitory friendship with Hamilton, moved over to an equally transitory association with Jefferson. In 1789 Governor Clinton, then in a political decline, made him his attorney general. Two years later, then aged thirty-five, Burr pulled enough legislative strings to take the United States Senate seat from Hamilton's father-in-law, General Philip Schuyler.

Financial genius though Hamilton might have been, at political intrigue he was a bungler. With his too obvious connivance the eight South Carolina electors agreed to cast their combined votes for Pinckney and Jefferson. Getting wind of this, eighteen of Adams' New England Federalist electors switched their votes from Pinckney to various minor candidates, with the result that although Adams was elected by 71 votes, Jefferson followed only 3 votes behind. Thanks to Hamilton, the United States—for the first and last time—found itself with a President and Vice President of opposing parties.

At the third inauguration the following March, Washington still remained the focus of all eyes, although this time he walked alone to Congress in a suit of plain black, as befitted a private citizen. Spontaneous applause broke out as his dignified figure crossed the threshold of the House. Jefferson received only slightly less applause on entering.

The new President arrived in his new carriage, without outriders and drawn by only two horses. In contrast to his usual simplicity, he wore a pearl-colored broadcloth suit, a sword, and a cockade. Slowly he proceeded to the speaker's dais and took his seat, with Jefferson on his immediate right and Washington two seats away.

At the moment of Washington's retirement, criticism of the first President had been muted. The figure with the sombre, yet serene, face seemed again to those present the Father of his Country. Adams noted the tears in many eyes, though—as he wrote his wife, Abigail, afterward—"whether it was from grief or joy, whether from the loss of their beloved President, or the accession of an unbeloved one, or from the novelty of the thing . . . I know not."

Adams had not slept much the night before. As he stepped forward to take the oath of office from the Chief Justice, he was noticeably pale, although he managed to conceal his trembling. He returned to his chair, sat for a moment, then stood, bowed to the close-packed room, and walked out to rising applause. Washington beckoned to the Vice President to follow, but Jefferson did not think it proper for him to precede Washington, and only after Washington beckoned more imperiously did he reluctantly obey. When Washington himself started toward the door, the crowd closed in on him. Remembering Washington's serene face while he sat near him, Adams noted down afterward that he seemed to be saying: "Ay! I am fairly out and you fairly in! See which of us will be happiest!"

The Young Navy

Despite spectacular American successes on the high seas during the Revolution, an economy-bent Congress disbanded the tiny Navy following the war as an idle luxury, and two years after the signing of the Treaty of Paris the last warship was sold. The shortsightedness of Congress was soon apparent. When American merchants, cut off from their usual markets by harsh British trade laws, sought new outlets in the Mediterranean, their vessels were captured and the crews enslaved by Barbary pirates. The United States began to pay tribute to the Barbary rulers for the safe passage of its ships.

These payments outraged the populace, and Congress, empowered by the Constitution to establish a Navy, authorized the construction of six frigates. Progress was dilatory, however, until a closer threat loomed: depredations by the French—now at war with England—on American shipping. Alarmed, the nation hastened construction and soon had a fleet able to defend its coastal waters. Out of self-interest, Britain aided the fledgling Navy in America's undeclared war with France, influencing its traditions and tactics. In fighting first France, then Tripoli, the Navy won a respect for American sea power that has never faded.

Construction of the 36-gun frigate Philadelphia *proceeds at a shipyard in Philadelphia during 1799. In the Tripolitan War, four years later, the ship drove hard onto a reef off Tripoli and was captured by pirates. Then, in a daring night exploit by Lieutenant Stephen Decatur, the ship was set afire and destroyed without the loss of a single American.*

*Shipboard work was hard and discipline severe
in the days of sail. However, under the
benign eye of President Adams, American tars
fared better than those of other navies.
Upper left, seamen aloft furl sail on a square-
rigger. The American sailor and officer at left wear uniforms of the early 1800's.*

OVERLEAF: *In the "Quasi-War" against France, armed merchant vessels served as warships in the small but growing American Navy. Here the merchantman* Planter *stubbornly beats off an attack by a French privateer. Such actions far outnumbered engagements between French and United States men-of-war.*

This gallery of heroes of the scrappy Navy includes Joshua Barney and John Barry, who both gained fame in the Revolution, and stern Commodore John Preble. Left, Stephen Decatur (in officer's uniform) leads his crew in an attack on a Tripolitan gunboat.

SACRED
to the Memory of
WASHINGTON
OB 11 Dec AD 1799.
Æ 168.

E PLURIBUS UNUM

Adams and Jefferson

The Republicans never let Adams forget that he was "President by three votes." Even more than Washington had in his second term, the new President would find his administration shadowed by Revolutionary France, then in its Directory phase. Angry at the American acceptance of Jay's pro-English treaty, the French government was doubly angered by the election of the Anglophile Adams. Acting in its irritation, it ordered American sailors impressed by the British to be hanged if captured. Any American ship with so much as a British handkerchief aboard found itself subject to confiscation without any compensation. Charles Cotesworth Pinckney, the newly appointed minister to France, was ordered to leave the country.

Adams moved cautiously. As President Washington had reacted pacifically to English provocations by sending Jay to London, so President Adams sent to Paris a conciliatory mission, consisting of Pinckney, John Marshall, and Elbridge Gerry. The Americans were authorized to make concessions to the recognized grievances of the French. The Federalists at the same time introduced bills in Congress to enlarge the Regular Army and to grant wide discretionary powers to the President. Jefferson and the Republicans opposed any such rearmament on the grounds that it would bring about the war it sought to avoid.

When the three American ministers arrived in Paris, they found no official prepared to receive them. For several weeks they cooled their heels in the anterooms of the directors, spoken to only by clerks and granted a single perfunctory and unofficial interview by the minister of foreign affairs, the cat-lived insinuating cripple Charles Maurice de Talleyrand-Périgord. Talleyrand had his own devious reasons for keeping the American envoys waiting, as they were soon to discover. Frustrated by sustained incivility, their mission appearing a failure, they received visits from three of Talleyrand's agents—later publicized as X, Y, and Z in President Adams' report to Congress. X, Y, and Z suggested that in spite of the corruption of the United States government, the Directory would officially receive the American envoys on the payment of $240,000 to Talleyrand together with a loan of some ten million dollars to the

George Washington died with the waning eighteenth century, in December, 1799. The symbolism was inescapable: in a new era the nation would have to turn to new leaders. This picture of Washington's apotheosis was made in China.

French government and an apology for Adams' recent harsh remarks.

For Talleyrand, known tongue in cheek as The Incorruptible, a bribe was a normal and necessary adjunct to negotiations, the more necessary to him because he, the former freethinking Bishop of Autun, had lost his original fortune in the Revolution. Austria had paid him a million francs for inserting secret articles in the Treaty of Campo Formio. Prussia added another million to learn about the articles. Bavaria, Tuscany, the Batavian Republic, even the Grand Vizier, had contributed to his thirty-million-franc nest egg.

"It is no, no; not a sixpence!" the outraged Pinckney told X, who had brought the demand. He and his colleagues would have been willing to consider paying a bribe *after* a treaty had been signed, but under no circumstances as a prelude to one. After several months of shilly-shallying, they broke off talks with X, Y, and Z and demanded their passports.

The publication of the envoys' X Y Z dispatches in April, 1798, in the United States swept the country into a fervor of indignant nationalism. Pinckney's words, translated by an imaginative newspaperman into the electric phrase "Millions for defense but not one cent for tribute!" became a national slogan. The Federalists, so long on the defensive as the stubborn foes of the progressive French Republic, became overnight the champions of American rights against foreign aggression, while the French fellow travelers with their catch phrases and their liberty-cap displays found themselves leading a parade from which the marchers had dropped out. Joseph Hopkinson, the composer of "Hail Columbia," observed that "American tunes and American sentiments have driven off those execrable French murder shouts which not long since tortured our ears in . . . every lane and alley in the United States." The President, reconciled to his lack of popularity, discovered, to his pleased surprise, that he had suddenly gained public approval. A few months earlier he could appear in public in Philadelphia "without receiving the slightest mark of attention." Now when the unprepossessing little man went to the theater, the audiences cheered "the eagle-eyed and undaunted Adams."

What succeeded the X Y Z Affair was, in effect, an undeclared war with France, a war for which the United States was prepared more with words than arms. While Congress was still struggling to revive an almost nonexistent Navy and an Army reduced to frontier-post garrisons, French picaroons from the West Indies swarmed up and down the Atlantic coast, capturing American merchantmen—often within sight of land. The French government's communications continued as insulting as its actions were arbitrary. President Adams, considering any further negotiations useless, declared that there was "no alternative between war and submission to the Executive of France."

Adams broke off commercial relations and repealed the French-American treaties. Yet, before the irrevocable step of declaring war, he and the Federalists hesitated. With Gerry remaining in Paris, a faint hope for peace persisted. Moreover, in 1798 the Directory's foremost general, Napoleon Bonaparte, was preparing for an invasion of England, and the thought that United States shores would be deprived of the protecting shield of the Royal Navy if he succeeded was a dismaying one. Already Britain's navy had undertaken to convoy American merchant ships in the Caribbean, off the coast of Europe, and even in American waters, while England supplied the United States with small arms, cannon, and ammunition.

Meanwhile, the United States continued to rearm. Early in 1798 Congress voted to put into service six frigates authorized four years earlier to fight Barbary pirates but never completed. They were the *United States*, the *Constitution*, and the *Constellation*, which needed only to be fitted out, and three others on which construction had been stopped. On April 30 of the same year, the Navy Department was created, with a Secretary, Benjamin Stoddert, of vision, energy, and sufficient persuasiveness to get from pinchpenny congressmen enough funds to create a fifty-ship Navy in a little more than two years.

Congress gave point to this rearming when, in May, 1798, it authorized the seizure of any armed French vessel—navy warship or privateer—found in American coastal waters and, in June, extended this authorization to cover all the high seas. The first fruit of this new American aggressiveness was the capture, in July, of the French privateer *Croyable* by the U.S.S. *Delaware*. The *Croyable*, a twelve-gun sloop, was renamed and added to the Navy, and as the U.S.S. *Retaliation*, took part in the first confrontation between warships, when she was forced to surrender in November to two enemy frigates that overwhelmingly outgunned her. It was the only defeat suffered by the American Navy during the course of what came to be called the Quasi-War.

The United States Navy was chiefly concerned with hunting French privateers and protecting American shipping, and operated mainly in the West Indies. During the two years of undeclared war, American ships captured some eighty enemy vessels. Engagements between men-of-war were few, for most of the French Navy was kept occupied in Europe by the British fleet, but of the encounters two of the most memorable involved the *Constellation*, Commodore Thomas Truxton commanding. On February 9, 1799, near the island of

Of all his accomplishments, John Adams was proudest of keeping his country from fighting a major war with France —a war his archenemy Hamilton fervently desired. This study for a portrait of Adams was made by John Copley.

St. Kitts, the *Constellation* pounded the frigate *Insurgente* helpless—while suffering only six casualties—until the French ship surrendered. And in the early morning of February 1, 1800, quite near the same spot, the *Constellation* fought the *Vengeance* for five hours, during which the French commander twice struck his colors. However, his act went unseen in the smoke and darkness, and at last the helpless vessel drifted out of sight in the gloom and so escaped.

To prepare against a possible French invasion by land, Congress voted to create an Additional Army of ten thousand men to be supplemented by a Provisional Army of fifty thousand. A private's pay was raised from four to six dollars a month to obtain more enlistments, although one congressman objected that "high pay would only serve to make the soldiers get drunk." Washington, summoned from retirement to assume command of the new Army, agreed to take the field, but only if an emergency arose, insisting—over Adams' objection—that the second-in-command and the active field commander be Alexander Hamilton.

With Nelson's defeat of the French in Egypt in 1798, the French threat seemed no longer acute. In America indignation and a sense of urgency both died down within the year. Warnings that American forces and homes were threatened "with fire, plunder and pillage, and your wives and sweethearts with ravishment and assassination, by horrid outlandish sans-culotte Frenchmen" brought no lines of young men to the recruiting places. Nor did the recruiting sergeants' promise of an elegant uniform, a generous bounty, and "rations that might tempt an epicure." The Additional Army never reached more than one-third of its authorized strength —although there was an excess of officer candidates.

Within the United States feeling against Revolutionary France developed into a drive against those who opposed the war effort. Republicans who had sung the "Marseillaise" and flaunted miniature guillotines, who saw the events in France as an extension of the American Revolution into a social revolution, found themselves pilloried as "democrats, mobocrats and *all* other kinds of rats." Jacobins, the Federalists called these "Gallic devotees" who would support France against their own country. Many believed that French agents, with their American accomplices, were preparing to set fire to Philadelphia and massacre the inhabitants. Foreigners became suspect, particularly the French-connected United Irishmen—"so many serpents within

SOUTH ELEVATION / Capitol / U.S.

your bosom," a Federalist newspaper called them.

Riding the wave of martial popularity, the Federalists passed the Alien and Sedition Acts to deal with what they considered an internal conspiracy. The Alien Acts gave the President power to order foreigners of dubious loyalty imprisoned or deported, and the Naturalization Act was changed, raising the residence requirement for citizenship from five to fourteen years. The Sedition Act, prescribing heavy fines and imprisonment for those judged guilty of writing, publishing, or speaking anything "in a scandalous or malicious way" against the government or any officer of the government, was a more harsh and active threat.

In defense of the latter act, it can be said that defamation had reached a level impossible to imagine today. Republican newspapers referred to the President as "the blind, bald, toothless, querulous Adams," "the blasted tyrant of America," "a ruffian deserving of the curses of mankind." Not that the Federalists were pen-tied in reply! Writing for them, Noah Webster described the Republicans as "such a pack of scoundrels as

. . . was never before collected into one country. . . .the refuse, the sweepings of the most depraved part of mankind from the most corrupt nations on earth."

As a result of the Sedition Act much of the Republican press was blasted into silence and ten journalists were convicted of violating the law. Perhaps the best-known victim of Federalist zeal was Congressman Matthew Lyon of Vermont, called the Spitting Lyon after an altercation in the House of Representatives during which he spat in the face of Connecticut's Roger Griswold. Lyon, charged with having published libelous statements against President Adams, was fined one thousand dollars and sentenced to four months in jail. Yet the Federalists, celebrating their defeat of "the licentiousness of the press," merely succeeded in making a martyr of Republican Lyon, who was re-elected to Congress from his cell.

Jefferson saw that the French menace was a convenient club that the Federalists could use to belabor their opponents. He hinted that Hamilton might use the Army, not to repel any hypothetical invasion, but—his

70

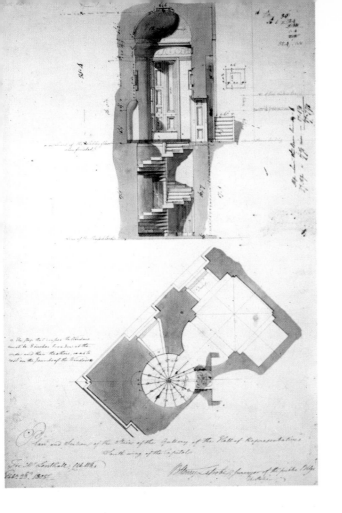

At President Jefferson's request, English-born architect Benjamin Latrobe modified the original designs of Dr. William Thornton (over Dr. Thornton's objections) for the south wing of the Capitol in Washington. Latrobe's sketch of the south elevation of this wing—to be used by the House of Representatives—is opposite. At left are his plan (bottom) and section (top) of the staircase to the gallery of the Hall of Representatives. Above is his modification of Dr. Thornton's design for the hall itself.

old obsession—to establish a monarchy. The Alien and Sedition Acts were a demonstration to him that the powers of the federal government must be curbed. As countermeasures he and Madison privately prepared resolutions for the Virginia and Kentucky legislatures.

The Virginia and Kentucky Resolutions brought up again the perennial matter of states' rights. Madison had swung so far from his earlier national position that he now advocated "Dual Federalism," with the states themselves responsible for common welfare, public morals, and general security. In his and Jefferson's interpretation the Constitution became a compact between sovereign states with narrowly defined powers reserved to the central government. Because the states had created the Constitution, they were the judges as to any federal usurpation. Jefferson maintained that the individual states had the right to nullify acts of the national government that they deemed unconstitutional. Other Virginians went further, claiming the right, if necessary, to leave the Union. Although Jefferson made no such claim, the Virginia and Kentucky Resolutions

implied this right. Washington so disapproved that he even persuaded the old firebrand Patrick Henry to come out of retirement as a declared Federalist.

By early 1799 the wind from France had shifted. As Talleyrand pointed out to the Directory, locked in its struggle with England, war with the United States would interfere with French plans to regain Louisiana and to use American shipping to break the strangle hold of the British blockade. In a conciliatory gesture the French halted the seizure of American ships and cargoes, released many vessels already seized, and called off the privateering picaroons. Adams was ready to accept the French overture. "The end of war is peace," he said, "and peace was offered me."

He reckoned without his Cabinet—inherited from Washington—and the Hamiltonian Federalists. A group of senators promptly informed him that they would never consent to the appointment of a minister to France. Let the French send an envoy to the United States if they wanted peace! But Adams was able to placate the senators by promising to appoint two men to

71

*General Anthony Wayne orders a charge at the critical
Battle of Fallen Timbers, near present-day Toledo, Ohio.
Here Wayne routed Chief Little Turtle of the Miamis
and his Indian allies, forcing the chiefs of the Northwest
Territory tribes to sign the Treaty of Greenville in
1795, which opened this fertile area to swarms of settlers.*

accompany William Vans Murray, the President's choice as minister to France. So in November, 1799, three ministers plenipotentiary left for France with the ill wishes of the Federalist leaders, though only in 1800 did the United States finally manage to sign an agreement with Napoleon—then First Consul—bringing the lagging undeclared war to an end.

Wars, even undeclared wars, cost money, as Jefferson realized when he remarked hopefully that the tax collector would drive out "a reign of witches." The morning-after effect of the Federalist government's direct taxes on houses, land, and slaves was to swing much popular sentiment against the Federalists. In Pennsylvania there was even a minor uprising, mostly among the Pennsylvania Dutch.

Adams dispatched the Additional Army into rebellious Pennsylvania, but the only rebel the soldiers encountered was a bull, the sole casualty of the expedition. They did seize John Fries, an auctioneer, who had set off the disturbances by leading an armed band to free some tax evaders—the records are unclear on the exact number—from a Pennsylvania jail. Fries and two companions were found guilty of treason and sentenced to death, and only Adams' pardon saved them from hanging. The Federalists wanted an example to be made that would eradicate "the principle of insurrection," and Hamilton felt that the pardon was the worst mistake of Adams' Presidency. Nevertheless, the Federalists could not help but be aware of the unpopularity of the idle Additional Army, and with the 1800 elections in the offing, they decided to reduce the Army to its pre-emergency size and lay up most of the Navy's ships.

While Federalists and Republicans were facing up to the election, the government itself had the chore of moving to the Federal City on the Potomac, which the commissioners of 1791 had decided would be called the City of Washington in the District of Columbia. The great boulevards with their sweeping vistas that the French engineer Major Pierre L'Enfant had drawn up with such vision were as yet paper phantoms. Reality showed a village of three thousand inhabitants built with haphazard indifference by slave labor—half-finished buildings set down in a raw landscape of reddish mud. "Houses scattered over a space of ten miles, and trees and stumps in plenty," Abigail Adams noted from the unfinished, half-furnished President's Palace, the East Room of which she at least found useful for drying the family wash. A causeway—optimistically labeled

Pennsylvania Avenue—running southeast across an alder thicket and Tiber Creek, led to the one completed wing of the Capitol and the unroofed rotunda. Seven or eight buildings surrounding the Capitol served as boardinghouses for congressmen and senators. The new Federal City might be all right for the future, Gouverneur Morris reported after picking his way through the mire of unpaved streets, but he was not posterity.

Heartened by the 1798 congressional elections, which had seemed to revivify their party, the Federalists faced the 1800 presidential election with wary optimism. They would have liked to have drafted Washington for a third term, but the former President refused to subject himself again to the vilifications of politics. Without him there was no choice but Adams. Charles Cotesworth Pinckney was chosen as Adams' running mate. The Republicans again picked Jefferson and Burr. Caucuses of both parties pledged that this time there would be no splitting of electoral votes.

Whatever the pledges, Hamilton wanted no more of Adams and plotted—as he had four years before—to elect another Pinckney in his place. Adams had removed two pro-Hamilton members of his Cabinet, Secretary of State Timothy Pickering and Secretary of War James McHenry. Aided by them, Hamilton and Treasury Secretary Oliver Wolcott prepared a letter entitled "The Public Conduct and Character of John Adams" to discredit the President among Federalist leaders. Though Hamilton described Adams as a person of "disgusting egotism," "distempered jealousy," and "vanity without bounds," he still urged that the President be supported equally with Pinckney, but it was easy to see that he had his fingers crossed. Nor was he too perturbed when Burr got hold of a copy of the letter and sent it to the newspapers. Adams and his supporters attempted unsuccessfully to form a third party, the Constitutionalists, leaving the Federalist rump to Hamilton. In the midst of their altercations came the news that New York, Federalist in the last election, had through its newly elected Republican legislature chosen electors pledged to Jefferson. Faced with possible defeat, the Federalists rallied. Unexpectedly they carried Rhode Island and one of the two Maryland electors. Accusing Jefferson of being an "intellectual voluptuary," an atheist, a vivisectionist, of having children by his own female slaves, they predicted "the just vengeance of insulted heaven" if he was elected.

Jefferson conducted his own strategic campaign from

Monticello, quietly, without attempting to answer Federalist slander. His platform emphasized states' rights, the liquidation of the public debt, a small Army and Navy, freedom of religion and the press, "little or no diplomatic establishment," and "a government vigorously frugal and simple." When in December the electors—the majority chosen by legislatures, the rest by public vote—met in their respective states, it was clear that the election would be close. After the votes of thirteen of the sixteen states were announced, the tally stood at 65 for Adams to 58 for Jefferson. If, as seemed probable, Adams could carry South Carolina, he would win the election. But another Charles Pinckney—this one a Republican—managed, with brisk promises of patronage, to swing enough electors to Jefferson to give him the state's 8 electoral votes. Although Georgia and the new state of Tennessee were yet to be heard from, their 7 votes were predictably Republican.

Jefferson would have been elected President then and there if the Republican electors had not followed their rigid instructions and given their 73 second votes to Burr. The ensuing tie threw the election into the House of Representatives, where each state had one vote. Disgruntled Federalists planned to spite Jefferson by throwing their votes to Burr, who himself made no move either to encourage or discourage them. Hamilton, considering Burr "the most unfit and dangerous man of the community," brought all his influence to prevent this. Jefferson, at least, was an honorable man, and Hamilton felt that with certain attached conditions he should be given the Presidency.

Not until February did the congressmen finally meet in the unfinished Capitol to elect a President. The first ballot—with 9 votes needed to win—stood 8 for Jefferson, 6 for Burr, with the votes of Maryland and Vermont void because of a tie. The balloting continued all the cold and overcast day and into the evening by candlelight, as a snowstorm swirled across the city. The House remained in session all night, not recessing until eight in the morning for a brief respite until noon. It was midday next before the House adjourned and only after a turbulent weekend, with a growing threat of mob action, was the deadlock finally broken when the Delaware Federalist James Bayard persuaded the lone Vermont Federalist to withhold his vote by casting a blank ballot. In return, Federalist congressmen were told, Jefferson had privately agreed to their minimum conditions: to uphold the public credit, maintain the

Army and Navy, continue the policy of neutrality, and remove no small-office holders. Jefferson later denied having made any such promises.

On the thirty-sixth ballot the Spitting Lyon of Vermont had the satisfaction of casting the deciding vote that elected Jefferson. Maryland also went to Jefferson after its Federalist congressman cast a blank. Four states remained with Burr, two others abstained from voting. Chagrined at his repudiation, Adams never forgave Hamilton, and it would be years before he could forgive Jefferson.

Always the continuing American thrust was westward, whatever the barriers. There were barriers enough after Harmar's ignominious defeat by the Indians in the Ohio country, and Washington had as a consequence taken the elderly Revolutionary general Arthur St. Clair out of military storage and sent him with a force of militia to put an end to the murderous raids along the Ohio. It was an unfortunate choice. St. Clair, advancing with stupid unconcern, was overwhelmed and put to flight by Chief Little Turtle—who had defeated General Harmar—in one of the worst disasters ever suffered by American arms. Not until almost three years later did General "Mad Anthony" Wayne's tough legion defeat Little Turtle at the Battle of Fallen Timbers, near Ohio's Maumee River. But after the beaten Indians had signed the Treaty of Greenville, by which they ceded southern Ohio and southeastern Indiana, the barriers were down and the settlers' way to the Northwest lay open.

By 1800 half a million Americans had settled beyond the Alleghenies—in Kentucky, Tennessee, and along the Ohio—often in conditions as primitive as those of their Saxon ancestors. Separated from the fourteen states along the Atlantic seacoast by the mountain barrier, they tended to think of themselves as a separate entity. Mannered Richmond, gracious Charleston, mercantile Boston, and the bustle of New York and Philadelphia were as remote to them as London.

Beyond the military and political events, the dates and the maneuverings that loom so large in written history, ordinary Americans on both sides of the mountain barrier were going about their daily affairs, reading in their newspapers the news of the new Federal City and the old world of Europe. In the ten years previous to 1800 the nation's population had grown from just under 4,000,000 to 5,300,000, of which 1,000,000 were Negroes. Yet 95 per cent of the people still lived in rural reas. Only five cities had more than 10,000 inhabitants—Philadelphia with 70,000, New York with 60,000, Boston with 25,000, Charleston with 18,000, and Baltimore with 13,000.

For Americans a belief in progress—that recent French fancy—became a kind of second nature. Never to be defined exactly, progress was the end, science, the means. As men watched, forests became clearings, clearings, settlements; settlements became villages and then in turn towns and cities. Progress seemed as inalienable a right as any named in the Declaration of Independence. Everywhere a rush of activity was transforming the face of the country.

Under the influence of France the very styles of the new republic were becoming republican. Although most men still wore their hair queued, they were discarding their wigs—Adams had left off wearing his— and some of the younger men even cut their hair short. Ruffles and ceremonial swords had gone out of fashion, and trousers were replacing knee breeches. As always, women's fashions changed even more quickly. Gone were the towering hairdos; dresses were shorter, narrower, without whalebone supports, and so revealing that moralists took alarm.

As yet the Eastern settlements did not touch the Western, and two-thirds of the population still lived within fifty miles of tidewater. Nine men out of ten were farmers, and farming itself had changed little in the eighteenth century from its generations-old pattern. The plowman still followed the rude and clumsy plow of his ancestors, planted and sowed as his father had done, cut grain with the same curved scythe used since Roman times. Farm animals were treated carelessly. Selective breeding was unknown. Few understood anything about drainage, the use of manures, or crop rotation. Midway in the eighteenth century the American Philosophical Society had begun to interest itself in agriculture as a science, and its early minutes are full of suggestions as to the value of new plants, the prevention of plant diseases, and the cultivation and conservation of the soil. Beginning with Jared Eliot's *Essay on Field Husbandry*, the society tried to make the latest developments in agriculture available to the farmer.

It was an inventive period, that decade before Jeffer-

The nation's fashions no less than its politics were in a state of flux during the early 1800's. The French republican influence on worldly Philadelphians can be seen in this detail from a painting by J. L. Krimmel: trousers replacing knee breeches, high hats and high collars in vogue, dresses high-waisted and more diaphanous.

75

Slaves on a South Carolina plantation—about 1800— dance to the rhythm of African musical instruments. Many Southerners who had favored freeing the slaves changed their mind after the cotton gin was invented.

son, but the most portentous invention was that of the cotton gin in 1793 by the mechanically minded young Eli Whitney. After graduating from Yale, Whitney had gone to Georgia as a private tutor. Observing that it took a slave all day to separate a pound of lint from the small tough cotton seeds, within ten days he invented his gin, which did the same work mechanically and which, when harnessed to water power, would eventually do the work of three hundred to a thousand slaves.

Eight years after Whitney had invented his gin, the Southern cotton crop had increased tenfold to fifty million pounds a year. From a luxury, cotton was on its way to becoming a cheap necessity. Whitney's invention made possible the looms of industrial England. But the ensuing demand for field hands on the large plantations necessary for cotton cultivation riveted the institution of slavery on the South. Reluctantly tolerated by Washington, decried but endured by Jefferson, slavery, after the introduction of the cotton gin, would come to be defended by Southerners as a positive benefit.

Imitations of Whitney's design came so rapidly that he made little money from the invention that, in Macaulay's words, did as much for the United States as Peter the Great did for Russia. But if Whitney's cotton gin may be said to have made the Civil War inevitable,

his later innovations in his Connecticut factory helped assure the North's victory. Having contracted to make muskets for the government, he conceived of producing them with interchangeable parts, and designed and built the machinery necessary to carry out his plan. He was among the originators of the system of mass production, which in a generation would make the North's industrial strength overwhelming.

Two years before Whitney's invention of the cotton gin, the English immigrant Samuel Slater had successfully constructed in Providence, Rhode Island, a cotton-spinning mill on the advanced British model. The flying shuttle, the spinning jenny, Arkwright's water frame, and Cartwright's power loom being English inventions, their export was forbidden. But Slater, an apprentice with a photographic memory, had carried the plans overseas in his head. Moses Brown, the owner of a cotton-spinning establishment, furnished the capital for Slater's successfully transported brain child. Production at first was limited by the small amounts of raw cotton available, but it expanded with explosive force after the invention of the cotton gin.

The art of road building, lost since Roman times, had been revived in Europe, and the revival quickly crossed the Atlantic. In the colonial period transportation for any distance had been by water, but now roads, ferries, and bridges were under construction in all the settled parts of the country. New York was the first state to aid in maintaining local roads, and the Philadelphia-Lancaster Pike was the first improved highway in the United States. In the decade before 1800 post roads increased in mileage from twenty-four hundred to twenty thousand. A new bridge across the Charles River in Boston was a wonder of its day. A few years after the bridge had been built, James Finley, a Pennsylvania engineer, erected America's first iron suspension bridge across Jacob's Creek in western Pennsylvania.

Travel by sea—still the easiest means of contact between the states—was aided immeasurably by Salem's Nathaniel Bowditch with his *The New American Practical Navigator*. The self-educated Bowditch had made five voyages as clerk, supercargo, and finally master while perfecting his knowledge of mathematics and navigation. Finding hundreds of errors in the British maritime table, he devised his own compilation in the classic volume published in 1802, which after seventy editions is still in use.

Bowditch and Whitney represented science at its

practical best. Among all classes, belief in science and the American future was replacing belief in tradition. Politics itself was seen as a science. In Virginia a constitutional society was founded to study government scientifically. In medicine the foremost proponent of the scientific method was the many-faceted friend of Adams' and Jefferson's, Dr. Benjamin Rush. Yet even Rush was so tied to the past in the treatment of disease that he bled many of his patients to death in the yellow-fever epidemic of 1793. A physician, teacher, and social reformer in one, he has been called the Father of American Medicine. As professor of the theory and practice of medicine at the University of Pennsylvania, he occupied the first chair of its kind in America, wrote the earliest medical books, and was also the first professor of chemistry in the colonies. Generations ahead of his day in diagnosing disease, he also pioneered in the science of sanitation, in the purification of water, in investigating the effects of tobacco and alcohol.

Noah Webster saw as great a future for English, but English purified and adapted to the vigor of a new country. Boldly he set out his phonetic system of spelling, clipping the u's from "errour," "honour," and "harbour," and making similar simplifications. In 1806 he published *A Compendious Dictionary of the English Language*, a first step toward his two-volume *American Dictionary of the English Language* of 1828, which helped set national standards of spelling and usage.

As late as 1820 Sydney Smith could ask waspishly in the *Edinburgh Review*: ". . . who reads an American book, or goes to an American play, or looks at an American picture or statue?" And ten years later Emerson would remark that fifty years of demands for a great American literature had produced none at all. Yet eager and ambitious men and women wrote their novels and poems, plays and essays, struggling with the dilemma of American substance and English form. Indeed, the sentimental novels in imitation of Richardson, the poetry in imitation of Pope, the essays in imitation of Addison, have only a vague historical interest, although in their day they were indiscriminately acclaimed. In 1786 John Adams found the Connecticut philosopher-poet Joel Barlow's *Vision of Columbus*, an epic of the discovery and colonization of America, a poem "which would do honor to any country and any age. . . . Excepting *Paradise Lost*, I know of nothing superior in any modern language."

But if no American made his mark in literature during the heyday of federalism, it was otherwise in art, for five painters born before the Revolution achieved a permanent reputation that extended to Europe. Benjamin West of Pennsylvania, enabled by wealthy sponsors to study in Europe, became a court painter to George III and created such stylized heroic battle scenes as *The Death of Wolfe*. John Trumbull, adapting West's grand style to the American Revolution, produced *Bunker's Hill* and his most celebrated painting, *Surrender of Cornwallis*. Charles Willson Peale, artist and naturalist, who commanded troops during the Revolution, was a good if not great artist—as can be seen in his portrait of Franklin at eighty-one and in his many portraits of Washington. His larger contribution was in founding the first museum as well as the Pennsylvania Academy of Fine Arts. The two great American artists of the age were the Tory John Singleton Copley and the patriot Gilbert Stuart. Copley, before his departure for England, left behind his unforgettable delineations of Boston merchant families on the eve of the Revolution. And it is through the eyes of Stuart, the painter of five Presidents, that we still see the severe paternal features of Washington.

In the last years of Washington's Presidency, Thomas Paine published *The Age of Reason*, his extended attack on orthodox religious beliefs and on the Bible. In doing so, he spoke for the most advanced liberal thinkers of his day. Eight American editions of his book appeared the first year. Though stating their opinions less bluntly, Franklin and Jefferson and perhaps a majority of the signers of the Declaration of Independence basically agreed with Paine. Paine was not the atheist he has been called, but a deist, believing in God the First Cause, who worked solely through the laws of nature.

For ordinary folk the idea of God the Great Watchmaker frozen in the immutable laws of His clockwork universe was not enough. They felt the need of a comforting and personal God attainable beyond the reasoning mind. Where intellectuals turned to Unitarianism—a polite amalgam of deism and Congregationalism—the masses sought the heady evangelism of the Baptists and the Methodists, which itself seemed a democratic form of religion. Itinerant preachers carried the gospel message beyond the Appalachians to the remote and lonely regions of the frontier. At camp meetings, in the light of flaring bonfires, they prayed and sang the gospel hymns and shouted their simple message of sin and repentance until the more fervent among them fell to the ground in spasms of emotion.

While New England was shifting from the rigidities of Calvinism to Unitarianism, the South, under the influence of its "peculiar institution," was moving toward a revival of Calvinist theology, buttressed by evangelism, in which there was no room for deviation or ranging thought. Liberalism in theology could lead to embarrassing questions about slavery, and the South, in sensing this danger, closed theological ranks. As for the Negroes, by the time of the Revolution they had begun to drift into separate churches conducted with primitive evangelistic zeal by their own clergy.

The religiousness of the century's end, known as the Second Awakening—the first, or Great Awakening, had been initiated by Jonathan Edwards fifty years earlier—though in a sense the ordinary man's reaction to the detached intellectuals of the Enlightenment, was above all an indication that the United States was in the main still religious-minded.

The country over which Jefferson was to preside had, by the time of his election, already assumed the basic outlines of its later characteristics. Within the nation two hundred years of settlement had formed the geographical distinctiveness of Northern, Middle, and Southern States, and now the increasingly significant Western division was taking form. Yet over and above the state and regional differences, common thought-patterns and attitudes asserted themselves. Americans had a sense of breaking away, of leaving behind, of beginning anew. Already ways of acting and thinking began to be classified as American or un-American. Because the future meant more, the past meant less. In a fluid society, where the discontented could move on, the class lines of the Old World were impossible to impose—except in the South with its paradox of slavery and freedom. Supercilious European visitors might comment on the crudities of the new nation and the squalor of travel in America, but Americans did not doubt themselves or their future. Self-confident, unaware of the difficulties of a more complex society and of the intellectual currents overseas, the ordinary American was convinced that Europe was decrepit and that his own emergent nation was the best, the most promising and progressive, country in the world.

The Revolution of 1800, Jefferson called his hair-breadth election, "as real a revolution in the principles of our government as that of 1776 was in form." It would have been difficult to find a Federalist who did

not agree with him. The narrow margin of his electoral votes, with South Carolina swinging the balance, failed to indicate the radical shift that had taken place. But the sixty-four Federalists in the House of Representatives had been reduced to thirty-six, while the Republicans had increased their number from forty-two to sixty-nine. Even in the Senate, supposedly insulated against the fickle winds of democratic opinion, the Federalist majority of six had been replaced by a Republican majority of four. The elections of 1800 were not just a defeat for the Federalists but the beginning of their extinction. Never again would an American political party openly express its distrust of the people, its belief in the rule of the wise, the rich, and the good.

For the eighteenth-century Federalist belief in reason and hierarchic order Jefferson substituted the nineteenth-century romantic trust in instinct and individual judgment. What brought him and his Republicans to power was the realization that ordinary men were no

longer content to be ruled by their self-appointed betters. As 1776 was a political revolution, so 1800 was a social revolution. Jefferson with his slaves and his Monticello was scarcely a man of the people, but he saw those of limited means and education, whose vote for the most part the Federalists would have despised, as the foundation of an expanding America.

Deliberately he made his inauguration a symbol of republican simplicity. On that sunny but mud-spattered March day in 1801 when he took his oath of office, he walked with a group of friends and colleagues and a few militiamen the hundred yards from Conrad's boardinghouse, where he had spent the night, to the Senate Chamber of the unfinished Capitol. In designed contrast to the elegance of his predecessors, he wore his everyday suit at his swearing-in.

Adams did not stay for the triumph of his rival. By the time Jefferson was strolling with his companions from Conrad's, Adams in his coach was already journeying along the roads northward. Adams had spent his last night in office filling all vacant legal posts and offices with loyal Federalists. Midnight appointments, Jefferson called them, and vowed he would purge as many as possible.

Aaron Burr was already presiding in the Senate when Jefferson entered the small, crowded room. Before taking the oath, the President-elect read his inaugural address in a voice so low that only those near could hear him distinctly. As an address it was lofty, conciliatory, and phrased with the same felicity as the Declaration of Independence. Mindful of those who had called him an atheist, he acknowledged the blessings of "an overruling providence, which . . . proves that it delights in the happiness of man here, and his greater happiness hereafter. . . ." Mindful of the bitterness of party strife, conscious in his moment of victory of being President of *all* his "friends & fellow citizens," he urged that differences of opinion were not differences of principle. "We are," he said hopefully, "all Republicans; we are all Federalists." Our common goal, he concluded, is "a wise & frugal government which shall restrain men from injuring one another, shall leave them otherwise free to regulate their own pursuits of industry & improvement, & shall not take from the mouth of labor the bread it has earned."

After finishing his address, Jefferson was sworn in by his distant cousin Adams' recently appointed Chief Justice, John Marshall, who then administered the oath to Burr. At the conclusion of the ceremonies, the new President left the chamber and returned on foot to his boardinghouse, where he took dinner at his usual place at the foot of the common table. When a guest tried to congratulate him, he smilingly advised the well-wisher to follow his own example of waiting until the end of the year after a wedding before congratulating the bridegroom.

Two weeks later Jefferson moved to the President's House—it would not be known as the White House until after it was painted to hide the scorch marks from its

79

burning during the War of 1812. That sandstone jewel in its setting of mud, designed by the Irish architect James Hoban and reminiscent of Dublin's Leinster House, was, in the new President's opinion, too large for a republican and too grandiose for a republic. Banished were the state coaches with their outriders, the formal levees, the stiff etiquette that the two first Presidents had considered incumbent on their office. Jefferson rode about on horseback unattended. Instead of levees, he held small informal dinner parties almost daily, with food prepared by his French chef and good wine and good talk to accompany each course. To the consternation of foreign diplomats and Federalist grandees, he issued new rules of presidential etiquette: ministers of foreign nations were to be considered equal; at public ceremonies no one, whatever his rank or title, would have precedence over any other invited guest; at dinners, public and private, gentlemen en masse would yield place to ladies en masse.

Jefferson eliminated all receptions—including the President's Birthday—except those of New Year's Day and the Fourth of July. On the Fourth the President's House was thrown open to the public, and merchants and mechanics mingled in the reception and dining rooms with diplomats and members of Congress. Punch, wine, and cakes were served to all while the Marine Corps band played "The President's March." Any stranger seized with curiosity to see Jefferson was free to drop in mornings at the President's House without appointment. Diplomats, in their gold-braided formality, were often shocked to find him dressed with studied untidiness, his hair not even queued, wearing carpet slippers, and with linen not as clean as it might be. Augustus Foster, the secretary of the British legation, described him after a visit as "a tall man, with a very red freckled face, and gray neglected hair; his manners good-natured, frank, and rather friendly, though he had somewhat of a cynical expression of countenance. He wore a blue coat, a thick gray-colored hairy waistcoat, with a red under-waistcoat lapped over it, green velveteen breeches with pearl buttons, yarn stockings, and slippers down at the heels—his appearance being very much like that of a tall, large-boned farmer."

Since the President was a widower with married daughters who had long before left home, and since Vice President Burr was also a widower, the position of administration hostess devolved on the sprightly Dolley Madison, the wife of Jefferson's clever but colorless Secretary of State. But if Madison appeared, in Washington Irving's eyes, "a withered little apple-john," his wife showed herself a hostess of unforgettable charm, beauty, wit, and liveliness. With her swan's-down-trimmed capes, her turban with ostrich feathers, her gold and enamel snuffbox, and her merry ways, she has survived the years, still a living memory in the White House.

Madison and Secretary of the Treasury Albert Gallatin were the outstanding members of Jefferson's Cabinet. Gallatin, though Swiss-born, was a Pennsylvania farmer who had lived with frontiersmen and knew them well. With a mind as mathematically sharp as Hamilton's, he scorned his predecessor's financial dogma. He understood economics as the political-minded Jefferson did not. For him a national debt was not a national blessing but something to be paid off. With Jefferson, he believed in economy at home and peace abroad.

As a republican innovation Jefferson submitted his messages to Congress in writing rather than speaking "from the throne." By the end of his administration in 1809, he had removed about one-third of all those in the federal government appointed by Adams. But his immediate concern was the Federalist-stacked judiciary. In his first message to Congress he had originally planned to denounce the Sedition Act as unconstitutional and to deny that the Supreme Court could be the sole arbiter of the Constitution. Instead, in line with his conciliatory inaugural address, he said nothing, and he pardoned those who were serving sentences under the act. With his backing, Congress reduced the residence requirement for citizenship to five years.

Among Adams' midnight appointments were commissions for several federal justices of the peace for the District of Columbia, signed and sealed by the President but not yet delivered. Jefferson, on taking office, discovered them on the desk of the Secretary of State. One of these commissions was for a petty Federalist politician, William Marbury, whose otherwise obscure name would thenceforth be stamped on the constitutional history of his country. Jefferson ordered Madison not to give Marbury his commission, whereupon Marbury applied to the Supreme Court for a writ of mandamus to force its delivery under the Judiciary Act of 1789.

The subtle Federalist Chief Justice, John Marshall, sensed in the case of *Marbury v. Madison* the instrument he needed to assert the judicial power of the Supreme Court. Marshall first was faced with a dilemma:

to reject Marbury's claim would be to admit the powerlessness of the judiciary; to uphold it would allow Jefferson to make a fool of the Court by ignoring the decision. The Chief Justice, in February, 1803, ruled that Madison had acted illegally in withholding the commission and that therefore Marbury had a right to appeal to the Court. Nevertheless, his ruling continued, the Supreme Court could not issue any writ under the Judiciary Act because the act itself was unconstitutional. And it was unconstitutional because the Court said it was! In *Marbury v. Madison* Marshall shaped the very structure of government by establishing that whatever laws Congress might pass, it was for the Supreme Court to decide whether or not they were authorized by the Constitution. Beyond the Supreme Court there was no appeal.

To Jefferson, Marshall's decision seemed an attempt by the judiciary to dominate the legislative and executive branches of the government. Jefferson believed that the power to decide what was and what was not constitutional should rest with the sovereign states that had established the Constitution. The Supreme Court's authority to pass on legislative acts, to his way of thinking, challenged the right of the people to pass, through Congress, laws they felt needful or desirable.

Striking back at the judicial power structure, Jefferson removed one drunken federal judge, but his culminating attempt to break the power of the judiciary came in the impeachment of Supreme Court Justice Samuel Chase, a signer of the Declaration of Independence. Chase was a bully, arbitrary and irascible, who, address-

Pavel Svinin, a visiting Russian artist and intellectual, painted this water color of an Anabaptist submersion near Philadelphia. The religious revival of the early 1800's caused immense growth among the more evangelistic denominations, like the Methodists and the Baptists.

ing a Baltimore grand jury in 1803, said: "The modern doctrines by our late reformers that all men . . . are entitled to enjoy equal liberty and equal rights, have brought this mighty mischief [mobocracy] upon us; and I fear it will rapidly progress until peace and order, freedom and property, shall be destroyed."

Prompted by Jefferson, the House of Representatives voted to impeach Chase on eight counts of misfeasance and malfeasance. Chase's trial took place in the Senate, with John Randolph of Roanoke—more brilliant in debate than learned in law—as prosecutor. Although more than half the senators considered Chase guilty on three counts, the two-thirds majority necessary to convict him was obtained on none of the eight counts. Jefferson angrily called the proceedings a farce. If Chase had been convicted, the President would have been ready to impeach the whole Supreme Court, but he was not willing to risk a second farce after Chase's acquittal.

Aaron Burr, making one of his rare appearances in the Capitol, had presided over the trial. The duties of Vice President weighed so lightly on him that it was almost a year after his election before he had again shown up in Washington. Long since a bankrupt and a political adventurer, he was at the time of Chase's trial a murderer as well. Snubbed by Jefferson in matters of patronage, he made overtures early in his term to the Federalists as well as to disaffected members of his own party. In the spring of 1804, while still Vice President, he ran for governor of New York on a third-party ticket, with the backing of Tammany and the secret support of many Federalists. Hamilton did his active best to persuade the members of his party not to vote for Burr.

There was more to the scurrilous New York election than met the eye. New England Federalist leaders, restive under the rule of Republican Virginia aristocrats and feeling, with Fisher Ames, that the nation was "too big for union, too sordid for patriotism, too democratic for liberty," were considering seceding to form a Northern confederacy. Timothy Pickering, senator from Massachusetts, schemed not only to elect Burr governor of New York but also to place him at the head of the confederacy. Although Tammany carried New York City for Burr, the opposition votes outside the city were enough to elect his colorless opponent. Burr blamed Hamilton for his defeat and challenged him to a duel. Though opposed in principle to dueling—the more since his eldest son had been killed in a senseless encounter—Hamilton felt honor-bound to accept the

challenge, although he himself was determined not to fire at Burr. The two men met at seven o'clock of a July morning at Weehawken on a ledge under the Palisades twenty feet above the Hudson. On the signal Burr—a skilled marksman—fired one shot, and Hamilton fell, his pistol going off harmlessly as his finger apparently tightened spasmodically on the trigger. Mortally wounded, he lived only a brief while.

If Jefferson had been able to do so, he would have erected a wall round the United States to protect the virtues of the New World from the Old World's vices; and he thanked God for the wideness of the Atlantic. Except for a necessary minimum of trade he wanted nothing to do with foreign nations, and he was determined to let all treaties lapse. Jefferson had already recalled the American ministers from Portugal, Holland, and Prussia. But no country can stand aside from history, as Jefferson was to discover, for he soon found himself more deeply involved in European affairs than either of his predecessors.

Long before he was President, Jefferson had written that it was "not our interest to cross the Mississippi for ages." And in his first inaugural address he said the nation had "room enough for our descendants to the thousandth and thousandth generation." The river, however, was vital to the settlers of Tennessee, Kentucky, and Ohio as their one highway to the outside world. During the French and Indian War, France had ceded Louisiana to Spain; New Orleans, French in name and aspect, had ever since remained in Spanish hands. But Spanish control of the port city at the river's mouth was not oppressive, and Americans were free to voyage up and down the Mississippi at will and to deposit their goods duty-free in New Orleans warehouses for shipment overseas.

When Napoleon, after his *coup d'état*, became First Consul, he revived the Bourbon dream of an overseas empire, one that would stretch in an arc from the homeland across the French islands of the Caribbean to New Orleans. Urged by Talleyrand, he pressed the Spanish government for the return of Louisiana. Spain, not valuing Louisiana greatly, was in any case in no condition to stand up to the victor of Marengo, and some months before Jefferson became President, by the secret Treaty of San Ildefonso in 1800, exchanged the territory for a part of the Italian peninsula.

To Jefferson the approaching replacement of the languid and indifferent Spaniards by the troops of the con-

By the 1800 Convention of Mortefontaine, America ended the naval war with France, which had feared an Anglo-American alliance. In this lithograph, after a Victor Adam painting, Napoleon (who was not present at the actual signing) formally presents a copy of the treaty to the American commissioners at the estate of his brother Joseph.

PATRICK GASS, *Journal*, 1811; BOTTOM: MISSOURI HISTORICAL SOCIET

*The first personal account of the Lewis and Clark expedition
published in book form was that of Sergeant Patrick
Gass, a barrel-chested ex-carpenter who had experienced all
the trials and triumphs of the two-and-a-half-year
journey to the Pacific and back. Later editions of the work
were enlivened with quaint illustrations, such as that
above: a member of the party is treed by a ferocious grizzly
bear apparently masquerading as a sheep dog. At right,
from Clark's own journal, is a sketch by the explorer of a
canoe used by the Indians of the Northwest coast.
He described the figures at bow and stern as "grotesque."*

quering First Consul Bonaparte in New Orleans seemed
a threat to Mississippi navigation and a prelude to war.
Much as he loved France and disliked England, he
wrote Robert R. Livingston, then minister to France,
that he was bound to regard the occupier of New Orleans as "our natural and habitual enemy. . . . The day
that France takes possession of N. Orleans. . . . From
that moment we must marry ourselves to the British
fleet and nation."

When the news of the cession of Louisiana became
public, it roused the country, particularly the West, and
indignation boiled over when the Spanish blocked the
Mississippi outlet by closing the port of New Orleans.

Jefferson maneuvered deftly between peace and the
threat of war. After getting a two-million-dollar appropriation from Congress for unspecified foreign dealings,
he instructed Livingston to sound out the First Consul
as to whether he would consider an offer for New Orleans and the Floridas.

Napoleon, preoccupied with putting down Toussaint
L'Ouverture's slave revolt in Santo Domingo, was not
interested, since he still planned to occupy Louisiana
after subjugating that island. Talleyrand received Livingston infrequently and with a minimum of civility.
Meanwhile in the summer of 1802 a large-scale French
expedition for Louisiana was fitting out in Holland.

84

Yet, before the year's end, Napoleon's dream of empire collapsed. A French army in Haiti had been destroyed in the pursuit of L'Ouverture, almost entirely wiped out in a yellow-fever epidemic. The Haitian bastion was becoming a grave, and without it Louisiana was useless. Even more ominously, Napoleon—as always short of money—found himself teetering on the brink of war with England, a war in which New Orleans would lie helpless before the British fleet.

Soon after Napoleon's stocktaking, Livingston, to his surprise, encountered a more affable Talleyrand. The slightly deaf American could scarcely trust his hearing when the Frenchman casually asked what the United States would give for the whole Louisiana territory. Livingston, momentarily awaiting the arrival of James Monroe as envoy extraordinary, replied cautiously that his country wanted merely New Orleans and the Floridas. Talleyrand said that without New Orleans the territory had little value, and told him to think it over.

Not until Monroe arrived did Livingston commit himself, but both men realized that the offer was far more than they had hoped for. The American envoys first offered fifty million francs for the territory and the city. The French minister of finance, the Marquis de Barbé-Marbois, thought it not enough, but a few days later agreed to accept sixty million francs—about fifteen million dollars. No one as yet knew the extent of the territory, how far west it ran, whether it included Texas. When Livingston questioned Talleyrand about the boundaries, the artful schemer told him: "I can give you no direction. You have made a noble bargain for yourselves and I suppose you will make the most of it."

The Louisiana Purchase was the outstanding act of Jefferson's two presidential terms. With a stroke of the pen and without firing one shot the area of the United States was doubled, adding land from which all or parts of thirteen states would eventually be carved. Yet the acceptance of the French offer put Jefferson in a dilemma. Desirable and necessary as the possession of Louisiana might be, did he have the right under the Constitution to acquire it? Only five years before, in 1798, he had written that when "a government assumes undelegated powers, its acts are unauthoritative, void, and of no force. . . ." He had accused the Federalists of usurping powers not specified in the Constitution and had maintained that such loose construction would destroy the Union. If he were now to agree that the government could acquire territory merely because this was not specifically forbidden by the Constitution, he would be replacing his principle that the federal government had only enumerated powers with Hamilton's doctrine that the national government had the right to assume whatever powers seemed necessary.

Jefferson's first reaction was to ask Congress for an amendment to the Constitution that would give the government the needed authority to purchase new territory. Livingston and Monroe were aghast. By the time Congress passed and the states ratified such an amendment, Napoleon might have changed his mind. The occasion was too fateful; they urged the President to sign the treaty at once.

Reluctantly Jefferson agreed, signing the treaty but admitting as he did so that it was an act beyond the Constitution. He begged Congress—in an argument that might have been plotted by Hamilton—to disregard "metaphysical subtleties." Still troubled by the precedent he had established, he trusted that "the good sense of our country will correct the evil of [broad] construction when it shall produce ill effects."

Despite an earlier disclaimer of American interest in the trans-Mississippi region, Jefferson had shown his sympathy for and interest in the West long before the Louisiana Purchase, early sensing the needs and importance of the land beyond the Alleghenies. While Louisiana was still French, he had obtained twenty-five hundred dollars from Congress for an expedition across the territory to explore the source of the Missouri and the region beyond. He chose his secretary, Captain Meriwether Lewis, to lead the expedition, with the frontier soldier William Clark, brother of George Rogers Clark, as second-in-command. Jefferson's instructions to Lewis called for the collection of both scientific and practical information. He wanted facts about the land, the soil, rock formations, minerals—particularly metals—animals, birds, reptiles, insects, and weather phenomena of all sorts. And he also wanted to know about "useful" plants and animals, as well as about the possibility of friendly relations with the Western Indian tribes. Lewis and Clark, with a party of forty-eight woodsmen, left St. Louis in May, 1804, on an epic exploration that would take them up the Missouri, across the Great Divide, and down the Columbia River to the Pacific. Two and a half years later they returned with bulging journals, much information about Western regions and resources, and two grizzly bear cubs for the President. Jefferson later sent Zebulon Pike, who had earlier explored the headwaters of the Mississippi, on a less publicized exploration into what is now Colorado and the Southwest.

Meanwhile during most of his term Jefferson, in spite of himself, was engaged in a desultory undeclared war against the Barbary pirates. For years all the European sea powers, as well as the United States, had been paying protection to the rulers of Morocco, Algiers, Tunis, and Tripoli. In return the North African rulers restrained their corsairs from attacking the Mediterranean shipping of the tribute-paying nations. Then in 1801 the pasha of Tripoli, feeling that United States payments had been too niggardly, ordered the flagpole of the American consulate chopped down. Jefferson's reaction was Hamiltonian. Without consulting Congress, he sent a squadron of frigates to blockade and bombard the Tripolitan coast. This naval war dragged on for three years without conclusion.

As Jefferson neared the end of his first term, he found himself at the height of popularity. Even the Tripolitan War seemed a not-too-costly demonstration of self-assertive patriotism. He had doubled the area of his country; he had upheld the honor of the flag while avoiding a major war; he had eliminated internal taxes, cut down the national debt, and satisfied the democratic instincts of his fellow countrymen. In spite of dire Federalist predictions, America was prosperous, with the promise of more prosperity to come.

Like Washington, Jefferson would have preferred his rural acres to the tumult of politics. The election of 1804 was such a foregone conclusion that the Federalist candidate, Charles Pinckney of the X Y Z Affair, was a nominal one. The Twelfth Amendment, then in the process of going into effect, separated the electoral votes for President and Vice President. Burr was by this time obviously impossible, and Jefferson replaced him with New York's fading George Clinton. Rufus King became the Federalist candidate for Vice President.

The election turned into a rout. Only in New England did the Federalists campaign actively, and even there they lost every state but Connecticut. Jefferson carried fourteen of the seventeen states—Maryland split evenly—with 162 out of 176 electoral votes. The ruin of the Federalist party was even more apparent in the new Congress, where the Democratic-Republicans won 116 seats in the House and 27 in the Senate, to 25 and 7 respectively for the Federalists.

The history of Jefferson's second administration is a frustrating footnote to the Napoleonic Wars, his hopeful domestic program strangled by the clash of England and France—the two leviathans, as he called them. His aim was peace with all, even though he had come to detest Napoleon far more than he had ever disliked England. However, he was to find that the two world powers locked in a death struggle would not be too particular about the rights of neutrals or the sensibilities of the small agrarian republic across the Atlantic. Jefferson's one minor foreign success in his second term was settling the war—still on terms of bribery—with the Barbary pirates after he had dispatched Commodores Edward Preble and Samuel Barron with a squadron to the Mediterranean.

Midway in his term Jefferson was faced with the enigmatic, and to this day mysteriously ambiguous, Burr conspiracy. In 1806 Burr, in his declining fortunes, approached the President for some kind of political appointment. On being refused, the former Vice President turned to a scheme of subversion he had long had in mind. His plan was twofold. First, he planned to raise a private army of discontented Westerners and lead them against Spain's colony Mexico, which he would detach from the Spanish crown. The administration, he hinted, would not be averse to such a step. Anti-Spanish feeling was so strong in the West that Burr was able to obtain the support of Henry Clay, General Andrew Jackson, and Governor William Henry Harrison of Indiana Territory. His second, more shrouded goal was to detach the West from the Union and combine it with Mexico in a vast Louisianian-Mexican empire, of which he would become emperor. Two conspirators shared this second plan: Harman Blennerhassett, an Irish eccentric of great wealth and simple mind, who had set himself up in Regency elegance on a large Ohio River island below Marietta; and the more sinister figure of General James Wilkinson of the United States Army in Louisiana, a friend successively of Washington, Adams, and Jefferson, and at the same time a paid agent of Spain.

The scheme was a harebrained one. Burr had even approached the British minister to ask for funds. When he finally launched his expedition from Blennerhassett's Island, the wily Wilkinson, in a successful maneuver to save himself, assumed the role of a sterling patriot by denouncing his fellow conspirator in a series of letters to Jefferson. Jefferson reacted by issuing a proclamation in which he called for Burr's arrest on

An American disaster in the Tripolitan War is shown above: the premature explosion of the powder-filled fireboat Intrepid *in the pirates' harbor before it could damage the enemy ships and fort. Captain Richard Somers and his crew were killed. Below is Somers' best friend, Stephen Decatur, an inspiring leader and brilliant naval tactician.*

charges of treason. Burr's supporters melted away to a few dozen before they reached New Orleans.

Burr was apprehended and went on trial before Chief Justice Marshall at Richmond. Marshall, more concerned with humiliating Jefferson's administration than with convicting a traitor, tried to favor Burr. But Burr, though acquitted, was never a figure of influence again, and sentiment was so hostile toward him that he felt forced to leave the country.

Far more ominous than Burr's monomaniacal fantasies were the depredations on American shipping by the two great warring powers. The English, with their larger navy, were more provocative, impressing American seamen on the suspicion of being British, seizing American ships merely suspected of trade that might be helpful to France. At Jefferson's request Congress passed a nonimportation act, giving him the power to throttle the flow of British commerce to the United States. Before putting this into effect, he sent Pinckney to join Monroe in London in the hope of negotiating a settlement with the new government. The treaty that Monroe finally managed to send back contained no specific guarantees of American rights, and though he maintained it was the best he could obtain, Jefferson and Secretary of State Madison rejected it.

Monroe, hurt and aggrieved, broke with Madison, and in spite of his lifelong friendship with Jefferson, gravitated to the hostile following of Randolph of Roanoke. With the growing crisis overseas, Randolph, from administration spokesman in the House of Representatives, had turned around to attacking Jefferson, and he announced that he was neither a Republican nor a Federalist but "a third something."

The crisis with Great Britain came to a head with the capture of the American frigate *Chesapeake* off the Virginia capes by the British ship of war *Leopard,* which was in search of deserters. The *Chesapeake's* commander hove to on British signal but refused to hand over any of his seamen, whereupon the *Leopard* opened fire at point-blank range, killing three American seamen, wounding eighteen others, and forcing the commander of the crippled ship to strike his flag. Although the British did not hold the *Chesapeake* as a prize, they did line up her crew and seized four sailors accused of being British deserters.

For the English, long troubled by naval desertions and desperately in need of men in their battle for survival, the *Chesapeake* affair was a minor, if arbitrary, incident in a relentless war. For Americans the violation of their Navy vessel seemed a national affront. All over the country there was a welling-up of anger, reinforced by a nascent national pride anxious to assert itself. A war declaration, as Jefferson realized, would be a very popular move. Yet he hesitated. Besides his personal repugnance to war there were practical considerations. Above all, the United States lacked a strong fleet and an effective army. The President temporized, excluding all British vessels from American waters but taking no other steps.

Meanwhile France and England engaged in a sequence of blockade and counterblockade. Napoleon closed European ports from Seville to Hamburg to British shipping. The British in turn demanded that all ships call at an English port before proceeding to a French-controlled one. Napoleon then announced that his navy would capture any vessel that sailed from a British port or allowed itself to be searched by a British warship. American shippers, who had profited hugely

from the war, found their vessels subject to seizure whatever they did. Still probing for an alternative to war, Jefferson, over the violent protests of merchants and shipping interests, persuaded Congress to pass the Embargo Act of 1807, which prohibited all American exports to foreign countries. The United States would live in peaceful, if austere, isolation, depriving the English of vital raw materials and essential markets until they mended their ways.

As soon as the Embargo Act went into effect, the great ports of Boston, New York, Philadelphia, and Baltimore shut down. Their ships rotted at the docks, their workers idled in the streets. Cotton, tobacco, and wheat piled up in warehouses. In a year American exports dropped by 80 per cent. In New York City thirteen hundred men were imprisoned for debt in 1809 after losing everything as a result of the embargo. As with most laws that run contrary to the will of the majority, widespread violations occurred. Shipowners and merchants were willing to take the long chance for the large profit, and smuggling became general. Maritime New England was hurt most by the embargo, and that region turned most bitterly against Jefferson. "You infernal villain," wrote one typically outraged New Englander to the President, "how much longer are you going to keep this damned Embargo on to starve us poor people?"

As an economic alternative Jefferson tried to encourage domestic industries, and indeed his Embargo Act gave a stimulus to manufacturing that Hamilton had never been able to achieve for all his efforts. Nevertheless the President had to face the fact that his sanctions were unenforceable. Even Gallatin had come out against them. Three days before leaving office he signed a bill for the repeal of the embargo, which was replaced by an act of nonintercourse with the French and British.

Jefferson, as he came to the end of eight years in the presidential office, was in his middle sixties, harassed by bickering and abuse, disappointed in his high hopes, declining in physical vigor, and weary of the drudgery of office. In spite of any adverse circumstances, he could still have had a third term for the asking, but—beyond any personal reluctance—he felt there was a danger to democracy in a President's continuing too long in office. "General Washington set the example of voluntary retirement after eight years," Jefferson wrote. "I shall follow it."

Emblem of the United States of America.

Peace with all Nations, Partiality to none.

Published according to act of Congress, by John Coles, sen. BOSTON. Sept. 7. 1804.

The First Years

The American Revolution created a new nation on earth—if nation it could be called, for the United States of the Confederation was more nearly an assemblage of thirteen semi-independent countries, moved by narrow self-interest. However, in a very important sense there was a single nation, for the common experience of pushing forward a frontier and settling a wilderness had shaped in America a new breed of men and women. In spite of regional differences, Americans were more like each other than they were the people of Europe, whence their forebears had come. Visiting Europeans found their ways strange, and Americans considered themselves a people unique and apart from their European cousins—as indeed they were. Benjamin Franklin tried to explain the American character to friends in the Old World.

. . . though there are in [America] few people so miserable as the poor of Europe, there are also very few that in Europe would be called rich: It is rather a general happy mediocrity that prevails. There are few great Proprietors of the soil, and few Tenants; most people cultivate their own lands, or follow some handicraft or merchandise; very few rich enough to live idly upon their rents or incomes; or to pay the high prices given in Europe, for Painting, Statues, Architecture, and the other works of Art that are more curious than useful. . . . Of civil offices or employments, there are few; no superfluous ones as in Europe; and it is a rule established in some of the States, that no Office should be so profitable as to make it desirable. . . .

These ideas prevailing more or less in all the United States, it cannot be worth any man's while, who has a means of living at home, to expatriate himself in hopes of obtaining a profitable civil office in America; and as to military offices they are at an end with the war, the armies being disbanded. Much less is it adviseable for a person to go thither who has no other quality to recommend him but his birth. In Europe it has indeed its value; but it is a commodity that cannot be carried to a worse market than to that of America, where people do not enquire concerning a stranger, *What is he?* but *What can he do?* If he has any useful art, he is welcome; and if he exercises it, and behaves well, he will be respected by all that know him; but a mere man of quality, who on that account wants to live upon the public, by some office or salary, will be despised and disregarded. . . . According to these opinions of the Americans, one of them would think himself more obliged to a genealogist, who could prove for him that his ancestors and relations for ten generations had been Ploughmen, Smiths, Carpenters, Turners, Weavers, Tanners, or even Shoemakers, and consequently that they were useful members of society; than if he could only prove that they were Gentlemen, doing nothing of value, but living idly on the labour of others. . . .

Benjamin Franklin
Information to Those Who Would Remove to America, 1784

A young army surgeon, Johann Schoepf, who had served with Hessian troops during the Revolution, was one of the first foreigners to visit the United States after the war. Although he had already spent seven years in America,

Columbia leads Franklin and Liberty; an early print on cloth

it had always been on territory occupied by redcoats and Hessians, amidst people hostile because he wore the uniform of an enemy mercenary. Then, in 1783, he set out on a long trip as an ordinary tourist and sight-seer.

Though a bit cruder, the national coat of arms in 1786 was much as it is today.

Tranquillity was now in some sort re-established in America. Ratification of the Peace had not yet come over from Europe, but under the guarantees of the provisional truce, there was already a certain intercourse opened between New York and the United States. Business and curiosity tempted a number of travellers from the one side and from the other. For near seven years I had been confined to the narrow compass of sundry British garrisons along the coast, unable until now to carry out my desire of seeing somewhat of the interior of the country. The German troops were embarking gradually for the return voyage; and having received permission, July 22 I took leave of my countrymen at New York, in order to visit the united American states, now beginning to be of consequence. . . .

People think, act, and speak here precisely as it prompts them; the poorest day-laborer on the bank of the Delaware holds it his right to advance his opinion, in religious as well as political matters, with as much freedom as the gentleman or the scholar. . . . Rank of birth is not recognized, is resisted with a total force.

Luxury, which is unavoidable in enlightened free nations, prevails here also, without, however, any dispossession of industry and thrift, being largely restricted to the luxury of the body; virtuosity, sensibility and other manifestations of soul-luxury are not yet become conspicuous here. . . .

The war has left no sign of want here; now, as before, the same exuberant plenty prevails. The inhabitants are not only well clothed but well fed, and, comparatively, better than their betters in Europe. Few families can be found who do not enjoy daily their fine wheat-bread, good meats and fowls, cyder, beer, and rum. Want oppresses but few. Work is rewarded and there is no need of catch-pole beadles. . . .

Nothing has so much damaged faith in the Congress, or so diminished regard for it, even among its friends and constituents, and nothing has caused more general and bitter indignation against it, than the debts heaped by it upon the states, and especially the woful after-pains left by the paper-money issued under its warrant. . . .

Johann David Schoepf
Travels in the Confederation, 1788

ichel Guillaume Jean de Crèvecoeur lived, worked, and traveled in America, became a naturalized citizen, married Meheteble Tippet of Yonkers, New York, and farmed in Orange County, New York, for eleven years. He returned to France in 1790, but in his Letters from an American Farmer *he has given us a discerning picture of the early republic and its citizens. Crèvecoeur saw not only that Americans were becoming a changed race from Europeans, but he recognized that it was the different environment of the New World that was responsible. Here Crèvecoeur gener-*

91

alizes on the influences that make an American, he looks at the rude and rough men and women who are in the vanguard of the advancing frontier, and he describes the New England character as he observed it on the island of Nantucket.

He is an American, who leaving behind him all his ancient prejudices and manners, receives new ones from the new mode of life he has embraced, the new government he obeys, and the new rank he holds. He becomes an American by being received in the broad lap of our great *Alma Mater*. Here individuals of all nations are melted into a new race of men, whose labours and posterity will one day cause great changes in the world. . . . Here the rewards of his industry follow with equal steps the progress of his labour. . . . Wives and children, who before in vain demanded of him a morsel of bread, now, fat and frolicsome, gladly help their father to clear those fields whence exuberant crops are to arise to feed and to clothe them all; without any part being claimed, either by a despotic prince, a rich abbot, or a mighty lord. . . . The American is a new man, who acts upon new principles; he must therefore entertain new ideas, and form new opinions. From involuntary idleness, servile dependence, penury, and useless labour, he has passed to toils of a very different nature, rewarded by ample subsistence. —This is an American. . . .

Now we arrive near the great woods, near the last inhabited districts; there men seem to be placed still farther beyond the reach of government, which in some measure leaves them to themselves. . . . as they were driven there by misfortunes, necessity of beginnings, desire of acquiring large tracks of land, idleness, frequent want of oeconomy, ancient debts; the re-union of such people does not afford a very pleasing spectacle. . . . The few magistrates they have, are in general little better than the rest; they are often in a perfect state of war; that of man against man, sometimes decided by blows, sometimes by means of the law. . . . men are wholly left dependent on their native tempers, and on the spur of uncertain industry, which often fails when not sanctified by the efficacy of a few moral rules. There, remote from the power of example, and check of shame, many families exhibit the most hideous parts of our society. They are a kind of forlorn hope, preceding by ten or twelve years the most respectable army of veterans which come after them. In that space, prosperity will polish some, vice and the law will drive off the rest, who uniting again with others like themselves will recede still farther; making room for more industrious people, who will finish their improvements, convert the log-house into a convenient habitation, and rejoicing that the first heavy labours are finished, will change in a few years that hitherto barbarous country into a fine fertile, well regulated district. Such is our progress, such is the march of the Europeans toward the interior parts of this continent. In all societies there are off-casts; this impure part serves as our precursors or pioneers. . . .

Idleness is the most heinous sin that can be committed in Nantucket: an idle man would soon be pointed out as an object of compassion: for idleness is considered as another word for want and hunger. This principle is so thoroughly well understood, and is become so universal, so prevailing a prejudice, that literally speaking, they are never idle. Even if they go to the market-place, which is (if I may be allowed the expression) the coffee-house of the town, either to transact business, or to converse with their friends; they always have a piece of cedar in their hands, and while they are talking, they will, as it were instinctively, employ themselves in converting it into something useful, either in making bungs or spoyls for their oil casks, or other useful articles. . . . You will be pleased to remember they are all brought up to the trade of coopers, be their future intentions or fortunes what they may; therefore almost every man in this island has always two knives in his pocket, one much larger than the other; and though they hold every thing that is called *fashion* in the utmost contempt, yet they are as difficult to please, and as extravagant in the choice and price of their knives, as any young buck in Boston would be about his hat, buckles, or coat. . . . As the sea excursions are often very long, their wives in their absence, are necessarily obliged to transact business, to settle accounts, and in short, to rule and provide for their families. These circumstances being often repeated, give women the abilities as well as a taste for that kind of superintendency, to which, by their prudence and good management, they seem to be in general very equal. This employment ripens their judgement, and justly entitles them to a rank superior to that of other wives; and this is the principal reason why those of Nantucket . . . are so fond of society, so affable, and so conversant with the affairs of the world. The men at their return, weary with the fatigues of the sea, full of confidence and love, chearfully give their consent to every transaction that has happened during their absence, and all is joy and peace. "Wife, thee hast done well," is the general approbation they receive, for their application and industry. . . .

Michel Guillaume Jean de Crèvecoeur
Letters from an American Farmer, 1782

Bonanza for a whaleman—
a sperm whale hard aground

The infant nation was overwhelmingly rural. Even its largest city, Philadelphia, probably had not reached a population of forty thousand in 1788, when Jacques Pierre Brissot de Warville visited the United States. Though Brissot was very favorably impressed by Boston and Philadelphia as centers of culture and commerce, both cities seem quaintly small-town from today's point of view.

. . . with what pleasure did I contemplate this town, which first shook off the English yoke! which, for a long time, resisted all the seductions, all the menaces, all the horrors of a civil war! How I delighted to wander up and down that long street, whose simple houses of wood border the magnificent channel of Boston, and whose full stores offer me all the productions of the continent which I had quitted! How I enjoyed the activity of the merchants, the artizans, and the sailors! It was not the noisy vortex of Paris; it was not the unquiet, eager mien of my countrymen; it was the simple, dignified air of men, who are conscious of liberty, and who see in all men their brothers and their equals. Every thing in this street bears the marks of a town still in its infancy, but which, even in its infancy, enjoys a great prosperity. . . .

Neatness without luxury, is a characteristic feature of this purity of manners; and this neatness is seen every where at Boston, in their dress, in their houses, and in their churches. Nothing is more charming than an inside view of the church on Sunday. The good cloth coat covers the man; callicoes and chintzes dress the women and children, without being spoiled by those gewgaws which whim and caprice have added to them among our women. . . .

Philadelphia may be considered as the metropolis of the United States. It is certainly the finest town, and the best built; it is the most wealthy, though not the most luxurious. You find here more men of information, more political and literary knowledge, and more learned societies. Many towns in America are more ancient; but Philadelphia has surpassed her elders. . . .

At ten o'clock in the evening all is tranquil in the streets; the profound silence which reigns there, is only interrupted by the voice of the watchmen, who are in small numbers, and who form the only patrole. The streets are lighted by lamps, placed like those of London.

On the side of the streets are footways of brick, and gutters constructed of brick or wood. Strong posts are placed to prevent carriages from passing on the footways. All the streets are furnished with public pumps, in great numbers. At the door of each house are placed two benches, where the family sit at evening to take the fresh air, and amuse themselves in looking at the passengers. It is certainly a bad custom, as the evening air is unhealthful, and the exercise is not sufficient to correct this evil, for they never walk here: they supply the want of walking, by riding out into the country.

Jacques Pierre Brissot de Warville
New Travels in the United States of America, 1792

Visitors from Europe expected to find regional differences among the peoples of the United States, but they seldom failed to be surprised by the austere Puritanism they found flourishing in New England. At no time was that stern and cheerless faith made so manifest to them as on a Sabbath day.

Sunday is observed with the utmost strictness; all business, how important soever, is then totally at a stand, and the most innocent recreations and pleasures prohibited. Boston, that populous town, where at other times there is such a hurry of business, is on this day a mere desert; you may walk the streets without meeting a single person, and if by chance you meet one, you scarcely dare to stop and talk with him. A Frenchman that lodged with me took it into his head to play on the flute on Sundays for his amusement; the people upon hearing it were greatly enraged, collected in crowds round the house and would have carried matters to extremity in a short time with the musician, had not the landlord given him warning of his danger, and forced him to desist.

Abbe Robin
New Travels Through North-America, 1783

New York in 1797; Broad Street and City Hall, earlier the first National Capitol

Herewith an anecdote: last Sunday morning I went out to take a ride in a chaise towards the fort which is a little further on than Dorchester Point, and as it was necessary to cross a small *ferry*, I started to call the boat, but they did not wish to send it to me as it was *Sunday*. Very patiently I retracted my steps along the same road which is quite good and came to a place, where the low-land was covered by a foot of water as it was high tide: quite a decent looking man came up at this moment, on horseback, with a woman on the pillon and immediately approached me and asked me if I would take his wife across in my chaise as she was afraid; I assented, and she then jumped from the horse and got in my chaise and I took her some two miles further on, where she asked me to let her get out and she then waited in a house for her husband, who was coming along on horseback at a certain distance behind us; who in Europe would have so favorably judged a human heart, that he would have entrusted to a perfect stranger his young and good looking wife? and who (in Europe) would have been so small minded to believe it a mortal sin to cross a river on Sunday?

Francisco de Miranda
Travels in the New Republic . . . in 1783–1784

But not all was well with the United States as the war ended. The soldiers who had done the fighting were disgruntled. They had gone unpaid for long periods; they had fought ill clothed, poorly armed, and often hungry. When it was proposed in 1782 to send the men remaining under arms home without paying them money still due, General Washington protested.

My Dear Sir:

Painful as the task is to describe the dark side of our affairs, it sometimes becomes a matter of indispensable necessity. Without disguise or palliation, I will inform you candidly of the discontents, which at this moment prevail universally throughout the army.

The evils, of which they complain, and which they suppose almost remediless, are the total want of money or the means of existing from one day to another, the heavy debts they have already incurred, the loss of credit, the distress of their families at home, and the prospect of poverty and misery before them. It is vain, Sir, to suppose, that military men will acquiesce contentedly with bare rations, when those in the civil walk of life, unacquainted with half the hardships they endure, are regularly paid the emoluments of office. . . .

While I premise, that no one I have seen or heard of appears opposed to the principle of reducing the army as circumstances may require, yet I cannot help fearing the result of the measure in contemplation, under present circumstances, when I see a number of men, goaded by a thousand stings of reflection on the past and of anticipation on the future, about to be turned into the world, soured by penury and what they call the ingratitude of the public, involved in debts without one farthing of money to carry them home after having spent the flower of their days, and many of them their patrimonies,

Moving a house in Philadelphia

in establishing the freedom and independence of their country, and suffered every thing that human nature is capable of enduring on this side of death. I repeat it, that when I consider these irritating circumstances, without one thing to soothe their feelings or dispel the gloomy prospects, I cannot avoid apprehending that a train of evils will follow, of a very serious and distressing nature. . . .

I am, my dear Sir, &c.,

George Washington
Letter to the Secretary of War, October 2, 1782

The great weakness of the Confederation was the lack of a strong central government. Each state was virtually independent, and most of the thirteen were quick to assert their sovereign rights. Thomas Jefferson, for one, noted with alarm the growing intransigency of the separate states, threatening disaster to the country as a whole.

. . . I find also the pride of independence taking deep and dangerous hold on the hearts of individual states. I know no danger so dreadful and so probable as that of internal contests. And I know no remedy so likely to prevent it as the strengthening the band which connects us. We have substituted a Congress of deputies from every state to perform this task: but we have done nothing which would enable them to enforce their decisions. What will be the case? They will not be enforced. The states will go to war with each other in defiance of Congress; one will call in France to her assistance; another Gr. Britain, and so we shall have all the wars of Europe brought to our own doors. Can any man be so puffed up with his little portion of sovereignty as to prefer this calamitous accompaniment to the parting with a little of his sovereign right and placing it in a council from all the states, who being chosen by himself annually . . . cannot possibly do him an injury? . . . My 'humble and earnest prayer to Almighty God' will be that . . . you will first lay your shoulders to the strengthening the band of our confederacy . . . and that you will see the necessity of doing this instantly before we forget the advantages of union, or acquire a degree of ill-temper against each other which will daily increase the obstacles to that good work. . . .

Thomas Jefferson
Letter to Edmund Randolph, February 15, 1783

James Madison; a portrait made while he was President

The weaknesses of the Confederation as a government became increasingly apparent as time passed—and as the thirteen states more and more asserted their independence of one another. William Davie, a North Carolina legislator, was among the many who commented on the growing impotence of the new United States.

The general government ought . . . to possess the means of preserving the peace and tranquility of the union. A striking proof of the necessity of this power recently happened in Rhode-Island: A man who had run off with a vessel and cargo, the property of some merchants in Holland, took sanctuary in that place; application was made for him as a citizen of the United Netherlands by the minister, but as he had taken the oath of allegiance [to the state], the state refused to deliver him up, and protected him in his villainy. Had it not been for the peculiar situation of the states at that time, fatal consequences might have resulted from such a conduct, and the contemptible state of Rhode-Island might have involved the whole union in a war.

The encroachments of some states, on the rights of others, and of all on those of the confederacy, are incontestible proofs of the weakness and imperfection of that system. Maryland lately passed a law, granting exclusive privileges to her own vessels, contrary to the articles of the confederation: Congress had neither power nor influence to alter it; all they could do was to send a contrary recommendation. It is provided by the 6th article of the Confederation, that no compact shall be made between two or more states without the consent of Congress; yet this has been recently violated by Virginia and Maryland, and also by Pennsylvania and New Jersey. North Carolina and Massachusetts have had a considerable body of forces on foot, and those in this state raised for two years, notwithstanding the express provision in the Confederation that no forces should be kept up by any state in time of peace.

William Davie
Speech in the legislature of North Carolina, 1787

The Confederation's most serious trouble occurred in 1786, and it struck in Massachusetts. New England's postwar depression had fallen especially heavily on the small farmers of Massachusetts because the legislature refused to give them any relief from seizure of their farms and possessions for taxes or overdue debts. At last in August of 1786 the Massachusetts farmers began to resort to force to prevent court action against delinquent debtors, a confrontation known as Shays' Rebellion from the farmer who led it.

In the following extract, George Washington writes from Mount Vernon to Henry Lee, a fellow Virginian and a delegate to Congress, deploring the violence and calling for a stronger government.

You talk, my good Sir, of employing influence to appease the present tumults in Massachusetts. I know not where that influence is to be found, or, if attainable, that it would be a proper remedy for the disorders. *Influence* is not *government.* Let us have a government by which our lives, liberties, and properties will be secured, or let us know the worst at once. Under these impressions, my humble opinion is, that there is a call for decision. Know precisely what the insurgents aim at. If they have *real* grievances, redress them if possible; or acknowledge the justice of them, and your inability to do it in the moment. If they have not, employ the force of government against them at once. If this is inadequate, *all* will be convinced, that the superstructure is bad, or wants support. To be more exposed in the eyes of the world, and more contemptible than we already are, is hardly possible. To delay one or the other of these expedients, is to exasperate on the one hand, or to give confidence on the other, and will add to their numbers; for, like snow-balls, such bodies increase by every movement, unless there is something in the way to obstruct and crumble them before their weight is too great and irresistible.

These are my sentiments. Precedents are dangerous things. Let the reins of government then be braced and held with a steady hand, and every violation of the constitution be reprehended. If defective, let it be amended, but not suffered to be trampled upon whilst it has an existence.

George Washington
Letter to Henry Lee, October 31, 1786

An *explanation of the causes of Shays' Rebellion was given to Washington by Benjamin Lincoln, who was leading the Massachusetts militia against the protesting farmers when he wrote to Washington. His view of events was the classic one of the powerful and arrogant: the farmers were shiftless ne'er-do-wells seeking a way out of honest obligations.*

I cannot . . . be surprized to hear your Excellency inquire, "are your people getting mad? are we to have the goodly fabric, that eight years were spent in raising, pulled over our heads? what is the cause of all these commotions? when and how will they end?" Although I cannot pretend to give a full and complete answer to them, yet I will make some observations which shall involve in them the best answers to the several questions in my power to give.

"Are your people getting mad?" Many of them appear to be absolutely so, if an attempt to annihilate our present constitution and dissolve the present government can be considered as evidences of insanity.

"Are we to have the goodly fabric, that eight years were spent in rearing, pulled over our heads?" There is great danger that it will be so, I think, unless the tottering system shall be supported by arms. . . .

"What is the cause of all these commotions?" The causes are too many and too various for me to pretend to trace and point them out. I shall therefore only mention some of those which appear to be the principal ones. Among those I may rank the ease with which property was acquired, with which credit was obtained, and debts were discharged in the time of war. Hence people were diverted from their usual industry and oeconomy. . . . The moment the day arrived when all discovered that things were fast returning back into their original channels, that the industrious were to reap the fruits of their industry, and that the indolent and improvident would soon experience the evils of their idleness and sloth, very many startled at the idea, and . . . complained . . . of the weight of public taxes, of the insupportable debt of the Union, of the scarcity of money, and of the cruelty of suffering the private creditors to call for their just dues. . . . the disaffected in the first place attempted, and in many instances succeeded to stop the courts of law, and to

Award for New England
sheep-breed improvement

suspend the operations of government. This they hoped to do untill they could by force sap the foundations of our constitution, and bring into the Legislature creatures of their own by which they could mould a government at pleasure, and make it subservient to all their purposes, and when an end should thereby be put to public and private debts, the agrarian law might follow with ease. In short, the want of industry, oeconomy, and common honesty seem to be the causes of the present commotions.

It is impossible for me to determine "when and how they will end;" as I see little probability that they will be brought to a period, and the dignity of government supported, without bloodshed. When a single drop is drawn, the most prophetic spirit will not, in my opinion, be able to determine when it will cease flowing.

Major General Benjamin Lincoln
Letter to George Washington, December 4, 1786

The shadow of Shays and his armed farmers thenceforth influenced the thinking of all American leaders. Many conservatives accepted the rebellion as a convincing argument against all forms of republican government. Most men, however, saw in it proof of the need for a stronger central government —and so Shays' Rebellion helped bring on the Constitutional Convention. Jefferson, though, professed to be unconcerned about the uprising.

A popular form of early folk art; this barnyard scene is an embroidered sampler.

Dear Sir:
. . . I am impatient to learn your sentiments on the late troubles in the Eastern States. So far as I have yet seen, they do not appear to threaten serious consequences. Those States have suffered by the stoppage of the channels of their commerce, which have not yet found other issues. This must render money scarce, and make the people uneasy. This uneasiness has produced acts absolutely unjustifiable; but I hope they will provoke no severities from their governments. . . . Even this evil is productive of good. It prevents the degeneracy of government, and nourishes a general attention to the public affairs. I hold it, that a little rebellion, now and then, is a good thing, and as necessary in the political world as storms in the physical. Unsuccessful rebellions, indeed, generally establish the encroachments on the rights of the people, which have produced them. An observation of this truth should render honest republican governors so mild in their punishment of rebellions, as not to discourage them too much. It is a medecine necessary for the sound health of government.

Thomas Jefferson
Letter to James Madison, Paris, January 30, 1787

Only three of the delegates refused to approve the new Constitution, which had been created after a summer of searching debate in 1787. But gaining acceptance by the people of the thirteen states was another matter. One of the most effective instruments of the pro-Constitution forces was The Federalist *papers, written by Hamilton, Madison, and John Jay. There were seventy-eight essays in the series; in this one Jay warns that a weak government at home can gain only contempt abroad.*

. . . whatever may be our situation, whether firmly united under one national government, or split into a number of confederacies, certain it is, that foreign nations will know and view it exactly as it is; and they will act towards us accordingly. If they see that our national government is efficient and well administered, our trade prudently regulated, our militia properly organized and disciplined, our resources and finances discreetly managed, our credit re-established, our people free, contented, and united, they will be much more disposed to cultivate our friendship than provoke our resentment. If, on the other hand, they find us either destitute of an effectual government (each State doing right or wrong, as to its rulers may seem convenient), or split into three or four independent and probably discordant republics or confederacies, one inclining to Britain, another to France, and a third to Spain, and perhaps played off against each other by the three, what a poor, pitiful figure will America make in their eyes! How liable would she become not only to their contempt, but to their outrage; and how soon would dear-bought experience proclaim that when a people or family so divide, it never fails to be against themselves.

The Federalist, Number 4

While a campaign was being waged to swing public support behind the Constitution other eloquent tongues and pens were raised against it. They ranged from the wild claim of Elbridge Gerry, a delegate to the Constitutional Convention, that the document was the result of a secret conspiracy, to the logical and measured arguments of Virginia's Richard Henry Lee. However, Lee's attack on the proposal for a Federal City shows that his insight was sometimes blurred.

The constitution provides, that congress shall have the sole and exclusive government of what is called the federal city, a place not exceeding ten miles square, and of all places ceded for forts, dock-yards, &c. I believe this is a novel kind of provision in a federal republic; it is repugnant to the spirit of such a government, and must be founded in an apprehension of a hostile disposition between the federal head and the state governments; and it is not improbable, that the sudden retreat of congress from Philadelphia, first gave rise to it. . . . the government of the union shall have secluded places, cities, and castles of defence, which no state laws whatever shall invade. . . .

The city, and all the places in which the union shall have this exclusive jurisdiction, will be immediately under one entire government, that of the federal head; and be no part of any state, and consequently no part of the United States. The inhabitants of the federal city and places, will be as much exempt from the laws and controul of the state governments, as the people

Countryman on Plodding Horse, *a penman's drawing by an unknown artist* of Canada or Nova Scotia will be. Neither the laws of the states respecting taxes, the militia, crimes or property, will extend to them; nor is there a single stipulation in the constitution, that the inhabitants of this city, and these places, shall be governed by laws founded on principles of freedom.

Richard Henry Lee
An Additional Number of Letters from the Federal Farmer to the Republican, 1788

Patrick Henry had been crying out against tyranny and the loss of liberty ever since the Stamp Act. Now he spoke out again to oppose adoption of the new Constitution, hinting that even Washington had hidden motives.

This proposal of altering our federal government is of a most alarming nature: make the best of this new government—say it is composed by any thing but inspiration—you ought to be extremely cautious, watchful, jealous of your liberty; for instead of securing your rights, you may lose them forever. If a wrong step be now made, the republic may be lost forever. If this new government will not come up to the expectation of the people, and they should be disappointed—their liberty will be lost, and tyranny must and will arise. . . . a wrong step made now will plunge us into misery, and our republic will be lost. . . . I have the highest respect for those gentlemen who formed the convention. . . . But, sir, on this great occasion, I would demand the cause of their conduct. Even from that illustrious man, who saved us by his valor, I would have a reason for his conduct. . . . That they exceeded their power is perfectly clear. . . . The federal convention ought to have amended the old system—for this purpose they were solely delegated: the object of their mission extended to no other consideration. You must therefore forgive the solicitation of one unworthy member, to know what danger could have arisen under the present confederation, and what are the causes of this proposal to change our government.

Patrick Henry
Before the Virginia ratifying convention, June 4, 1788

The battle had been fought and the Constitution adopted by the time Hugh Henry Brackenridge published his novel, Modern Chivalry, *in which he caricatured backwoods democracy. Here he describes a stump debate between an earnest candidate and an illiterate but vocal backwoodsman.*

When they looked on the one, they felt an inclination to promote him. But when, again, on the other hand, they saw two kegs which they knew to be replenished with a very cheering liquor, they seemed to be inclined in favour of the other. The candidates were called upon to address the people, and the grave person mounted the stump of a tree, many of them standing round, as the place was a new clearing. His harangue was listened to by some of the older and more sedate, and one man, hard of hearing, seemed to make great

101

effort to catch the sounds. As soon as the man of the two kegs took a stump, he was surrounded by an eager crowd. —"Friends," said he, in the native Scotch-Irish, "I'm a good dimicrat, and hates the Brattish—I'm an elder of the meetin, forby, and has been overseer of the roads for three years. —An' ye all know, that my mammy was kilt o' the Ingens—now all ye that's in my favour, come forit an' drenk." —Appetite, or rather thirst, prevailed, and the voters gave their votes to the man with the two kegs.

Hugh Henry Brackenridge
Modern Chivalry, 1792–1797 (4 vol.)

What was the United States like in its first years under the Constitution? In general, those who had wanted to change the Articles of Confederation found the new government good and those who had opposed change looked on the new order with a sour eye. As for observers from outside, they found pretty much what their own prejudices had prepared them for, as the following selections from the accounts of two Englishmen prove. Both visited the United States to see if it would be a good place to settle.

At the American taverns, as I before mentioned, all sorts of people, just as they happen to arrive, are crammed together into the one room, where they must reconcile themselves to each other the best way they can. On the present occasion, the company consisted of about thirteen people, amongst whom were some eminent lawyers from Virginia and the southward, together with a judge of the supreme court, who were going to Philadelphia against the approaching sessions: it was not, however, till after I quitted their company that I heard who they were; for these kind of gentlemen in America are so very plain, both in their appearance and manners, that a stranger would not suspect that they were persons of the consequence which they really are in the country. There were also in the company two or three of the neighbouring farmers, boorish, ignorant, and obtrusive fellows. It is scarcely possible for a dozen Americans to sit together without quarrelling about politics, and the British treaty, which had just been ratified, now gave rise to a long and acrimonious debate. The farmers were of one opinion, and gabbled away for a long time; the lawyers and the judge were of another, and in turns they rose to answer their opponents with all the power of rhetoric which they possessed. Neither party could say any thing to change the sentiments of the other one; the noisy contest lasted till late at night, when getting heartily tired they withdrew, not to their respective chambers, but to the general one that held five or six beds, and in which they laid down in pairs. Here the conversation was again revived, and pursued with as much noise as below, till at last sleep closed their eyes, and happily their mouths at the same time; for could they have talked in their sleep, I verily believe they would have prated on until morning. Thanks to our stars! my friend and I got the only two-bedded room in the house to ourselves.

Isaac Weld, Jr.
Travels Through the States of North America, 1799

Billiard players in a Virginia tavern, by Benjamin Latrobe

102

Sketch from memory by Benjamin Latrobe, 1796

I left this kingdom expressly to determine whether America, and what part of it, was eligible for a person, like myself, with a small fortune, and a large family, to settle in. During my residence in Philadelphia, the Congress sat, and I had therefore the means of acquiring satisfactory information respecting every part of the continent which I had not a personal opportunity of visiting. I had no other employment, while in America, than to make observations and inquiries to this purpose; I therefore made this my business, and having compleatly satisfied my own mind upon this subject, I left part of my family there, and have returned (probably for the last time) to this country to fetch away the rest. . . .

You ask what appear to me to be the general inducements to people to quit England for America? In my mind, the first and principal feature is, *"The total absence of anxiety respecting the future success of a family."* There is little fault to find with the government of America, either in principle or in practice: we have very few taxes to pay, and those are of acknowledged necessity, and moderate in amount: we have no animosities about religion: it is a subject about which no questions are asked: we have few respecting political men or political measures: the present irritation of men's minds in Great Britain, and the discordant state of society on political accounts, is not known there. The government is the government *of* the people, and *for* the people. There are no tythes nor game laws: and excise laws upon spirits only, and similar to the British only in name. There are no men of great rank, nor many of great riches. Nor have the rich there the power of oppressing the less rich, for poverty, such as in Great Britain, is almost unknown. Nor are their streets crouded with beggars. I saw but one only while I was there, and he was English. You see no where in America the disgusting and melancholy contrast, so common in Europe, of vice, and filth, and rags, and wretchedness in the immediate neighbourhood of the most wanton extravagance, and the most useless and luxurious parade. Nor are the common people so depraved as in Great Britain. Quarrels are uncommon, and boxing matches unknown in our streets. We have no military to keep the people in awe. Robberies are very rare. . . .

In Great Britain, perpetual exertion, incessant, unremitting industry, daily deprivation of the comforts of life, and anxious attention to minute frugality, are almost incumbent on a man of moderate fortune, and in the middle class of life: and the probabilities of ultimate success, are certainly against a large family. In England, no man has a right (calculating upon the common chances) to expect that five or six children shall all succeed.

In America it is otherwise; you may reasonably reckon upon a comfortable settlement, according to your situation in life, for every part of a family, however numerous. I declare I know nothing in your country equivalent to the taking off this weight upon the mind of a father of a family. It is felt in the occurrences of every day; and I have seen with pleasure the countenance of an European emigrant, in America, brighten up on this very comfortable reflection; a reflection which consoles even for loss of friends, and exile from a native country.

Thomas Cooper
Some Information Respecting America, 1794

The War of 1812

James Madison had long looked forward to succeeding his friend Jefferson in the Presidency. Yet, though Jefferson as President was strong enough to secure his trusted subordinate's succession, he was not able, in the election of 1808, to prevent a contest within his own party. To insure the allegiance of the New York political machine, controlled by the Clinton clan, he had reluctantly agreed to the patriarchal George Clinton as Madison's vice-presidential running mate. But the seventy-year-old Clinton, whose ambitions had not shrunk with age, insisted as well on presenting himself as a presidential candidate. Randolph of Roanoke and his "third somethings" were bent on swinging Virginia's electoral votes to Monroe. The Federalists, hoping to benefit from the Republican schism, again nominated Pinckney and Rufus King. The election outcome, in spite of Republican rifts, was almost as foreordained, if not as overwhelming, as Jefferson's victory in 1804. Monroe withdrew from the race, and Madison received 122 electoral votes to Pinckney's 47 (39 of those from Federalist New England). Clinton captured 6 of New York's 19 votes. Capitalizing on the reaction against the Embargo Act, the Federalists managed to increase their seats in the House of Representatives from 24 to 48.

Jefferson's relation to Madison was much like that of an older brother to a younger one. They had been Virginia neighbors, of the same gentry stock and with similar attitudes. Madison was a fifth-generation American, the third of his line to live on the family estate of Montpelier east of the Blue Ridge. Like other Virginia plantations, Montpelier relied on slave labor, and like most Virginians of the Enlightenment, Madison felt dubious about slavery—although he would still sell slaves when pressed for money. He believed that the solution to the South's peculiar institution was gradual emancipation and the resettling of the freed Negroes in Africa.

In 1769, at the age of eighteen, he had entered Princeton—then called the College of New Jersey—more interested in the arts than in science, for he wrote verse and numbered among his friends the young poet Freneau. A decade later he was elected to the Continental Congress, and following his close association with

This stylized version of the "Glorious Battle of New Orleans," printed on a handkerchief, bears little relation to the actual event, from the number of stripes on the American flag to the narrow meander of the Mississippi.

105

Benjamin Latrobe's sketch of Pennsylvania Avenue— Washington's main thoroughfare—carefully excludes the stumps and swamp grass that disfigured it at the time.

Hamilton from the drafting of the Constitution to its ratification, he became a recognized spokesman for the Federalists. Then, influenced by Jefferson, he swung gradually over to the Republicans.

Yet, on that morning in March, 1809, at the moment of reaching his goal, Madison found himself apprehensive and reluctant. The Presidency he had so long sought seemed like one of those fairy wishes that, once granted, bring misfortune instead of happiness. Any brightness of his Inauguration Day was shadowed by international and domestic problems. Britain's Orders in Council, placing restrictions on shipping to the Continent, and Napoleon's Decrees of Berlin and Milan, closing European ports to ships trading with Britain, made America's neutral position intolerable. American ports were turning into ghost towns. The Republican party seemed ready to dissolve into angry and jealous factions, and a secessionist storm was gathering over the stagnant harbor cities of New England, where armed mobs tramped the empty streets.

In keeping with the times, the inauguration was semimilitary. Madison arrived at the Capitol in his carriage, escorted by cavalry units from Washington and Georgetown. Minute guns fired as the Chief Justice administered the oath, and the new President walked to his carriage past long lines of militiamen.

That evening the first inaugural ball was held at Long's Hotel, "the most brilliant and crowded [assembly] ever known in Washington." Dolley, in a yellow velvet gown—her favorite color—with a train, strings of pearls, and a velvet turban with bird-of-paradise plumes, "looked a queen." Madison, dressed in black, his sparse hair heavily powdered in the old-fashioned manner, seemed listless, old, and woebegone in the crush. Jefferson, present at his first ball in forty years, was full of high spirits, moving from group to group, talking with everyone, sunny and carefree.

With the entrance of the Madisons to the President's House, much of the formality of an earlier day returned. Liveried footmen reappeared, along with a French master of ceremonies. The President rode in a four-horse state coach trimmed inside with yellow lace and displaying a most "elegant Cypher" on the door. His wife furbished and furnished the Mansion. Her Wednesday evening levees became international in their tone, for foreign diplomats found the President's House under its new First Lady an oasis of gracious living in the lonely half-finished Capital. Ladies, on being presented to the President, were expected to curtsy as to royalty. Dolley Madison, in spite of her forty-one years and her increasing girth, still managed to keep her wide-eyed charm. At Madison's frequent dinner parties she presided in a blaze of candlelight, relieving her shrunk and silent husband of the burden of small talk.

While Dolley's charm pervaded social Washington, relations of the government with England and France continued to deteriorate. Napoleon had progressed from seizing to burning American ships. British Orders in Council forced American vessels to pass through England even if bound for Russia or Denmark. British captains, desperate for man power, searched American ships on the high seas for deserters from the Royal Navy—of which there were many—whether or not such seamen might be considered Americans. In retaliation the United States decreed that British and French merchant ships entering American ports be confiscated. As one way out of the imbroglio, Madison was ready to resume trade with the first belligerent prepared to drop its attacks on American shipping.

That first one to do so appeared to be England. After long talks, the English minister David Montagu Erskine agreed that his government would make reparations for the *Chesapeake* attack and repeal the Orders in Council in exchange for a resumption of American trade. On April 19 Madison issued a proclamation that on June 10 all trade with Great Britain would be renewed.

The proclamation cleared the air across the country like a thunderstorm on a hot day. In rare political unity, men of all parties praised the President. Even the more rabid Federalist journals joined in the chorus. Hundreds of American ships laden with goods from bursting warehouses sailed for England, pacing themselves to arrive on the magic date. Shielded against Napoleon by the British Navy, Madison felt free to lay up all United States gunboats, except for a few at New Orleans, and to discharge one hundred thousand militiamen being readied for service. Less than two months in office, the President had achieved heights of popularity unrealized since Washington's day.

Madison's proclamation was premature, for Erskine was not long afterward denounced in London as having exceeded his authority. The British government repudiated his agreement and he was recalled in disgrace. Madison thereupon issued another proclamation in August, 1809, restoring the state of nonintercourse with England. Erskine was succeeded by Francis James Jackson, known as Copenhagen Jackson, a hard-boiled representative of the Foreign Office who considered Erskine a complete fool.

The next two years saw a turbulent seesawing of embargoes, repeals of embargoes, grumbling by merchants with unsold goods, vaguely conciliatory gestures by France and England followed by hostile acts at sea, American hopes for peace, and the drums of the West beating for war. In 1810, with the nonintercourse law of the previous year expiring, Congress, after much bickering, passed Macon's Bill No. 2—named oddly enough after a man who did not write it or even favor it—which reopened trade with England and France while providing that if either one should, before March 3, 1811, remove or revise its restrictions against American commerce, a trade ban would go into effect within three months against the other belligerent.

Among other tensions the struggle of England and France brought the problem of Florida to the foreground. East Florida remained an unpeopled wilderness, but West Florida—later the southern sections of Alabama, Mississippi, and Louisiana—was already filling with American farmers, settlers, and eager land speculators. Although England's ally Spain continued to maintain a loose control over the region, the United States claimed West Florida under the terms of the Louisiana Purchase. With the region's American population restive and with the threat either of annexation by Napoleon or occupation by the British, Madison decided he must assert his country's dormant claim. On October 27, 1810, he signed a proclamation taking possession of West Florida as far east as the Perdido River.

Taking advantage of the Macon Bill, by which he had little to lose, Napoleon revoked the Decrees of Berlin and Milan, saying that "His Majesty loves the Americans" while on the very same day secretly ordering the seizure and sale of all American ships still in French ports. Accepting Napoleon's slippery word for the deed, the United States government, in November, 1810, issued a proclamation threatening to ban British imports if the British Orders in Council were not repealed. It was becoming increasingly clear that the Orders were directed as much against the United States as a commercial and maritime rival as they were against Napoleon, for under their terms all American ships trading directly with Continental Europe were subject to seizure and confiscation. British men-of-war lay in wait in American waters, often within the three-mile territorial limit. To all appeals Britain's Tory Prime Minister, Spencer Perceval, remained impervious.

Bitterly the Federalists accused Madison of being a vassal of Napoleon. The debate grew so savage in Congress that Randolph of Roanoke formed the habit of bringing two pointers into the House with him and would set them barking at any Republican speaker he disliked. With his reputation as a duelist, nobody dared to interfere. Meanwhile, in 1811, Monroe made his peace with Madison by accepting the office of Secretary of State. In January of that same year the Virginia legislature had elected him governor on his assurance that he would support the national administration. Madison had been much troubled by his incompetent and secretly disloyal Secretary of State, Robert Smith, and had determined to ease him out of office by offering him the post of minister to Russia. Monroe, still smarting from the rejection of his 1806 treaty with England, saw his appointment to head the State Department as a vindication, and eagerly accepted the post though he had earlier condemned Madison's foreign policy.

The grounds of the War of 1812 were, wrote Woodrow Wilson ninety years later, "singularly uncertain." Ostensibly it was the refusal of the British government to repeal its Orders in Council that drove the United States to war. But were the Orders a necessity in the struggle against Napoleon, or were they more a weapon to restrain United States commercial growth? Madison's 1811 message to Congress, while offering peace and friendship, seemed pointed toward war—even though it had been toned down by Treasury Secretary Gallatin, who had removed its more bellicose passages. Most Republicans remained fearful of war and its consequences for an unprepared country, whereas some Federalist leaders were prowar in the hope of ruining Madison and driving him from office at the end of his first term. Paradoxically, pro-English, antiwar sentiment was strongest in the Northeastern maritime states, whose ports had suffered most from embargoes and restrictions, whose ships had been seized and sailors impressed by the British, while the real drum-beating fervor came from the new landlocked states of the West.

The 1810 congressional elections had brought a sea of new faces in a campaign dominated by belligerent antiforeign resentments. In reaction to the mannered Eastern Federalists, with their British commercial ties, British ways, and their antipathy to the leveling tendencies of democracy, came the young men of the West and the South, who grouped round Henry Clay of Kentucky. Called with some exaggeration War Hawks, they were more easily persuaded than men of the coastal states to move against England—out of national pride, out of the expansionist urge to seize Canada in the North and East Florida in the South, out of anger

against the British, whom they accused of stirring up the Indians against them. The new House was about 3 to 1 Republican, and in New England Madison's supporters had even captured New Hampshire.

With Henry Clay a new generation was emerging. Madison and Monroe were the last of the eighteenth-century Virginia gentry to dominate the young republic. They were of the rococo generation, when men wore silver-buckled shoes and carried swords and modeled their English style on Addison and Steele; Monroe would, in fact, be the last President of the United States to wear his hair in a queue. Henry Clay was a new breed. Harry of the West represented the new romantic nationalism, and when he spoke in his soaring rhetoric, ladies twittered in the galleries. He wore a sober frock coat, tight trousers, and a black cravat below his high collar. American expansion was written on his face.

As a young man with no more capital than a law license, Clay had made his way through the Cumberland Gap to Lexington, Kentucky, where he soon established himself as a brilliant trial lawyer. Yet, for all his legal skills, his true interest lay in politics. Even time spent in gambling, drinking, and conviviality he knew how to turn to political account. After two interim appointments to the United States Senate, he found his real place in the House of Representatives, where in his first term he was promptly elected Speaker—a position he transformed from that of mere presiding officer to one of leadership. Almost at once he showed his mettle against Randolph of Roanoke when that insolent aristocrat strolled into a session of the House with his huge pointer bitch at his heels. Clay, from the Speaker's chair, ordered the doorkeeper to remove her from the floor of the House because she was a female. And out the dog went!

While Clay and such newcomers in Congress as the young Calhoun moved toward war, the same war spirit, irrational and compelling, spread through the country. It was further increased by General William Henry Harrison's defeat of the one-eyed Shawnee chief, the Prophet, at Tippecanoe Creek in Indiana Territory. In itself the victory was a dubious one, for Harrison, contrary to presidential orders, had marched his thousand-man force one hundred and fifty miles into Indian territory. Then, before the Prophet's Town, he had allowed himself to be surprised by the one-eyed leader, and although he had been able to rally his men the next day and destroy the Indian settlement, he had already lost

The launching by Napoleon of fresh European campaigns after his 1804 coronation, embroiled America in the fierce commercial war between France and Britain, both countries highhandedly violating American rights on the open sea. In this painting by David, the newly crowned emperor presents battle standards to his regiments

MAJOR GEN! W™ H. HARRISON.

No. 1. *ENSIGN HARRISON*. 19 years of age, with his knapsack on his back, in the winter of 1791, at the fatal battle field of St. Clair, to which he marched at the head of his Detachment, to Inter the bones of his slaughtered Countrymen.

2. *LIEUT! HARRISON* as the aid-de-camp of Gen! Wayne, 20th of August 1794, at the Victory at the Maumee Rapids.

3. *GOVERNOR HARRISON*, in August, 1810, at the Council of Vincennes with Tecumseh, at which an attempt was made to assassinate him.

4. *GOVERNOR HARRISON* making a treaty with the Sacks and Fox Indians.

No. 5. *GENERAL HARRISON*, in 1812, at the head of 7000 Troops in his first Campaign against the combined British and Indians on the North Western frontier.

6. *GEN! HARRISON* in the Winter of 1812 hastening at night to the assistance of Gen! Winchester to prevent the Massacre at the River Raisin.

7. *GEN! HARRISON* and his Army going into Winter quarters at the Maumee Rapids, in 1812.

8. *HARRISON'S Victory at Tippecanoe*, over the combined Indian tribes under the Prophet, November 7th 1811.

No. 9. *HARRISON'S Victory at the Thames* in upper Canada, over the combined British and Indian forces under Proctor and Tecumseh, October 5th 1813.

20 per cent of his men in the first day's fighting. Tippecanoe stirred up the Indians all the way to the Mississippi, while making certain that if war did come, the Prophet's brother, the great Indian leader Tecumseh, would side with the British. Nevertheless Madison deftly used the whole episode to push war preparation through Congress, and the battle itself provided a national slogan that would later elect a President.

Involved as were the diplomatic maneuverings, the various and complicated issues boiled down to the simple fact that if the British government did not repeal its Orders in Council, the United States would sooner or later declare war. Calhoun, in his maiden speech in the House late in 1811, asked: "Which shall we do, abandon or defend our own commercial and maritime rights, and the personal liberties of our citizens employed in exercising them? These rights are essentially attacked, and war is the only means of redress."

"Our swords leap, flaming from their scabbards," Shenandoah Valley militiamen announced to the President. Although still ready to listen to any peace overtures, Madison had in his heart decided, and was preparing for war. But the English minister Augustus Foster, with his ear attuned to the Federalists, was never really convinced that Madison intended to do more than threaten, even while Monroe, as the President's spokesman, was telling the House Committee on Foreign Relations, "Without war, public expectations would be defeated and our character destroyed abroad."

On May 11 Prime Minister Perceval, who seemed to fear American commercial rivalry more than he did Napoleon, was shot to death by a madman. A month later the British foreign minister, Lord Castlereagh, announced the suspension of the Orders in Council. It came too late: the House of Representatives had already voted 79 to 49 for war, and the Senate followed with a 19 to 13 confirming vote.

Madison's war message of June 1 had been read in closed session. In it he listed the British actions hostile to the United States: forcible seizure of persons sailing under the American flag, the commerce of the United States "plundered in every sea" under a pretended blockade, the Orders in Council enforced in spite of the repeal of French edicts, British encouragement of Indian warfare in the West. "Such," he concluded, "is the spectacle of injuries and indignities which have been heaped on our country, and such the crisis which its unexampled forbearance and conciliatory efforts have not

been able to avert. . . ."

It was one thing to declare war. It would be another thing to wage it. After such a tense period of waiting, the actual war declaration brought a sense of relief. Throughout much of the country it was welcomed with celebrations, parades, illuminations, and salutes. Henry Clay struck a more sober note. "God grant us," he wrote, "a happy result to this new & untried experiment to which the only free government on earth is about to be subjected!" In the Northeast, however, the declaration was greeted with tolling church bells and anti-Madison sermons from New England pulpits.

The war, never more than half-expected by the general public, came to a nation wretchedly unprepared for it. The Regular Army, enlarged to thirty-five thousand on paper, was in actuality less than one-third that size. Congress balked at the cost of naval expansion. Soldiers lacked essential clothing and supplies. There were not, it was said, even enough fifes and drums to stir up martial feeling in the land.

Weeks before the actual declaration of war, preparations had been made to invade Canada. Madison had no intention of permanently annexing the Canadian provinces. He saw Canada as a pawn to be traded back to the British for the repeal of the Orders in Council and an agreement on impressment. The jubilant War Hawks, on the other hand, wanted to annex both Canada and East Florida.

Madison favored an all-out strike at Montreal, but found himself thwarted in this plan when the New England militia—the best in the country—refused to march, on the grounds that the Constitution required them to repel but not to undertake an invasion. Plans were then improvised to thrust north from the forts at Detroit, Niagara, and Sackets Harbor on Lake Ontario, with an accompanying drive toward Montreal. It was left for Brigadier General William Hull, governor of Michigan Territory, to strike the first blow from Detroit. Hull, whose general's stars dated from the Revolution, was described as a "short, corpulent, good natured old gentleman, who bore the marks of good eating and drinking." His skills were more oratorical than martial; he liked to address his troops, and in moments of tension he had a nervous habit of stuffing quid after quid of tobacco in his mouth until the juice ran down his beard and vest.

In April at Dayton, Ohio, he assumed command of three militia regiments, later joined by a regiment of

William Henry Harrison was one of the few capable commanders America managed to put in the field in the War of 1812. This portrait, of unknown date, may have been done for his presidential campaign; the border vignettes illustrate incidents from his military career.

regulars that had fought at Tippecanoe, and led them through the wilderness toward Detroit. Reaching the Maumee River, unaware as yet of the war declaration, he hired the schooner *Cuyahoga* to carry most of his baggage and medical supplies plus his confidential military papers. Since the British controlled Lake Erie, they soon captured the *Cuyahoga*.

Hull reached Detroit on July 5 and prepared to move into Canada. But the inept general, although overwhelmingly superior in man power, was faced by a most able British professional, Major General Isaac Brock. Brock had long been preparing for an American invasion, and though handicapped by the small number of his regulars, the unreliability of his militiamen, and his temperamental Indian allies, he nevertheless knew how to use every man to best advantage. A week after arriving, Hull crossed the Detroit River with two regiments and issued a proclamation to the people of Canada demanding their allegiance and promising to protect their persons, property, and rights. At first, luck seemed to favor him. Deserters from the Canadian militia began to appear at his strong point, Fort Hope, in considerable numbers. After securing his position, he sent out foraging parties while preparing to attack the Canadian Fort Malden. If he had moved on Malden at once, he might have succeeded in capturing the fort and its garrison of only about fifty men, but his nature was to hesitate. Quid after quid dissolved in his mouth as he thought of his supply lines along Lake Erie open to British gunboat attacks and Indian raids. His imagination peopled the wilderness with thousands of redcoats. To unnerve him still further, news arrived of the fall of the American Fort Michilimackinac, in the straits between Lakes Huron and Michigan, captured with its garrison of sixty officers and men. Then a supply column from Ohio was beaten back by Indians. After three weeks of inaction, Hull at last ordered an attack on Fort Malden, then canceled it the next day when he heard that British reinforcements were expected. He suggested a retreat, and when his Ohio officers threatened to rebel, compromised by leaving a small garrison at Fort Hope and withdrawing to the fort at Detroit.

Having sized up Hull, Brock, for all his deficiencies in man power, saw the withdrawal as his big chance. Crossing over to the American side with his Indian ally Tecumseh and a force half as big as Hull's, he surrounded Detroit while warning the American general of the dangers of an Indian massacre if he did not surrender.

Brock also arranged for a document exaggerating the size of his forces to fall into American hands and paraded his militia near the fort dressed in the red coats of regulars. When two British gunboats bombarded Detroit, Hull lost whatever remained of his nerve and any further capacity to act. On August 16—on the grounds that the fort was filled with women, children, and "the old and decrepid"—he surrendered. The flag was lowered, the captive Americans marched out, and the victorious British marched in. Brock took twenty-five hundred American prisoners, sending the regulars to Lower Canada but contemptuously allowing the militia to return home.

If Hull's capitulation was a disgrace, other expeditions were a farce. When Governor Isaac Shelby of Kentucky sent two thousand volunteers—the best "in the western country or anywhere else"—commanded by Samuel Hopkins, a congressman turned general, on a punitive expedition against the Indians of the Illinois country, the Indians routed the volunteers by setting fire to the prairie. Major General Henry Dearborn, Jefferson's former War Secretary, commanding Fort Niagara and all the country to the east, could not make up his mind whether he should be preparing to attack Montreal or overseeing New England coast defenses.

At Fort Niagara itself, Stephen Van Rensselaer, a Federalist leader totally without military experience, commanded a force of some six thousand New York militiamen. Plagued by lack of supplies, poor food, bad discipline, and much illness, the men grew restive, and as summer gave way to fall, threatened to go home unless they saw action. Brock's strategic sense warned him of an impending attack in the Niagara area and he made his preparations for it. Van Rensselaer's plan was to cross the swift-moving Niagara River and storm the village of Queenston on the steep heights 275 feet above the river. Meanwhile General Alexander Smyth at Buffalo with 1,650 regulars, was to attack Fort George six miles north at the entrance to Lake Ontario.

The second part of Van Rensselaer's plan got off to a bad start when Smyth declined to serve under a militia general and kept his men at Buffalo. Then on the morning of October 11, when Van Rensselaer had at last decided to launch an independent assault, the attempt had to be called off after a militia officer rowed across the river in a boat containing all the oars and by some stupid misadventure abandoned it on the Canadian side. The following night Van Rensselaer made another attempt, but what with a shortage of boats and oars and the swiftness of the current, only about two hundred militiamen were able to cross the river before they were discovered by a Canadian sentry. At daylight the premature engagement took place. Colonel Solomon Van Rensselaer, the general's cousin and the leader of the assault party, was wounded on the shore, and his place was taken by Captain John Wool, who, despite the enemy fire, managed to ferret out a fisherman's path up the cliff. By the time Brock and his men arrived, the Americans had established themselves on Queenston Heights. At once Brock placed himself at the head of a company of regulars to counterattack, but before he could reach the Heights, a bullet pierced his heart.

With Brock dead, the Americans might have won an easy victory if they had been reinforced by their comrades across the river. But the militiamen watching the smoke of battle from the opposite bank lost their taste for combat, and when Van Rensselaer ordered them to cross over, they refused to go. The abandoned Americans fought bravely, but the British reinforcements arriving from Fort George were too much for them. With their whooping Indian allies, the redcoats and the Canadian militia swung around to attack from the land side and, with fixed bayonets, pressed the Americans toward the river. The American ranks broke. Some men tried to hide in the shrubbery and gullies along the cliffs; others attempted to swim the river. Most were forced to surrender.

The only cheerful news in that dismal year came from the Atlantic. There, in a series of individual ship combats, American courage, seamanship, and design had overcome units of the greatest navy in the world. Captain Isaac Hull, commanding the frigate *Constitution* out of Boston, in quick, bloody battle had destroyed the smaller H.M.S. *Guerrière* only three days after his uncle had surrendered Detroit. The bold young Captain Stephen Decatur, sailing six hundred miles west of the Canaries in the *United States*, outmaneuvered, outfought, and finally brought back as a prize the British frigate *Macedonian*. And even in defeat Captain James Lawrence inspired the nation when, taking the *Chesapeake* out of Boston Harbor with a new crew, with his ship shattered by the guns of H.M.S. *Shannon*, he gave his dying command: "Don't give up the ship. Fight her till she sinks!"

However reviving to American spirits individual victories at sea might have been, they were no more than

A *resplendent American militia officer consults his map. Reliance on the militia resulted in many disgraceful defeats in battle.*

pinpricks to the British Navy, with its 120 ships of the
line and 116 frigates. The American Navy, with only a
dozen seaworthy vessels, had no ships of the line and
only the 7 frigates built two decades earlier when
war with France threatened. The few battles won by the
American frigates had no important effect on the direction of the war. At first the British had left American
trade undisturbed in the expectation that repeal of the
Orders in Council would bring peace and, more particularly, in the knowledge that American foodstuffs were
needed to supply Wellington's armies on the Iberian
Peninsula. Gradually, however, the British blockade expanded along the American coast as more British ships
became available after Napoleon's Russian disaster.
American exports, which had once reached a peak of
$130,000,000, fell to $25,000,000 by 1813 and $7,000,-
000 a year later. Coasting trade suffered equally. The
blockade bottled up the famous frigates, and only the
Constitution was able to slip away and sail the seas
again. America's greatest success was with her privateers, which swarmed over the Atlantic while dodging
the seventeen ships of the line and the twenty-seven
frigates of the British blockade. During the war the
privateers took thirteen hundred prizes and at one point
were capturing merchantmen at the rate of two a day.

Disastrous though most of the year 1812 had been
in a military sense, politically it carried Madison to
election to a second term. Vice President Clinton having died in office, the war-minded Republican Elbridge Gerry—recently defeated for re-election as
governor of Massachusetts—was chosen his successor.

The Federalists, no longer willing to go through the
vain motions of nominating a candidate, supported the
dissident Republican peace candidate, DeWitt Clinton,
long-time mayor of New York and nephew of the late
Vice President. Clinton's running mate was the ancient
Pennsylvania Federalist, Jared Ingersoll, once a member of the Continental Congress. The issue of the election was Madison and war versus Clinton and peace,
and the results were regional. Federalist New England—except for Vermont—voted for Clinton, as did
New York, New Jersey, Delaware, and half the electors
of Maryland. All the other states, including the Solid
South and the West with newly admitted Louisiana,
gave their votes to Madison.

The military lessons of 1812 were harsh and obvious.
To wage the war successfully the United States would
have to gain control of the Great Lakes, develop strate-

gic objectives rather than vaguely grandiose invasion schemes, and find better leaders. The first of the deadwood to be swept from office were the parsimonious Secretary of War, William Eustis, and the bibulous Secretary of the Navy, Paul Hamilton, who had demonstrated their gross incapacity even to Madison's indulgently friendly eye. The new Secretary of War, John Armstrong, though a New York politician brought in to maintain the New York-Virginia alliance, was nevertheless a man of energy and vigor who at once began to clear out the ancient generals.

In September, 1812, Madison appointed the hero of Tippecanoe, the thirty-nine-year-old William Henry Harrison, commander in chief of the new Northwestern Army, a mixed force of regulars and militiamen. With these ten thousand soldiers the new brigadier general was expected to remove the threat of Indian attack from the West and to retake Detroit. Heavy autumn rains held up the start of Harrison's expedition, but he hoped with freezing weather to move his artillery and baggage across the icebound rivers and lakes. He planned to assemble his army in three columns converging at the Maumee Rapids, some fifty miles below Detroit. The winter was a cruel one. Blizzards swept down on the soldiers as they constructed causeways and blockhouses. Rations often had to be cut to one-half, and at night the men shivered in their crudely built huts. The Kentucky militia, forming the left wing under the command of the elderly James Winchester, suffered most.

Winchester's men, huddled in fortified misery at their camps on the bank of the Maumee, learned that the settlement of Frenchtown, thirty-five miles to the northeast on the banks of the Raisin River, contained an abundance of food supplies as well as a number of American civilian prisoners, and was garrisoned by only fifty Canadian militiamen and about a hundred Indians. To the famished and frozen Kentuckians in that bitter January the opportunity seemed too good to miss. Winchester sent an advance detachment of half his troops to make a surprise attack on Frenchtown. After a brief skirmish they succeeded in taking possession of the precious stores. What he failed to consider was that a British force larger than his own, under command of Brock's old subordinate Colonel Henry Procter, was garrisoned at Fort Malden only eighteen miles to the north. When Procter learned how perilously the Americans had overextended themselves, he moved out with his mixed command of redcoats and Indians.

Captain Lawrence's Chesapeake *was manned by a green crew; the* Shannon *was one of Britain's best ships. In this detail from a British version of the fight, boarders swarm over the* Chesapeake. *In only minutes, despite Lawrence's dying orders, the Americans gave up the ship.*

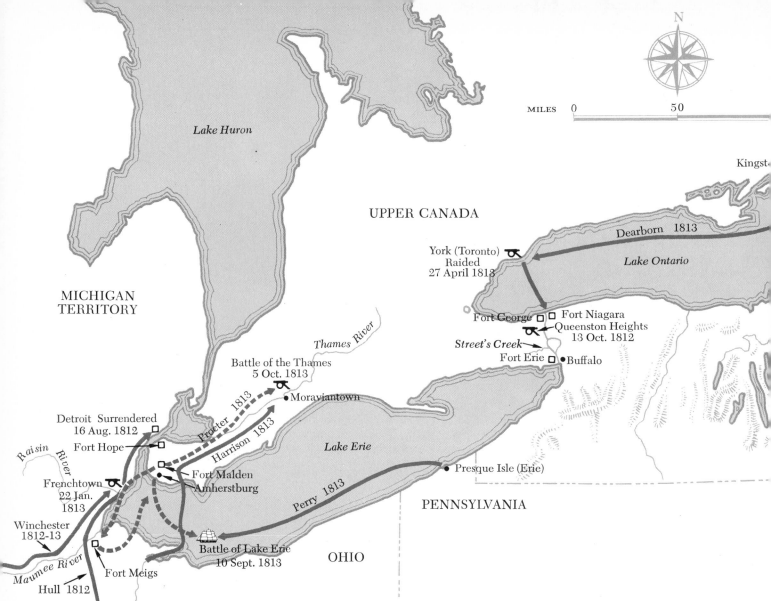

Belatedly sensing the danger, Winchester hurried toward Frenchtown with the rest of his troops. There, while Procter advanced, the bumbling American did all the wrong things: dividing his men on both sides of the river, failing to prepare adequate entrenchment, neglecting even to set out night patrols and pickets. Procter, the professional, overwhelmed Winchester's militia on the right at the beginning of the engagement and in a few minutes his Indian auxiliaries removed more than a hundred Kentucky scalps. Winchester's left surrendered on the promise of protection, a promise badly kept, for the Indians, after becoming drunk on the liquor stores at Frenchtown, attacked the American wounded left behind at the settlement, plundering, tomahawking, and scalping. At least thirty Americans were said to have been murdered, and the number grew with the telling. "Remember the River Raisin" became a rallying cry for the soldiers of the Northwestern Army.

That army, assembled at Fort Meigs on the Maumee, was reduced to only about a thousand through the loss of Winchester's troops and through winter attrition—death, sickness, and desertions. With the spring Procter laid seige to Fort Meigs. Harrison had appealed to Governor Isaac Shelby of Kentucky for reinforcements, and Shelby had responded with twelve hundred additional militiamen. Half of these troops were killed or captured in a British ambush on the way to Fort Meigs, but the rest managed to reach and save the fort.

Action on the water turned out to be more decisive than on the land. Perhaps England's most telling error of the war was, through inertia, to allow control of the Great Lakes to pass to the Americans. On Madison's orders, Captain Isaac Chauncey had built up a fleet at Sackets Harbor that soon outmatched the British vessels on Lake Ontario. Then, setting his sights on Lake Erie, Chauncey had built a shipyard at Presque Isle (lat-

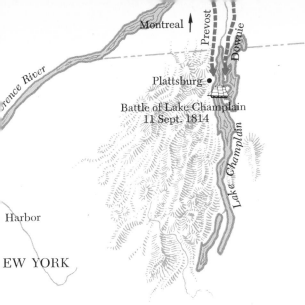

Montreal
Prevost
Downie
Plattsburg
Battle of Lake Champlain
11 Sept. 1814
Lake Champlain
rence River
Harbor
EW YORK

Thrust and counterthrust marked the war in the north, with vast distances preventing a final decision. America's first invasion of Canada was halted by General Brock, who easily captured Detroit; a second attempt, across the Niagara, was smashed at Queenston Heights. Victorious at Frenchtown, the British were stalled at Fort Meigs, which resisted siege. Americans, meanwhile, had taken York (Toronto), burned some of it, and captured Fort George. Perry's Lake Erie triumph enabled Harrison to chase the British from Detroit to Canada, where he won the Battle of the Thames. At Street's Creek, American militiamen earned enemy respect. Macdonough's Lake Champlain victory made the British abandon invasion plans. Before either side could launch another offensive, the war ended.

er Erie, Pennsylvania) and had begun the construction of two 50-foot gunboats and two 480-ton brigs—subsequently named the *Niagara* and the *Lawrence*. Anxious to place the command of the developing Lake Erie squadron in the hands of a competent regular officer, he was delighted to receive an application from Master Commandant Oliver Hazard Perry. Although only twenty-eight years old, Perry was an experienced sailor, brave, resourceful, and exacting. The son of a sea captain, he had already spent seventeen years at sea, fighting against the Barbary pirates when he was scarcely more than a boy.

Not until the shipyard at Presque Isle had been operating for half a year did the British belatedly take notice of the growing American threat. Then they sent Captain Robert Barclay of the Royal Navy to Amherstburg on the lake to start a rival building program. By that time it was too late. The British still kept a precarious hold on the lake with their six small vessels, but after the redcoats had been forced to evacuate Fort Erie, Perry managed to outnumber his rivals by pulling four small gunboats and a brig up the Niagara River.

Barclay and Procter—the latter by then promoted to general—found themselves under blockade in their joint headquarters at Amherstburg. Since Procter had taken on the responsibility of feeding some fourteen thousand Indians, his supply situation rapidly grew desperate. Barclay, relying on his superior long-range firepower, determined to engage the American squadron and break the blockade. His *Detroit*, with seventeen long guns, was larger than any vessel under Perry's command. His thirty-five long guns formidably overmatched his opponent's fifteen. Perry, however, had the advantage in short-range armament.

The British fleet weighed anchor early in the morning of September 10 and was sighted by the Americans, at first light. Sailing out to meet it, Perry made meticulous preparations for battle. The decks of his vessels were sprinkled with sand to keep them from becoming slippery with blood. As the enemy's sails grew larger, he had food served so that his men could fight on a full stomach. His flagship, the *Lawrence*, displayed a banner with its namesake's famous order, "Don't give up the ship." In line just ahead of him were his schooners *Scorpion* and *Ariel* and behind him the *Niagara*, commanded by Captain Jesse Elliott. Shortly before noon the British long guns opened fire, with such damaging effect that Perry made sail directly toward the enemy in order to bring his carronades into range. Barclay in the *Detroit*, joined by the *Queen Charlotte*, accepted the challenge and headed for the *Lawrence*. For reasons never wholly clear, Elliott in the *Niagara* kept his distance during the whole engagement, using nothing but his long-range guns. Perry soon found himself hemmed in. For two hours the smoke billowed across the bright water as the two flagships exchanged cannon shots. Under such a galling attack Perry's ship was reduced to a blood-soaked hull, all the rigging shot away and every gun out of action. He might well have surrendered with honor. Instead, after hauling down the *Lawrence*'s banner, he sprang into a boat, and with his brother and four seamen, rowed to the *Niagara*, the water round him churning with shot.

Unharmed, he reached the *Niagara* and took command. What he said to Elliott can only be guessed. Drifting helplessly, her commander gone, the *Lawrence* struck her colors. Before Barclay could secure his prize, Perry in the *Niagara* broke the British battle line and

117

sent the *Detroit* careening into the *Queen Charlotte*, after which he shot the two fouled ships to pieces. Barclay, a veteran of Trafalgar who had already lost an arm, had his remaining arm shattered. With all five commanders and the seconds-in-command of his other vessels either dead or wounded, he surrendered at three in the afternoon. Two still-serviceable British vessels attempted to escape but were captured. With his victory Perry hastily scribbled a note to General Harrison: "We have met the enemy and they are ours: two ships, two brigs, one schooner and one sloop."

"The loss of the fleet is a most calamitous circumstance," wrote General Procter. "It is my opinion that I should retire on the Thames without delay." Procter, short of men and supplies, was aware that Harrison was readying a force of forty-five hundred, most of them Kentucky militiamen supplied by Governor Shelby, for a "last effort" against Canada.

Harrison followed in pursuit, sending cavalry to undefended Detroit while the rest of his army crossed the liberated lake and landed below Fort Malden. He found Amherstburg a smoking ruin, put to the torch by Procter's rear guard. The Americans advanced rapidly, capturing supplies, ammunition, and finally two gunboats. With the enemy nipping at his heels, Procter finally decided to make a stand in a wooded area near Moraviantown. To compensate for his inferiority in man power he picked his location with a river on his right and on his left a large swamp, to force the Americans into a frontal attack. British regulars were deployed on the river side, while the Indians massed in the underbrush on the left. Procter had by then only four hundred regulars and about a thousand Indians to oppose a force of almost three thousand, which included a regiment of a thousand mounted riflemen.

In an improvised scheme of attack that Harrison later admitted was sanctioned by no principle of tactics he had ever heard of, he ordered his mounted regiment to charge the line of British and Indians and get to their rear. However unorthodox, the attack was an overwhelming success, with the British breaking and fleeing before the galloping troops. Thick undergrowth prevented a similar quick success against Tecumseh and his Indians on the American right. The Indians did not fire until the troopers were almost on them, but in spite of a withering first volley, the Americans dismounted and pressed on in hand-to-hand encounters through the tangle of shrubs and vines. In this close combat

Chief Tecumseh was killed. With their leader dead and their ammunition running out, the Indians broke and fled into the swamp. Moving from this success, Harrison hoped to continue his invasion of Canada, but the hero of Tippecanoe and the Thames was less than a hero to Secretary of War Armstrong. The Secretary, for reasons best known to himself, transferred him to the inactive Cincinnati area, where, after a few months of idleness and rebuffs, Harrison resigned.

By the end of 1813 the Americans had won control of Lake Erie, retaken Detroit, and broken up Tecumseh's long-threatening Indian confederation. Yet their year's accomplishments scarcely more than restored the status of things as they were at the moment of Madison's war declaration. Such limited successes were unimportant to Secretary of War Armstrong, whose vision was the capture of Montreal and the control of all Canada to the west. Armstrong had conceived of an attack on Kingston, with York as an alternative, and Forts George and Erie as a third choice. General Dearborn and Commodore Chauncey, in their timidity, had grossly overestimated the Kingston garrison and insisted instead on an attack on the strategically less important capital of Upper Canada, York (Toronto). Brigadier General Zebulon Pike, the Western explorer and a competent soldier, had led the attack, but its success had been marred by the explosion of a powder magazine that caused over three hundred American casualties and killed Pike. After some desultory looting, the Americans had set fire to the two parliament buildings and made off with the royal standard and speaker's mace.

The year 1814 brought a smoldering stalemate along the Canadian border while the Americans of the Eastern seaboard cities waited apprehensively for spring to bring renewed and increased raids by the Royal Navy. The climactic event of the year was the fall of Napoleon. With the disappearance of the Corsican tyrant, it would have been reasonable for the British to settle their differences with America, to renounce the no-longer-necessary impressment of sailors, to do away with the Orders in Council. But in war, emotions replace logic. The English believed themselves betrayed in their struggle against Napoleonic despotism and felt that America must be punished for "her perfidy and ingratitude."

Wellington's cold, military mind was dubious about any American campaign. America was too vast a region, in his opinion, and there was no one vital point at which one could strike. Civilian minds felt otherwise. Looking

118

for a quick, decisive victory, the British government determined on a tightening of the blockade, an invasion of New York by way of Canada that would make the Northern states clamor for peace, an amphibious attack on New Orleans, and punitive raids against the Eastern coastal cities. In June fifteen thousand red-coated veterans of the Peninsula Army—the scum of the earth, they had been called in ironical affection—bearing their proud regimental standards with the battle honors from Marlborough's to Wellington's campaigns, boarded transports for the New World.

In the Niagara theater, 1814 was marked by forays and skirmishes, sharp but indecisive in the war's larger pattern and remembered best for Brigadier General Winfield Scott's defeat at Street's Creek of British under Major General Phineas Riall. Scott's men, in militia gray—the uniform later adopted in his honor for West

Point cadets—faced the redcoats' concentrated volleys with resolute firmness, closing ranks over their fallen, reloading and firing with a drilled precision. When Riall's force began to give way, Scott's men followed up with the bayonet. Riall, previously contemptuous of the Americans, watched with stunned audible respect: "Those are Regulars, by God," he remarked.

Three weeks later the two armies clashed again at Lundy's Lane. Each side suffered more than eight hundred casualties in the hard fight in which both Scott and Riall were wounded. The outcome was inconclusive, but American invasion plans for 1814 were thwarted.

The main British thrust was to come along Lake Champlain, the old route of armies since Amherst's day. General George Prevost crossed the Canadian border on September 3 with fifteen regular regiments, Ca-

Striking right and left at British troops and their Indian allies, the mounted riflemen of Colonel Richard M. Johnson—under the command of General Harrison—helped defeat the British at the Battle of the Thames, north of Lake Erie, and restored American dominance in the Northwest. Johnson himself is credited with having slain America's great enemy, Shawnee Chief Tecumseh.

nadian militia, and artillery—fifteen thousand of the best soldiers ever to serve in America. His immediate goal was to seize the American base at Plattsburg, denuded of the bulk of its garrison by Secretary Armstrong, who had sent the best soldiers to the Niagara region. The base contained a patched-up force of some fifteen hundred recruits, convalescents, and militiamen. Plattsburg should have proved an easy objective. But Prevost was a defensive military leader who was governed by fumbling caution. By the time he reached the Saranac River on the outskirts of Plattsburg, American Brigadier General Alexander Macomb had managed to build his fortifications and gather in some four thousand defenders, mostly militiamen. At the sight of Macomb's works bristling with cannon and the American fleet anchored in Plattsburg Bay, Prevost hesitated and decided to wait for the Royal Navy and make a joint attack.

The two fleets on Lake Champlain were small. The British fleet, commanded by Captain George Downie, consisted of a thirty-six-gun frigate, barely finished in time for the battle, a brig, two sloops, and twelve gunboats and row galleys. Downie, handicapped by a shortage of sailors, was forced to fill out his crews with castoffs and draftees. The American fleet, under Captain Thomas Macdonough, was better manned and of about equal strength, with the twenty-six-gun *Saratoga*, a brig, a schooner, a sloop, and ten gunboats. Macdonough's strategy was to stay within the bay and force the English to attack him, taking advantage of the wind and placing his squadron in a maneuverable position. Downie's plan was a simple one: to sail in on the American squadron and destroy it at close range. As the mist rose on the morning of September 11, the British squadron, in battle formation, rounded Cumberland Head at the entrance to the bay. Several hundred yards from the enemy, Downie, on his flagship, the *Confiance*, found himself becalmed but within range of the foe. His was the first broadside. After that the fire became general. Downie was killed within fifteen minutes. Macdonough, with one-quarter of his crew soon out of action, directed the fire from his *Saratoga*, often sighting a gun personally. The American ships, having previously rigged anchors and hawsers, were able to swing round from port to starboard after the guns on one side were disabled and rake the enemy with fresh broadsides. The disabled *Confiance* was forced to surrender, and the morning ended with an American victory that cost the British their entire Lake Champlain fleet.

Prevost's coordinating land attack did not even find the Americans. Two of his four brigades got lost while looking for a ford, and a third brigade never reached the river at all. Downie's defeat took place as the redcoats were thrashing about in the thickets. That naval defeat overwhelmed the wavering Prevost. Discouraged, convinced that he could not supply and protect his men without cover from the lake, he abandoned his mission and led his dispirited army north again.

While Prevost was making his preparations to invade the United States from the north, another invasion was taking place farther south. Although the Royal Navy was poised to strike anywhere along the coast and although Chesapeake Bay was particularly vulnerable, Secretary Armstrong had concerned himself little with any possible threat to Washington. The threat suddenly loomed like a black thundercloud over the bay with the sudden appearance of the British fleet of Vice-Admiral Sir Alexander Cochrane convoying four thousand men, twenty-five hundred of them Wellington's veterans, under command of Major General Robert Ross.

No more than a thousand regulars were on hand to protect the Capital, plus one hundred and fifty marines and the five hundred sailors of the Chesapeake Bay gunboat flotilla, led by the aggressive former Revolutionary privateer Commodore Joshua Barney. Madison hurriedly appointed Brigadier General William Winder to defend the Capital, more because that sedentary soldier was related to the governor of Maryland than out of regard for his military abilities.

On August 18 Cochrane's fleet pursued Barney's flotilla up the Patuxent River. The next day four regiments of redcoats and a marine battalion commanded by General Ross landed in pursuit of Barney. The American flotilla was finally cornered in the upper river at Pig Point by a naval force under Cochrane's second-in-command, Rear Admiral George Cockburn, and Barney was forced to blow up his gunboats. Winder managed finally to assemble two thousand regulars and militiamen in Washington and marched them out of the city toward the enemy while a party of dragoons commanded by War Secretary James Monroe—turned soldier overnight—scouted the British flanks.

The Americans made their stand at Bladensburg, a small town strategically athwart the road to Washington, with hills on either side and a bridge behind the town leading over a branch of the Potomac to the Capital, five miles away. Across the river a brigade of Mary-

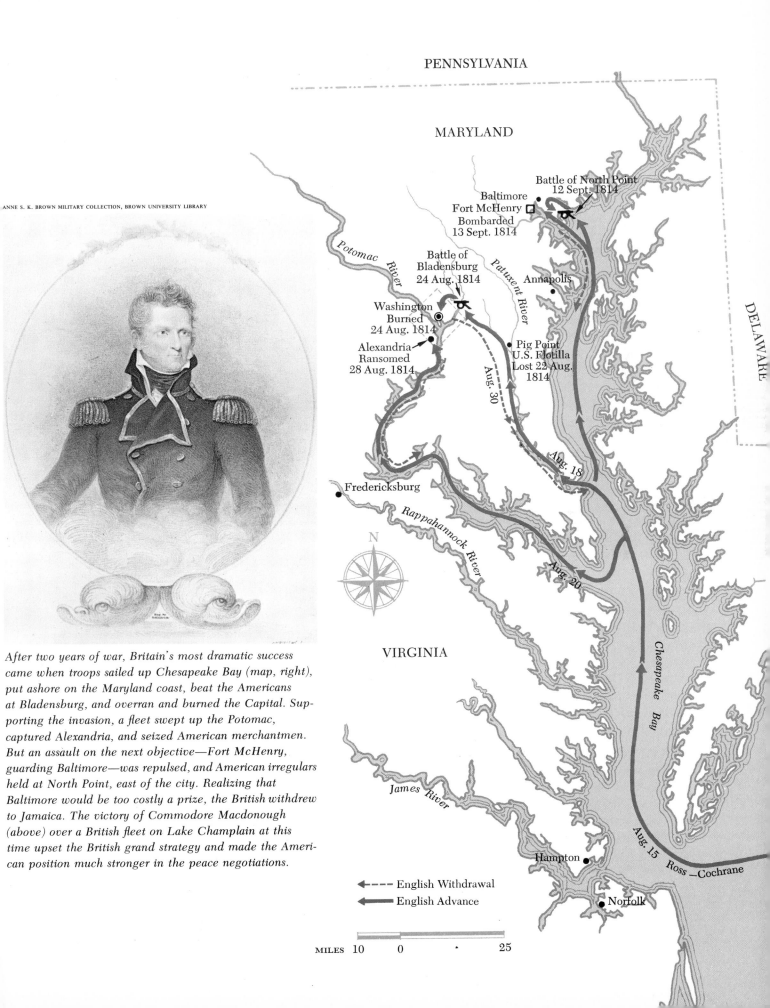

PENNSYLVANIA

MARYLAND

Battle of North Point
12 Sept. 1814

Baltimore
Fort McHenry
Bombarded
13 Sept. 1814

Battle of
Bladensburg
24 Aug. 1814

Potomac River

Patuxent River

Annapolis

Washington
Burned
24 Aug. 1814

Alexandria
Ransomed
28 Aug. 1814

Pig Point
U.S. Flotilla
Lost 22 Aug.
1814

Aug. 30

Aug. 18

Fredericksburg

Rappahannock River

Aug. 20

N

VIRGINIA

DELAWARE

Chesapeake Bay

James River

Aug. 15 Ross —Cochrane

Hampton

Norfolk

*After two years of war, Britain's most dramatic success
came when troops sailed up Chesapeake Bay (map, right),
put ashore on the Maryland coast, beat the Americans
at Bladensburg, and overran and burned the Capital. Supporting the invasion, a fleet swept up the Potomac,
captured Alexandria, and seized American merchantmen.
But an assault on the next objective—Fort McHenry,
guarding Baltimore—was repulsed, and American irregulars
held at North Point, east of the city. Realizing that
Baltimore would be too costly a prize, the British withdrew
to Jamaica. The victory of Commodore Macdonough
(above) over a British fleet on Lake Champlain at this
time upset the British grand strategy and made the American position much stronger in the peace negotiations.*

← - - - English Withdrawal
←——— English Advance

MILES 10   0 · 25

Although they set fire to many federal buildings in Washington, as shown above, the British spared the Patent Office because of the protests of Dr. William Thornton, the superintendent, who charged them with vandalism.

land militiamen had dug in on a high ridge, and other militia units kept trickling in to take up whatever positions their individual commanders thought best. Winder came with some regulars, a detachment of Virginia militiamen, and Barney's tough boatless sailors. As the British continued to advance, the American general seemed near collapse.

The American forces entrenched beyond the river contained two thousand more men than the British had and nineteen more field guns, but there any advantage stopped. For the most part the Americans were civilian soldiers, and more civilians than soldiers. Many of the British were toughened veterans of the battlefields of Spain. Six abreast they marched in their red coats and black shakos through Bladensburg and stormed the bridge. At first the American fire brought them up sharply as redcoats sprawled in the brown dust, but the British deployed, outflanking the Americans. When Winder attempted a counterattack against the enveloping red tide, his inexperienced troops broke and ran. Barney's Navy men alone stood steady. Aided by five guns, they held three assaults by Ross's light infantrymen at bayonet range, and with cries of "Board 'em, board 'em!" launched their third counterattack, which forced the British to retreat. Only when Barney had been wounded and Winder had ordered a general retreat did they withdraw.

Winder's rapid and confused retreat left Washington

122

open to the enemy. As the victorious troops, led by Ross and Cockburn, marched into the Capital on the evening of August 24, refugees were still fleeing from the other side of the city. "You may thank old Madison for this," Cockburn told some ladies he passed, "it is he who has got you into this scrape. . . . We want to catch him and carry him to England for a curiosity." When the general and the admiral reached the President's House, they found the table spread in the State Dining Room, places set for guests, and decanters of wine cooling on the sideboard. Cockburn poured himself a glass and drank "Jemmy's health." Dolley, in her belated exit, had slipped away what presidential silver she could in her reticule. Just before she left in the yellow-trimmed coach, the French master of ceremonies removed the Stuart portrait of Washington from its frame in the State Dining Room. In the brief interval between her departure and the British arrival the house was pillaged by the city rabble. The British officers, after their impromptu meal, inspected the premises and ordered all the furniture piled up in the Drawing Room. Burning coals were brought from Frenchy Nardin's saloon across the street. "Our sailors were artists at the work," one officer noted as the kindling flames raged up Jefferson's grand staircase.

Ross, a landed Irishman and a meticulous officer, would have preferred ransom money to destruction, but could find no one to bargain with. Forbidding all looting, doing his best to protect private buildings, as reprisal for the burning of York he had torch and gunpowder applied to the Capitol, the War-and-State and the Treasury buildings, and the arsenal.

Washington did not seem a healthy place in which to linger. Rumors spread that thousands of Maryland and Virginia militiamen were massing to avenge the humiliation of the capture of their Capital. After issuing an order forbidding the inhabitants on pain of death to leave their houses after dark, Ross slipped away that evening from the still-smoldering city. It took him four days to march his men the fifty miles to their ships, carrying with them 540 barrels of captured powder, 206 cannons, 100,000 rounds of American cartridges, and a drove of some 60 or 70 cattle.

While Ross had been on the road to Washington, a British naval squadron had come up the Potomac to capture Alexandria, which the city fathers had then ransomed to prevent its destruction. The British ships' return downstream was not so easy, as the aroused Americans showered them with cannon shot and fire from the banks.

Cochrane refused to risk any more inland thrusts, but both he and his second-in-command, Cockburn, thought that Baltimore, with its sea approach, might offer a quick, profitable capture. Cockburn, who had been harrying the Chesapeake Bay region off and on for a year and a half, was all for clearing out the privateers in that "nest of pirates." Ross remained dubious. Although Washington had been a great propaganda victory, it had been a precarious success, and he did not wish to tempt fate again. But the admirals overruled him.

Baltimore, the fourth largest city of the United States, found a far abler defender than Winder in the person of a former Revolutionary officer, militia general, and United States senator, Samuel Smith. His energy was matched by his military capacity. Smith also had the good fortune of having the three naval subordinates Commodores John Rodgers, David Porter, and Oliver Hazard Perry. By the time the British were ready to launch their attack, he had prepared a formidable defense network, whose keystone was Fort McHenry.

Ross's redcoats landed on September 12 below the city and began their advance. At the initial contact the Maryland militia gave way, and as the British followed up, Ross was killed—by a militiaman picking peaches. The news of his death spread dismay through the army, and the British advance halted after a brisk but inconclusive engagement called the Battle of North Point.

The British spent the next day moving up to the American defense line, their advance slowed by trees felled across the roads. A cold and rainy evening followed, with redcoats dug in before the outer defenses and the Royal Navy preparing a night assault on the water front. The overcast sky was crisscrossed with streaks of varicolored light as bombs, Congreve rockets, and shells rained on Fort McHenry. In a bombardment that lasted twenty-five hours the Americans lost forty men; in the fort itself the well-concealed defenders lost only four men, with twenty-four wounded and two buildings destroyed. The night's naval assault was beaten back. Morning showed the red-and-white-striped flag still flying over the fort, and later in the day Cochrane came to the conclusion that the taking of Baltimore would not be worth the cost.

During that rainy night, as shells and rockets had traced their fiery arcs, a worried young Georgetown lawyer, Francis Scott Key, and a physician, Dr. William

Beanes—whose release from British captivity Key had just negotiated—had stood on the deck of a small American dispatch boat in the harbor just beyond the British fleet. In the failing evening light, Key, a writer of pleasant impromptu verse, had watched his country's flag flying over the fort. Then, through the rocket-seared hours, he had waited with fear and hope until the clearing air of morning had shown the familiar banner still flying. Intensely moved at the sight, he at once wrote the first draft of a poem on the back of a letter, continuing to jot down lines as he was rowed ashore after the British fleet's departure. All that evening in his room at the Fountain Inn he worked at his poem—which was later set to the old English drinking song "To Anacreon in Heaven," a tune that had earlier carried other patriotic verses. The next morning Key's finished poem—later to become the national anthem, "The Star-Spangled Banner"—was printed as a handbill, "The Defence of Fort McHenry," and distributed in the city.

The War of 1812 was a conflict that neither side could win, and the painful realization of this finally led to a peace that did little more than restore the pre-war state of things. In the early days of the war Great Britain, after repealing the Orders in Council, attempted to negotiate a cease-fire, but Secretary Monroe refused to bargain until the British agreed to stop impressment. However, by the spring of 1813 Madison had many reasons for looking for a way out. His planned invasion of Canada had failed. The country's financial position was becoming increasingly precarious. Congress was hesitant to raise taxes to support the rapidly rising public debt. With the drop in import duties the Treasury—already badly overdrawn—was forced to borrow by selling bonds at a discount. In addition, the man power promised for the Army had not materialized, and the possibility of conscription loomed.

After attempts to negotiate at Moscow with the Czar as mediator proved fruitless, five commissioners —John Quincy Adams, Henry Clay, James Bayard (Federalist senator from Delaware), Jonathan Russell (diplomat), and Albert Gallatin (till then Treasury Secretary)—began meeting with the British in Ghent, Belgium, during the summer of 1814. Triumphant in conquering Napoleon, resentful of the Americans who had failed to stand by them in their desperate struggle, the British were in no hurry for a settlement. At first they demanded territory in eastern Maine and

northern New York as well as an Indian buffer state in the Northwest as the price of peace. Madison refused to consider any concessions except, on Gallatin's advice, to yield on impressment as a bargaining point during the sessions.

As summer moved into autumn, the British grew more conciliatory. Russia, their ally of May, had by October turned into a new threat. News of Macdonough's victory on Lake Champlain and Prevost's retreat from Plattsburg made it clear to London that the war overseas had developed into a costly stalemate. The duke of Wellington, whose opinion weighed more than that of any man in England, was all for liquidating the war and settling with the Americans on the best terms obtainable. The Americans in turn came to realize that they lacked the resources to take Canada and to challenge the Royal Navy. With both parties in this soberly realistic mood, the British and American commissioners at Ghent signed a treaty on Christmas Eve, 1814, bringing the war to an end. The causes of the war—neutral rights and impressment—were not even mentioned. The main object, the ending of a futile war, had been attained.

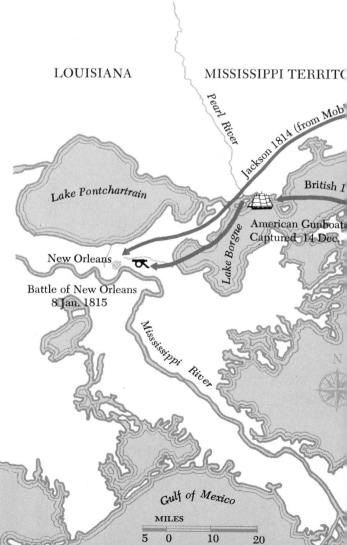

While the rival commissioners were reaching agreement at Ghent, twenty-six New England Federalists—"the Wise and Good of those States, which deem themselves oppressed"—elected by their respective legislatures, were meeting in secret convention at Hartford, Connecticut, to discuss their discontent with Mr. Madison's War and various proposals for "a radical reform in the national compact."

Disaffection and secession had become household thoughts in New England ever since Jefferson's election. The New England Federalists, unlike their more tactless Tory predecessors, formed a close-knit social system of clergymen, lawyers, judges, merchants, and bankers who, even while limiting the franchise, managed to conciliate the plebeian sons of the men who had rioted with Sam Adams and ridden with Daniel Shays. The new aristocracy had found its most intransigent expression in the Essex Junto, named after the wealthy group of Federalists in Essex County, north of Boston. Fisher Ames, their spokesman, felt that the new nation was destined to fail, "too big for union, too sordid for patriotism, and too democratic for liberty."

With the outbreak of the War of 1812, the New England Federalists all but boycotted the war effort. Although Massachusetts was the second state in the number of recruits it gave to the Regular Army, it was among the last in subscribing to national loans. Federalist bankers forwarded specie to Canada. Canadian armies lived on beef sent by New England contractors, and New England merchants furnished supplies for the offshore British fleet. Long after Madison's war declaration, New England shippers continued to supply Wellington's armies in Spain. To the Federalists, the 1813 Embargo Act closing the New England ports was an act of robbery. Seeing nothing but French influence in Madison's efforts to establish American rights at sea, they demanded trade on British terms.

The Hartford Convention, called by Harrison Gray Otis and dominated by the more moderate leaders of his type, for all its talk of secession did not go to the extremes of the Essex Junto. In their report the delegates demanded protection from any national conscription, national financial support for the state militia, and seven amendments to the Constitution. These amend-

From Jamaica the British sailed to Lake Borgne, where the fleet defeated American gunboats, and then went on toward New Orleans. The disembarked army was met east of the city by Jackson's forces, most of whom had come from Mobile, Alabama. Above, General Sir Edward Pakenham dies amidst the carnage of battle—the worst defeat the British suffered in the entire war.

ments would have prohibited all embargoes exceeding sixty days, required a two-thirds vote of both houses of Congress for a declaration of war, prevented naturalized citizens from holding federal office, and made the President ineligible for a second term. The convention voted to hold another convention if these amendments should not be adopted, with the broad hint that the secession of New England would follow. The Treaty of Ghent made the proceedings at Hartford irrelevant and ridiculous, but for a time the convention had seemed a very real threat to the Union.

The great battle of the war, around which the heroic myths have clustered, was fought at New Orleans, ironically two weeks after the signing of the Treaty of Ghent. There Andrew Jackson, the boldest and most energetic of the young American generals, commanding a mixed army of Tennessee and Kentucky militiamen, Indians, Negroes, and Gulf pirates, almost annihilated a larger army of Wellington's Peninsular veterans.

Old Hickory, Jackson's men had called him for his tough determination in leading a militia army home from an abortive Florida campaign after the Secretary of War had dismissed the volunteers in Natchez "with thanks" but without pay or transportation. In his Southern campaign against the Creeks, who had shocked the country by their massacre of the Fort Mims garrison in what is present-day Alabama, Jackson demonstrated his own ruthlessness in his extermination of the Creek warriors gathered behind fortifications at Horseshoe Bend on the Tallapoosa River. As subsequent commander of the military district that included Tennessee, Louisiana, and Mississippi Territory, he carefully prepared New Orleans against assault when he learned that a British expedition, three-quarters of them Wellington's veterans, was on its way, led by Wellington's brother-in-law Sir Edward Pakenham.

Late in December, Admiral Cochrane's fleet landed some seventy-five hundred soldiers—later increased to ten thousand—on a small island in Lake Borgne, thirty miles from New Orleans, after capturing five defending American gunboats. Through drizzling days and freezing nights twenty-four hundred men made their way by naval barge and on foot to within nine miles of the river city before Jackson learned of their presence. Several inconclusive engagements followed while the British—suffering much from the weather, short rations, Indians, and American shelling—brought up their artillery and reinforcements.

The decisive battle took place on the foggy morning of January 8, when Pakenham launched a direct frontal assault on the main American position. Jackson's forces, though numerically inferior, had the protection of a ditch and an earthen rampart. The British, with a cypress swamp on their right and a river levee on their left, had no protection at all. The colonel leading the British attack discovered that the sugar-cane fascines prepared to fill the ditch and the ladders to scale the American wall had been forgotten, and while his troops waited, Pakenham's rocket signal to advance went up.

As a breeze tore away patches of fog, the pale first light showed the British advancing across the cane stubble toward the American lines as if on parade, drums beating, the pattern of the massed red coats, with the white cross bars and glittering buttons, edged here and there by the green black-trimmed uniforms of the Rifle Brigade. Like doomed automatons they came on, until at five hundred yards the American cannon opened fire with grape and canister. For the British the long, level field turned into a bowling alley of death, with themselves as ninepins. And when the cannon left off, volley after volley from well-concealed riflemen tore them to pieces. Only a handful of redcoats reached the ramparts, and even Wellington's battle-hardened regulars at last panicked. Two thousand redcoats were dead or wounded; Pakenham lay lifeless in the mud. Among the slain were five hundred more who had prudently played dead and later rose like ghosts to surrender. Jackson had only eight dead and thirteen wounded.

News of the Peace of Ghent, with the New Orleans victory as a happy encore, was celebrated throughout the United States with an exuberant relief, in which even Federalist New England joined. A renewed sense of nationalism blotted out the memory of earlier frustration and reverses. On a practical level the war brought about the reorganization of the Army and Navy on a much more efficient basis. Protected involuntarily by the blockade, native manufactures had expanded to meet democratic needs, until even the most Jeffersonian Republicans were forced to admit the desirability and, in fact, the inevitability of industrial development. The end of the war marked the end of American dependence on European political fluctuations. Foreign affairs and national defense would no longer be the primary concern of United States policy. Shielded by the Royal Navy through mutual interests stronger than flag-waving prejudices, the country could work out its destiny.

The Rigors of Travel

Overland travel at the outset of the nineteenth century was slow, strenuous, and often dangerous. What roads existed—mainly linking population centers near the East coast—were rutted, potholed, and frequently studded with stumps. In wet weather the mud was sometimes belly-deep on a horse. A stage took five days to reach Baltimore from Philadelphia, as long as a month to get to Washington from Boston. Despite the building of turnpikes, principally by private companies, horseback remained the most popular mode of travel. The desperate cry for better communication between the East and the West prompted the federal government to build the first section of the Cumberland Road—from Cumberland, Maryland, to Wheeling in what is now West Virginia—facilitating wagon travel as far as the Ohio River.

Lacking roads, the West was fortunate in being laced with a network of long, navigable rivers—such as the Mississippi and its tributaries—which served in their stead, although traffic was chiefly down-river. Flatboats, after the down-river trip, were sold for lumber, the crews returning to their home ports by land. More-maneuverable keelboats were sailed, poled, and towed upriver, usually a hard task of many months. Only after the steamboat appeared on Western waters in 1811 did the transport of passengers and cargo north and east as well as south and west become feasible.

OVERLEAF: *Cattle, Conestoga wagons, and a stagecoach jam the Frederick Road west of Baltimore. The road in the early 1800's was an important route west to the Alleghenies.*

MARYLAND HISTORICAL SOCIETY; ABOVE: *Harper's New Monthly Magazine*, VOL. XII, JAN., 1856

A four-horse stage bowls downhill on its scheduled run between Trenton and Philadelphia, above. Stagecoach drivers were not noted for their sobriety. Left, travelers while away the hours at a stage depot awaiting their transportation. Accommodations were much more primitive far from the coast, however. A lone pioneer leading his pack horse, right, trudges along a time-worn mountain trail in eastern Pennsylvania.

Water transport, by flatboats and keelboats, was much easier and cheaper than that ventured overland. Above, a Missouri river-boat man rests on his pole. At right, emigrating settlers glide down the Ohio on a flatboat loaded with livestock.

OVERLEAF: *Fulton's* Clermont *and its successors, like this one on the Hudson, proved steamboats practical and opened Western rivers to steam navigation. The aquatint,* Palisades, *was done in the 1820's by John Hill.*

New Frontiers

By the end of the War of 1812 the Federalists had ceased to be a national political party. They did not even choose official candidates for the presidential election of 1816, although the perennial Federalist vice-presidential candidate, Rufus King, was willing to bear the dubious honor of his party's label. Madison wished Monroe, that trusty civil servant, to succeed him, but there was much Northern objection to the self-perpetuating Virginia dynasty, and it was only after an acrimonious caucus of Republican congressmen that Monroe was finally designated his party's choice over Madison's Secretary of the Treasury, William H. Crawford. A Republican victory was inevitable. The Federalists carried only Massachusetts, Connecticut, and Delaware while losing a third of their seats in the House of Representatives.

Monroe was not quite fifty-nine years old when he became President. "James the Lesser," his critics called him as he succeeded James Madison. A tall man with a large mouth and an inexpressive face, he was indeed less brilliant than Madison or Jefferson, although an abler administrator for whom the Presidency was the culmination of a long life of public service.

As a very young man he had left the College of William and Mary to enlist in Washington's army, had served through the Revolution, and had been wounded. Later he married the daughter of a British officer who had served in the occupation forces in New York. As a close friend of Jefferson's he had built a modest house, Ashlawn, overlooking Monticello. Formal in the manner of the previous century, at his second inauguration he wore knee breeches, silk stockings, and silver shoe buckles. Yet, though the last of the Virginia dynasty and ambivalently conservative as the other Virginians in the matters of slavery and voting qualifications, he tended increasingly to separate himself from his inherited background and to emphasize the new America. One of his first acts as President was to make John Quincy Adams his Secretary of State—the first Yankee to take a high position in the government since the elder Adams' day.

Monroe took his oath of office out of doors, on the steps of the temporary

John Searle, an obscure painter, made this water color of a November, 1822, performance at New York's Park Theater. The time was one of general national expansion, not only on the pioneers' frontiers but also in the arts, the sciences, and industry.

capitol. Although this came about more or less by chance, to prevent arguments over seating arrangements indoors, the open-air ceremony became from then on an American tradition. Inauguration Day found the restoration of the President's House still incomplete. Some of the more extreme republicans would have preferred it left a ruin. "The destruction of the President's house cannot be said to be a great loss in one point of view," the Washington *City Gazette* observed sourly, "as we hope it will *put an end* to drawing-rooms and *levees*." The *Gazette's* observations were vain, for once belatedly installed in the restored Mansion—now redecorated in Louis XVI style—the Monroes lived in courtly elegance. Unlike the ebullient Dolley Madison, who had called on everyone, Elizabeth Monroe felt that the dignity of her position required her not to pay visits.

Soon after his inauguration Monroe made a goodwill tour from Baltimore to Detroit, which took him through the so recently disaffected Northeast, ostensibly to inspect coastal and border fortifications. In Boston the Federalist *Columbian Centinel* referred locally to the visit as an Era of Good Feelings. That casual designation, meant merely for the occasion, would become a political cliché, embedded in the popular mind as a description of Monroe's presidential years. Actually the time was one of hope matched by confusion and of vigor by uncertainty, with much more ill than good feeling evident. It was, among much else, a period of consolidation, during which the population grew to ten million. Following Indiana, Mississippi became a state in 1817, Illinois in 1818, Alabama in 1819, Maine in 1820, and Missouri in 1821.

The eclipse of the Federalists resulted from an absorption, a change of labels along with a change of mind. Even under Madison the Republicans had chartered the Second Bank of the United States, resurrecting Hamilton's buried arguments to justify themselves. Old agrarians began to show a novel solicitude for manufactures, tariffs, an established army and navy, while even New England Federalists were to be found sheltered under the patched umbrella of Jeffersonian Republicanism.

Political exigencies had determined the continuation in office of Monroe's presidential rival Crawford as Secretary of the Treasury. John Caldwell Calhoun, "the cast-iron man, who looks as if he had never been born," became Secretary of War. Calhoun was then simply a

Southern nationalist, a Unionist who would conquer space and "bind the republic together with a perfect system of roads and canals." Only later would he become the subtle and impassioned champion of slavery. To Adams, Crawford, and Calhoun, the bright stars in a dim Cabinet, their office seemed a way station to something higher. They assessed the situation pragmatically: Washington's precedent limited a President to two terms, and so the Presidency would be available at the conclusion of Monroe's second term. The three Secretaries would also be available. Henry Clay, in the House of Representatives, furious at being passed over for Secretary of State, was arranging every detail of his own political behavior with those facts in mind.

The underlying constant in Monroe's administration was the westward thrust, the steady shift of the center of the population toward the Alleghenies. After the Treaty of Ghent the migration that took place in the United States was one of the greatest in history. Tecumseh's Indian confederation had turned to dust, the boundaries were quiet, and the roads open.

Farmers, mechanics, artisans, tradesmen, the obscure and the anonymous, driven by taxes and hard times and by their own personal discontents, took the path west, with its dream of riches and freedom beyond the farthest hills. Along the Mohawk and Genesee turnpike they moved toward Lake Erie—by wagon if they could afford it, otherwise on horseback or on foot. They followed the Catskill turnpike to the headwaters of the Allegheny. They took the old road from Philadelphia to Pittsburgh, the Baltimore turnpike to join the new National Road at Cumberland, which carried them as far as Wheeling. Through the mountain passes they went, crossing the Appalachians into the Western lands. Flatboats carried them down the Indian-named rivers, the Allegheny, the Monongahela, the Ohio, the Mississippi.

For the most part they were forest-minded, avoiding the flat openness of the prairies, following the woodsman's pattern of girdling, cutting, clearing, building log cabins, planting, and hunting. Where they stopped, swamp fever overran them, and ague, and milk sickness, and their diet of pork and corn and whiskey left them pallid. Self-contained, isolated, they lived in squalor and endured corrosive loneliness, relieved at intervals by combat, drunkenness, and the wild ardor of their religious camp meetings. God became again a vengeful Old Testament deity, far removed from the Great Watchmaker of the Enlightenment. When they moved into the wilderness, the pioneers left behind them everything of culture or refinement. In their struggle for survival, formal learning beyond the basics of reading and writing counted for little. Locke, Montesquieu, the classical allusiveness, held no meaning for the clearings. Those westward-bound to seek more from life resented those who had already achieved a comfortable life—the mannered Virginians on their slave-kept estates, the seaboard merchants in their brick mansions with furniture and china and silver imported from England. The pioneers' resentments made them reject formal education. Every man on the frontier was equal and fully equipped, mentally and physically, and that was, they felt, enough to acquire property, to vote, to raise a family. He did not need to learn through books what he felt by instinct. The American pioneer's distrust of the cultivated mind would be long-enduring.

The Era of Good Feelings, if it had any precise limits, can be said to have been encompassed in Monroe's first two years in office, the years of Andrew Jackson's impulsive conquest of Florida and the great land boom that was ended by the Panic of 1819. Early in 1817 trouble broke out between the Seminoles of Spanish Florida and the frontiersmen of lower Georgia. Many of the Creeks, after their defeat and the loss of most of their land in the Treaty of Fort Jackson, had crossed the border to join the Seminoles. Conflict between the aggrieved Indians and the belligerent whites was constant, their mutual killings culminating in the massacre by the Seminoles of the men, women, and children of a hospital ship on the Apalachicola River. Even before this, Monroe had directed that a punitive expedition be sent into Spanish territory. When the expedition set out, General Andrew Jackson was in command.

If the President's intention was to intimidate the Seminoles without disturbing the country's pacific relations with Spain, his choice of Jackson was a curious one, for Jackson's reckless courage was matched only by his impulsiveness. He detested Indians and Spaniards and made no secret of his belief that East Florida—that refuge for runaway slaves—should be annexed to the United States. Self-interest reinforced his patriotism, since his friends and relatives had speculated heavily in Florida lands.

With fifty years, Jackson's temperament and his appearance had come to coincide. His long, lined face, the brush of stiff gray hair above his small blue eyes, his arched nose, resolute chin, and wide mouth, combined to give an effect of fierce dynamism. That he was always right remained his most unswerving conviction. Whether in speech or writing or action, he expressed himself in terms of cutting throats, caning, or dueling. His was a simple world of right and wrong, regulated by his professed principle "An eye for an Eye, Toothe for Toothe, and Scalp for Scalp."

When Jackson led his two thousand men into Florida, he had already determined that the Spanish, in harboring hostile Indians, were enemies of his country. His problems were more those of supply, transportation, and sickness than of confrontation with the primitive tribes or the supine Spanish. Almost without resistance he captured the Spanish fort St. Marks, at the same

This, the second Trinity Church to stand on the site on Manhattan's lower Broadway, was painted about 1824 by D. D. Foot, otherwise unknown. Like today's church, it faced the end of Wall Street, then becoming an important financial center with a boom in Erie Canal stocks.

time seizing a British trader named Alexander Arbuthnot, whose chief crime had been to deal fairly with the Indians and whom he accused rightly of disapproving of the Treaty of Fort Jackson. He next attempted to surprise a Seminole town but was enraged to find the Indians had been forewarned and had fled. Near the town he captured a Lieutenant Robert Ambrister, late of the Royal Colonial Marines, whom he suspected of having warned the Seminoles. Even though Ambrister and Arbuthnot were British subjects, Jackson had them tried by a special military court as "unprincipled agents" who had stirred up the Indians to war, and at the expected verdict of guilty he hanged Arbuthnot and had Ambrister shot. With equally intemperate dispatch he went on to seize Pensacola, after a token defense by the Spanish governor, and replaced the Spaniard by an American colonel. The campaign successfully completed, Jackson returned home a hero once again.

To the British and the Spanish, Jackson was something less than heroic. There was agitation in London on the news of the execution of the two Englishmen. Spain's minister Luis de Onís demanded an explanation for an invasion that could have been considered an act of war if Spain had been in any condition to take up the challenge. Onís had been negotiating with Secretary of State Adams over the boundaries of Spain's possessions in the West and the Southwest, but the Spaniard was thrown off balance by Jackson's aggression. With the Spanish Empire revolt-ridden, dying, and helpless, he feared the Americans would recognize the rebelling colonies, seize all Florida, and invade Mexico. Even Adams' hard-driven demands were preferable to that. Unlike the other members of Monroe's Cabinet, Adams, a continentalist and an expansionist, had defended the actions of Jackson in Florida, seeing the General as a lever for American claims. Onís agreed to cede all Florida and to give up his country's claims to land beyond the Rockies north of the 42nd parallel. On its part, the United States gave up its claims to Texas and assumed payment of up to five million dollars in claims brought by American citizens against Spain. The treaty also established the western boundaries of the Louisiana Purchase. The Adams-Onís Treaty, its signing delayed by futile chicanery on the part of the king of Spain, was, as Adams wrote, "a great epocha in our history." With it the Secretary of State carried American claims to the Pacific. North of the 42nd parallel the United States and Great Britain agreed amicably to a joint occupation of

140

An unidentified artist, possibly a visiting Frenchman, filled his sketchbook in 1818 with characteristic American types, mostly New Yorkers. Here are four of his impressions: above, a Negro, probably a rich man's servant; at top, opposite, a group of solid citizens being harangued by one of their number; below, a chaise and its driver drawn by a weary horse; at bottom, opposite a gentleman identified as Mr. Fouchet. Fashion decreed top hats and cutaways; parasols, while fairly common, were considered optional.

the Oregon country for ten years, postponing, if not avoiding, an eventual confrontation.

As continental in its way as Adams' treaty, was Chief Justice Marshall's decision in *McCulloch v. Maryland*, in which he ruled that the Constitution of the United States was superior to the constitutions and laws of the states. The case depended on the question whether the state of Maryland had a right to tax a branch of the Second Bank of the United States, established by act of Congress. The defendant was the otherwise obscure cashier of the Baltimore branch, James McCulloch.

Held in the basement of the Capitol in February, 1819, the hearings aroused enormous political and legal interest. The thin, loose-jointed Chief Justice, with his untidy hair and not-too-clean linen, hardly seemed a man to make history. But the old Federalist who looked to the past would in his decisions foreshadow the advance of the new nationalism. In the McCulloch case he and his fellow justices ruled against Maryland while Marshall, going beyond the immediate, set down for all time the "great principle that the constitution and the laws thereof are supreme; that they control the constitution and laws of the respective states, and cannot be controlled by them." The United States, by Marshall's definition, was a nation and not a confederation.

The speculative cycle of Monroe's first year and a half, with its hectic prosperity, had seemed—like all such cycles—eternal. Although the end of the Napoleonic Wars had brought about a world-wide fall in prices, the United States managed to insulate itself from the consequences through the rapid circulation of vast quantities of paper money. Though even the Bank of the United States would have been unable to halt the paper flood, its incompetent president, far from trying, did his best to increase it. State banks issued their notes on dubious security or on none at all. A land bubble like the South Sea Bubble of a century before followed. The price of cotton soared.

By the end of 1818 the bubble had broken. Even before then there had been warning signs. As European land had come back into cultivation, the need for American agricultural products had faded. English manufactures had flooded the American market, undercutting the blockade-stimulated domestic industries. With the collapse, land lost up to three-quarters of its value. The price of cotton fell by more than half. Farmers and planters, caught between falling prices and heavy fixed charges, in many cases lost their property. Trade stag-

nated, markets were ruined, industries closed down, and in the cities the unemployed tramped the streets.

As always, those who saw their money wilt away with their hopes, who faced or experienced ruin, sought a scapegoat. And the most obvious one was the Bank of the United States, with its new president embarked on a deflationary policy that through foreclosures made it the unwilling owner of hotels, warehouses, stores, factories, and even vacant lots. In the Panic of 1819 the Bank became the Monster, attacked by hard-money advocates for its paper policies, assailed by private interests jealous of its power, denounced in the debt-ridden West and the Southwest for keeping local banks from issuing cheap money.

To many Southerners the unemployed of the industrial North in their uncared-for wretchedness were wage slaves, far less fortunate than the actual slaves of the agricultural South, who were under the paternalistic care of their owners. For the Southerner of Jefferson's generation slavery had roused mixed emotions, and Jefferson himself after much agonizing thought was finally forced to admit that the Negro placed in the white man's environment would become his equal. Calhoun in the next generation would move in the opposite di-

142

rection until eventually he could conclude that as he told Adams, "manual labor was the proper work of slaves" and slavery was "a good—a positive good." It was during the mid-period of Monroe's Presidency that Southern and Northern attitudes began to polarize, that the South and the North as entities began to emerge.

After Louisiana had been admitted as a state in 1812, the rest of the Louisiana Purchase had been organized as Missouri Territory. The Territory of Arkansas was organized and detached from Missouri Territory in 1819, and that same year the settlers of Missouri Territory petitioned for statehood. Settled mostly by Southerners, the region had grown rapidly in population. In 1810 it had contained three thousand slaves. By 1820 the number of slaves had increased to ten thousand out of a total population of sixty-six thousand. Geographically Missouri Territory did not have the attributes of a slaveholding society, being more suitable for diversified farming than for cotton.

Ever since the Northwest Ordinance of 1787, the admission of territories to statehood had been routine. The slave territories of Mississippi and Alabama were admitted with as little question in 1817 and 1819 as were the free states of Indiana and Illinois in 1816 and

1818. Eleven slave states were then balanced by eleven free states. Nevertheless, and in spite of the million and a half slaves who for the purposes of congressional representation each counted for three-fifths of a man, the population balance was swinging sharply away from the South. Since Northern control of the House of Representatives was all but inevitable, it seemed to Southerners vital to keep the Senate a Southern bastion. Clay considered it fair enough—except possibly for the slaves—to admit Missouri as a slave state while admitting the District of Maine as a free state. The Missouri Enabling Bill might indeed have passed in February, 1819, without debate had it not been for the amendment proposed by James Tallmadge, Jr., of New York. Tallmadge's motives are as obscure as the rest of his career, but his amendment would have banned "the further introduction of slavery" into Missouri and would have freed all slaves born after Missouri had become a state when they reached the age of twenty-five. The amendment passed the House on a strictly sectional vote, but was rejected overwhelmingly by the Senate shortly before the Fifteenth Congress came to an end.

What Tallmadge had done in his amendment was to challenge the doctrine of white supremacy, and in so doing he waked a wolf that had been sleeping uneasily for forty years, one that the South would have preferred to let sleep for forty more. Whitney's invention of the cotton gin—followed by the introduction of upland, or short-staple, cotton, which would grow over vast areas of South Carolina, Georgia, Alabama, Louisiana, and Mississippi where sea-island cotton could not flourish—had brought a quick expansion of slavery. Throughout the South what had been considered a necessary evil came to seem a positive good. The wolf that Tallmadge had waked was soon howling.

The Sixteenth Congress, with its expanded Northern membership in the House of Representatives of 105 to the slave states' 81, was the first Congress to meet in the Capitol since its burning by the British. For the occasion the Hall of Representatives was resplendent with crimson curtains, a crimson silk canopy, surmounted by a gilt eagle, above the Speaker's desk, and new brass cuspidors for the legislators. There was a new spirit in Congress to match the decor. For the first time the legislative halls echoed with the oratory of those defending slavery. Southerners were even willing to argue that the clause of the Ordinance of 1787 prohibiting slavery in the Northwest was no longer binding. Some went so far as to use the Bible to justify their peculiar institution, arguing that "Christ himself gave a sanction to slavery."

Those Northern congressmen who attacked slavery were by no means abolitionists. No politician was yet ready to suggest that slavery be abolished in the states in which it was rooted. The opposition to its expansion was more a power struggle than a matter of principle. Eventually in regard to Missouri a compromise was reached. After much weary and repetitious debate the Senate finally adopted the Maine-Missouri Bill, admitting Missouri as a slave state but prohibiting slavery "forever" elsewhere in the Louisiana Purchase above the 36° 30′ parallel, Missouri's southern boundary. Southerners acquiesced, believing it vital to have Missouri enter the Union as a slave state and convinced that west of the Missouri River, where slavery was prohibited, lay nothing but "a prairie, resembling the steppes of Tartary" from which no more than one state could be formed.

At first the House of Representatives was less amenable, backing and filling with antislavery amendments, separating Maine's statehood from that of Missouri; but after some adroit juggling by Mr. Speaker Clay, the Missouri Compromise became law. Yet the wolf question of slavery would never sleep again. At Monticello the aged Jefferson heard it like a "fire-bell in the night." He thought it the knell of the Union, hushed, but only for a moment, by the Compromise.

Monroe signed the Missouri Compromise Bill with hesitation, uncertain whether Congress had the right to prohibit slavery in a territory and whether such a prohibition should carry over when the territory became a state. No sooner had the Compromise gone into effect than the controversy sprang up with renewed bitterness when the Missouri constitution was submitted to the Senate. Under its provisions the Missouri legislature was enjoined to pass such laws as were necessary "to prevent free Negroes and mulattoes from coming to and settling in this State, under any pretext whatsoever." Most states, even in the North, had restrictions against

Zachary Taylor leads his men, aided by bloodhounds, in an attack on the Seminoles during the bitter seven-year-long war in Florida.

Negroes and Indians, but Missouri's gesture brought up the issue squarely: Was a free Negro free or was he not? Could Missouri bar a citizen of the United States from crossing its border? Or must that clause be dropped before Missouri could be admitted to the Union?

Clay, the deft compromiser, with his sunny, persuasive personality, provided the conciliatory exit. With his American System he had done his best to make Northern capitalism acceptable to the West and the South. Missouri would now be admitted with her unamended constitution, provided the clause in question "never be construed to authorize the passage of any law . . . by which any citizens . . . shall be excluded from the enjoyment of any of the privileges and immunities" to which they were entitled under the Constitution, and providing that the Missouri legislature give its assent "to the said fundamental condition." With defiant logic the legislature passed a bill that, while giving assent, at the same time declared itself an unnecessary law and therefore not binding on the state! This paradox being considered satisfactory, Missouri was admitted to the Union. Twenty-seven years later Missouri lawmakers would pass an act providing that "no free Negro nor mulatto shall under any pretext emigrate into this State from any State or Territory."

While Clay was moving through his minuet of compromise, the electoral votes for the ninth presidential election were being counted with brisk debate as to whether Missouri's electoral votes should be considered. Not that Missouri made any difference in the result, for Monroe was unopposed, the single electoral vote against him being cast for John Quincy Adams by Monroe's personal enemy, former Governor William Plumer of New Hampshire, ostensibly on the grounds that only Washington was deserving of a unanimous election.

Monroe believed his re-election represented unity. But what his unopposed election really represented was indifference. The Federalists had disappeared as a national party, and controversy had not yet split the Republicans. Though the President had incurred some resentment as a result of the extended depression, he was far from becoming its scapegoat. There was simply no other choice. So lackluster was the election that only a minority of voters bothered to go to the polls. In Richmond, the story is, a mere seventeen people voted.

Monroe's second inauguration day was one of wind and sleet, and few gathered in the streets to watch as he drove in a plain carriage with a single Negro footman from the President's House to the Capitol. In his inaugural address he brushed aside the "present depression in prices" as temporary, pointed to the payment of nearly sixty-seven million dollars of the public debt as proof of the country's "extraordinary prosperity," and concluded that "there is every reason to believe that our system will soon attain the highest degree of perfection of which human institutions are capable."

Though Monroe the man has become a vague anachronistic figure in knee breeches and with queued, powdered hair, his name is perpetuated in the Monroe Doctrine, evoked by him as a temporary response to an immediate crisis. Washington in his Farewell Address had warned his countrymen against entangling themselves in the web of Old World politics; Monroe warned the nations of Europe against spinning their webs in the Western Hemisphere. Of course, the warning would have been an empty one without the good will of England, but the recent war bitterness was being pushed aside with surprising rapidity as mutual interests drew the two countries together. "Great Britain," Jefferson wrote in mellowed words to Monroe, "is the nation which can do us the most harm of any one, or all on earth; and with her on our side we need not fear the whole world."

From across the water Lord Liverpool, England's Tory Prime Minister, had become convinced that the prosperity of England depended on the prosperity of a low-tariff United States. Liverpool was a Tory with a difference—an opponent of the War of 1812, who sensed the mighty industrial potential of his country and never forgot that America was the chief single customer for the British manufacturer. Even Perceval, Liverpool's more reactionary predecessor, had known the value of the United States market, had been willing to concede much in the trade and shipping disputes between the two countries, and had refused to make an issue of the Arbuthnot and Ambrister executions in spite of public clamor. George Canning, Britain's foreign secretary and a cousin of the minister to the United States, stifled his dislike of republics and republicans in the friendliness of his overtures to the American minister, Richard Rush, and in his freely expressed opinion that the United States and Britain were "the two chief commercial and maritime states of both worlds."

It was the sudden collapse of Ferdinand VII's Spanish Empire that had brought about a resolution of

OVERLEAF: *In the fall and winter of 1821–22 Samuel F. B. Morse worked as many as fourteen hours a day to complete this painting of an evening session of the House of Representatives. Among the eighty-six men he portrayed were members of the Supreme Court, on the dais at rear left, and a Pawnee chief in the gallery at right.*

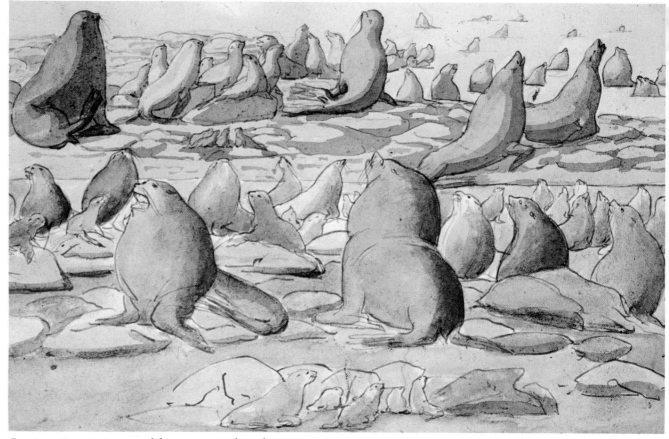

Russian attempts to control fur resources of northwest
America were one major reason for the Monroe Doctrine.
A Russian painted these Alaskan sea lions about 1815.

American and British antipathies. In the aftermath of
the Napoleonic era, revolts broke out in the Spanish
American colonies from the Argentine to Mexico. Ferdinand's own absolutist government was overthrown in
Spain in 1820 and he himself made prisoner by liberal
constitutionalists.

To the Holy Alliance of Russia, Austria, and Prussia,
formed with the pious intention of keeping states and
dynasties as they were, revolution anywhere was the ultimate evil. At the Congress of Verona, these powers—
over England's objections—gave restored Bourbon
France a free hand to suppress the new Spanish government. Equally disturbing to the Holy Alliance was the
revolutionary flame in Spanish America, which they
were eager to extinguish before it could spread. Here
also England disagreed with her late allies, for far more
important than any so-called principle of legitimacy
was her flourishing trade with South America.

Secretary of State Adams believed that the independence of Spain's New World colonies was necessary to
the well-being of the United States. Monroe, like Adams, resolved that the breakup of the Spanish Empire
should offer no threat to the westward expansion of his
country. In March, 1822, Monroe sent a special message
to Congress recommending the recognition of the independence of Argentina, Colombia, Chile, Peru, and
Mexico. Recognition was more symbolic than anything
else, for Monroe would promise no practical help to the
rebels either in men, money, or supplies. The threat of
foreign intervention remained.

The year following these events, Canning wrote to
Rush that he felt that the independence of Spain's colonies was inevitable. England would not interfere between them and the mother country but "could not see
any portion of them transferred to any other Power with
indifference." Canning suggested that these opinions,
common to "your government with ours," be made into
a pact between the two friendly governments. Minister

Rush countered by suggesting that if the British government would first recognize the new Spanish American countries, he would pledge his country to a joint declaration with Britain on the status of Spanish America. Canning, faced with opposition from within his own party, was not yet ready to agree to this.

Since the possibility of a Holy Alliance against South America remained, Monroe prepared a message to Congress for December 2, 1823, that was in a sense a sequel to Canning's note. In his message, which was strongly influenced by Adams, Monroe observed that the United States would remain neutral between Spain and her colonies as long as the European powers did the same. In the Alaska region he was willing to negotiate any conflict of rights and interests with Russia. But "the American Continents, by the free and independent condition which they have assumed and maintain, are henceforth not to be considered as subjects for future colonization by any European Power."

The United States would refrain from taking part in any European wars, but would consider any European intrusion in this hemisphere "dangerous to our peace and safety." Although not in Monroe's message, the principle that the United States would not permit the transfer, by one European power to another, of any possession in the New World is an additional point of the Monroe Doctrine. It was stated by Adams in a note to the Russian government shortly before Monroe's message was delivered.

Monroe's message would have been so much wind without the power of the Royal Navy behind it. But the power was there and would remain there until the First World War. European countries, discounting the young republic, did not take the message seriously. In Spanish America it was enthusiastically received, though there were second thoughts when the United States turned down proposed alliances with, or requests for assistance from, five of the new states. Canning was pleased at first to see his ideas being implemented, but became less so when he considered the unfriendly implications of the noncolonization clause. England, however, soon recognized the new countries. The message would become known as the Monroe Doctrine, a lasting commitment to United States leadership in world politics.

Though formed by the eighteenth century, though the last of the Virginia dynasty, Monroe found himself forced by circumstances to turn away from the pastoral dreams of Jeffersonian agrarianism. Before the end of his second term he had endorsed and signed a protective tariff measure raising the relatively low rates of the 1816 tariff bill. Like Lord Liverpool in England, he sensed that the future was an industrial one. Others like Clay sensed it more exuberantly.

The Panic of 1819 had stirred Clay to hasten development of a system of economic self-sufficiency, which he had first conceived in 1816. What he demanded in his flowing rhetoric was an alliance between the undeveloped West and the industrial North that would create an American prosperity independent of world markets. In March, 1824, he made his famous two-day speech in Congress in which he explained and urged on the country his American System. That system was in essence a planned national economy with the government taking on the burden of internal improvements—a vast network of roads and canals to speed the agricultural products of the West to Eastern cities. A high tariff would protect developing American industries from foreign competition and at the same time would bring in revenue for necessary public works. American farmers, in Clay's vision, would wear American cotton spun in American mills, American cotton spinners and mechanics would eat Western food and drink Western whiskey! With the population growing, with the domestic market constantly expanding, Clay hoped with his American System to link all sections of the United States together in a prosperous, mutually dependent whole.

Clay's romantic vision was continental, looking to a future when "the wave of population, cultivation and intelligence shall have washed the Rocky Mountains and have mingled with the Pacific." His system was feared by the South, with its enormous cotton exports that no domestic market could absorb. Old Virginians like John Randolph of Roanoke saw in the system the iron yoke of a central government. Clay's support of the Bank of the United States made him not wholly trusted in his own West. New England was dubious about internal improvements that did not improve New England. But for Northern capitalism, the American System was the music of the spheres.

After the War of 1812, shipping and foreign commerce no longer remained the easy means to quick wealth that they had been for the venturesome. New England merchants, for all their distaste for Mr. Madison, had profited most by the war. Now the money-conscious representatives of the great Massachusetts merchant families—the Lowells, the Lawrences, the

Lees, and the Jacksons—began to withdraw their capital from foreign trade and reinvest it in manufacturing. About 1814 Francis Cabot Lowell and a group of canny Boston associates established the world's first full-process cotton mill at Waltham, Massachusetts. Lowell, on a visit to England just before the war, had toured the English mills and inspected the new power looms, and like Samuel Slater a generation before him, had carried away the designs in his head. Returning to New England, he planned a mill where both spinning and weaving would be done under one roof, where Southern cotton bales would be delivered at one end and finished yard goods would emerge at the other.

Unlike England, where land enclosure had left large numbers of unemployed agricultural laborers as a supply of cheap labor for the expanding industries, the rural-based United States, with its easily available land, suffered from a chronic labor shortage. To provide the workers to tend the new machines, American employers evolved two systems. The first and more haphazard originated in the Slater mills. It involved the hiring of whole families—though women and children predominated—for the spinning process. Most of the weaving was done on hand looms on nearby farms. Generally the mills were small, since they were dependent on local labor. Faced with this built-in labor problem, Lowell and his associates evolved the Waltham system, which they extended from Waltham to such Merrimack River water-power sites as Lowell and Lawrence and Nashua. The system was one of large-scale coordination, each factory producing a standardized cloth of coarse weave that required little skill on the part of the operator. The most spectacular feature of the system was its method of obtaining labor. From all over New England, Lowell recruited farmers' daughters, housing them in special dormitories for the few years that they worked to provide themselves with a dowry.

The city of Lowell on the Merrimack became the show place of the Waltham system. Where the village of East Chelmsford with a population of 200 had existed sleepily in 1820, Lowell with a population of 6,477 flourished ten years later. Most of the newcomers were farm girls, respectable and self-respecting. They lived in neat white rows of boardinghouses, each house supervised by a matron who watched carefully over the conduct and morals of her charges. They worked six days a week, thirteen hours a day in summer and eleven in winter, with half-hour breaks for breakfast and noon-

While the North was making the transition from an agricultural to a partly industrial economy, Southerners continued to depend on the soil for their livelihood. Above, a view of the cotton capital of Charleston, South Carolina, in the early part of the century; at right, women tend machines in a Northern bookbinding plant.

day dinner—not excessive hours to those accustomed to a farm routine. The girls were in bed at ten yet still found time to read, attend improving lectures, and even publish a magazine, *The Lowell Offering*. In a few years they would return home, still in the freshness of youth. If they were frugal—as Yankee farmers' daughters were—they could save up to nine dollars a month. When President Jackson visited Lowell, twenty-five hundred factory girls—pretty women "by the Eternal," Jackson observed—paraded in his honor, carrying parasols and wearing silk stockings. Dickens, who liked neither industrialism nor the United States, was much impressed by his visit to Lowell, writing in *American Notes:* "The rooms in which [the girls] worked were as well ordered as themselves. In the windows of some there were green plants, which were trained to shade the glass; in all, there was as much fresh air, cleanliness, and comfort as the nature of the occupation would possibly admit of. . . . From all the crowd I saw in the different factories that day, I cannot recall or separate one young face that gave me a painful impression. . . ."

Gradually, unspectacularly, but inevitably shop and handicraft production gave way to the factory system. With the advent of piecework and labor-saving machinery, household fabrication declined. Whitney's inter-

150

changeable parts were found to be the key to industrial progress. Glassworks and ironworks grew to large plants. Innovations, such as the iron-rolling mill, were brought from Britain. Hydraulic turbines replaced cumbersome water wheels, and steam appeared as a mover of factory machinery, although it did not generally replace water power until after the Civil War. Inventions such as food canning came into being.

Industrialism, of course, scarcely touched the frontier. Cities like New York and Philadelphia and Baltimore, in spite of their increasing number of factories, retained their mercantile and maritime aspects. But the industrial process was an irreversible one, and it made inevitable an urban proletariat that would bring the trade-union movement.

In the colonial period skilled workmen had had their own craft associations and combinations, and with the perennial shortage of labor, were relatively well paid. The onset of industrialism in the new century undermined their position. Even in small workshops production became directed more to the market than to the individual, leading to the delegation of simpler tasks to women and children, with a consequent lowering of wages. Before 1815 some of the more skilled workers were beginning to organize and even to engage in

strikes. In 1806 there had been the famous case of the Philadelphia cordwainers brought into court charged with unlawful conspiracy and found guilty of "a combination to raise their wages."

Later, as economic conditions improved following the depression of 1819–20, workingmen's societies or unions increased in number, but they were still largely associations of skilled workers. One of the notable strikes of the period was that of the Boston carpenters who walked out in 1825, demanding a ten-hour day and overtime pay. The Boston employers expressed shock over this demand by the "industrious sons of Massachusetts" for a change in "the time of commencing and terminating their daily labor, from that which has been customary from time immemorial." By the end of the decade there were the first beginnings of a real labor movement, with workers of various occupations uniting for economic purposes and political action.

Though industrial slums were festering in the cities, 90 per cent of the United States remained rural. Farm life still was the standard and had not altered greatly since the Revolution. The most spectacular agrarian advance was in the improvement of stock. In 1790 a New England farmer considered eighty-five pounds of butter a good annual yield for a cow. With better care and breeding, that yield had been doubled by 1830. Starting in 1820, the Quakers of Chester County, Pennsylvania, developed a famous breed of swine from a strain originally obtained from Bedfordshire, England. Other strains were introduced to improve the breed, culminating in the superior Berkshires that had arrived by 1830. Even more notable was the introduction of merino sheep from Spain, through the efforts of, among others, Robert Livingston and the French-born Pierre DuPont de Nemours.

In 1807 the first agricultural show and country fair was organized in Berkshire County, Massachusetts, after a local farmer had exhibited his imported merinos on the Pittsfield green. More directly beneficial to the farmers was the appearance of agricultural journals with sound, simple, and practical advice on plant care and stockbreeding. The *American Farmer*, founded by John P. Skinner, the Baltimore postmaster, in 1819, was soon followed by the *Ploughboy*, the *New England Farmer*, the *New York Farmer*, and the *Southern Agriculturist*. Written as they were for the "real, unsophisticated American," they brought a freshness of outlook, an impulse to break ingrained rural habits and try

151

new ways of raising both crops and livestock.

Whatever prosperity the farmer enjoyed depended on his ability to transport his products to market. By 1815 a network of roads covered the settled parts of the country. Most were scarcely more than broad paths, rutted, stump- and boulder-strewn, mudholes in wet weather, yet serving to connect farms with villages.

Even before 1812 considerable progress had been made in linking the larger commercial centers by means of turnpikes. The best new American roads were built on the classical model, with a solid stone foundation covered by gravel. The Lancaster Pike, between Philadelphia and Lancaster, completed in 1794, was a rousing commercial success and started a craze for toll roads. Such roads, with their toll stations, crisscrossed New England and reached out beyond Albany to Lake Erie. In New York and Pennsylvania they attained their greatest mileage. Costing anywhere from five thousand to ten thousand dollars a mile, they were for the most part financed privately.

Most toll roads were financially disappointing. For travelers by stagecoach and for westward-bound emigrants they were a blessing, but they failed to provide cheap, advantageous freight-hauls. By the mid-twenties the toll-road boom was over.

Most famous, most durable of the roads, and a free one, was the Cumberland Road, a truly Roman way built by the federal government—with considerable doubt as to whether the government had the right to do any such thing. Its first section—from Cumberland, Maryland, to Wheeling, West Virginia—was completed in 1818. It was later extended westward. The section west of Wheeling was usually called the National Road; it reached Columbus, Ohio, in 1833 and continued to its eventual end in Vandalia, Illinois, after mid-century.

Such federally sponsored improvements were looked at ambivalently as both necessary and unconstitutional. Madison, though he had believed the national government should build a network of roads and canals, nevertheless vetoed on constitutional grounds an 1817 bill sponsored by Clay and Calhoun for internal improvements. And Monroe in his time refused to sign a bill to erect toll gates on the National Road.

Water continued to offer the cheapest and surest means for transporting freight and produce, and the expansion of the country led to the building of canals that from a venture became a craze. The prototype was New York's Erie Canal, DeWitt Clinton's long-cherished dream. Jefferson as President had thought such a project, the linking of the Great Lakes and the Atlantic by a canal connecting Lake Erie and the Hudson River, a harebrained scheme, and President Madison, while more sympathetic, could not persuade Congress to vote any government funds for what Clinton's enemies called Clinton's Ditch. In 1817 Clinton stumped the state and got himself elected governor on the promise of having the state itself build the canal.

On the Fourth of July, three days after Clinton took the oath of office, the first shovelful of earth was turned over for his Grand Canal. The canal—40 feet wide, 4 feet deep, and 363 miles long—was the greatest piece of engineering yet undertaken in the United States. Clinton was buoyantly convinced that the tolls would not only pay for the canal but free New Yorkers from all personal and real-estate taxes from then on.

Even in the Panic of 1819 Governor Clinton pressed on with the work, financing his project through lotteries and taxes on salt and on auctions as well as by selling canal stocks. In October, 1825, the last link in the Big Ditch was completed and the triumphant governor, aboard the canalboat *Seneca Chief*, led a ceremonial flotilla from Lake Erie to New York Harbor, accompanied on his voyage by the daily roar of cannon and the nightly flare of fireworks from canalside towns. New York City staged a gaudy procession down Broadway.

Many of the canal laborers had been brought over from Ireland, the beginning of the mass emigration that would become a flood in the famine years. Poor Paddies were met at the New York docks and hired to work on the canal on the promise of "roast beef guaranteed twice a day, regular whiskey rations, and wages eighty cents." Eighty cents a day—later raised to a dollar—was a high wage for common labor at the time. They dug the canal, working from dawn to sunset, in sun and heat, in cold and wet, dying like flies, leaving only the canal bed as their memorial.

The Erie Canal was an immediate success, carrying the emigrants through the gateway to Michigan, Wisconsin, Indiana, and Illinois. Other canals followed, in Maine and Massachusetts and Connecticut, the Delaware and Hudson in Pennsylvania and New Jersey, the Lehigh, the Morris, the Union, the Susquehanna and Tidewater, the 395-mile Main Line, running through Pennsylvania and crossing the Alleghenies with a cable railroad to carry the canalboats over the mountains. In the West there were the 308-mile Ohio and Erie Canal and the Miami and Erie, with their many branches. From 1816 to 1840 the people of the United States built 3,226 miles of canals. While the canals helped develop the nation, none except the Erie was a real financial success. Three states almost went bankrupt in the canal boom. The Wabash and Erie was the longest canal—453 miles—and the greatest canal failure in the country. In the end the canals proved more useful to the public than to the stockholders, more useful to the expanding nation than to the states that had built them. The coming of the railroads marked the beginning of their decline.

From the earliest days Americans had used rivers to transport their products, floating them on keelboats, rafts, or flatboats. Upriver transportation was impossible except for the type of craft called a keelboat. A boat from Pennsylvania could drift down the Ohio and the Mississippi to New Orleans in a month, but to get a keelboat back required three or four months of poling, towing, and sailing by the toughest and brawniest crew.

By the end of the eighteenth century American inventors had applied steam power to river craft. The result was still only a rather elaborate toy, but steam-engine design continued to improve. In 1807 the toy gave way to the practical as Robert Fulton's *Clermont* made her successful voyage up the Hudson. Two years later John Stevens constructed the first completely American built steamship, which he operated on the Delaware. Fulton and Chancellor Robert Livingston obtained the exclusive rights to navigate New York waters with steamboats, a monopoly they managed to keep until it was declared invalid by the Supreme Court in

In awarding diplomas during this time of scientific advance, "agricultural" societies made little distinction between achievements in the industrial arts and in farming. The certificate above was granted for work in carburetion—adding carbon compounds to various gases to increase their illuminating power.

1824. Before the War of 1812 they succeeded in acquiring the same monopoly rights for the lower Mississippi, and during the autumn of 1811 their *New Orleans*, supervised by Theodore Roosevelt's great-granduncle Nicholas, made the first steamboat voyage from Pittsburgh to New Orleans. The age of steam on Western rivers began with that epic run as the *New Orleans*, accompanied by earthquakes, astonishing the settlers with night showers of sparks, made her amazingly speedy way to the great river port. Steam navigation became general after the War of 1812 on waterways from Maine to Florida, on the Great Lakes, and in the vast area traversed by the Mississippi and its tributaries.

Through the period of the westward surge, of nationalist political and economic expansion, American writers continued to toil over novels and essays and poems that they hoped would confound and astonish the condescending European critics. Their names are forgotten or half-forgotten; passing satirists, imitators of Scott—overwhelmingly the most popular writer in America—

romantic versifiers, who had turned from Pope's couplets to the rhythms and modes of Byron, Ossian, and Moore. Not until the appearance of Washington Irving and James Fenimore Cooper did the United States succeed in producing indigenous literary figures who could hold their own against those of Europe.

Van Wyck Brooks summed up Irving as "the first high literary talent the country had known." Born into a prosperous New York Federalist family, he had been christened Washington when the British evacuated New York. As a young man of fashion in Manhattan, he showed himself Tory by temperament, loving the English tradition, loving the past, haunting the old Dutch world still lingering on near Tarrytown, where he picked up the tales that he later would retell for the world. In a desultory way he studied law, then gave it up with the advent of his first client. Together with his friends he turned out the witty occasional magazine *Salmagundi*, modeled after the *Spectator*. His burlesque *A History of New York . . . by Diedrich Knickerbocker*, in

Despite public enthusiasm, a special council in 1817 approved the New York legislature's appropriation to build the Erie Canal by only a single vote—one of the most important in American history. Above is the trial proof for an aquatint of the busy canal as it looked in the 1830's.

which he assumed the alter ego of the brisk antiquary Diedrich Knickerbocker with his outmoded clothes and old-fashioned ways, brought him his first fame. Ten years later his *Sketch Book,* written in England though published first in America, made him an international literary personage. Europeans were as surprised by the American's elegantly simple style as if—Irving said so himself—a Chinese had expressed himself in pure English. Translated into French and German, *The Sketch Book* and its successor, *Bracebridge Hall,* were read all over Europe. Considered a New World classic on both sides of the Atlantic, *The Sketch Book* would be used for the next hundred years as a first reader for students of English all over the world. *Rip Van Winkle* and *The Legend of Sleepy Hollow* became an American legacy.

Like Irving, although six years younger, James Fenimore Cooper was a New Yorker of Federalist background but was born to grander surroundings, for his father was a great landowner and he himself would assume the life of a Westchester County squire. His early life had been adventurous. Expelled from Yale for tying a donkey in his tutor's chair, he had gone to sea for a year and then had spent three years in the Navy. Later he had wandered over the state of New York, absorbing its history, reliving in imagination the savage past of the French and Indian War. He had sailed and traveled and talked with old men and had spent hours in the old Dutch inns along the Mohawk in the countryside he would make his literary domain. Yet till he was thirty he had written nothing, content to live on his inheritance at Angevine, the manor house he had built at Scarsdale. As a country squire he read much—above all Scott's Waverley novels—rode, visited, and wrote his first novel as a wager. His second, *The Spy,* was written under Waverley influence; it was the first novel successfully to adopt Scott's techniques to American subjects.

Although a clumsy writer, Cooper has survived his careless style and awkward plots through his magical ability to capture the mood and feeling of forest and sky and space and the sea. In his Leatherstocking tales he

caught the moment of conflict between the wilderness savage and the restless new American, expressing it as no one had yet been able to do. Indeed, when Natty Bumppo, the forest man with his long rifle, walked into Cooper's pages, American fiction came of age.

Until the Revolution, American architecture had derived almost unconsciously from England, although there were regional Dutch, Swedish, and French influences. Builders following Georgian books of architecture produced such restrained and dignified buildings as Philadelphia's Independence Hall and Boston's King's Chapel and viceregal Shirley Place. Following the Revolution, Boston's Charles Bulfinch continued a modified British style in New England, while Jefferson turned back to Roman examples.

The English-born Benjamin Latrobe, surveyor of public buildings and later rebuilder of the Capitol, did not care much for the Roman manner. For Latrobe, who was, next to Jefferson, the most distinguished architect of America's new century, Greek democracy and art were more akin to the American scene. "The days of Greece," he told the Philadelphia Society of Artists, "may be revived in the woods of America." In 1801 his Bank of Philadelphia became the first Greek Revival public building in the United States and was copied so widely that he could boast a few years later that he had changed a whole city's tastes. He could have included the whole country, for with him and his followers came the Greek Revival, which would leave its mark on every region, from the massive porticoes of the new-rich cotton planters of the Deep South to the diminutive wooden Ionic columns on New England village porches. Everywhere post offices, banks, railroad stations, schools, and houses would assume the façades of Athenian temples, until the style collapsed shortly before the Civil War.

Education beyond the elementary level became the province of the new private academies. By 1815 Massachusetts had thirty of them and New York thirty-seven, and the Attic movement rapidly expanded south and west. They varied greatly in quality, some doing little more than training bumpkins in reading and writing, others preparing the sons of the well to do to enter Harvard or Yale. Most were supported by public subscription or endowed by wealthy philanthropists, though some were the offshoots of churches. Secondary education for a classical-minded elite had existed in the eighteenth century; as early as 1765 there were at least

forty-eight Latin schools in Massachusetts. General public secondary education began in Boston in 1821 with English Classical School, the first high school in the United States, designed not to teach Latin and Greek but to fit its graduates "for active life." Three years after the founding of English Classical School, the Massachusetts legislature required every community of more than five hundred families to establish a high school.

At the elementary school level it was firmly held that every young white American was entitled to a public education. Legislatures passed laws to insure it. Yet not until after the War of 1812 did any part of the country have a general public-school system except on paper. Local officials, faced with raising taxes for schools, frequently failed to act. Even where schools existed, thanks to taxes and state subsidies, there was seldom enough money to maintain the buildings and pay the teachers' small salary as well. School boards raised funds by assessing families according to the number of school-age offspring. Parents who could not pay were usually allowed to enter their children as "charity pupils." Illiteracy was widespread in the poorer sections of the cities, where the existing educational facilities were provided for the most part by sectarian charitable associations. Since children without church connections were those most in need of schooling, two New York Quakers, Thomas Eddy and John Murray, Jr., founded the Free School Society in 1805, with DeWitt Clinton as the first president and the largest subscriber. The leaders of the society announced that they would furnish instruction in what was "essentially requisite for the due management of the ordinary business of life" without regard to church or sect. In time the society became known as the public-school system and assumed charge of all the schools of New York City, making no distinction between the children of the poor and those of the well to do.

Opposition to free schools remained. Some objected to paying taxes to educate "other people's children." Those who sent their children to private schools did not see why they should pay to support public schools they did not use. This double taxation was particularly felt by immigrant groups who had established parochial schools from their small earnings to insure that their religion and their heritage be passed on to their children. There were some Americans who even doubted the wisdom of teaching all men to "read, write and cipher," feeling that such accomplishments could be a detriment

America's brightest literary light in the early part of the century was Washington Irving, right, whose irreverent and amusing descriptions of the colorful Dutch who settled New York gained him an international reputation. The portrait of Irving is by John Vanderlyn, a student of Gilbert Stuart. Many of the fictional characters Irving created became the inspirations of artists: above, Katrina Van Tassel (the plump heroine) and Ichabod Crane (the angular schoolmaster) of The Legend of Sleepy Hollow *are depicted by Daniel Huntington, a student of the painter and telegraph inventor, Samuel F. B. Morse.*

The summit attained.
Jolly companions.
A confirmed drunkard.

STEP 5.

STEP 4. Drunk and riotous

STEP 6. Poverty and Disease

STEP 3. A glass too much.

STEP 7. Forsaken by Friends

STEP 2. A glass to keep the cold out.

STEP 8. Desperation and crime.

STEP 1. A glass with a friend.

STEP 9. Death by suicide.

DISTILLERY

*Fear—laced with appeals to the conscience—was the main
weapon of temperance leaders of this period and later,
who endeavored to make Americans forswear the bottle.*

to "a plain farmer, or a mechanic."

The spread of public education in the United States was part of the spread of nineteenth-century democratic feeling. Despite the anomaly of slavery, despite the rise of an industrial proletariat in city slums, the rhetoric of the Declaration of Independence translated itself, however haltingly, into fact; the worth of the individual, whatever his circumstances, was increasingly recognized. Treatment of the insane is a case in point. Where eighteenth-century Londoners had visited Bedlam to find amusement in the poor lunatics gibbering in their chains, doctors were now beginning to consider the insane not as beasts but as human beings suffering from disease.

The many-sided Dr. Benjamin Rush was the leader in America of this approach to the mentally afflicted. Much impressed by the success of Philippe Pinel in France in freeing lunatics from their filthy cells and by similar work by William Tuke in England, Rush established new procedures in his Philadelphia Hospital. The so-called lunatics were not to be punished nor were they to be shackled or for the most part restrained. Keepers and nurses were to have formal training, and above all they were to treat the patients with kindness. In 1812

Rush published the first American treatise on mental disease. Following its publication, various new-model mental institutions were founded: Thomas Eddy's Bloomingdale Hospital in New York, the McLean Asylum in Massachusetts. State mental hospitals were established along the same lines.

Progress was slow. A generation after the publication of Rush's book, most of the insane were still hidden away by their families in barred rooms or outhouses, or else locked up as public charges in poorhouses and jails. The frail young schoolteacher Dorothea Dix became the dedicated and militant champion of the insane, the person in the middle of the nineteenth century who did most to force the states to recognize their responsibility to the deranged. She first noticed the dreary fate of mental cases in public institutions in Massachusetts while conducting a women's Sunday-school class in the East Cambridge House of Correction in 1841. With the help of Dr. Samuel Gridley Howe and Charles Sumner, she began an investigation of state facilities, reporting to the legislature in 1843.

"I tell what I have seen," her memorial to the legislators began. With documented indignation she called their attention "to the *present* state of insane persons confined within the Commonwealth, in *cages, closets, cellars, stalls, pens! Chained, naked, beaten with rods* and *lashed* into obedience." Although the keepers and officials concerned did their bureaucratic best to defend themselves and to discredit the frail young woman with the fiery pen, the facts she produced were too overwhelming. A cowed legislature voted funds to enlarge and improve the hospital for the insane at Worcester.

From Massachusetts Dorothea Dix went on to Rhode Island, to New Jersey, to Pennsylvania, then west and south, investigating as she had in Massachusetts, presenting her carefully documented charges in a most decorous manner, gathering allies and support as she moved along. Between 1844 and 1854 she traveled more than thirty thousand miles. By 1860 she had gone through Indiana, Illinois, Louisiana, Tennessee, Mississippi, Missouri, North Carolina, Michigan, Wisconsin, visiting jails, hospitals, and poorhouses. Wherever she went she stirred up public opinion and goaded politicians. "I encounter nothing," she wrote, "which a determined will created by the necessities of the cause does not enable me to vanquish."

Dr. Benjamin Rush had been a valiant worker on behalf of the insane; equally dedicated were his efforts in the cause of temperance. America was a hard-drinking country in a hard-drinking century, and particularly on the frontier the consumption of raw whiskey was brutal and its effects devastating. To combat the notion that rum and whiskey were necessities in a rugged climate, a curative of everything from pneumonia to snake bite, Rush published *An Inquiry into the Effects of Spiritous Liquors on the Human Mind and Body.* In it he described the deleterious effects of hard liquor on the mind and body of the drinker, gave mortality statistics for those addicted, and suggested remedies and alternatives. Not a teetotaler, Rush favored wine, cider, beer, and coffee as substitutes for distilled spirits. His book went through eight editions between 1784 and 1815, the American Tract Society alone printing 172,000 copies. Joining him in his moderation appeal was Parson Weems, amiable itinerant bookseller and popularizer of the Washington cherry-tree legend, who in his *Drunkard's Looking Glass* recommended coffee in the morning and a good wife in the evening as two antidotes to the whiskey keg.

Reformers increasingly drew attention to alcohol's link with poverty and crime. The Presbyterian clergyman Lyman Beecher, disturbed by the cups of cheer he found circulating so freely at ministerial ordinations, persuaded the General Association of Presbyterian Churches to take a much stricter stand against the use of any kind of strong drink. "Intemperance," he wrote, "is the sin of our land." In Boston, where there was one licensed grogshop for every twenty-one males over the age of sixteen, the Congregational and Presbyterian churches formed in 1813 the Massachusetts Society for the Suppression of Intemperance, the prototype of many such societies.

Early temperance societies were not very effective. They were succeeded by much more militant organizations, such as Boston's American Society for the Promotion of Temperance, founded in 1826, made up of clergymen and determinedly dry laymen, which called for complete abstention from alcoholic beverages. After 1825, as an offshoot of religious revivalism, a temperance crusade swept the country, making over a million converts by 1834. Beecher, in a series of six sermons, demanded complete abstinence, calling the traffic in "ardent spirits" as sinful and dishonorable as slavery.

The crusade was launched with all the fervor of a revival and the adroitness of a political campaign. Following it, temperance societies sprang up everywhere, and persons of alcoholic habits were urged by every kind of persuasion to sign the pledge. Women were foremost in zeal, boycotting stores that sold intoxicants, goading their husbands and sons to put their name on the list. The effect was soon noticeable in the falling off of grogshop business, the failures of distilleries. Temperance hotels were founded. Students formed dry societies. College commencements, from their inherited Middle Age ribaldry, took on an ecclesiastical solemnity that they have kept ever since.

The dividing line in the temperance crusade came between those content to abstain and take the pledge and those whose moral conviction was so strong that they felt obliged to inflict it on any who thought otherwise. That same dividing line ran through the issue of slavery. The question remained in each case as to what would happen when the irreconcilables of both sides confronted each other.

Jefferson, pondering the bitter legacy of slavery, came to feel that the answer to the problem would be to return the blacks to Africa. Many slaveowners from the border states, uncomfortable with slavery but fearing the free Negro, came to agree with him. After a discussion by such varied national leaders as Madison, John Marshall, Clay, and Randolph of Roanoke, the American Colonization Society was organized in Washington in 1817 "to promote and execute a plan for colonizing (with their consent) the Free People of Colour residing in our country, in Africa, or such other place as Congress shall deem it most expedient." The society, under its first president, Washington's slaveholding nephew and Supreme Court Justice Bushrod Washington, recruited members, raised funds—mostly through clergymen—maintained paid agents, and even published a newspaper, the *African Repository*. Yet, beneath its benevolent intentions, the underlying assumptions of the society remained racist—that the Negro was an inferior being and that the United States, North and South, would be better off without him.

With the help of the United States government, an area on the west coast of Africa was picked as the site of the new colony—symbolically named Liberia—that would check the slave trade and spread the gospel of Christ through all Africa. Henry Clay hoped optimistically to repatriate fifty-two thousand Negroes each year, though even that would have been scarcely more than the annual increase in the number of Negroes in the nation. The society never sent to Africa more than an in-

significant fraction of that number, for it lacked both money and resources for any such large-scale effort. In addition many free Negroes showed a marked reluctance to return to the barbaric land of their ancestors, and even some slaves refused their freedom on such terms. Between 1820 and 1830 only fourteen hundred American Negroes were shipped to Liberia, of which a mere two hundred were slaves. Two million slaves still remained behind.

These same years saw the rise of extremist associations that would do away with slavery altogether. Still considered a crackpot fringe, these early abolitionist societies held twenty-four joint conventions between 1794 and 1829. Already by 1817 an abolitionist paper, *The Philanthropist*, was appearing in Ohio. Then in 1829 a free Negro from North Carolina, David Walker, who earned his living in Boston as an old-clothes dealer, published a pamphlet for distribution to Negroes— *Walker's Appeal*—in which he called for an end to slavery through insurrection and violence, and he scattered copies of his pamphlet through the South.

Southerners demanded Walker's arrest as a subversive. In reaction, various Southern states decreed heavy penalties for the circulation of such incendiary pamphlets. Georgia passed a law making it illegal to teach slaves to read. Negroes were forbidden to gather together in groups without the presence of a white. Reaction in the South was even sharper two years later, in 1831, when the Boston reformer and abolitionist William Lloyd Garrison began to publish the *Liberator*.

Garrison made the uncompromising claim that the Declaration of Independence's "life, liberty and the pursuit of happiness" applied to all men regardless of race and color. For him the only answer to slavery was instant liberation. In the first issue of his paper he threw down his passionate words with defiance: "I am in earnest—I will not equivocate—I will not excuse—I will not retreat a single inch—AND I WILL BE HEARD."

Heard indeed he was, but much more in the apprehensive South than by his handful of subscribers in the North. The *Liberator*, mailed to Southern editors, set the presses humming from Maryland to Mississippi. Garrison's name became an evil omen, a symbol of Northern recalcitrance. Unreasoning and unreasonable, he had succeeded. The issue of slavery, which had smoldered so long under a layer of silence and compromise and evasion, he had brought to an unextinguishable blaze. Only war would burn it out.

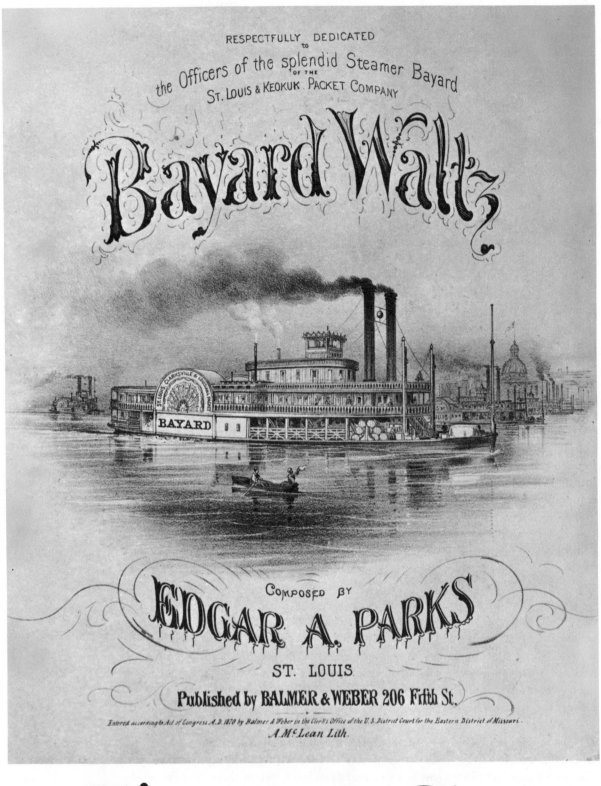

RESPECTFULLY DEDICATED
to
the Officers of the splendid Steamer Bayard
OF THE
ST. LOUIS & KEOKUK PACKET COMPANY

Bayard Waltz

COMPOSED BY

EDGAR A. PARKS

ST. LOUIS

Published by BALMER & WEBER 206 Fifth St.

Entered according to Act of Congress A.D. 1870 by Balmer & Weber in the Clerk's Office of the U.S. District Court for the Eastern District of Missouri.

A. McLean Lith.

West with the Frontier

Even before the Revolution hardy pioneers had been drifting through the passes of the Appalachians to chop out their small clearings and make their homes in the apparently endless Western wilderness. By the end of the war the trickle became a tide, a great migration, which would continue to carry the frontier westward for more than a century, beyond forests, prairies, plains, and mountains. To the Mississippi and farther, the land was covered with a forest so tall and thick that the sun hardly ever reached the ground; all this would have to be conquered with the woodsman's axe. It was said that a squirrel could have traveled from the Alleghenies to the Mississippi without once coming to earth. Yet, incredibly, most of this huge tract had been settled and most of the towering forests cleared away well before the Civil War. However, the three observers below saw the wilderness when it was largely untouched by man. French statesman Talleyrand moving toward the Appalachians in 1794, American missionary Timothy Flint traveling through a Southern swamp, and English novelist Harriet Martineau viewing the forests along the Mississippi were all struck by the vastness of the great woods.

A backwoodsman and his wi sketched by Joshua Shaw

I was struck with astonishment; at less than 154 miles distance from the capital [Philadelphia] all trace of men's presence disappeared. Nature, in all her primeval vigour confronted us. Forests old as the world itself; decayed plants and trees covering the very ground where once they grew in luxuriance; others shooting forth from under the *débris* of the former, and like them destined to decay and rot; thick and intricate bushes that often barred our progress . . . and here and there the traces of former tornadoes that had carried everything before them. Enormous trees, all mowed down in the same direction, extending for a considerable distance, bear witness to the wonderful force of these terrible phenomena. . . . To be riding through a large wild forest, to lose one's way in it in the middle of the night, and to call to one's companion in order to ascertain that you are not missing each other; all this gives impressions impossible to define. . . . When I cried, "So-and-so, are you here?" and my companion replied, "Unfortunately I am, my lord," I could not help laughing at our position.

Charles Maurice de Talleyrand-Périgord
Memoirs, 1892

Beyond these lakes, there are immense swamps of cypress, which swamps constitute a vast proportion of the inundated lands of the Mississippi and its waters. No prospect on earth can be more gloomy. The poetic Styx or Acheron had not a greater union of dismal circumstances. Well may the cypress have been esteemed a funereal and lugubrious tree. When the tree has shed its leaves, for it is a deciduous tree, a cypress swamp, with its countless interlaced branches, of a hoary grey, has an aspect of desolation and death, that often as I have been impressed with it, I cannot describe. In summer its fine, short, and deep green leaves invest these hoary larches with a drapery of crape. The water in which they grow is a vast and dead level, two or three feet deep, still leaving the innumerable cypress "knees," as they are called, or very elliptical trunks, resembling circular bee-hives, throwing their points above the waters. This water is covered with a thick coat of green matter, resem-

A grizzly-bear hunt on the plains

bling green buff velvet. The musquitoes swarm above the water in countless millions. A very frequent adjunct to this horrible scenery is the moccason snake with his huge scaly body lying in folds upon the side of a cypress knee; and if you approach too near, lazy and reckless as he is, he throws the upper jaw of his huge mouth almost back to his neck, giving you ample warning of his ability and will to defend himself. I travelled forty miles along this river swamp, and a considerable part of the way in the edge of it, in which the horse sunk at every step half up to his knees. I was enveloped for the whole distance with a cloud of musquitoes. Like the ancient Avernus, I do not remember to have seen a single bird in the whole distance except the blue jay. Nothing interupted the death-like silence, but the hum of musquitoes.

Timothy Flint
Recollections of the Last Ten Years, 1826

A few miles farther on, we went ashore at the wooding-place, and I had my first walk in the untrodden forest. The height of the trees seemed incredible, as we stood at their foot, and looked up. It made us feel suddenly dwarfed. We stood in a crowd of locust and cotton-wood trees, elm, maple, and live oak: and they were all bound together by an inextricable tangle of creepers, which seemed to forbid our penetrating many paces into the forest beyond where the wood-cutters had intruded. I had a great horror of going too far; and was not sorry to find it impossible: it would be so easy for the boat to leave two or three passengers behind, without finding it out: and no fate could be conceived more desolate.

Harriet Martineau
Retrospect of Western Travel, 1838

Morris Birkbeck, who came from England in 1817 to settle in Illinois, was impressed by the large number of emigrants moving down the roads toward Pittsburgh. That town was the jumping-off-place for the frontier. Most of the pioneers would continue on by boat down the Ohio, for the roads in the West were mere trails, passable only by humans afoot or by pack animals.

We have now fairly turned our backs on the old world, and find ourselves in the very stream of emigration. Old America seems to be breaking up, and moving westward. We are seldom out of sight, as we travel on this grand track towards the Ohio, of family groups, behind and before us, some with a view to a particular spot; close to a brother perhaps, or a friend, who has gone before, and reported well of the country. Many, like ourselves, when they arrive in the wilderness, will find no lodge prepared for them.

A small waggon (so light that you might almost carry it, yet strong enough to bear a good load of bedding, utensils and provisions, and a swarm of young citizens,—and to sustain marvellous shocks in its passage over these rocky heights), with two small horses; sometimes a cow or two, comprises their all; excepting a little store of hard-earned cash for the land office of the district; where they may obtain a title for as many acres as they possess half-dollars,

163

being one fourth of the purchase money. The waggon has a tilt, or cover, made of a sheet, or perhaps a blanket. The family are seen before, behind, or within the vehicle, according to the road or weather, or perhaps the spirits of the party.

The New Englanders, they say, may be known by the cheerful air of the women advancing in front of the vehicle; the Jersey people by their being fixed steadily within it; whilst the Pennsylvanians creep lingering behind, as though regretting the homes they have left. A cart and single horse frequently afford the means of transfer, sometimes a horse and pack-saddle. Often the back of the poor pilgrim bears all his effects, and his wife follows, naked-footed, bending under the hopes of the family.

Morris Birkbeck
Notes on a Journey in America, 1818

For many years the only roads into the wilderness, except for the few narrow trails scarcely wide enough for a pack horse, were the rivers that flowed west and south. But they provided broad and reasonably safe highways on which a man could drift with his family for hundreds of miles—all the way down to New Orleans if necessary when it came time to market his harvest. Although French visitor F. A. Michaux was chiefly interested in botanizing during his 1802 trip through the West, he found time to make notes about the people he saw, including the emigrants and their flatboats.

The amazing rapidity of the Ohio has an influence on the shape of the boats that navigate upon it, and that shape is not calculated to accelerate their progress; but to stem the current of the stream. All the boats or barges, whether those in the Kentucky or Mississippi trade, or those which convey the families that go into the eastern or western states, are built in the same manner. They are of a square form, some longer than others; their sides are raised four feet and a half above the water; their length is from fifteen to fifty feet; the two extremities are square, upon one of which is a kind of awning, under which the passengers shelter themselves when it rains. I was alone upon the banks of the Monongahela, when I perceived, at a distance, five or six of these barges, which were going down the river. I could not conceive what these great square boxes were, which, left to the stream, presented alternately their ends, sides, and even their angles. As they advanced, I heard a confused noise, but without distinguishing any thing, on account of their sides being so very high. However, on ascending the banks of the river, I perceived in these barges several families, carrying with them their horses, cows, poultry, waggons, ploughs, harness, beds, instruments of agriculture, in fine, every thing necessary to cultivate the land, and also for domestic use. These people were abandoning themselves to the mercy of the stream, without knowing the place where they should stop, to exercise their industry, and enjoy peaceably the fruit of their labour under one of the best governments that exists in the world.

F. A. Michaux
Travels to the West of the Alleghany Mountains, 1805

164

One of the best observers of the Western scene was Timothy Flint, a New England missionary who traveled, lived, and even farmed for a time on the lands that were being turned with axe and sweat from wilderness into farms and settlements. Flint wrote a book about his experiences; in that volume he described the various river craft in use in 1826.

Many travellers and emigrants to this region, view the first samples of the modes of travelling in the western world, on the Allegany at Oleanne point, or the Monongahela at Brownsville. These are but the retail specimens. At Pittsburg, where these rivers unite, you have the thing in gross, and by whole-sale. The first thing that strikes a stranger from the Atlantic, arrived at the boat-landing, is the singular, whimsical, and amusing spectacle, of the varie-ties of water-craft, of all shapes and structures. There is the stately barge, of the size of a large Atlantic schooner, with its raised and outlandish looking deck. This kind of craft, however, which required twenty-five hands to work it up stream, is almost gone into disuse, and though so common ten years ago, is now scarcely seen. Next there is the keel-boat, of a long, slender, and ele-gant form, and generally carrying from fifteen to thirty tons. This boat is formed to be easily propelled over shallow waters in the summer season, and in low stages of the water is still much used, and runs on waters not yet fre-quented by steam-boats. Next in order are the Kentucky flats, or in the vernac-ular phrase, "broad-horns," a species of ark, very nearly resembling a New England pig-stye. They are fifteen feet wide, and from forty to one hundred feet in length, and carry from twenty to seventy tons. Some of them, that are called family-boats, and used by families in descending the river, are very large and roomy, and have comfortable and separate apartments, fitted up with chairs, beds, tables and stoves. It is no uncommon spectacle to see a large family, old and young, servants, cattle, hogs, horses, sheep, fowls, and animals of all kinds, bringing to recollection the cargo of the ancient ark, all embarked, and floating down on the same bottom. Then there are what the people call "covered sleds," or ferry-flats, and Allegany-skiffs, carrying from eight to twelve tons. In another place are pirogues of from two to four tons burthen, hollowed sometimes from one prodigious tree, or from the trunks of two trees united, and a plank-rim fitted to the upper part. There are common skiffs, and other small craft, named, from the manner of making them, "dug-outs," and canoes hollowed from smaller trees. These boats are in great numbers, and these names are specific, and clearly define the boats to which they belong. But besides these, in this land of freedom and invention, with a little aid per-haps, from the influence of the moon, there are monstrous anomalies, reduci-ble to no specific class of boats, and only illustrating the whimsical archetypes of things that have previously existed in the brain of inventive men, who reject the slavery of being obliged to build in any received form. You can scarcely imagine an abstract form in which a boat can be built, that in some part of the Ohio or Mississippi you will not see, actually in motion. The New York canal is beginning, indeed, to bring samples of this infinite variety of water-craft nearer to the inspection of the Atlantic people.

Timothy Flint
Recollections of the Last Ten Years, 1826

Part real, part legendary, Mike Fink, king of the keelboat-men, as he was pictured in Davy Crockett's Almanack

The flatboats carried not only emigrants on their way to make a new home but also the commodities of the Western lands: the farm crops, lumber, and other goods being sent down-river by those who had already established themselves as producers on their new lands. Timothy Flint describes a congregation of flatboats on the Mississippi as they carry their freight to market.

In the spring, one hundred boats have been numbered, that landed in one day at the mouth of the Bayan, at New Madrid. I have strolled to the point on a spring evening, and seen them arriving in fleets. The boisterous gaiety of the hands, the congratulations, the moving picture of life on board the boats, in the numerous animals, large and small, which they carry, their different loads, the evidence of the increasing agriculture of the country above, and more than all, the immense distances which they have already come, and those which they have still to go, afforded to me copious sources of meditation. You can name no point from the numerous rivers of the Ohio and the Mississippi, from which some of these boats have not come. In one place there are boats loaded with planks, from the pine forests of the southwest of New York. In another quarter there are the Yankee notions of Ohio. From Kentucky, pork, flour, whiskey, hemp, tobacco, bagging, and bale-rope. From Tennessee there are the same articles, together with great quantities of cotton. From Missouri and Illinois, cattle and horses, the same articles generally as from Ohio, together with peltry and lead from Missouri. Some boats are loaded with corn in the ear and in bulk; others with barrels of apples and potatoes. Some have loads of cider, and what they call "cider royal," or cider that has been strengthened by boiling or freezing. There are dried fruits, every kind of spirits manufactured in these regions, and in short, the products of the ingenuity and agriculture of the whole upper country of the west. They have come from regions, thousands of miles apart. They have floated to a common point of union. The surfaces of the boats cover some acres. Dunghill fowls are fluttering over the roofs, as an invariable appendage. The chanticleer raises his piercing note. The swine utter their cries. The cattle low. The horses trample, as in their stables. There are boats fitted on purpose, and loaded entirely with turkeys, that, having little else to do, gobble most furiously. The hands travel about from boat to boat, making inquiries, and acquaintances, and form alliances to yield mutual assistance to each other, on their descent from this to New Orleans. After an hour or two passed in this way, they spring on shore to raise the wind in town. It is well for the people of the village, if they do not become riotous in the course of the evening; in which case I have often seen the most summary and strong measures taken. About midnight the uproar is all hushed. The fleet unites once more at Natchez, or New Orleans, and, although they live on the same river, they may, perhaps, never meet each other again on the earth. . . .

While I was at New Madrid, a large tinner's establishment floated there in a boat. In it all the different articles of tin-ware were manufactured and sold by wholesale and retail. There were three large apartments, where the different branches of the art were carried on in this floating manufactory. When they had mended all the tin, and vended all that they could sell in one place, they floated on to another. A still more extraordinary manufactory, we were told,

166

was floating down the Ohio, and shortly expected at New Madrid. Aboard this were manufactured axes, scythes, and all other iron tools of this description, and in it horses were shod. In short it was a complete blacksmith's shop of a higher order, and it is said that they jestingly talked of having a trip-hammer worked by a horse power on board. I have frequently seen in this region a dry goods shop in a boat, with its articles very handsomely arranged on shelves. Nor would the delicate hands of the vender have disgraced the spruce clerk behind our city counters. It is now common to see flat-boats worked by a bucket wheel, and a horse power, after the fashion of steam-boat movement. Indeed, every spring brings forth new contrivances of this sort, the result of the farmer's meditations over his winter's fire.

Timothy Flint
Recollections of the Last Ten Years, 1826

Any description of Western roads of the early nineteenth century explains why the rivers were so important for travel and commerce. Fortescue Cuming, who made his journey through the West in 1807–9, describes a stream crossing in Ohio on Zane's Trace. The trace was one of the famous roads of the early frontier, although it was no more than a trail wide enough for a horse— there was not then a wagon road anywhere west of the Appalachians. In another excerpt, a Scottish civil engineer gives some idea of land travel in 1837, when wagon roads were beginning to traverse the new country.

After getting safely through the plains, and a mile further over a ridge, I came to Will's creek, which is a small muddy river with a slow current. The banks are steep and the bottom muddy, so that it has to be crossed by a wooden bridge, which has become extremely dangerous, from some of the posts having been unplaced by floods, so that it is shelving, one side being a good deal higher than the other, and the balustrade is so much decayed that it would not support a man, much less a carriage, yet bad as it was, I had to pay a toll of an eighth of a dollar for my horse.

Fortescue Cuming
Sketches of a Tour to the Western Country, 1810

On the road leading from Pittsburg on the Ohio to the town of Erie on the lake of that name, I saw all the varieties of forest road-making in great perfection. Sometimes our way lay for miles through extensive marshes, which we crossed by corduroy-roads, formed [of logs] . . . cut in lengths of about ten or twelve feet, and laid close to each other across the road, to prevent vehicles from sinking . . . at others the coach stuck fast in mud, from which it could be extricated only by the combined efforts of the coachman and passengers; and at one place we travelled for upwards of a quarter of a mile through a forest flooded with water, which stood to the height of several feet on many of the trees, and occasionally covered the naves of the coach-wheels. The distance of the route from Pittsburg to Erie is 128 miles, which was accomplished in forty-six hours, being at the very slow rate of about two miles and three quar-

A double-cabined flatboat of 1829

167

ters an hour, although the conveyance by which I travelled carried the mail, and stopped only for breakfast, dinner, and tea, but there was considerable delay caused by the coach being once upset and several times "mired."

David Stevenson
Sketch of the Civil Engineering of North America, 1838

In the autumn of 1811 the first steamboat on a Western river, the New Orleans, started down the Ohio and reached New Orleans in January. The era of steamboating had begun. The flatboats did not disappear—hundreds of them drifted down the river each year for decades carrying bulk freight— but with steam power men at last had a means of traveling with ease against the current. By 1860 there were more than a thousand steamboats on the Mississippi and the Ohio and a large number on the various tributaries, and in the competition for elegance and passengers, some had become floating palaces, towering wedding cakes of wooden scrollwork. In legend they were pleasure domes, but the following accounts, one by Timothy Flint, the other by naturalist-artist John James Audubon, show that the quality of service differed.

A stranger to this mode of travelling, would find it difficult to describe his impression upon first descending the Mississippi in one of the better steamboats. He contemplates the prodigious establishment, with all its fitting of deck, common, and ladies' cabin apartments. Over head, about him and below him, all is life and movement. He sees its splendid cabin, richly carpeted, its finishings of mahogany, its mirrors and fine furniture, its bar-room, and sliding tables, to which eighty passengers can sit down with comfort. The fare is sumptuous, and everything in a style of splendour, order, quiet, and regularity, far exceeding that of taverns in general. You read, you converse, you walk, you sleep, as you choose; for custom has prescribed that everything shall be "sans cérémonie." The varied and verdant scenery shifts around you. . . . At other times you are sweeping along for many leagues together, where either shore is boundless and pathless wilderness. And the contrast, which is thus so strongly forced upon the mind, of the highest improvement and the latest invention of art, with the most lonely aspect of a grand but desolate nature,—the most striking and complete assemblage of splendour and comfort, the cheerfulness of a floating hotel, which carries, perhaps, two hundred guests, with a wild and uninhabitable forest, one hundred miles in width, the abode only of owls, bears, and noxious animals,—this strong contrast produces, to me at least, something of the same pleasant sensation that is produced by lying down to sleep with the rain pouring on the roof, immediately overhead.

Timothy Flint
Recollections of the Last Ten Years, 1826

The weather has been bad ever since we left Baltimore. . . . We first encountered ice at Wheeling, and it has floated down the Ohio all around us, as well as up the Mississippi to pleasant St. Louis. And such a steamer as we have

A coach has trouble fording a stream during high water

A side-wheeler docks at the mouth of the Mobile.

come in from Louisville here!—the very filthiest of all filthy old rat-traps I ever travelled in; and the fare worse, certainly much worse, and so scanty withal that our worthy commander could not have given us another meal had we been detained a night longer. I wrote a famous long letter to my Lucy on the subject, and as I know you will hear it, will not repeat the account of our situation on board the "Gallant"—a pretty name, too, but alas! her name, like mine, is only a shadow, for as she struck a sawyer one night we all ran like mad to make ready to leap overboard; but as God would have it, our lives and the "Gallant"—were spared—she from sinking, and we from swimming amid rolling and crashing hard ice. THE LADIES screamed, the babies squalled, the dogs yelled, the steam roared, the captain (who, by the way, is a very gallant man) swore—not like an angel, but like the very devil—and all was confusion and uproar, just as if Miller's prophecy had actually been nigh. Luckily, we had had our *supper*, as the thing was called on board the *"Gallant,"* and every man appeared to feel resolute, if not resolved to die.

I would have given much at that moment for a picture of the whole. Our *compagnons de voyage*, about one hundred and fifty, were composed of Buckeyes, Wolverines, Suckers, Hoosiers, and gamblers, with drunkards of each and every denomination, their ladies and babies of the same nature, and specifically the dirtiest of the dirty. We had to dip the water for washing from the river in tin basins, soap ourselves all from the same cake, and wipe the one hundred and fifty with the same solitary one towel rolling over a pin, until it would have been difficult to say, even with your keen eyes, whether it was manufactured of hemp, tow, flax, or cotton. My bed had two sheets, of course, measuring seven-eights of a yard wide; my pillow was filled with cornshucks. Harris faired even worse than I, and our "state-room" was evidently better fitted for the smoking of hams than the smoking of Christians. When it rained outside, it rained also within, and on one particular morning, when the snow melted on the upper deck, or roof, it was a lively scene to see each person seeking for a spot free from the many spouts overhead.

John James Audubon
Letter to James Hall, March 29, 1843

A river steamboat was not the safest means of traveling from place to place. Michael Chevalier, a Frenchman who visited the United States in 1833–35, was another of the seeming multitude of Europeans who came to see the American West. He was appalled by the perils of steamboat travel.

Besides, the voyage on the Mississippi is more dangerous than a passage across the ocean; I do not mean merely from the United States to Europe, but from Europe to China. In the former, you are exposed to the risk of explosions, and of fire, and in ascending, to that of running against snags and planters. Then there is the danger of your boat falling afoul of another, running in an opposite direction, in a fog, to say nothing of the inconvenience of getting aground on sand-bars. . . . Explosions of the boilers are frequent, either on account of the ignorance and want of skill of the engineers, or on account of the defective nature of the boilers themselves, and they are always attended with serious injury, because the boats are so much crowded with passengers. A few days ago, sixty persons were killed and wounded aboard a single boat. . . .

There have been many accidents by fire in the steamers, and many persons have perished in this way, although the river is not very wide. The Brandywine was burnt near Memphis, in 1832, and every soul on board, to the number of 110, was lost. The Americans show a singular indifference in regard to fires, not only in the steamboats, but also in their houses; they smoke without the least concern in the midst of the half open cotton-bales, with which a boat is loaded; they ship gunpowder with no more precaution than if it were so much maize or salt pork. . . .

. . . so much the worse for those who perish in the steamboats! The essential point is not to save some individuals or even some hundreds; but, in respect to steamers, that they should be numerous; staunch or not, well commanded or not, it matters little, if they move at a rapid rate, and are navigated at little expense. The circulation of steamboats is as necessary to the West, as that of the blood is to the human system.

Michael Chevalier
Society, Manners and Politics in the United States, 1839

The Mississippi River was too huge, too wild, too elemental, for the tastes of most European visitors. English author Charles Dickens expresses a reaction to the mighty stream that was quite common among foreigners.

But what words shall describe the Mississippi, great father of rivers, who (praise be to Heaven) has no young children like him! An enormous ditch, sometimes two or three miles wide, running liquid mud, six miles an hour: its strong and frothy current choked and obstructed everywhere by huge logs and whole forest trees: now twining themselves together in great rafts, from the interstices of which a sedgy lazy foam works up, to float upon the water's top; now rolling past like monstrous bodies, their tangled roots showing like matted hair; now glancing singly by like giant leeches; and now writhing round and round in the vortex of some small whirlpool, like wounded snakes. The banks low, the trees dwarfish, the marshes swarming with frogs, the wretched cabins few and far apart, their inmates hollow-cheeked and pale, the weather very hot, mosquitoes penetrating into every crack and crevice of the boat, mud and slime on everything: nothing pleasant in its aspect, but the harmless lightning which flickers every night upon the dark horizon.

Charles Dickens
American Notes, 1842

Though foreign visitors may have been repelled by the Mississippi, Western Americans looked on it and its tributaries as one of the most important facts of their existence, the highway system that tied the great central valley

You see, this has got to be learned; there isn't any getting around it. A clear starlight night throws such heavy shadows that if you didn't know the shape of a shore perfectly you would claw away from every bunch of timber because you would take the black shadow of it for a solid cape; and you see you would be getting scared to death every fifteen minutes by the watch. You would be fifty yards from shore all the time when you ought to be within fifty feet of it. You can't see a snag in one of those shadows, but you know exactly where it is, and the shape of the river tells you when you are coming to it. Then there's your pitch-dark night; the river is a very different shape on a pitch-dark night from what it is on a starlight night. All shores seem to be straight lines, then, and mighty dim ones, too; and you'd *run* them for straight lines only you know better. You boldly drive your boat right into what seems to be a solid, straight wall (you knowing very well that in reality there is a curve there) and that wall falls back and makes way for you. Then there's your gray mist. You take a night when there's one of these grisly, drizzly, gray mists, and then there isn't *any* particular shape to a shore. A gray mist would tangle the head of the oldest man that ever lived. Well, then, different kinds of *moonlight* change the shape of the river in different ways. . . . You only learn the shape of the river; and you learn it with such absolute certainty that you can always steer by the shape that's *in your head* and never mind the one that's before your eyes.

Mark Twain
Life on the Mississippi, 1883

From Harper's, 1858, *some Western steamboating perils: hitting a snag, going aground, rushing down a rapids*

The frontier promised cheap land and independence. To the firstcomers it meant backache and often heartbreak. Morris Birkbeck in 1817 visits a backwood family in the wilderness beyond the frontier in Illinois and comments, as other travelers had, on the pallor of dwellers in the sunless, deep woods.

Wandering without track, where even the sagacity of our hunter-guide had nearly failed us, we at length arrived at the cabin of another hunter, where we lodged.

This man and his family are remarkable instances of the effect on the complexion produced by the perpetual incarceration of a thorough woodland life. Incarceration may seem to be a term less applicable to the condition of a roving back-woodsman than to any other, and especially unsuitable to the habits of this individual and his family; for the cabin in which he entertained us is the third dwelling he has built within the last twelve months; and a very slender motive would place him in a fourth before the ensuing winter. In his general habits the hunter ranges as freely as the beasts he pursues; labouring under no restraint, his activity is only bounded by his own physical powers:

still he is incarcerated—"Shut from the common air." Buried in the depth of a boundless forest, the breeze of health never reaches these poor wanderers; the bright prospect of distant hills fading away into the semblance of clouds, never cheered their sight: they are tall and pale, like vegetables that grow in a vault, pining for light.

The man, his pregnant wife, his eldest son, a tall half-naked youth, just initiated in the hunters' arts, his three daughters, growing up into great rude girls, and a squalling tribe of dirty brats of both sexes, are of one pale yellow, without the slightest tint of healthful bloom.

In passing through a vast expanse of the backwoods I have been so much struck with this effect, that I fancy I could determine the colour of the inhabitants if I was apprised of the depth of their immersion; and, *vice versa*, I could judge of the extent of the "clearing" if I saw the people.

Morris Birkbeck
Notes on a Journey in America, 1818

English authoress Frances Trollope had almost nothing good to say about anything American, and her word picture of woodcutters living in the swampy wilderness along the Mississippi may have been drawn in the worst possible colors. In the main, however, it agrees with that of other observers.

But still from time to time appeared the hut of the woodcutter, who supplies the steamboats with fuel, at the risk or rather with the assurance of early death, in exchange for dollars and whiskey. These sad dwellings are nearly all of them inundated during the winter, and the best of them are constructed on piles, which permit the water to reach its highest level without drowning the wretched inhabitants. These unhappy beings are invariably the victims of ague, which they meet recklessly, sustained by the incessant use of ardent spirits. The squalid look of the miserable wives and children of these men was dreadful, and often as the spectacle was renewed I could never look at it with indifference. Their complexion is of a bluish white, that suggests the idea of dropsy; this is invariable, and the poor little ones wear exactly the same ghastly hue. A miserable cow and a few pigs standing knee-deep in water, distinguish the more prosperous of these dwellings, and on the whole I should say that I never witnessed human nature reduced so low, as it appeared in the woodcutters' huts on the unwholesome banks of the Mississippi.

Frances Trollope
Domestic Manners of the Americans, 1832

If the deep forest was gloomy, the first clearings were bleak and desolate. The British Captain Basil Hall, who visited the frontier regions in 1827–28, gives his impression of the first openings made by settlers.

The cleared spaces, however, as they are called, looked to our eyes not less desolate, being studded over with innumerable great black stumps; or, which was more deplorable still, with tall scorched, branchless stems of trees, which

172

Top, girdling and burning trees for a clearing
Right, pioneer diversion in Missouri in 1820

had undergone the barbarous operation known by the name of girdling. An American settler can hardly conceive the horror with which a foreigner beholds such numbers of magnificent trees standing round him with their throats cut, the very Banquos of the murdered forest! The process of girdling is this: a circular cut or ring, two or three inches deep, is made with an axe quite round the tree at about five feet from the ground. This, of course, puts an end to vegetable life; and the destruction of the tree being accelerated by the action of fire, these wretched trunks in a year or two present the most miserable objects of decrepitude that can be conceived. The purpose, however, of the farmer is gained, and that is all he can be expected to look to. His corn crop is no longer overshadowed by the leaves of these unhappy trees, which in process of time, are cut down and split into railings, or sawed into billets of firewood,—and their misery is at an end.

Even in the cultivated fields, the tops of the stumps were seen poking their black snouts above the young grain, like a shoal of seals. Not a single hedge or wall was to be seen in those places, all the enclosures being made of split logs, built one upon the top of another in a zig-zag fashion, like what the ladies call a Vandyke border. These are named snake fences, and are certainly the most ungraceful-looking things I ever saw.

Basil Hall
Travels in North America, 1829

Frontier settlements were rude and unpolished. When they happened to be river towns, they were usually rowdy as well, and often lawless. Charles A. Murray, who took time off in 1834–36 from his duties as master of the household to the queen to see America—including a summer spent with the Pawnee Indians—was repelled by Keokuk, Iowa, and some of its citizens.

This village of Keokuk is the lowest and most blackguard place that I have yet visited: its population is composed chiefly of the watermen who assist in loading and unloading the keel-boats, and in towing them up when the rapids are too strong for the steam-engines. They are a coarse and ferocious caricature of the London bargemen, and their chief occupation seems to consist in drinking, fighting, and gambling. One fellow, who was half drunk, (or, in western language, "corned,") was relating with great satisfaction how he had hid himself in a wood that skirted the road, and (in time of peace) had shot an unsuspecting and inoffensive Indian, who was passing with a wild turkey over his shoulder: he concluded by saying, that he had thrown the body into a thicket, and had taken the bird home for his own dinner. He seemed quite proud of this exploit, and said that he would as soon shoot an Indian as a fox or an otter. I thought he was only making an idle boast; but some of the bystanders assured me it was a well-known fact, and yet he had never been either tried or punished. This murderer is called a Christian, and his victim a heathen!

Charles Augustus Murray
Travels in North America, 1839

St. Louis in 1835 was no longer a frontier village—in fact, it was then seventy-one years old. Nevertheless, it was still rough and unfinished enough to offend Captain Frederick Marryat's English sensibilities. The town could hardly be blamed for the heat and humidity, which still afflict St. Louis in mid-summer, but the squalor was typical of the West, where men found it more important to keep moving and expanding than to tidy up what had already been done.

In point of heat, St. Louis certainly approaches the nearest to the Black Hole of Calcutta of any city that I have sojourned in. The lower part of the town is badly drained, and very filthy. The flies, on a moderate calculation, are in many parts fifty to the square inch. I wonder that they have not a contagious disease here during the whole summer; it is, however, indebted to heavy rains for its occasional purification. They have not the yellow-fever here; but during the autumn they have one which, under another name, is almost as fatal—the bilious congestive fever. I found sleep almost impossible from the sultriness of the air, and used to remain at the open window for the greater part of the night. I did not expect that the muddy Mississippi would be able to reflect the silver light of the moon; yet it did, and the effect was very beautiful. Truly it may be said of this river, as it is of many ladies, that it is a candlelight beauty. There is another serious evil to which strangers who sojourn here are subject —the violent effects of the waters of the Mississippi upon those who are not used to them. The suburbs of the town are very pretty; and a few miles behind it you are again in a charming prairie country, full of game, large and small. Large and small are only so by comparison. An American was asked what game they had in his district? and his reply was, "Why, we've plenty of *baar* (bear) and deer, but no *large* game to count on."

. . . Thank Heaven I have escaped from St. Louis; during the time that I remained in that city, I was, day and night, so melting away, that I expected, like some of the immortal half-breeds of Jupiter, to become a tributary stream to the Mississippi.

Frederick Marryat
A Diary in America, 1839

Two English commentators on America: Frances Trollope (an American impression) and Frederick Marryat. Opposite, bottom, the village of Piqua, Ohio, on the Miami River

Frances Trollope, with her anti-American bias, complained bitterly of the barbarous table manners of Westerners. However, many other Europeans remarked with just as much distaste as Mrs. Trollope on the tobacco chewing and incessant spitting they found everywhere.

The total want of all the usual courtesies of the table, the voracious rapidity with which the viands were seized and devoured; the strange uncouth phrases and pronunciation; the loathsome spitting, from the contamination of which it was absolutely impossible to protect our dresses; the frightful manner of feeding with their knives, till the whole blade seemed to enter into the mouth; and the still more frightful manner of cleaning the teeth afterward with a pocket knife, soon forced us to feel that we were not surrounded by the generals, colonels, and majors of the old world; and that the dinner hour was to be any thing rather than an hour of enjoyment.

Frances Trollope
Domestic Manners of the Americans, 1832

John Mason Peck, who wrote a guide for those planning to settle in the West, disagreed with Mrs. Trollope's low opinion of the frontier American. Accept the Westerner on his own roughhewn terms, he advised.

The characteristic property of our western population, is blunt, unaffected hospitality. They will make every stranger welcome, provided he will accept of it in their own way. . . . Enter whatever house or cabin you may, if it is the time of meals, you are invited to share a portion; but you must eat what is set before you, asking no questions, and making no invidious comparisons. Nor must you offer remarks on the accommodations you have had, or the unpleasant things you may have encountered at other places where you have tarried, as such remarks are considered as reflections upon the people, and those by whom you are now hospitably entertained will infer that you will thus slander them when you have departed.

John Mason Peck
A Guide for Emigrants, 1831

American pioneering experience since the beginning had been gained in the deep forest; the frontier economy was based on having plenty of wood for fuel, houses, fences, tools and implements. The first pioneers in Illinois avoided the rich, treeless prairies and settled in the wooded river valleys. In 1820 Major Stephen Long crossed the Great Plains, and three years later published a report that created the legend of the Great American Desert.

In regard to this extensive section of the country, I do not hesitate in giving the opinion, that it is almost wholly unfit for cultivation, and of course, uninhabitable by a people depending on agriculture for their subsistence. . . . This region, however, viewed as a frontier, may prove of infinite importance to the United States, inasmuch as it is calculated to serve as a barrier to prevent too great an expansion of our population westward, and secure us against the machinations or incursions of an enemy that might otherwise be disposed to annoy us in that part of the frontier.

Major Stephen Long
Report, 1823

Jackson and the Common Man

*I*f the presidential election of 1824 had been decided by popular vote, General Jackson would have been elected by a large plurality over any of his three opponents. Though no one really knew the run of his opinions, men saw and hailed the victor of New Orleans as the one military hero of an unheroic war, as the People's Friend. While Jefferson had appealed to the ordinary man, Jackson spoke to the frontiersman, to the dispossessed, to those with real or fancied grievances. When he talked of "the people," everyone knew that he was not referring to Boston merchants or Virginia squires but to farmers, mechanics, miners, rivermen, and sailors.

Yet this spokesman of the people was an aristocrat—if of the raffish recent variety that had emerged on the frontier—a Tennessee planter living on his acres above the Cumberland River in his fine brick house with his slaves and his racing stables. As a general he had been the strictest disciplinarian since Von Steuben. His appeal was that of a man of action. He felt before he thought. Men knew that he would fight a duel at the drop of a loose word, that he bore a dueling bullet in his body, that for all the mahogany and silver of his Hermitage, his wife still smoked a clay pipe. The dynastic Virginians were men apart. Any man might measure himself against Jackson. Any man in that fluid society might feel hopeful of attaining such a high house by the river. If Jackson was not the common man, he was the common man's ideal.

Jackson's father had been a Scotch-Irish tenant farmer who had emigrated from the north of Ireland to the "Garden of the Waxhaws," the upland frontier region of the Carolinas. On Ligget's Branch of Twelve Mile Creek the elder Jackson, with his wife and two children, staked out two hundred acres of thin red soil. Then in 1767, the month before his son Andrew was born, he died. Nevertheless the Jacksons held their own, respectable and respected among the settlers of that rough community. Andy was the bright boy of the local church-school, reddish-haired, freckled, thin, impetuous. Unfortunately he could not control his "slobbering," but at any mention of it he fought. As a desultory schoolboy during the Revolution he was profane, pugnacious, reckless as a rider and with his fists, and more interested in horses and cockfighting

A leader of strong prejudices and uncompromising character, Andrew Jackson stepped down hard on institutions and causes of which he disapproved. This poster for the presidential campaign of 1832 features a paternal candidate whose greatest political asset was his appeal to the Common Man.

than in grammar. When Philadelphia papers arrived at the Waxhaws with news of the Revolution, he was often selected as the public reader. Shrill-voiced, he "could read a paper clear through without getting hoarse . . . [or] stopping to spell out the words."

It was inevitable that he would join the Continental Army, the more so because a family friend, Robert Crawford, was serving as a major. At the age of thirteen, with his sixteen-year-old brother, Robert, he joined up. He was taken prisoner; an arrogant British officer ordered the boy to clean his boots and on his refusal struck at him with his sword. Andy raised his hand to ward off the blow. The blade cut to the bone, then glanced aside and laid open his head. The white scar that remained would serve as a token of Jackson's hatred for England as long as he lived.

At fifteen, his mother having died of typhus, he went to stay with Major Crawford, where his preoccupations are said to have been horse racing, cockfighting, and gambling. Finally Crawford apprenticed him to a saddler. Then a grandfather in Ireland left him a legacy of several hundred pounds, and while money lasted he lived in postwar Charleston as a horseman and a gambler. When out of funds he taught school, then moved on to Salisbury, North Carolina, where he mingled with the town's elite and read law. In Salisbury he was long remembered as "the most roaring, rollicking, game-cocking, horse-racing, card-playing mischievous fellow that ever lived in Salisbury." Nevertheless he found time to pass his law examination and was admitted to practice before he was old enough to vote.

North Carolina then extended to the Mississippi, and its Western District, that vague area beyond the reaches of civilization, drew him. When his friend John McNairy, with whom he had studied law in Salisbury, was elected judge of the Western District's superior court, McNairy appointed Andy his public prosecutor.

With Bacon's *Abridgement of the Law* and a Negro girl he had bought for two hundred dollars, Jackson set out for the West in 1788. Crossing the Blue Ridge, moving through the almost state of Franklin, lingering at Jonesborough, in September Jackson and McNairy joined the first caravan over the new Nashville Road. They reached the Cumberland River settlement—two taverns, two stores, a distillery, a broken-down courthouse, and a fringe of cabins—that was Nashville on October 26, 1788. A rough fence, meant to keep out stray buffalo, still surrounded the settlement.

Nashville at the time of Jackson's arrival was a town of and for debtors. Within a month the young prosecutor changed all that, enforcing seventy writs of execution. Creditors and property owners were delighted, and clients flocked to him. Though money was scarce, land was cheap, and Andy found himself a landowner before he knew it. Most of his fees went into deals in land and slaves. He boarded at the Widow Donelson's blockhouse across the river and ten miles down the Kentucky Road from Nashville, a twice-daily ride that would have been tedious if it had not been for the landlady's dark-eyed, full-lipped daughter Rachel Donelson Robards. The dimpled, pipe-smoking Rachel managed to infuriate her jealous husband by her casual manner of fascinating men, not the least of them being Andrew Jackson. Her married life was a succession of quarrels. In 1790 she went to Kentucky with Robards following a reconciliation, but the harmony was brief and she sent an unhappy letter home. Jackson appeared and took her home, with the approval of the Donelson tribe. When the aggrieved Robards showed up in Nashville, Jackson threatened to cut off his ears. Robards thereupon petitioned the Virginia legislature—Kentucky was not yet a state—for permission to sue for divorce.

After her flight Rachel went on to Spanish Natchez. During the Confederation, and even afterward, the trans-Appalachian region had shown a preference for Spain as the controller of the Mississippi, and there were American settlers on the Cumberland who would have been content even to see the whole area drift into the Spanish orbit. The young Jackson, his feelings toward the Spanish not yet having hardened, had built a log house and a trading post at Bayou Pierre, on the Mississippi thirty miles above Natchez, where he planned to sell slaves and supplies to the wealthier American settlers. On learning of the divorce proceedings, he followed Rachel to Natchez. In August, 1791, they were married in the columned brick mansion Springfield, belonging to a friend and slave customer of Jackson's. The twenty-four-year-old couple spent their honeymoon at Bayou Pierre, on a high bluff overlooking the great river, unaware that Robards had let his divorce action lapse.

Jackson brought his bride back to Poplar Grove, a plantation he had bought from Rachel's brother John Donelson. Settled in his new home, he traded in cotton, slaves, horses, land. His clients increased in number, and he was constantly at court in Nashville and Jones-

Typical of the pioneers who poured from the Carolinas and Virginia into the frontier West was this emigrating North Carolina family, portrayed by James Beard.

borough. The rising young planter-lawyer seemed far more interested in wealth and position at this time than in politics. When the territory became a state, he is said to have proposed its name, Tennessee. John Sevier, who had once ruled the outlawed state of Franklin, became its first governor, while Jackson was named its first representative in Congress. From the opening of the session in December, 1796, the urbane Gallatin remembered Jackson as a "tall, lanky, uncouth-looking personage . . . queue down his back tied with an eelskin . . . dress singular . . . manners those of a rough backwoodsman."

Jackson refused another term, but when Tennessee's Senator William Blount was expelled for "a high misdemeanor," he took Blount's place in the United States Senate, only to relinquish it not long afterward because

of financial difficulties. Although Jackson himself was fiercely honest, his business affairs soared and sagged with all the varying fortunes of a speculator. He built a new house for his "little Rachael" at Hunter's Hill, then was forced to sell it and move to a blockhouse on a six-hundred-and-forty-acre tract that he had acquired in his earlier land hunger. But for the luck of his race horse, Truxton, he might have gone to jail as a debtor.

After his term in the Senate, he became, in 1798, a justice of the state superior court, really a supreme court. On the bench Justice Jackson was quick, impatient of legal subtleties, belligerently fair. Yet even his judge's robes did not prevent his challenging Sevier to a duel after the governor had referred sneeringly to "a trip to Natchez with another man's wife." Jackson had gone through the legal forms of a second marriage in

179

A few of the activities of the Common Man
are depicted by three American artists: above,
David Blythe, noted for his satiric painting,
mocks a country lawyer and his comatose jury;
below, George Bingham illustrates a political discussion at the grass-roots level; at right,
cider makers pausing to savor their prod-
uct are portrayed by William Sidney Mount.

*As an artist-scientist with Major Stephen Long's 1819–20
expedition to the Rocky Mountains, Titian R. Peale
made this water-color sketch of the Missouri River at sunset. At right are his drawings of a burrowing owl
and a cliff swallow (top)—both Western birds—along
with the mud nests of the latter. Major Long pessi-
mistically reported that east of the Rockies lay a "great
American desert," useful only as a protective frontier.*

1794, but it had been a humiliation for Rachel. Her
deepest sorrow, however, was that she was barren. She
filled her house with other people's children, brought
up children of friends and relatives as if they were her
own, and finally adopted her brother's infant son, giving the baby her husband's name.

In 1802 the field officers of the Tennessee militia
elected Judge Jackson their major general, an office on
which the martial Sevier had set his heart. Not until the
War of 1812 did Jackson become a major general of volunteers, and not until after the Battle of New Orleans,
when he became a major general in the regular
United States Army, was he *the* General. By the time
Jackson left on his Florida expedition, even Rachel
was referring to him by his military title.

182

Returning from Florida, weakened by dysentery but triumphing over Clay's attack on his conduct of the war, he built a rectangular brick house to replace the Hermitage blockhouse. The rise in the price of cotton and tobacco brought him an unwonted, if temporary, prosperity. Something of the grace of the Tidewater was coming to the Cumberland as the frontier moved on. By 1821 Nashville had a theater and street lamps and the city owned fifty slaves to keep the streets tidy.

The 1819 Panic found Jackson deep in speculation. A single court action had him suing one hundred and twenty-nine of his debtors. When Monroe offered him the governorship of newly acquired Florida, he took it reluctantly and over Rachel's objections. Another governor might have relaxed in Pensacola while awaiting congressional approval for the implementation of American government in the territory. But not Andrew Jackson! While Rachel was learning to smoke Spanish cigars, he was shutting down gambling houses, closing shops and bazaars on Sunday, even arresting the former Spanish governor—who had stayed on as his king's commissioner—and throwing him in jail overnight. John Quincy Adams, in the State Department, came to dread the arrival of the Florida mail, for he never knew what the impetuous Jackson might be up to next.

The thought of that unpredictable man of the people, General Jackson, and Rachel—grown stout with the years—in the President's House was enough to trouble the sleep of any conservative. Polite eyes looked wistfully toward Adams, who as Secretary of State was occupying the office that had come to seem the final step in the succession to the Presidency. One could scarcely imagine the scholarly Adams on a dueling field or charging through a tavern with a horsewhip or risking what was left of his fortune on a horse race. Yet, for all their differences in temperament, background, and upbringing, Adams supported and defended Jackson in his truculent nationalism. One fundamental article of faith brought the disparate men together—their belief in the independence and unity of the United States.

No American of John Quincy Adams' day had seen as much of the world, and of history and the men who made it, as he had. As a little boy he had watched the far-off cannon flash from the Battle of Bunker Hill. At ten he had accompanied his father on a mission to France and had then spent seven years in Europe. As a young man he had gone, as a secretary, with Francis Dana on his mission to St. Petersburg. He spoke French fluently and understood Italian and Dutch and German. He knew the courts of Europe and the great cities— Paris, London, St. Petersburg, the Hague, Berlin. In 1794, when he was twenty-six, Washington made him minister to the Netherlands. In 1803 the Federalist Massachusetts legislature sent him to the United States Senate, where he served until 1807, when he broke with his party over its opposition to Jefferson's embargo. But an Adams was always an Adams first and a party member second, and old John, in his retirement, did not disapprove when his son became a Republican.

In 1809 Madison appointed the younger Adams minister to Russia. At the negotiations leading to the Peace of Ghent he acted as the chief of the American commission. He served as minister to Great Britain from 1815 to 1817, when Monroe called him home to make him Secretary of State in order to balance his Cabinet with a New Englander. A short, plump man, growing bald, a classicist and a scholar, Adams had been among other things Boylston professor of rhetoric and oratory at Harvard and might have become president of the college if he had not become President of his country. He is probably the greatest diplomatist that the United States has ever produced.

For Adams 1824 was his year of opportunity. To become President had long been his deepest wish, as it had been his father's ambition for him ever since he was a boy. Jackson had no further ambition than to live out his years at the Hermitage. "I have no desire, nor do I expect ever to be called to fill the Presidential chair," he declared, "but should this be the case, contrary to my wishes or expectations, I am determined it shall be without any exertion on my part." The General's friends, willing to make the exertions for him, in 1823 sent him back to the battlefield of the United States Senate for the political seasoning that was so important to a presidential candidate.

The 1824 election was a singular one—without an opposition party, without an issue (in regard to slavery even Adams stood mute), without a campaign, with nothing but presidential candidates eager to fill Monroe's shoes. Earlier there had been seventeen, but as the election month neared, they were whittled down to five. Henry Clay, brilliant and burning for power, found himself again in the strategic position of Speaker of the House. Calhoun concealed his burning ambition from his friend Adams. The devious Secretary of the Treasury, Crawford, controller of patronage, whom Monroe had once threatened with a pair of fire tongs, was the Virginia dynastic choice. Though detested by Monroe, though ailing and his mind uncertain after a stroke, he was endorsed by Jefferson and Madison.

In February a congressional caucus nominated Crawford for President and Gallatin for Vice President. But the days of selecting in this manner were waning, and only sixty-six congressmen showed up at the caucus. A country-wide outcry resulted. If there was any issue in the campaign beyond personalities, it was that of the caucus system. In March a nominating convention at Harrisburg, Pennsylvania, defied the system by choosing Jackson, with Calhoun as his running mate. By accepting, Calhoun eliminated himself from the race for the higher office. At a meeting in Boston's Faneuil Hall, Adams was chosen as the candidate of Massachusetts and soon received the backing of the rest of New England. Clay, the candidate of the West, had his chief strength in Kentucky, Ohio, and Missouri.

For all its lack of party differences and issues, the campaign was fiercely partisan. With each state having its own election day, anywhere from October 29 to November 22, the results were not known until December. Jackson—the predicted winner—had 99 electoral votes, with 84 for Adams, 41 for Crawford, and 37 for Clay. Since Jackson lacked 32 of the votes necessary for a majority, the election moved to the House of Representatives, where, according to the Constitution, each state would be allowed one vote. Although too low in the electoral scale to be further considered as a candidate, Clay, with the votes of three states secure in his pocket, was seen as the President maker.

In the House Jackson controlled the votes of eleven states—two short of the necessary majority—while Adams controlled seven, and Crawford and Clay each three. Adams had the choice of following the obvious will of the people and throwing his votes to Jackson, or maneuvering to have himself elected as a minority President. He chose the latter way. To win he would need not only the support of Clay's three states but also that of three more states. Clay was in the flattering position of being solicited from all sides. In a long private conversation with Adams he promised to support the New Englander. Though Adams' voluminous diary is for once silent, the implication is that in return Clay was offered Adams' old post as Secretary of State.

The two months before the election was a period of backstairs bargaining, dealing, and maneuvering. The austere and withdrawn Adams suddenly became a convivial glad-hander, dropping in at boardinghouses and hotels to call on obscure congressmen, cultivating members. Balloting took place on a snowy February afternoon in 1825. Thirteen states voted for Adams, including those of Clay and three more that had somehow been lured from the Jackson camp. Adams was elected on the first ballot, with Calhoun—the choice of the Jacksonians and the Adamites as well—as Vice President. "So you see the *Judas* of the West has closed the contract and will receive the thirty pieces of silver," Jackson wrote after learning that Clay would receive the appointment as Secretary of State. "His end will be the same. Was there ever witnessed such a bare-faced corruption?"

Monroe gave his last official levee that evening. Among those present were General Lafayette, as the Nation's Guest; the President-elect and the Vice President-elect; and Clay, the President maker. But all eyes were drawn to the thin martial figure of the Hero of New Orleans as with self-contained courtesy he made his way through the crowd, a lady on his arm. When he came face to face with Adams he hesitated, then gallantly stretched out his hand. "How do you do, Mr. Adams?" he said. "I give you my left hand, for my right as you see is devoted to the fair; I hope you are very well, sir." "Very well, sir," the high-spirited Adams answered. "I hope General Jackson is well."

By the following day, when Daniel Webster and his congressional committee of notification waited on the President-elect, Adams' high spirits had given way to his New England conscience. As he listened to Webster's sonorous voice announcing that on March 4 he, John Quincy Adams, would be the next President of the United States, he trembled all over and sweat rolled down his face. He chose to reply not in words but in writing, and in the privacy of his diary he admitted that the election had not taken place in "a manner satisfactory to pride or just desire; not by the unequivocal suffrages of a majority of the people; with perhaps two-thirds of the whole people adverse to the actual result."

Henry Adams, philosopher of history, reflecting on his grandfather's unfortunate single term, observed: "To me the old gentleman's Presidency appears always as lurid." To Jacksonians, Adams would remain the usurper and Clay his agent. In his inaugural address the new President asked for political magnanimity, a sacrifice of partisan "prejudice and passion." He was to get

184

In this portrait sketch of John Quincy Adams, English-born artist Thomas Sully has captured the introspective, reserved quality of the sixth President, which prevented him from communicating easily with the people.

neither. To carry out his concepts of nationalism and continental expansion, he would need the cooperation of his adversaries. He would not even be able to retain the loyalty of his Vice President.

In a sense the second Adams was a reversion to Federalism. He believed in a strong national government to administer the country's resources and felt that political parties had an unhealthy effect on political life. His first annual message was a singular one for a minority President, an amplification of Clay's American System. "Liberty is power," he told Congress, and he warned of being "palsied by the will of our constituents." He asked for a network of national highways and canals that would bind all sections of the country together, a Department of the Interior to aid in the conserving and developing of the public domain, a national university, a national observatory to emulate the European "light-houses of the skies," a naval academy, exploration of the Pacific Northwest, a uniform national bankruptcy law and a uniform militia law, a uniform system of weights and measures, and improved patent laws.

Adams' demands for internal improvements came at a time when the South was beginning to realize the dangers to its "peculiar institution" of such a pervasive national control. Randolph of Roanoke, swinging his riding whip as he strode down the aisle of the House followed by a small Negro carrying a jug of porter, periodically denounced the President in lacerating terms. Adams had no real leaders in the House or Senate, and Congress paid no attention to his program. Supporters of Jackson, Calhoun, and Crawford began to combine against the President in what came to be called the Democratic-Republican party. Chief manipulator was New York's wily politician Martin Van Buren, successor to Burr as leader of Tammany Hall and a man determined on Adams' ruin. His astute partisan mind

anned the defeat of Adams through a combination of outhern planters and the "plain republicans of the orth." At the mid-term elections the opposition cap- ured the House of Representatives, leaving the Presi- ent politically high and dry for the remaining two ears of his term.

Four months before those elections, on July 4, 1826— he fiftieth anniversary of the signing of the Declaration f Independence—the last flickering ember of the Rev- lution was snuffed out with the death of the two for- er Presidents Adams and Jefferson. Old John Adams, ying in his Quincy mansion, had managed to respond o his fellow townsmen's request for a toast to be used n Independence Day with "Independence Forever!" our days later, on July 4, he had died quietly late in he afternoon, not long after murmuring, "Thomas Jef- erson still survives." Jefferson had died a few hours ear- er at Monticello. Men were awestruck at such an or-

dered turning of the great wheel of fortune—although one inflexible Boston Federalist was convinced that Jef- ferson had taken an overdose of laudanum in order to die on that sacred day. To the religious-minded the double deaths were a sign that Divine Providence still guided the destiny of the republic.

Little of the awe inspired by his father's passing rubbed off on John Quincy Adams. Public opinion, astutely aided by the Van Buren clique, steadily turned against him. The shrill reiteration of "bargain and corruption" managed to convince more and more citi- zens that Adams and Clay had cheated them out of the President of their choice. Adams, for all his trying, lacked the politician's touch. He bothered too much with ad- ministrative details, saw too many cranks, job hunters, favor seekers, and visitors. In opposing Georgia's ef- forts to dispossess the Indians of their remaining lands, he stirred up the states' rights opposition.

American military history shows that local and state militias, unless inspired by brilliant leadership, often fought poorly in battle, and as this David Johnston lithograph suggests, drilled even worse—facts prompting President Adams to recommend an overhaul of the system.
AMERICAN ANTIQUARIAN SOCIETY

Like Clay, Adams favored a protective tariff, and found himself faced in 1828 with what became known as the Tariff of Abominations. Southern agriculturists insisted that the Constitution did not grant the federal government the power to levy a *protective* tariff, that any such tariff would subject them to the economic tyranny of the North. Northerners demanded protection for their new industries. To discredit Adams, Van Buren and his Jacksonian associates concocted such a grotesquely high tariff schedule that even the New England protectionists could scarcely vote for it. With this Tariff of Abominations they hoped to pose as friends of both sides. Unexpectedly the tariff, with its bizarre schedule of duties, did pass both the House and the Senate, leaving the President the dilemma of signing it and alienating the South or vetoing it and strengthening the Jacksonians in the Northeast. Placing the responsibility for the bill on Congress, Adams signed it, signing with it his political extinction in the South.

In March, 1828, Adams was at his writing table in the President's House when the table began to shake, the floor quivered, and the windows rattled. At once he realized that it was an earthquake. The shaking lasted several minutes and was felt from western New York to the Shenandoah Valley. It was like an ancient portent in that election year, the earth shaking under the marching legion of General Jackson.

Adams had a program; Jackson had no more than his Jeffersonian belief in "a plain system, void of pomp, protecting all and granting favors to none." But by 1828 Jackson had become a symbol of change. The population had grown; the qualifications for voting were less severe; ordinary people felt that something was wrong without being able to say what. So feeling, they were more ready to vote *against* Adams than *for* Jackson. Popular discontent focused on the polished, lonely, learned man who had become the personification of the upper classes and snobbery.

From the Republican chrysalis, two new parties were emerging: Adams' National Republicans and the Jacksonian Democrats. The campaign turned bitter. Jackson was called a gambler, a cockfighter, a drunkard, a duelist, a slave trader, even insane. Adams found himself labeled a monarchist, a spendthrift, a sybarite, even a procurer. Such terms fell within the limits of accepted political abuse, but Adams' adherents went beyond this when they accused Jackson in print of having knowingly lived in adultery with Rachel before her divorce. "Ought a convicted adulteress and her paramour husband be placed in the highest offices of this free and Christian land?" one Adams supporter asked in a pamphlet. Plain, stout, goodhearted Rachel was devastated by such political infamy. "I had rather," she said on several occasions, speaking of the President's House, "be a doorkeeper in the house of God than to live in that palace at Washington."

Adams had come to disbelieve in the possibility of his re-election, but he was overwhelmed by the extent of his defeat. He kept his New England stronghold, but little else, Jackson defeating him by 178 to 83 electoral votes. "The ruin of our cause," Adams wrote, "the overwhelming ruins of the Administration."

Once his combative nature had been aroused, Jackson had wanted to be President, but his satisfaction with the election result was short-lived, for within a month his beloved Rachel died full of sorrow at the slander that had pursued her name. When he arrived in Washington three weeks before his inauguration, he seemed to have aged ten years, a worn, thin, heartbroken old man in deep mourning. He stayed at Gadsby's Hotel; and place hunters, favor seekers, and other parasites descended on it like a swarm of flies. Lobby, corridors, and stairways were jammed with applicants for an audience. The Wigwam, Jackson's enemies labeled the place.

From the South and the West and even from the North the crowds streamed into Washington for the great day—politicians, editors, old soldiers, mechanics, farmers, immigrants, in brief, the people. They called him Old Hickory, making him the first President of the United States to bear a nickname. The American Revolution had been political rather than social. Jefferson's revolution had been basically that of the middle class against an entrenched aristocracy. Jackson's, the third American revolution, was a rising of the masses in a country still fundamentally agrarian.

To celebrate this revolution the masses made their way in triumph to the Capital. They overflowed the city and the towns beyond. In Georgetown and Alexandria tourists were sleeping five in a bed. Men adopted Jackson's old-style stocks for their neckwear, and Washington barbers were giving Jackson haircuts. The President-elect refused to pay a courtesy call on the President, and Adams could not bring himself to stay for the inauguration of the man who for three years had been stridently accusing him of corruption. Like his father efore him, he fled the city to avoid the victor.

On Inauguration Day Jackson walked bareheaded rom his hotel to the Capitol, accompanied by a few iends and followed by a cheering, shouting crowd. In is short inaugural address, which he read in a very low oice, he promised economy and the liquidation of the ational debt, but avoided committing himself on the ariff and internal improvements. Then he rode on orseback down Pennsylvania Avenue to the building hat was becoming known as the White House.

In the East Room long tables had been spread with akes, ice cream, and orange punch for those officially ivited to the inaugural reception. Heedless of invita- ons, the mob followed their hero into the White House, surging through the doors, engulfing the re- eshment tables, breaking the furniture, roistering hrough the rooms. Women fainted in the crush. Men

bloodied each others' noses. "A profusion of refresh- ments had been provided," one observer recorded. "Orange punch by barrels full was made; but as the waiters opened the door to bring it out, a rush would be made, the glasses broken, the pails of liquor upset. . . . Wine and ice-creams could not be brought to the ladies, and tubs of punch were taken from the lower story into the garden to lead off the crowd from the rooms. . . . It was mortifying to see men with boots heavy with mud, standing on the damask-satin-covered chairs and so- fas." Supreme Court Justice Joseph Story, a Boston Federalist, observed that "the reign of King Mob seemed triumphant." Buffeted and almost suffocated by the crowd, Jackson appeared listless and exhausted. As the din rose, his friends locked arms to clear a way so that he could slip out the back entrance to go to his rooms at Gadsby's, leaving the mob in possession.

President Jackson, pictured in silhouette and water color s a mounted general, several times risked foreign vars—against Britain over West Indian trade and against The Two Sicilies and France over debts owed to Americans. Conflict was averted, but American rashness n diplomatic affairs disturbed European nations.

*Lying along the Mississippi on the Missouri frontier, this
lonely log cabin and its orchard and fields were
sketched in 1826 by the French artist Charles Lesueur.*

Jackson looked old and sad at his inauguration, and many thought he would last only one term. But, as Daniel Webster noted, "Nobody knows what he will do." He did not know himself, for he took office without any definite plan or program. What he felt, what he was to develop, was a sense of kinship with the majority. He was sure that when he followed his instincts a majority of the voters would agree with him—and usually he was right. The fundamental things he believed in were simple and unvarying: he distrusted banks and paper money, he held that the Union was indissoluble, and he believed that the interests of the majority were the real measure of national interests. For all his acquired membership in the planter-slaveholder aristocracy, for all the harshness of his military discipline, he sustained an extraordinary rapport with the people, a sense that he belonged to them and they to him. That was why they cheered him, why they had come in droves to see him become their President, why they had stormed after him to their White House.

Except for Van Buren, who had resigned as governor of New York to become Secretary of State, Jackson's Cabinet was composed of nonentities. Four years before, Van Buren, as the political dictator of New York, had been the leader of the Crawford faction, but after Adams' minority election—with a politician's gift of the ability to read the handwriting on walls—he had thrown in his lot with the friends of Jackson.

Where Jackson was fiery and direct in manner, Van Buren was suave, adroit, devious. A small, graceful man, blond until he became bald, Van Buren was something of a dandy, favoring snuff-colored coats, lace-tipped cravats, and yellow gloves. Yet underneath his grace and wit lurked the feeling of inadequacy inherent in the self-made man. His father had been a Dutch tavern keeper at Kinderhook and he himself would bear all his life such opprobrious nicknames as the Red Fox of Kinderhook and the Little Magician. After leaving the village school, he became a clerk in a lawyer's office at the age of fourteen and read law with sufficient assiduity that by the time he was twenty-one he could start a practice. Politics, however, was closer to

190

his heart than law. At first he sided with the Clinton-Livingston faction in New York in their opposition to Burr, and early showed his talent for political manipulation. As he made his way up the political ladder, he became an intense rival of DeWitt Clinton. Through Tammany he managed to get himself appointed attorney general of New York until Clinton, elected governor in 1817, removed him from office. An anti-Clinton legislature sent him to the United States Senate in 1821, and he was elected governor of his state in 1828, the year of Jackson's election. He remained the chief of a group of New York leaders called the Albany Regency, formidable in their Tammany-based monopoly of patronage. Toward Jackson he is said to have had the "perfect bedside manner," and he became in time the old man's most trusted adviser and confidant.

The most controversial member of the Cabinet was the Secretary of War, Jackson's long-time friend former Senator John Henry Eaton of Tennessee. A thirty-eight-year-old widower, Eaton had made himself notorious through his liaison with Peggy O'Neale Timberlake, the wife of a Navy purser. Peggy, the daughter of a boardinghouse keeper, had a past at an age when most young ladies had scarcely begun to look to the present. Before she was fifteen, a man had killed himself for her sake, two Army officers had exchanged challenges to a duel over her, and an elderly general had been driven into a state of distraction. At sixteen she married the handsome John Timberlake, and after his handsomeness had worn off, Senator Eaton pulled strings to see that the purser spent most of his time at sea. When Timberlake died, it was rumored he had cut his throat because of his wife's affair with Eaton. A few months after his death and a few months before Jackson's inauguration, Eaton married Peggy, then thirty-two years old, at the naïve insistence of the President-elect.

Eaton, it was felt by those more worldly-wise than Jackson, had disgraced himself for good. Tennessee's congressional delegation begged the President not to take him into the Cabinet. The bride found herself snubbed by the ladies at the inaugural ball, among them the new hostess of the White House, Emily Donelson, the wife of Rachel's nephew Jack Donelson, who had come to Washington as his uncle's able and devoted private secretary. No Cabinet wives could be induced to call on the new Mrs. Eaton despite all the President's pugnaciously gallant attempts to make her socially accepted. At one point Jackson even summoned

a special Cabinet meeting to lay the rumors about Peggy Eaton's private life. "She is chaste as a virgin!" Old Hickory told his Cabinet, showing himself a better judge of horses than of women. Donelson wrote that the affair "has done more to paralize his energies than 4 years of the regular and simple operations of the Govt." Jackson finally gave his nephew and niece the choice of receiving Mrs. Eaton or going back to Tennessee.

The social breach soon turned political. Van Buren earned Jackson's gratitude by his assiduous sponsoring of the Eatons. Calhoun, brooding in his undemanding post of Vice President and never a Jackson enthusiast, became the leader of the anti-Eaton faction. Jackson began to measure the prestige of his Presidency by the Eaton imbroglio, viewing Van Buren as his champion and Calhoun as his enemy. The Eaton Malaria, Van Buren called the affair.

When Jackson was inaugurated, many of his supporters had carried hickory brooms as tokens of the "clean sweep" of officeholders that they anticipated. Over the years the average federal worker had come to accept as a matter of course the permanence of his position through changes of administration. Many had become old and inefficient in their security, some indifferent, some alcoholic, some corrupt. One example that Jackson uncovered was that of the register of the Treasury, who had been employed by the government since the Revolution and was in default for about ten thousand dollars. The new President promised retrenchment and reform. He did not see the process of government as a continuity of civil service but as a matter of individuals. Public office, in his emphatic opinion, was not a kind of property to be retained until death or retirement. To avoid an entrenched bureaucracy, he felt that appointments should be made for four years only.

Jackson's political remedy turned out to be worse than the bureaucratic disease. His enemies managed to foster the belief that he introduced the spoils system to American public life. But he neither introduced it nor did he employ it as much as he was accused of doing. Of the eleven thousand federal workers he could have replaced, he had removed only about one-tenth by the end of his first year. Yet it was undeniable that pre-election opposition to Old Hickory did not add to security of tenure, that Jackson applied the spoils system nationally as Van Buren and his associates had applied it locally in New York, that he established a precedent of favoritism that would long outlive him, to the detriment

OVERLEAF: *For all the mudslinging and the argument over contestable votes, rural elections in the 1820's and 1830's were rowdily festive affairs, characterized by last-minute canvassing on the part of party workers and by dedicated drinking. The painting is by George Bingham, himself a sometime stump orator and candidate.*

*In 1831, when this painting of the Charleston water
front was made, the rice crop had made the city prosperous
and its planter aristocracy gave political leadership
not only to South Carolina but to the entire agrarian South.*

of efficient and honest government.

On the corrosive issue of the tariff, the South had
looked hopefully to Jackson until it became clear that
little could be expected of him. Calhoun in his vehe-
mence declared the Tariff of Abominations to be "unconstitutional, unequal, and oppressive, and calculated
to corrupt the public virtue and destroy the liberty of
the country." He claimed that each state retained the
right to interpose and nullify "unconstitutional" acts of
the national government.

Besides this threat of nullification, the Southerners
forged another weapon through their alliance with the
West. Westerners wanted public lands distributed for
next to nothing, as opposed to Jackson's inherited policy
of using such lands as a source of revenue. The hoarse-

voiced Thomas Hart Benton of Missouri, "Old Bul
lion," the hard-money man, who had once engaged
Jackson in a shooting brawl, denounced land-sale limi
tation as a means of retaining cheap labor in Easter
factories. Robert Y. Hayne, the urbane senator from
South Carolina, agreed to support the Western deman
for cheap land in return for Benton's support of tariff re
duction; and both senators attacked the East.

It fell to New England's Daniel Webster—a nationa
ist, a hypnotic orator, possessed of the most sonorou
and rhythmic voice that ever echoed in the Senat
Chamber—to answer them. He lashed out at states
righters, denied that the moneyed East was hostile t
the rest of the country, advocated the sale of publi
lands at low but not give-away prices, and disputed tha

194

evenue from land sales could ever become a source of corruption. Hayne answered him with bitter brilliance, defending his state's right to nullification while assailing not only New England's dubious role in "Mr. Madison's War" but Webster himself.

Webster's second reply to Hayne would become an American classic of the romantic period of oratory, declaimed by schoolboys till the end of the century. The Senator from Massachusetts—swarthy, heavy-built, in his familiar blue coat with the large brass buttons—took the Senate floor and began in a tone of ordinary conversation. Then the deep voice developed intensity, the dark, luminous eyes seemed to glow. For two days, beginning on January 26, 1830, he spoke to a spellbound Senate, climaxing with his tribute to the Union:

When my eyes shall be turned to behold, for the last time, the sun in heaven, may I not see him shining on the broken and dishonored fragments of a once glorious Union; on States dissevered, discordant, belligerent; on a land rent with civil feuds, or drenched, it may be, in fraternal blood! Let their last feeble and lingering glance, rather, behold the gorgeous ensign of the republic, now known and honored throughout the earth, still full high advanced, its arms and trophies streaming in their original lustre, not a stripe erased or polluted, nor a single star obscured, bearing for its motto no such miserable interrogatory as, What is all this worth? Nor those other words of delusion and folly, Liberty first, and Union afterwards: but everywhere, spread all over in characters of living light, blazing on all its ample folds, as they float over the sea and over the land, and in every wind under the whole heavens, that other sentiment, dear to every true American heart—Liberty *and* Union, now and forever, one and inseparable!

For all Jackson's planter background, he sensed that Hayne's doctrine implied the destruction of the Union he loved. Though Hayne was his friend, tacitly he approved of Webster's speech. Several hours later the antagonists met at a White House reception.

"How are you this evening, Colonel Hayne?" Webster asked him.

"None the better for you, sir," said the Southerner.

In the summer of 1829 Jackson had been so ailing that he had written Rachel's brother: "My time cannot be long upon earth. . . . My earthly house [is] in order and [I am] prepare[d] for another & I hope a better world." But by December he had recovered enough to deliver his vigorous first annual message to Congress. In regard to the tariff, so abominated by the South, he was conciliatory and suggested a compromise. In other mat-

ters he was less so. He asked that the national debt be paid off, the remaining Indians ousted from Georgia, and he suggested tartly that the Bank of the United States be replaced by a more amenable agency. To the dismay of Westerners, he came out against indiscriminate federal internal improvements.

The shift in Jackson's attitude toward internal improvements derived from Van Buren—long an opponent of Clay and his system—who had managed to convince the President that such public spending would lead to "a torrent of reckless legislation." As the months of office wore on, the ailing Jackson had come to lean more and more on the ever available Little Magician. It was Van Buren's idea to nip the budding internal-improvements program by a demonstration of presidential opposition, and he found the opportunity in the Maysville Road Bill, which called for the federal government to construct a twenty-mile highway from Maysville to Lexington, Kentucky. The bill easily slipped through both houses of Congress, but Jackson vetoed it.

Southerners, dismayed by Webster's tremendous speech, had been more dismayed by the approving silence from the White House. Calhoun and his associates formed a plan to use a Jefferson's Birthday subscription dinner on April 13, 1830, as an opportunity for defending Hayne's nullification stand.

The banquet was held in the dining room of Brown's Indian Queen Hotel. Jackson, as the guest of honor, would offer the first voluntary toast after the regular toasts—twenty-four in number—had been given. He had drafted several preliminary versions before he was satisfied. When, after the formalities, the toastmaster introduced the President of the United States and the diners rose, Van Buren, at the far end of the next table, had to stand on his chair to see his chief. The erect white-haired Jackson, his face like steel, fixed his eye on Calhoun and said with measured emphasis: "Our Union: It must be preserved."

There was no sound in the long room. Then the President raised his glass as a signal for the toast to be drunk standing. Calhoun's hand trembled so that drops of wine trickled down the side of his glass. When the room had again quieted down, the chairman called on the Vice President for a second toast. Slowly Calhoun stood up, glass in hand.

"The Union," he said, "next to our liberty, most dear." Then, hesitating a moment to form his ideas, he continued redundantly: "May we all remember that it can only be preserved by respecting the rights of the States and by distributing equally the benefits and burdens of the Union."

It was not Andrew Jackson's nature to shirk any difficulty in his path, and when he brought up the subject of the Bank of the United States in his first message, he was serving notice that he did not intend to avoid that emotion-fraught issue. To his mind the Bank of the United States—the Monster of the 1819 Panic—was a gross Hamiltonian survival flourishing at the expense of the people.

The Second Bank had been established to combat the financial chaos resulting from the War of 1812. Its president, the easy-mannered Philadelphia aristocrat Nicholas Biddle, probably was as astute a banker as could be found in the country and was cultivated and honest if at the same time arrogant. For all the 1819 outcry, the Bank with its branches had served the nation well, providing in its notes the soundest currency the country as yet had had, as well as disciplining the state banks to keep their currency in order. Through its quick and cheap exchange the Bank aided commercial operations and helped move crops. It offered a market for government bonds and other Treasury operations. A present-day economist has concluded that "the Bank often served the public and on a few occasions this was done at the expense of the stockholders."

The Bank was scarcely the monopoly that its enemies charged. In 1830, a good year, it issued only about one-fifth of the nation's bank notes and held only one-third of the total bank deposits. Moreover, its charter could be revised. But it did have the aspect of a vested interest where wealth served the wealthy. It was not subject to effective government regulation. It controlled state bank currencies and dominated the domestic- and foreign-exchange markets. And Nicholas Biddle, as its president, had enormous leverage on the country's economy. The Bank was not above lending money to deserving politicians. Clay and Webster were both among the deserving, and Webster served for a time as the Bank's legal counsel.

In Jackson's simplistic view the Bank was a "hydra of corruption," and his determination to destroy it grew. Biddle tried at first to placate the President by appointing Democrats to the board of directors and by presenting a plan for accelerating the payment of the national debt. But faced with Old Hickory's implacable hostility, he accepted the advice of Clay and Webster that the

election year of 1832 would be the most auspicious time to attempt to renew the Bank's charter. The recharter bill, sponsored by Clay and Webster, easily passed the Senate and the House, with the opposition coming chiefly from the South and the Southwest. The old soldier in the White House scented combat and reacted predictably. "The Bank is trying to kill me," he told Van Buren, "*but I will kill it.*"

That the Bank had been of great service to the economy, that the President offered no adequate substitute for it, were as nothing in the balance of his emotions. With the help of his Kitchen Cabinet he drew up a veto message—perhaps the most widely read one in our history—in which he asserted that the Bank was a monopoly and therefore unconstitutional and a dangerous centralization of power. But the core of his attack came in his impassioned conclusion that the Bank was a truckler to "the rich and powerful." He, the champion of the people, pledged himself to stand against "the advancement of the few at the expense of the many." His message said, in part:

Distinctions in society will always exist under every just Government. Equality of talents, of education, or of wealth cannot be produced by human institutions. . . . But when the laws undertake to add to those natural and just advantages artificial distinctions . . . to make the rich richer and the potent more powerful, the humble members of society, the farmers, mechanics, and laborers, who have neither the time nor the means of securing like favors to themselves, have a right to complain of the injustice of their government.

For Webster the veto, which inflamed "the poor against the rich," was a threat to the Constitution. But Jackson's skilled publicist Francis Preston Blair, editor of the Washington *Globe* and member of the Kitchen Cabinet, could scarcely find words to describe "the sublimity of the moral spectacle now presented to the American people in the person of Andrew Jackson." Old Hickory, as the leader of the masses, had dared to challenge the "monied aristocracy," the "insidious enemy," the "creeping poison," the "germ of an American nobility."

Combat and struggle seemed to reinvigorate Jackson, restoring the sparkle to his eye and to his talk. As his term neared its end, he reversed his earlier decision and planned to run for a vindicating second term, with Van Buren as his running mate. Then after a year or two he planned to resign and turn over the Presidency to Van Buren. The Little Magician sensed danger to himself in such a succession. When he had found a way out of the Eaton dilemma by resigning his office and maneuvering Eaton into doing the same, the President had then appointed his Secretary of State minister to England. Van Buren was already functioning there when the Senate refused to confirm his appointment. Vice President Calhoun, his efforts to heal the breach with the administration having failed, cast the deciding vote against Van Buren. "It will kill him dead, sir," he remarked with satisfaction, "kill him dead."

Calhoun in his estrangement assumed the leadership of the South Carolina nullifiers, who were unappeased by a new tariff act that lowered duties to what they were before the Tariff of Abominations. In July, 1832, Hayne and the South Carolina congressmen called on the people to decide whether their liberties should be "tamely surrendered without a struggle or transmitted undiminished to posterity." Jackson's reaction was wholly characteristic. "Tell . . . [them] from me," he said to a South Carolina congressman about to return home, "that they can talk and write resolutions and print threats to their hearts' content. But if one drop of blood be shed there in defiance of the laws of the United States I will hang the first man of them I can get my hands on to the first tree I can find."

The approach of the 1832 election found Jackson the leader of an energetic party united through discipline, patronage, and the personality of the President. The nomination of presidential candidates by caucuses had been discontinued, and the party choices were made through conventions. With mechanical enthusiasm the Democratic-Republicans picked Jackson. Old Hickory, outraged by the Senate's rejection of his minister to England, insisted on Van Buren as his running mate. Much less united, the National Republicans nominated Clay, with John Sergeant, a lawyer friend of Biddle's and a legal and political adviser to the Bank, as Vice President. A strange third party—America's first—appeared with the Antimasons, who based their appeal on a common belief that the Masonic lodges represented an undue concentration of power and privilege. As their candidate they chose Adams' Attorney General, William Wirt. Editor Blair reduced the National Republicans' name to Nationalists, and the Nationalists riposted by labeling their opponents Democrats.

The overriding issue of the campaign was the Bank, with the Democrats posing as defenders of liberty in opposition to "Czar Nicholas" and a renewed aristocracy.

The Nationalists tried to make what issue they could of the spoils system, internal improvements, and the dangers of the veto; and they caricatured Jackson as King Andrew I, a power-mad tyrant trampling the Constitution underfoot.

Even the most partisan Nationalist must have been forewarned of the election results. Jackson's landslide victory gave him a 2 to 1 popular majority over Clay and a broad margin over his two opponents combined. He received 219 electoral votes to 49 for Clay, while Wirt received only Vermont's 7 votes. "My opinion," Wirt observed, "is that he [Jackson] may be President for life if he chooses."

Scarcely had the votes been counted when Jackson found himself faced with the Nullification Crisis in South Carolina. The Nullies, as they were called, had stubbornly given their electoral votes to their own candidate, John Floyd. Wearing blue cockades, they had swept the state for nullification, winning a two-thirds

Jackson's attack on the Senate for its opposition to his war on the Bank of the United States was blunted by Clay, who induced the Senate to declare the presidential protest unconstitutional. The muzzling of Jackson inspired this contemporary cartoon.

majority in both houses of the legislature. In a special session the new legislature voted for a state convention. Dominated by Hayne—now governor—and other Nullies, the convention proceeded to declare that the tariff would not be enforced within the state and that at any federal attempt to enforce it the people of South Carolina would dissolve their connection with the Union and set up a separate government. To demonstrate their seriousness the legislators voted to stock arms and to authorize the enlistment of volunteers.

Privately Jackson raged at what he considered "positive treason," but publicly he showed himself conciliatory, sponsoring a new tariff bill that would lower objectionable duties by one-half. While Calhoun continued to argue that the states had entered the Union of their own free will and had retained the right to leave of their own free will, Jackson, in his "Proclamation to the People of South Carolina," asserted that no state had the right to annul a federal law and that the people and not the states had formed the Union. "To say that any state may at pleasure secede from the Union is to say that the United States is not a nation," he told the Nullies, warning them that "disunion by armed force is *treason.*" With the Force Bill—called in South Carolina the Bloody Bill—Congress made ready to employ military means if necessary to collect tariff duties.

Beyond the nullification issue lurked the shadow of the hydra-headed Bank of the United States. Jackson, on the pretext that the Bank was insolvent, informed his Cabinet that he intended to withdraw government deposits and place them in state banks. When William Duane, Secretary of the Treasury, opposed this decision, the President replaced him with his Attorney General, the fifty-six-year-old Marylander Roger B. Taney. Taney drew on the Treasury balance in the Bank while making deposits in "pet banks" in the larger cities. Biddle, as he saw the Bank's funds diminish, called in loans and refused credit. Money grew tight, times hard. Merchants and businessmen petitioned Congress. Those who managed to get to see Jackson found him angry and adamant. "Go to the Monster, go to Nicholas Biddle," he told a New York business delegation, "I never will recharter the United States Bank, or sign a charter for any other bank, so long as my name is Andrew Jackson." And he wrote to Van Buren: "Providence has a power over me, but frail mortals who worship Bale and the golden calf, can have none."

Backed by Webster and Calhoun, Clay attacked Jackson's arbitrary removal of government deposits from the Bank, accusing him of subjecting the Treasury to his despotic will and of shifting the country from a republic to a dictatorship. He predicted an eventual elective monarchy if the trend continued. For three months the Senate's three most brilliant opposition leaders attacked Jackson and his administration. Calhoun, who had resigned the Vice Presidency to resume his seat as senator from South Carolina, saw "the approach of despotic power." Webster declared that the country's welfare and its very Constitution were at stake. "The premonitory symptoms of despotism are upon us," Clay told the Senate in offering a resolution of censure for the removal of the Treasury deposits. "If," he continued, "Congress does not apply an instantaneous and effec-

The 1832 Antimason candidate, William Wirt, received few votes but cut into Clay's total, increasing Jackson's margin of victory. Agitation against the Order of Masons, fomented in papers like that above, ceased in about 1838, when the Antimasonic party merged with the Whigs.

198

ive remedy, the fatal collapse will soon come on, and we shall die—ignobly die! base, mean, and abject slaves. . . ."

The Senate passed the resolution, but the Democratic-controlled House turned it down. Jackson was able to enjoy the vindication of the mid-term election, when the Democrats increased their House majority and managed to gain control of the Senate by 2 votes. For three years Senator Benton worked to get the censure resolution expunged from the Senate records—not annulled or revoked but physically removed, although Webster objected that a record of what the Senate had done could not be wiped out as though it had never happened. By January, 1837, Benton at last had his majority, and in a curious ceremony after midnight the 1834 journal was brought out and opened to the offending page. The Senate clerk drew heavy lines around the resolution and wrote across its face: "Expunged by order of the Senate, this 16th day of January, 1837."

While the National Republicans were following the downward path of the Federalists, and the Democratic-Republican party was transforming itself into the mass-appealing Democrats, the new Whig party was coming into being. The name, contrived in New York as an anti-"King Andrew" term, first appeared on a ballot in that city in 1834, and the party grew. The Whigs took shape from a coalition of National Republicans, Antimasons, and disgruntled Democrats. As a party it was middle-class in tone, attracting businessmen, merchants, up-and-coming lawyers, promoters, farmers eager for internal improvements, the nullifiers of the South, supporters of Clay's American System, and many antiforeign American workmen. Whigs distrusted the city mob, frontiersmen, and the right of the ignorant and illiterate to vote. (Jackson angrily defined a Whig as a completely untrustworthy man devoid of principle and honesty.) But the Whigs also attracted men of vision, who saw the vast possibilities of Clay's American System, nationalists, who looked beyond sectional interests to an interrelated national economy.

Less expansionist in outlook, drifting toward political and economic equalitarianism under Jackson's guidance, the Democratic party took on increasingly the tone of the party of the "common people." Artisans, mechanics, farmers—those who believed in unlimited franchise, free public schools, and equal opportunity—gave Old Hickory's party an emotional allegiance that the Whigs were unable to muster among their supporters. Van Buren's Tammany Hall, having somewhat belatedly realized the political potential of the foreign-born, brought their voting weight into the party. Small planters and dirt farmers of the South were drawn to Jackson rather than to Calhoun. The Democratic party was not a party of social democracy, for it contained many conservative elements and lacked doctrinaire class consciousness, but it offered a clear contrast to Whig conservatism.

By the election year of 1836 the federal government was out of debt and money was beginning to pile up in the Treasury as Western land sales soared in a new bubble of easy-credit speculation. Slavery remained the insolvable issue. Antislavery petitions became increasingly frequent in Congress, particularly those to abolish slavery in the District of Columbia. Though Calhoun would have forbidden all action hostile to the "peculiar institution," the House merely voted to table all such petitions while declaring that it would be inexpedient to interfere with slavery in the District. Jackson, disturbed by the violence of the Northern antislavery literature that was being shipped South, proposed a stringent law to prohibit sending through the mails any material that tended to incite slaves to revolt. When the Senate deadlocked on the measure, Van Buren, as presiding officer, cast the deciding vote in its favor. Such action did not endear him to the North.

"Get behind me, Mr. Van Buren," Jackson had called out to his Vice President at the National Jockey Club when a frisky stallion had broken away from its trainers. So the President saw the Little Magician—the lesser figure whom he would protect. The Vice President had shown no leadership in the Bank and nullification battles, and many of the Democrats were reluctant to accept the man whom Old Hickory had hand-picked as his successor. To avoid any outward demonstration of inner reluctance, the President so thoroughly rigged the Democratic convention that the Little Magician was its unanimous choice. There was no formal party platform. The real platform would be the record of Jackson's eight years in office.

The Whigs, unable to achieve such unanimity, did not even hold a convention. Clay, branded by his previous defeat, was not an acceptable candidate. For their candidate the Whigs resurrected the sixty-three-year-old hero of Tippecanoe, William Henry Harrison. The Massachusetts legislature nominated Webster. South-

CAPITOL BUILDING, AUSTIN, TEXAS

The crude but spirited woodcut above—one of the many representations of the fall of the Alamo—is from Davy Crockett's Almanack. The Almanack, first published in 1835, usually showed humorous incidents from the life of the tall-tale-telling backwoodsman, but Crockett is here pictured as he falls beneath Mexican bullets. Left, Sam Houston, victor at San Jacinto and the first president of Texas, is portrayed in classic garb as Marius, his favorite Roman general. The Texans' fight for independence did not win universal praise; the malevolent young man on the page opposite, his deeds tattooed on his arm and sitting on a prostrate slave, is from a Northern cartoon of the period that expressed resentment over the extension of slavery into the Southwest.

ern Whigs and anti-Jackson Democrats chose Hugh Lawson White, a former Democrat from Tennessee who disliked Jackson's policies and disliked Jackson's political heir, Van Buren, even more.

As the last months of his Presidency slipped away, the old and ailing soldier in the White House looked forward above all to the peace of the Hermitage. More by instinct than by reason he had changed the face of American politics and had brought about the emergence of the "common man." No major party in the United States would again campaign without an appeal to "the people." And he had succeeded in paying off the national debt. "The apparition so long unseen on earth—a great nation without a national debt!—stands revealed to the astonished vision of a wondering world!" exclaimed Old Bullion Benton.

In foreign affairs the Jackson administration had done well, coming to an agreement with Britain on the West Indian trade and settling claims against Denmark, Spain, the Kingdom of Naples, and—after belligerent exchanges of notes—France. Texas—its swarms of settlers, adventurers, and land speculators having broken away from Mexico to form a Texas republic under Jackson's old friend Sam Houston—remained a problem.

For a time in 1836 it seemed that there would be neither a Texas republic nor a Houston after the Mexican General Santa Anna, with a force of seven thousand, had advanced across the Rio Grande into Texas, annihilating the Alamo garrison (and giving Texas an undying slogan) on the way north. But Houston, with a greatly inferior force, surprised and overwhelmed the Mexicans at the San Jacinto River and captured Santa Anna. The news electrified Washington. Calhoun demanded instant recognition of the new republic, to be followed by its admission to the Union. For the Southerners Texas seemed a vast area for the expansion of slavery. Jackson hesitated, cautious for once. Like Adams before him, he had long considered the possibility of acquiring Texas. But recognition just before the election would stir up the slavery issue and damage Van Buren's chances in the North.

During his two terms Jackson had been able to appoint six of the eight Supreme Court justices, and when Chief Justice Marshall died, he named Taney his successor. Taney was a Marylander, nearsighted, stooped, and untidy, with uneven tobacco-stained teeth, but under his direction the Court would move—even as the administration had moved—toward a greater consid-

eration for human rights. The new Chief Justice showed less respectful regard for corporations and contracts than had his Federalist predecessor, establishing the principle—as in the famous case of Boston's Charles River Bridge Company—that where private property rights conflicted with the community, the public's right was paramount.

Jackson could reflect, as he sat in the White House study, on his achievements of setting the nullifiers back on their heels and of breaking the power of the Bank of the United States. The implications of the latter accomplishment were beyond him: the United States, from being one of the leading nations in the development of bank techniques, would become one of the most backward; the Bank's decline would foster unbridled speculation, financed by state banks; inflation and currency debasement would follow; the economic development of the country would be hindered; a depression was already in the wings.

The earlier Presidents had been men of cultural attainments, intellectually rooted in the age of reason, interested in the sciences, the arts, education. Even Washington, no academic intellectual, had had books sent to Mount Vernon from England and France. Jackson, the once-reluctant schoolboy, read little more than the newspapers. Any thought of a national university was dropped in his administration. A national observatory was not even worth considering. Jackson found more aesthetic appeal in a race track than in a museum. When a Whig senator proposed to use a half million dollars, which an English admirer of the republic had left to the United States, to found a scientific and literary institution in Washington, Jacksonians defeated the measure. More-farseeing politicians later put the money to use and founded the Smithsonian Institution. From this time on a vindictive anti-intellectualism, the suspicion of the educated man, would run like a thread through American political life; and for this Old Hickory, the voice of the people, bears his share of responsibility.

The day after he had left office and just before he left Washington, the former President dropped in to talk with his Kitchen Cabinet crony Frank Blair. Smoking a pipe, Old Hickory reminisced about his "reign." Getting rid of the Bank was, he felt, the best thing he had done. The tariff question had been only half resolved. Texas would solve itself. Had he any regrets about his eight years in office? The old man had only two: he had not been able to shoot Clay and hang Calhoun!

202

Nation of Farmers

In the nation's early years, farming was a profession of both great men and small. To Jefferson, who invented a plow, farmers were God's chosen people. Washington practiced soil conservation. Henry Clay imported the first Hereford cattle into America. In 1800 nine out of ten Americans lived and worked on farms; even villagers raised crops and livestock.

Farmers were of many types, ranging from Southern plantation owners, who specialized in cash crops, like rice, corn, cotton, or tobacco, to the small landholder of New England, who scratched bare subsistence from rocky ground. Frontier settlers used rifles more than plows to obtain their food. Because of the limitless unsettled lands to the west, most farmers wasted the soil. They disdained scientific methods, like crop rotation, and when the soil became exhausted, moved on to new land. With the agricultural revolution of the 1840's the farmer began to utilize scientific knowledge as well as the new laborsaving machinery. As the productivity of the individual farmer increased, the number of farmers decreased; those remaining could support the growing cities. By 1860 only five out of ten Americans worked on farms.

OVERLEAF: *Under a benevolent sun, New England farmers gather sheaves of wheat, pitch hay, and, using cradles, laboriously harvest grain. The engraving is from* Gleason's Pictorial, *the country's first illustrated weekly.*

Gleason's Pictorial, JULY 15, 1854; ABOVE: *Gleason's Pictorial,* APRIL 22, 1854

J

Farming, whether by slave or freeman, was most often backbreaking labor and did not always lend itself to picturesque tableaux. Clad in stripes for easy identification, Louisiana field slaves, above, cut sugar cane under the eye of an overseer. Molasses made from this demanding crop was their reward for hard work. At right, a Missouri pioneer chops wood for his fire. Until the advent of good roads, many Western farmers settled on bottom land, despite the risk of calamitous floods, to insure the transport of their excess produce to market by water. So dependent were pioneer farmers on wood—for cabins, fences, furniture, and fuel—that many of them were reluctant to settle on the fertile prairies of the West until the middle of the century.

OVERLEAF: The country fair, like this one in Pennsylvania in 1824, gave gentlemen farmers a chance to appraise livestock, discuss agricultural innovations, and (left, background) even watch plowing contests. Despite the urging of farm societies and journals, however, the small landholder was usually unwilling to change old ways.

Janssonists—immigrant farmers from Sweden—use primitive methods to sow grain and plow (above). Below, males help prepare for a holiday feast by plucking fowl. The farmer at right pours corn onto a cloth to let the wind carry away the chaff—a process called winnowing.

OVERLEAF: *Inventions like Cyrus McCormick's reaper and John Deere's steel plow changed the face of American farming and opened the West to agricultural conquest. In this romanticized advertisement for McCormick reapers, pioneers come upon grain fields being harvested.*

Countryfolk of the early nineteenth century made pleasant social occasions out of workaday tasks. At the quilting bee, above, and the cornhusking bee, right, songs were sung, gossip was exchanged, and swains paid court to their ladies.

The Rise of the Whigs

With the prestige and party organization of Jackson behind him, Van Buren's victory was a foregone conclusion, and the election was dull. He collected 170 electoral votes to the combined 124 of his opponents, but won only a small popular majority and failed to carry Jackson's own state of Tennessee. Jackson's hand-picked vice-presidential candidate, Richard Johnson, lacked even the necessary majority, although he was later elected by the Senate. In New York a new group emerged, the Equal Rights party—a radical wing of the Democrats opposed to banks, paper money, corporations, tariffs, slavery, and labor-saving machines "by which drones are enabled to grow rich without honest industry." These Neo-Jeffersonian reformers became known as Locofocos after a Tammany conservative turned off the gaslights to regain order when they threatened to take control of a Democratic meeting in Tammany Hall. Left in the dark, they continued proceedings by lighting candles with pocket matches called locofocos. Named so casually, the Locofocos were to make their mark on the Democratic party. For all its lack of fire, the 1836 election indicated two things: the Jackson "reform" wave had all but spent itself and a fairly evenly balanced two-party system was taking shape in the United States.

The crowds that pressed on to Washington for the inauguration did so more for the sake of the old President than for the new one. They had sent Jackson gifts of all kinds during his last weeks in office—pipes for his collection, walking sticks, a hickory sulky with the bark still on it, a phaeton made from the oak timbers of the frigate *Constitution*. Most spectacular of all was a cheese, four feet in diameter and weighing fourteen hundred pounds.

The President's last few months in office had been saddened by the death of his favorite niece, Emily, whom he had loved unwaveringly in spite of her temporary banishment for snubbing Peggy Eaton. He himself had had a hemorrhage that had nearly carried him away. On Washington's Birthday he had recovered sufficiently to hold his last public reception. Though more decorous, it was like his first inauguration in offering the freedom of the White House. The doors were open to all, and each person

Pioneers heading for Oregon—the Promised Land for armies of emigrants in the 1840's—pause on the east bank of the Mississippi opposite the bustling river port of St. Louis before resuming their westward trek. Independence, Missouri, jumping-off-place for the Oregon Trail, lay 250 miles farther on.

present sliced himself a souvenir piece of the giant cheese before leaving.

Between Van Buren's election and inauguration, Jackson had been importuned almost daily by William Wharton, envoy extraordinary and minister plenipotentiary of the Republic of Texas, for recognition of Sam Houston's new nation. Finally, on the President's last day in office, in the bustle of departure, with the White House a confusion of slaves coming and going, Jackson sent to the Senate his nomination of a chargé d'affaires to the Texas Republic. By evening the nomination had been confirmed. Just before midnight Jackson and Wharton, standing in the dismantled study, drank a toast to the Lone-Star Republic. "Texas," the old soldier said with fire, "*must claim the Californias!*" Then he went to bed, and as was his custom, read a chapter from Rachel's Bible before going to sleep.

Inauguration Day was mild and sunny, yet with a melancholy cast, as if the sadness of time's passing were summed up in the changing of a regime. Jackson rode up Pennsylvania Avenue with Van Buren in the *Constitution* carriage, drawn by his four grays. As the frail, upright, indomitable figure passed, the cheers stopped and men removed their hats in silent respect. "For once," Senator Tom Benton wrote, "the rising was eclipsed by the setting sun." A bullet from the pistol of Benton's brother Jesse had lodged for years in Jackson's arm after the early Benton-Jackson public brawl, but time and politics had brought Senator Thomas

Benton to affectionate collaboration with the man he and his brother had once tried to kill. After Van Buren had been sworn in and had delivered his inaugural address from the Capitol's portico, Jackson walked slowly down the broad steps, paused, took off his hat, and bowed. Benton never forgot the great shout that rose from the crowd at that point, "[a cry such] as power never commanded, nor man in power received. It was affection, gratitude and admiration . . . the acclaim of posterity breaking from the bosoms of contemporaries. . . . I felt an emotion which had never passed through me before."

Plump, cheerful, dandified, five and a half feet tall, Van Buren was the first President born under the American flag and the first machine politician—an honorary Grand Sachem of Tammany, no less—to enter the White House. He saw his Presidency as a less aggressive continuation of Jacksonian policies, committing himself in his inaugural address to follow in Old Hickory's footsteps. Cautiously handling the issue that he knew could shake the foundations of the republic, he promised no interference with slavery where it existed, including no attempt to abolish it in the District of Columbia without the consent of the South.

His careful aim for consensus availed him nothing in the face of the depression that was spreading like a blight across the country, congealing commerce and business activities, plummeting prices, shutting the doors of banks, turning men out of factories, and foreclosing farms. Like all depressions, the Panic of 1837 had many facets, many causes. In part it was brought about by land speculation. The Treasury deposited its receipts in state banks, and the banks lent these funds to speculators to buy land. The money went back to the Treasury and then out again to "pet banks" and from them once more to speculators, in an endless chain. Jackson broke the link in this particular chain in 1836, when he issued his Specie Circular, requiring that land purchased from the government be paid for in gold or silver. The boom received another impulse from the Treasury surplus lent to the states, which used such funds to build roads and canals and to lend money to private businesses.

For a time the hectic fever of business could be mistaken for the glow of health. Men bought on credit and prices soared. American merchants quadrupled their imports of European luxury articles between 1831 and 1836, creating a balance of payments deficit, which increased when European wheat had to be brought in following the failure of the American crop in 1835. After a similar boom gave way to depression in England, merchants there demanded payment from American debtors in hard money, bringing the brisk import trade to a standstill. The deflationary effect was cumulative. As English mills slowed down, English cotton purchases fell off and American raw cotton prices tumbled. Southern planters cut down on their purchases of Western farm produce; Western farmers cut down on their orders for Northern manufactured goods; Northern factories closed. In New York there were riots of the unemployed. Then, to make matters worse, on January 1, 1837, the pet banks were required to pay to the states the first installment of the surplus revenue that had been deposited with them by the Treasury; most were speculating with the money and were unprepared to pass it on to the states. Two months after Van Buren's inauguration every bank in the country had been forced to suspend specie payments.

With the ending of the boom, money became so tight that the planters of the South found themselves paying up to 30 per cent annually for a loan. The price of prime Negro slaves—the South's most stable commodity—dropped from eighteen hundred to five hundred dollars. Many blamed the panic on the Specie Circular, and Democrats as well as Whigs pressed Van Buren to repeal it, arguing that such action would restore confidence, increase revenues, and bolster land values. Even

Van Buren's Cabinet was divided, but he held out against all protests. Nevertheless, within weeks of taking office he found himself forced to call a special session of Congress.

What he demanded chiefly of this "panic session" was the creation of an independent treasury system, free of all and any banks. The government would keep its own receipts in its own vaults and issue its own notes. Like Jackson, Van Buren believed in the traditional currency one could touch—gold and silver for all transactions under twenty dollars, readily redeemable notes for anything over that amount. It was not, he told the legislators, the function of the government to manage domestic or foreign exchange. He wanted no new national debt, no government works or program to fight the depression. Whatever the general-welfare clause of the Constitution might signify, it did not in his opinion mean that the government should make plans for "relieving mercantile embarrassments," since such steps, besides being unconstitutional, "would not promote the real and permanent welfare of those they might be designed to aid." In his Jeffersonian view the Founding Fathers had "wisely judged that the less government interferes with private pursuits the better for the general prosperity." A panic was like a frost or a whirlwind—however one cared to regard it—but in any case it had to run its course. The President resolutely declined to interfere in what he considered a transient problem in the life of the nation.

Webster and Clay were convinced that it was the duty and function of the government to provide relief, through banks and through works. Despite their opposition, Van Buren's Independent Treasury Bill was passed by the Senate, but was twice defeated by the House. In the following year, 1838, the economic clouds seemed to lift a little, but in 1839 the congealing depression spread even further. There would be five more lean years before prosperity returned. The boastful expansionist mood of America, commented on so caustically by so many European travelers, had grown subdued, doubtful, hesitant.

Old Bullion Benton's Western remedy for the depression was readily available, cheap land. He wanted land sales restricted to settlers, with speculators barred; preemption, the protection of the rights of squatters already on the land; and graduation, the step-by-step reduction in the price of public lands remaining unsold. The Whigs, on the other hand, wanted the revenue from public lands used for a vast program of internal improvements—Clay's American System expanded—which they maintained would unite the country in a renewed prosperity.

In June, 1840, the Independent Treasury Bill—an economically backward step—finally passed both houses of Congress by a narrow margin. A bill extending and broadening an 1838 pre-emption act also passed, but a graduation bill was defeated. Van Buren had at last managed a shaky success with his legislative program, but the shadow of the coming election was already on him. The President became the focal point of general discontent. The public's resentment was not helped by his private manner of life, as described with lurid relish by his opponents. In the midst of a depression he had spent over twenty-seven thousand dollars in refurnishing the White House—an enormous sum in those days. It was noised about maliciously that he gave elegant little dinners, with elaborate French menus, at which finger bowls were provided and that he had brought his chef over from London. No longer was the White House the "People's House" of Jackson's day but an aloof residence from which the public was barred by the newly introduced police.

While the depression was spreading across the country a series of conflicts on the Canadian border threatened for a time to develop into a third war with England. Canada's incrusted conservative society had found itself challenged by two rebellious leaders, William Lyon Mackenzie in Upper Canada and Louis Joseph Papineau in Quebec. Both aimed at revolt and independence, and when their movements failed, they fled to the United States. In spite of American failure to conquer Canada during the War of 1812, Americans still cherished the notion that most Canadians would welcome the chance to shake off the trappings of feudal England and join the United States. More-adventurous Americans felt it was their duty to aid the cause of freedom. Secret societies sprang up along the frontier in New York and Vermont to aid the insurgents, who established a base on Canada's Navy Island in the Niagara River near the Falls. For some time the rebels and their American friends used the steamer *Caroline* to ferry their supplies from the American side to the island. Then, toward the end of December, 1837, Canadian soldiers rowed out to the island, set the *Caroline* on fire, and cast her adrift. In the skirmish an American citizen was killed. The *Caroline* herself went aground above the Falls and burned to the water line, although a legend has grown up that she was swept over the cataract, a spectacular flaming torch.

Van Buren, though sympathetic to what he considered the cause of freedom, wanted no difficulties with a friendly power and warned that any American citizens captured fighting against Canada would be left to their fate. He also sent General Winfield Scott with a minuscule force to patrol eight hundred miles of the frontier and do what he could to prevent exuberant American patriots from committing hostile acts. The acts nevertheless continued, brief and bloody, with raids into Canada. A British steamer, the *Sir Robert Peel*, was seized and burned by the Americans to avenge the *Caroline* and an American steamer was fired on in the St. Lawrence. Rebellious Hunters' Lodges were formed in both the United States and Canada. In 1838 Hunters from both sides of the border met in convention in Cleveland and elected a Clevelander named Smith the first President of the Republic of Canada.

Surprising though it may seem to Americans, the majority of Canadians neither then nor afterward wanted to become part of the United States. Many of the English-speaking Canadians were descendants of the loyalists who had fled north at the time of the American Revolution. The French Canadians feared for the uniquely privileged status of their church. For all their martial pronouncements, the Hunters' Lodges represented only a small minority of the population.

When the United States government demanded recompense for the *Caroline*, the British refused. Then a Canadian deputy sheriff, Alexander McLeod, on a visit across the border, boasted in a New York tavern that he had killed the American aboard the *Caroline*. He was at once arrested and charged with murder. To Canadian and British protests the American government announced that it could not interfere. McLeod's trial was still pending at the end of Van Buren's term, and many feared that his conviction might lead to war.

While the temperature of belligerency rose on both sides, the old border dispute between Maine and Canada—in abeyance since 1783—came up again. The Treaty of Paris had been ambiguous. Twelve thousand square miles of disputed territory, much of it rich in timber, hung on the question of whether the St. John River in emptying into the Bay of Fundy also emptied into the Atlantic. In 1826 the two countries agreed to alow the king of the Netherlands to arbitrate. He found he 1783 treaty "inexplicable and impracticable" and ecommended that two-thirds of the disputed area go to he United States and one-third to Canada. The state of Maine refused to accept the recommendation, and for he next decade a series of border incidents stirred up he men of Maine on one side and the men of Nova Scotia and New Brunswick on the other. Canadian woodsmen entered the Aroostook River valley and began cutting timber. Maine's Governor Fairfield sent ten thousand militiamen two hundred miles through the wilderness in deep snow to drive them out. Congress authorized the President to call up fifty thousand volunteers, Nova Scotia and New Brunswick called up their militia, and the Aroostook War was on. Before it led to any actual passages at arms, General Scott, the pacifier, arrived and persuaded Governor Fairfield to withdraw his frost-nipped militiamen, and the Canadians to leave the Aroostook area temporarily a no man's land until its ultimate owners could be decided around a conference table by men with cooler heads.

Taking several leaves from Jackson's 1828 election book, the Whigs in 1840 picked a military hero—if of somewhat antique vintage—as their presidential candidate and ran him as the champion of the people. Clay had long fixed an eager eye on 1840, and he had written his son that he felt sure of the nomination. But he had acquired too many enemies among the disparate elements that made up the Whig party. Although he had a plurality of votes at the Whig convention, the delegates discarded him for a figurehead candidate of much wider appeal. They found him in their standard-bearer of four years earlier, the innocuous William Henry Harrison. "I am the most unfortunate man in the history of parties," Clay sighed after a consoling drink of whiskey, "always run by my friends when sure to be defeated, and now betrayed for a nomination when I, or anyone, would be sure of election."

Clay was indeed right about the election, for any Whig could have defeated Van Buren that year. The President was renominated because as Jackson's heir he controlled the party machinery, but even the more optimistic Democrats had given up hope of his winning. In the campaign, issues gave way to slogans. Harrison had the advantage of having done nothing and of having offended no one since the Battle of Tippecanoe. Though an old Federalist, a rich man, the possessor of two thousand fertile Ohio acres, he was portrayed by

A victim of the general tightening of credit as a result of hard times after the 1837 Panic looks aghast at his long-unpaid bill for merchandise on the day of reckoning.

OVERLEAF: *President Harrison's inauguration was marked by bitter weather as well as pomp and circumstance. The President was treated so violently by his physicians for the cold he caught that he died within a month.*

the Whigs as the homespun hero, in contrast to the silken "Old Kinderhook." Granny Harrison, the Democrats called him. "Give him a barrel of Hard Cider," a Baltimore newspaper jeered, "and settle a pension of $2,000 a year on him and, my word for it, he will sit the remainder of his days in his Log Cabin."

The gibe was seized on by the Whigs as an inspiration. Harrison, the wealthy governor's son, found himself transformed into a simple backwoodsman sitting before the doorway of his log cabin with a keg of hard cider beside him. The cabin and the keg became the omnipresent symbols of the campaign. To rally the disgruntled Clay supporters, Virginia's John Tyler—who had shed tears at the convention defeat of Harry of the West—was chosen Harrison's running mate. "Tippecanoe and Tyler too!" was the Whigs' jingling slogan.

Tippecanoe handkerchiefs, log-cabin badges, song sheets, circulars, appeared by the thousands. Cider barrels and coonskin caps were flaunted everywhere. On the day before the Democratic convention in Baltimore a crowd of a hundred thousand watched a Whig parade wind past, complete with real log cabins on floats, each drawn by six horses, with real smoke curling from the chimneys, and with real hard cider on tap for thirsty spectators. A group of stalwarts from Allegany County rolled a ball along the street, ten feet in diameter and covered with Whig slogans; and they sang to the tune "The Little Pig's Tail":

> It is the ball a-rolling on
> For Tippecanoe and Tyler too, for Tippecanoe and
>   Tyler too,
> And with them we'll beat little Van, Van
> Van is a used-up man;
> And with them we'll beat little Van.

The delirious campaign of slogan and symbol, though it added little to political clarification, at least gave several expressions to the language. "Keep the ball rolling" very probably gained currency from the Allegany ball rollers of the Baltimore parade. The E. C. Booz Company of Philadelphia distributed its Old Cabin Whisky in bottles shaped like a log cabin, and Old Tippecanoe supporters handed them out so generously that they brought the word "booze" into being. "O.K." is said to have originated in one of Van Buren's nicknames, Old Kinderhook; there are also, however, a dozen other explanations.

There were spasmodic efforts at serious discussion.

Democrats defended Van Buren's independent treasury; Webster came back at them with the demand for an effective national currency; Harrison himself called for a strong Union, a protective tariff, internal improvements, a national bank. But their words were drowned out by "Tippecanoe and Tyler too," engulfed in cider, obscured by the lamplit transparencies of log cabins. Farmers took to naming their horses Tip and Ty. Hens in the West were said to cackle "Tip-tip! Tyler!"

Harrison, as predicted, won the election easily, capturing 19 of the 26 states, including 7 in the South, although he received only 53 per cent of the popular vote. "The honest old Farmer of Ohio takes the reins of government into his own pure hands," the Springfield *Republican* applauded. "The voice of the People wills it." The Whigs also reversed the Democratic majorities in the House and Senate. Almost buried from sight, the Liberty party, formed by antislavery groups from six states, polled 7,069 votes, out of a total of almost two and a half million, for its candidate, James G. Birney, a former Alabama slaveholder who had turned abolitionist and had, for obvious reasons, moved north.

By March almost as many office seekers had made their way to Washington as at Jackson's first triumphant entry. General Harrison, with an escort that included two aides from the Battle of Tippecanoe, rode to his inauguration on what John Quincy Adams described as a "mean-looking white horse." In spite of the bitter weather he wore no overcoat and kept doffing his top hat to the crowd. It may be then that he caught the cold that turned to pneumonia. In any case a month later he was dead.

His Accidency, they would call "Tyler too," the first Vice President to succeed to the Presidency. John Tyler called himself a Whig, but it soon became clear that he did not always think like a Whig. A Virginia aristocrat, a long-faced man with a hawk nose, he was, at fifty-one, the youngest President the country had yet had. In his home state he had held every major office, and had been nominated for Vice President by the Whigs mainly to secure Virginia for Harrison. At heart he remained a Jeffersonian states' rights Democrat, turned Whigward because of Andrew Jackson, yet disagreeing with the Clay Whigs in most things: a protective tariff, internal improvements, public-land sales. Honest and conscientious, His Accidency was a troubled, indecisive man.

Clay saw Tyler as a political misfit. Harry of the

TEXT CONTINUED ON PAGE 228

224

A New England Village

Franklin Poole was a house painter in South Reading, Massachusetts; as a pastime he began, before 1840, to paint the village scenes he knew. It was a simple world, centered in the village common (overleaf, center), and one seldom disturbed by any sound louder than the clop of a horse crossing a wooden bridge or the squeak of a wagon wheel on an ungreased axle. On these three pages are some of the many Poole paintings that survive. They picture a world so long gone that many of its ways are now foreign: the town pond (overleaf, top right) was not only a place for fishing and skating but also the supplier of ice for summer cooling; the odd arched structures beside the church (overleaf, bottom right) sheltered the horses of churchgoers. South Reading, though, was not isolated. For one thing, it was moved by the slavery issue, and Poole was an abolitionist. But the world intruded in a more direct way in 1845 when the railroad came. Industry followed; before long, Poole was painting the new rattan factory (above, top). And soon South Reading was renamed Wakefield, for a man who had helped bring in the factories.

OVERLEAF, MIDDLE RIGHT: COLONEL JAMES HARTSHORN HOUSE ASSOCIATION; REST: WAKEFIELD HISTORICAL SOCIETY, WAKEFIELD

Where the state of Maine ended and Canada began was a geographical puzzle that might have led to war. Here American surveyors check the nation's Northeast terrain.

TEXT CONTINUED FROM PAGE 224

West's influence in the Cabinet, which Tyler had kept unaltered after Harrison's death, was great. Although Clay had previously been on good terms with Tyler, he now demonstrated his lack of concern for the views of the new President. Through his own imperious presence in the Senate, and through his friends in the House—whose Speaker was now a Clay man—he assumed the leadership of his party. His immediate goal was to replace Tyler in 1844. When the Secretary of the Treasury sponsored a bill for a new deposit bank that could establish branches with the consent of the states concerned, Clay countered with his own bill for a national bank with unlimited power to set up branches, and forced it through Congress. Repelled by Clay's ar-

rogance, Tyler, after much hesitation and over the objections of most of his Cabinet, vetoed the national bank measure. When a second, modified bank bill was presented to him, he again vetoed it, as much to challenge Clay as because of his objections to the bill. As a protest against this second veto all the Cabinet resigned except the Secretary of State, Daniel Webster, then involved in negotiations with England. Tyler, determined on a loyal Cabinet, would have preferred to see even Webster go, and in fact had already offered the State Department to Jackson's former Secretary of the Treasury, Louis McLane, who had declined it. Webster did not know this when, at a private meeting with the President, he asked if he should stick to his post. Tyler told

228

him he must decide for himself. "I will stay where I am," Webster said with sonorous emphasis. The President, so overcome that he forgot all thoughts of McLane, stood up and stretched out his hand: "Give me your hand on that," he told the Secretary of State, "and now I will say to you that Henry Clay is a doomed man from this hour!"

But Tyler boasted too soon. Clay, in the haughty assurance of his leadership, rallied the Whigs around him, determined to destroy the President. Tyler, his Cabinet purged of all but Webster, moved steadily toward the Democrats while at the same time indulging in fanciful speculations about starting a party of his own. Some of his supporters bought newspapers and through them began to persuade the public that he was really a Democrat after all. However the party tides might run, Tyler's political career was finished. Yet Clay, in spite of his absolute leadership and the almost certain knowledge that he would be the Whigs' choice in the next presidential election, had no extraordinary success with his legislative program. True, he had done away with the hated independent treasury, but he had not succeeded in replacing it by any Third Bank of the United States. The bankruptcy act that he sponsored required all the subterranean efforts of New York's Whig boss Thurlow Weed to get it through Congress. His pet distribution bill, by which the money from public-land sales would go to the states, was emasculated by being tied to tariff concessions to the South. In March, 1842, Clay resigned his Senate seat.

With the advent of Tyler's administration, relations with Great Britain had taken a turn for the better. McLeod's trial, which had seemed almost a signal for hostilities, proved him no more than a barroom boaster who had never been near the *Caroline*, and he was contemptuously acquitted. Secretary of State Webster, unlike his predecessor, carried no anti-English chip on his shoulder, and prospects for success seemed bright when his friend Lord Ashburton arrived as Britain's special representative to negotiate all the differences between the two countries. Besides his friendship with Webster, Ashburton had the advantages of an American wife and a pacific nature. With relative ease the two representatives agreed on a compromise boundary west of Lake Superior and on rectifications of the New York and Vermont borders. The most difficult and most important dispute they faced was that of the emotion-weighted Maine boundary. That difficulty was quietly, if inadvertently, smoothed over through the chance discovery of two maps.

Some time before, the historian Jared Sparks, it was said, had come across a map of the disputed territory in French government archives, with a boundary line drawn in red that gave most of the area in question to the British. The line had supposedly been drawn by Franklin as peace commissioner in 1783. On being shown a copy of this, the most adamant senators and State of Mainers were ready to climb down from their high claims. At about the same time a map of the region, in which most of the disputed territory had been conceded to the United States, was discovered in the British Museum. Whether the maps were authentic or were forged and then opportunely discovered to soften opposition no one will ever know, but they left both sides deprived of assurance and in an unusually conciliatory mood. Webster and Ashburton agreed to give Maine seven thousand of the twelve thousand disputed square miles. Although from the Hermitage Jackson denounced the concessions as "disgraceful, and disreputable to our national character," the Senate ratified the Webster-Ashburton Treaty 39 to 9. In England the treaty was attacked with equal indignation as "Ashburton's Capitulation"—perhaps an indication of its inherent fairness. In any case it ushered in a period of easier Anglo-American relations. It provided for joint naval action to suppress the slave trade—although Americans would allow this provision to become a dead letter—and it ended for good, sixty-three years after the close of the Revolution, the troublesome situation on the Northeast boundary.

Webster, satisfied with his accomplishment, resigned from an administration that was growing increasingly distasteful to him. He was succeeded by Abel Upshur of the Virginia Whig group that now remained Tyler's almost sole support. Upshur served as Secretary of State for nine months, until he was killed by the explosion of a cannon while inspecting the battleship *Princeton*. His place was, to the astonishment of the public, taken by Calhoun. Both Tyler and Calhoun in their separate ways had long been moving toward some meeting point within the Democratic party. Twice previously Calhoun had declined to serve under Tyler, but in 1844, at the beginning of an election year that had brought the dimming of his own presidential hopes, with the long-postponed Texas question coming to the fore, he saw in the office of Secretary of State a means of securing the annexation of Texas as a slave state, a step that he felt was necessary for the peace and security both of the South and of the Union.

For Van Buren, balanced precariously between his Northern and Southern supporters, the question of Texas annexation had been one he had preferred to tuck away in some dark political cubbyhole. During his years in the White House he had found Sam Houston, the president of Texas, annoyingly ambivalent. Sometimes the Raven—as the Indians had called Houston from the time he had lived with them in his young manhood—was all for immediate annexation. At other times he seemed to have absorbed Burr's old dream of an independent empire in the Southwest. Midway in Tyler's administration another of the Raven's ambassadors arrived, an envoy extraordinary and minister plenipotentiary, to press the matter of annexation, and the Texas question could no longer be tucked away. The proslavery Upshur, fearing British maneuvers to bring Texas within Britain's sphere of influence and to do away with slavery in Texas, gave an ultimatum to the Mexicans, who still had not reconciled themselves to the loss of Texas: they must either reconquer Texas at once or recognize its independence. Clay, like other Whigs, opposed annexation, arguing that it would mean war with Mexico. Benton considered the whole agitation to be motivated by land speculators. Northern abolitionist sentiment was passionately opposed to the admission of slave territory. John Quincy Adams, who with brave unconcern for appearances had returned to Washington as a Massachusetts congressman, said that admitting Texas would be "identical with dissolution" of the Union.

Facing the disparate opposition of Whigs, abolitionists, and Locofocos, Calhoun, on taking over the State Department, felt that he had to act quickly. Just before the Whig National Convention of 1844 he concluded a treaty of annexation with Houston by which Texas would come into the Union as a territory, ceding its public lands to the United States in exchange for the federal government's assumption of its public debt up to ten million dollars. Debate in the Senate over ratification of the treaty was bitter, with the Northerners accusing the South of trying to extend slavery and the Southerners denouncing Northern prejudice against the nation's destined expansion.

The Whig convention, meeting in Baltimore, had all the carnival trappings of four years earlier: live coons— the Whig symbol—and caged Van Buren foxes (both "raising the Old Harry"), flags, slogans, and parades. But there was no real contest. Henry Clay was the unanimous choice.

For a time it seemed that Van Buren, smarting from his last defeat and eager for vindication, would be the all-but-unanimous choice of the Democrats. Jackson favored him, and the convention favored Jackson. Privately the Little Magician and Clay had come to some sort of informal agreement not to make Texas an issue in the campaign. No candidate, Jackson had said, could be elected President who opposed the annexation of Texas, and when he learned that Harry of the West had written an open letter against annexation, he remarked with satisfaction, "Clay is a dead political duck." How much greater was his dismay—he is said to have shed tears—when he learned a few days later that Van Buren had written a letter equally antagonistic to annexation and three times as long. Jackson remarked grimly that Van Buren had been misled and appealed to his old protégé to reverse himself.

In spite of the disastrous impact of his Texas letter, Van Buren could still muster a majority of the votes at the Democratic convention—146 to 83 for Lewis Cass, Jackson's old Secretary of War. But the two-thirds rule adopted by the convention made it impossible for him to overcome the annexationists' opposition. With Van Buren written off as an apostate, Jackson saw his fellow Tennessean James K. Polk as "the most available man." Hard-working but humorless, Polk as a congressman had been one of Jackson's floor leaders, aiding in the attack on the Bank. After leaving Congress he had served a term as governor of his state, and in the vice-presidential free-for-all of 1840 had received a solitary electoral vote. Old Hickory, aiming at a Jacksonian restoration, at first had wanted him nominated Van Buren's running mate in 1844.

After seven inconclusive ballots in an increasingly disorderly convention, the Democratic leaders finally decided on Jackson's dark horse as the compromise candidate. After one more ballot Van Buren withdrew his name, and on the ninth ballot Polk was unanimously nominated. Senator George Dallas of Pennsylvania was chosen his running mate, giving the Democrats their slogan "Polk and Dallas—Texas and Oregon." News of Polk's nomination was flashed to Washington by Mr. Morse's electromagnetic telegraph, the instrument itself causing as much amazement as the news it carried, for the wires between Washington and Baltimore, the first in the nation, would not even be formally opened for more than three weeks.

While the Democrats were in the process of rejecting Van Buren, a splinter group nominated the abandoned President to run on an independent "Tyler and Texas" ticket, but on word from the Hermitage Tyler withdrew. Not so easily deterred was James G. Birney of the Liberty party, who had been once more nominated by the abolitionists. In spite of his ludicrous showing in 1840—he had not carried a single county—he insisted on running on righteousness, demanding "the absolute and unqualified divorce of the general government from slavery. . . ."

Much of the bombast of 1840 carried over into the 1844 campaign. Clay was by far the more popular man, but the dark horse Polk had the more popular cause, for—except in New England—the spirit of annexation and expansion was in the air, and Texas was the real issue before the voters. "Who is James K. Polk?" the Whigs asked, as if nobody had ever before heard of the former Tennessee governor. The Democrats countered by calling Clay a duelist, a gambler, and a friend of abolitionists, and by providing their supporters with hickory pokers while proclaiming Polk "Young Hickory."

It was the closest presidential election yet in terms of the popular vote, and the most fraudulent. In New York Tammany transformed twenty thousand aliens into citizens just before Election Day, and in Louisiana a boatful of Democrats steamed upriver and voted in three separate towns. Not counting New York's 36 electors, Polk received 134 electoral votes to Clay's 105. Polk won the Empire State by only 5,106 popular votes, with 15,812 going to Birney, the Liberty party candidate. Thus, had it not been for Birney, Clay would very probably have carried New York and become President. In the country-wide popular voting Polk did not win a majority, defeating Clay by a mere 38,000 votes out of more than 2,500,000 cast, with the Liberty party increasing its total ninefold over its 1840 showing to 62,300. A Clay supporter in Illinois, Abraham Lincoln, observed ruefully: "If the Whig abolitionists of New York had voted with us . . . Mr. Clay would now be President, Whig principles in the ascendant and Texas not annexed; whereas, by the division, all that either had at stake in the contest was lost."

The Democrats' slogan "Re-occupation of Oregon," deftly pitched to the North, balanced their "Re-annexation of Texas" appeal to the South. Oregon, occupied

jointly with the British since 1818, had been a dormant issue until the period of national expansion ushered in during the eighteen-forties. Manifest destiny, a phrase first used in 1845 by John L. O'Sullivan in the *Democratic Review,* was the term that came to characterize the westward push. Nothing must interfere, O'Sullivan wrote, with "the fulfillment of our *manifest destiny* to overspread the continent allotted by Providence for the free development of our yearly multiplying millions." There were some completely swept away by the heady visions aroused by manifest destiny. Congressman John Wentworth of Illinois dreamed a hemispheric dream of a United States that covered half the globe; he told his colleagues in the House that he hoped to see the day when the Speaker would recognize not only the members from Nova Scotia, Canada, Cuba, and Mexico but "aye, even the gentleman from Patagonia."

The push was constant, increasing in times of depression and panic as the thwarted and the discontented abandoned the settled areas. The nation grew like a

Joel T. Hart, a self-taught sculptor, fashioned this bust of Henry Clay in classic style and journeyed to Florence, Italy, in 1848 to oversee its rendering in marble.

young organism, pushing forward its frontiers as it drew life into itself. In 1820 the population was 9,600,000. Twenty years later it had almost doubled, and in 1850 it would reach 23,000,000. Arkansas came into the Union in 1836, Michigan in 1837, and Florida in 1845 to make twenty-seven states in all.

The United States had expanded its internal commerce first by road and canal and coastal shipping. But only a cheap and speedy means of transportation could conquer the great unsettled spaces with their forest and mountain barriers. The means was at hand in the forties with the development of that most revolutionary of inventions, the steam railroad.

America's first railway, the Granite Railroad, dated from 1826, a two-mile stretch of roadbed over which horse-drawn cars rolled on wooden rails, carrying granite from Quincy to Boston Harbor. The first steam locomotive—the famous *Stourbridge Lion,* imported from England—was tried on the tramway of the Del-

aware and Hudson Canal Company a few years later but proved too heavy for a track designed for horsecars. By 1830 the Baltimore and Ohio, the first important American railroad, had laid down thirteen miles of track, while three years later the longest railroad in the world—extending 136 miles—had been constructed in South Carolina. By the mid-thirties a number of short lines were operating in New England.

The growth of the railroads was phenomenal. By 1840 there were 3,328 miles of track—almost exactly as many miles as there were of canals—although scarcely any yet ran west of the Appalachians. In spite of the depression of the early forties, railroad construction continued, much of it in New England and New York. Some states—among them Pennsylvania, Georgia, Virginia, Michigan, and Indiana—built and in some instances operated their own railroads as part of their program for internal improvements. Troy, New York, even built a twenty-mile municipal line to Schenectady.

For the first few decades of the nineteenth century the centers of communal life in California were the Franciscan missions, staffed by friars who, in addition to their religious duties, supervised the work of docile Indians. At right is a proud ranchero of California—one of the rulers of the prosperous but feudal empire of the time.

What had started as a spectacular novelty soon became matter-of-course. When Jackson left the White House for the last time, in March, 1837, he took a Baltimore and Ohio train from the depot at Second Street and Pennsylvania Avenue, the first President to leave Washington by steam.

Where the iron rails ended beyond the Alleghenies, men continued on by wagon, on horseback, or on foot. The country was full of restless men—those who had lost their holdings in the depression, those who had never had anything. In the decade of the thirties Arkansas's population increased from 30,000 to 100,000, more than 200,000 newcomers entered Missouri, Michigan grew from 32,000 people to more than 212,000, Ohio's population reached 1,500,000. Yet even the empty lands in Wisconsin and Minnesota had to be bought. Beyond the territories, beyond the mountain ranges, lay the bright enticement of California and Oregon, the lands of promise, those sunny, fertile tax-free re-gions of easy winters where land cost nothing. The dream, stimulated by travelers' tales and such books as Richard Henry Dana's *Two Years Before the Mast* with its California locale and Washington Irving's Oregon-based *Astoria*, found its expression in Polk's campaign slogans and in the belligerent cry of the expansionists, "Fifty-four forty or fight!"—the claim and clamor for the Oregon region northward all the way to the south boundary of Alaska.

California was still a feudal backwater between the mountains and the sea, with its missions and its im-mense ranchos and its proud families of Spanish blood who called themselves *Californios*. Their idle, gracious, courtly life was sustained by the labor of Indians—a more tractable and enduring breed than the tribes of the Northeast. Into the sunny valleys came from time to time the mountain men, American trappers—rough, hard-drinking, frightening to the mannered *Californios*, but fortunately few in number. By 1836 there were

*Swift-flowing rivers with treacherous bottoms that had to
be forded were among the perils pioneers faced
on the Oregon Trail—the longest wagon trail in history.*

about two hundred foreigners, mostly Americans, living in California. Among them was a Swiss adventurer, John Augustus Sutter, who, having gone bankrupt in his native country as a dry-goods merchant, had abandoned his wife and children and fled across the Atlantic. After having stayed for a while in St. Louis, he had assumed the military title captain and had followed a band of trappers across the continent. He had lived for a time in the Oregon country, had sailed from Hawaii to Alaska, and had finally settled in California's empty Sacramento Valley as a Mexican citizen, with fifty thousand acres granted him—as a virtual personal empire—by the indulgent governor.

Under the distant and ineffectual control of Mexico, California governors came and went without leaving any impression. The band of allegiance was so frail that finally Governor Juan Alvarado proclaimed California a "free and sovereign state." When a new governor, Don Carlos Antonio Carillo, arrived from Mexico City to replace Alvarado, the latter refused to be replaced. From his capital at Monterey he marched a task force swiftly down the coast, and in an engagement in which one

man was accidentally killed, defeated Carillo's army. Carillo was placed under arrest after his capture but was soon released after he "accepted the change of fortune with equanimity."

When Alvarado's term ended, he was succeeded by General Manuel Micheltorena, who arrived by ship from Mexico with three hundred vagabond soldiers. After enduring their plundering and roguery for two years, the *Californios*, under the brothers Pío and Andrés Pico, revolted. Both sides engaged mountain men as mercenaries, but when the two armies met, the Americans recognized one another and refused to fight. The ensuing engagement, resulting in the loss of two horses and a mule, became known as the Battle of Cahuenga Pass. Discouraged, Micheltorena resigned, returning to Mexico with his *soldados* and leaving Pío Pico as California's new governor. Indolent and innocent, the land lay waiting for the American advance. The wait would not be a long one.

Lewis and Clark had reached the Oregon country in 1805, and half a dozen years later John Jacob Astor had set up a trading post near the mouth of the Columbia

234

Especially harrowing was the passage through the beds of quicksand in the Platte River. Some 34,000 emigrants died on the trail from various causes in the pioneer years.

River. The huge region, mostly unexplored, embraced what is today Oregon, Washington, Idaho, the southern part of British Columbia, and the western sections of Montana and Wyoming. The Hudson's Bay Company, after setting up forts and trading posts, tried to encourage agricultural settlements, but the few settlers who arrived were interested only in the fur trade. South of the company's Fort Vancouver on the Columbia River a number of French Canadians did settle in the Willamette Valley, where they were later joined by a scattering of American missionaries and mountain men.

As early as 1836 Jackson, in his dream of advancing the nation's borders to the Pacific, had sent his secret service agent William Slacum to report on the Oregon country. Two years later the missionary Jason Lee brought east a settlers' petition to Congress to make Oregon part of the Union. Many a Western missionary was showing himself more zealous for land acquisition than for the souls of the Indians. In 1843 Senator Thomas Benton's new son-in-law, Lieutenant John C. Frémont, of the Army Topographical Corps, set out on trail-exploration expeditions in Oregon and California,

and his reports became guides for later immigrants. The Pathfinder, they would call him.

In the early forties Americans began arriving in Oregon in growing numbers, most of them on the Oregon Trail, which, outlined in part by mountain men and fur traders, stretched from Missouri across the Great Divide to that fair and fertile region. Forerunner of the pioneer treks across the continent by covered wagon was the Great Emigration that left for Oregon from the elbow bend of the Missouri at the frontier town of Independence in May, 1843. There had been three small expeditions during the previous three years, but in none had the travelers gone by wagon all the way. The great expedition of 1843 was a family affair, with women and children brought along, and household goods, farm tools, and spare parts carefully stacked in the covered wagons. The elected captain of the expedition was Peter Burnett, a Missouri lawyer destined to be the first governor of the state of California. Jesse Applegate— lawyer, surveyor, and trail blazer, who would prove one of the great leaders of the West—took command of the "cow column," the section made up of those

OVERLEAF: *The grandeur and wild beauty of the Far West are expressed in this view from the Wind River Mountains in Wyoming, painted by Albert Bierstadt. Indians regarded these mountains, with their shimmering vista of plains and distant peaks, as the crest of the world.*

settlers who had cattle to drive and take care of.

About 1,000 emigrants set out—no one is entirely certain of the number—and 875 straggled into Oregon at the end of the year. Their cattle, oxen, mules, and horses numbered anywhere from two to five thousand. Sixty wagons with the women and children went on first, guided by bewhiskered Marcus Whitman, missionary and physician, who had been to Oregon before. The caravan followed the broad muddy shallows of the Platte River, "a mile wide and six inches deep." Each afternoon scouts went ahead to select a camping ground for the night. Then as the light faded, the emigrants would make their camp within a protective circle of wagons, cooking their supper, visiting, settling disputes by impromptu courts, while the children played in and out among the shafts and wagon wheels. Shifts of horsemen guarded the cattle until morning.

Daily the wagons moved westward under the enormous arching sky, until the flat horizon was at last broken by mountain ranges. The canvas-topped wagons passed the friendly stockade of Fort Laramie, reached the Sweetwater River, and climbing higher in chill mountain air, crossed the Great Divide at South Pass. A child was born along the way, delivered by Dr. Whitman. It had been a safe, tightly run journey until the party reached the Hudson's Bay Company trading post of Fort Hall in what is now southeast Idaho.

At Fort Hall the resident factor warned the dismayed emigrants that their wagons could never reach the Pacific. But Whitman reassured them. At a night meeting within the wagon circle he told them that he knew they could get through, and taking courage from his experience, they set off again. Forty axemen hacked a way through the woods of the supposedly impassable Blue Mountains, while others behind them graded the trail. But at the farther barrier of the Cascade Mountains Whitman found that he had been wrong. The wagons were blocked, and the party had to abandon them for the river route of the Columbia Valley. Several persons drowned and most of the baggage was lost in the voyage. When the settlers in the Willamette Valley heard of the newcomers' distress, they sent help, as did the Hudson's Bay Company factor at Fort Vancouver, and most of the emigrants and some livestock finally reached the valley of the Willamette River.

Later caravans were not always as fortunate. One delayed by a wet season the following year was snowed in within the Walla Walla Valley, those who survived ar-

Hated for their creed or envied for their prosperity, the Mormons were driven westward till they finally found a haven in Salt Lake Valley, Utah. This lithograph shows members of the sect, their temple gleaming in the background, being expelled from Nauvoo, Illinois, in 1846, after the murder of their leader, Joseph Smith.

riving destitute in Oregon the next season. Appalled by the sequence of disasters, Applegate, with fifteen companions, set out to locate a trail over the Cascade Mountains that a wagon could travel. Working south and east, he finally found a pass that took him to Klamath Lake and from there across the Nevada desert to the Humboldt River. It was not any easy trail, not even wholly safe, but it was at last a possible one all the way to Oregon. Each season the wheel ruts cut deeper as more and more wagon trains moved westward in the wake of the Great Emigration. The growing colony of Americans in the Willamette Valley even formed a loose civil government for themselves, and the cry "Fifty-four forty" swelled.

Just beyond Fort Hall one branch of the trail turned south. Called the California Trail, it edged the Humboldt River until that river lost itself in marshland, then swung up across the towering Sierra Nevada at the Truckee Pass. It was a hazardous trail, one to avoid if possible, yet in 1846 some five hundred emigrants made their way over it to California. Sometimes the Sierra crossing led to disaster, as with the long-remembered Donner party, which in the spectacular horror of its journey gave a name to a pass, a summit, a lake, and a moment of history.

In the summer of 1846 the Donner emigrants, in twenty-three wagons, parted from a larger group at Little Sandy Creek in Wyoming and proceeded alone under the leadership of the elderly George Donner. From the beginning luck was against them. The Wasatch Mountains exhausted the strongest among them, and the party nearly died of thirst in crossing the desert west of Great Salt Lake. Two men were murdered, another died of accidental gunshot wounds, still another was abandoned. Many of the cattle had perished crossing the desert. Indians killed or stole more. The winter, the worst in memory, came early, catching Donner's caravan just short of the Sierra crest. The advance party took cover from the snow in three abandoned cabins near what is now Donner Lake. Five miles down the trail the rest sheltered as they could in hutches under canvas and buffalo robes. Finally fifteen of the advance party, including five women, contrived snowshoes of hides and ox bones and managed to cross the summit through mounting blizzards and the cold glare that caused snow blindness. Five died, and the others ate the dead. One man went mad and killed their two Indian guides. These, too, were eaten. Another man fought his way through the snow and down the slopes to give the alarm at Sutter's Fort. Rescuers set out from the fort at intervals. When they finally pushed across the snow barrier, they found that the survivors in the lower camp had turned cannibal. Of the eighty-seven who had started out with Donner, only forty-seven survived.

The best-planned migration of those years was that of the Mormons, the Latter-day Saints, the more ironical in that their goal was not to expand the Union but to get away from it. Ever since their founder, Joseph Smith, who had conversed with angels on the hills of Palmyra, New York, had been lynched by a mob and the Saints had been forced from Nauvoo, the thriving city they had built in Illinois, their goal had been to shelter themselves and their unique beliefs beyond reach of the laws of the United States. The single-minded energy, ability, and spirit of Smith's successor, Brigham Young, alone made their goal possible. President Young's purpose was to take his Saints into some nominally Mexican territory close to Great Salt Lake where they could live out Smith's revelation. He planned each step carefully, first establishing winter quarters across the Mississippi from Council Bluffs, Iowa, then setting up way stations where the migrating Saints would rest, make wagon repairs, and collect their livestock. Caravans, run with military precision, were to be large enough to discourage marauding Indians.

In April, 1847, Young led out his first caravan of seventy-two wagons across the Elkhorn River and into the valley of the Platte, following the northern bank instead of the Oregon Trail on the southern bank to avoid non-Mormons. The president had drilled his young men as military units. Each morning a bugle sounded at five for prayer, and again in the evening. A newly formed choir sang during their religious services. "Joking, nonsense, profane language, trifling conversation and loud laughter do not belong to us," he sternly informed some of the more high-spirited, younger Saints, who were growing restive at the monotony of the prairie crossing. The Saints passed Fort Laramie, took the resident agent's advice and crossed over to the Oregon Trail, then went up the Sweetwater River and across the Great Divide. Some of the travelers suffered from mountain sickness as they climbed higher, and Young came down with a fever. Not until the last week of July did the pious, martial caravan reach the Great Salt Lake Valley. President Young, weak but recovering, had himself brought forward in a wagon so that he could look out over the barren plain and the salt lake beyond that was so much like the sea. "This is the right place," he said.

Other carefully projected caravans followed to the Great Basin, to the empire the Mormons called Deseret, meaning "land of the honeybee," a word from their scriptures, the Book of Mormon. Within two years six thousand Mormons arrived, almost as many settlers as existed in either California or Oregon.

Jefferson had thought the North American continent too large for one Union and felt there should eventually be two American nations, divided by the Rocky Mountains. Benton as a young man had shared this feeling, but as a senator his vision, like that of so many of his countrymen, grew imperial. Pointing grandly to the West, he would say, "There lies the East—there lies India!" As the covered wagons moved toward Oregon and California, America's natural boundaries came to seem the Rio Grande and the Pacific. They had always seemed so to Andrew Jackson.

Nevertheless, after the political conventions of 1844, when the treaty to annex Texas finally came to a vote in the Senate, it was not only opposed solidly by the Whigs but by half a dozen Democrats, including Benton, who saw annexation as of benefit chiefly to planter expansionists. After Polk's election but before his inauguration, the Senate rejected the treaty for the second time. "If Texas goes begging again for admission to the United States, she will only degrade herself," said Sam Houston testily, implying that England's friendship and guidance would next be sought. Faced with this threat, the President-elect went to Washington to confer with Tyler. At the Hermitage a half-blind, dying old man wrote on and on, appealing, commanding, never losing sight of his great dream of an empire reaching to the shores of the Pacific.

Tyler, interpreting Polk's victory as an endorsement of annexation, bypassed the Senate by calling on Congress to take Texas into the Union through a joint resolution. Three days before the President left office, the resolution passed by the simple majority required, and he had the satisfaction of signing it as one of his last official acts. Houston, caught in a shimmering dream of independence, hesitated, then yielded to the Union. They brought Old Hickory the news and congratulated him as he sat in his invalid's chair. "I congratulate my beloved country," he told them. Three months later he died, content with the course the Union was on.

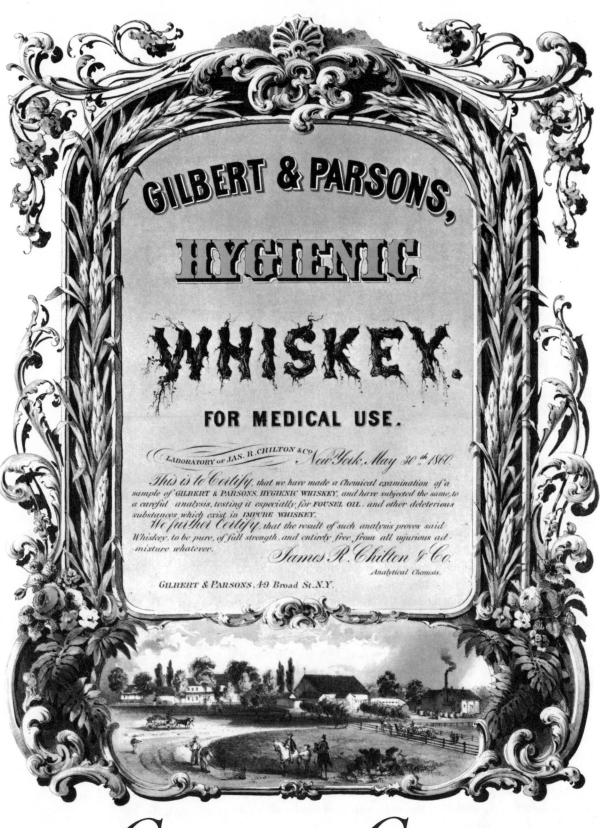

Cures and Comforts

Ideas about man's soul and knowledge of his body were changing rapidly in the decades between the Revolution and the Civil War. American citizens were free to question old beliefs about God without being burned at the stake, and many found comfort in earnest new faiths, such as Mormonism or Unitarianism, while others turned to the occult and to pseudo religion and looked for answers in table rappings or in the special virtues of eight-sided houses. At the other extreme, men withdrew into the eternal and grim verities of old-fashioned, hard-shelled fundamentalism.

As for the science of medicine and the treatment of man's body, a strange blend of knowledge, ignorance, and superstition existed. In 1800 the germ theory of disease lay in the future, surgery was largely limited to amputations, the meaning of asepsis was unknown, anesthetics were unheard of, drugs were often ineffectual and sometimes even harmful. Where so little was known, incompetents flourished, purveyors of nostrums thrived, and the line was often thin between the quack and the dedicated doctor plying his patient with useless remedies because no one knew better.

James Fenimore Cooper, in his novel The Pioneers, *describes the training of a country doctor in upper New York in the 1790's. Though Cooper's doctor is fictitious, the situation he describes is not.*

[Elnathan Todd] was removed to the house of the village doctor, a gentleman whose early career had not been unlike that of our hero, where he was to be seen, sometimes watering a horse, at others watering medicines, blue, yellow and red; then again he might be noticed, lolling under an apple tree, with Ruddiman's Latin Grammar in his hand, and a corner of Denman's Midwifery sticking out of the pocket of his coat; for his instructor held it absurd to teach his pupil how to despatch a patient regularly from this world, before he knew how to bring him into it.

This kind of life continued for a twelvemonth, when he suddenly appeared at meeting in a long coat (and well did it deserve the name) of black homespun, with little bootees, bound with uncoloured calf-skin. . . .

Another year was passed under the superintendence of the same master, during which the young physician had the credit of "riding with the old doctor," although they were generally observed to travel different roads. At the end of that period, Dr. Todd attained his legal majority. He then took a jaunt to Boston, to purchase medicines, and, as some intimated, to walk the hospital; we know not how the latter might have been, but if true, he soon walked through it, for he returned within a fortnight, bringing with him a suspiciously looking box, that smelt powerfully of brimstone.

The next Sunday he was married; and the following morning he entered a one-horse sleigh with his bride, having before him the box we have mentioned, with another filled with home-made household linen, a paper-covered trunk, with a red umbrella lashed to it, a pair of quite new saddle-bags, and a bandbox. The next intelligence that his friends received of the bride and bridegroom was, that the latter was "settled in the new-countries, and well to do as a doctor, in Templetown, in York state."

James Fenimore Cooper
The Pioneers, 1823

Dentistry was not even the beginning of a profession at the start of the nineteenth century. The country doctor usually carried a tooth forceps in his bag and took care of patients with aching teeth. Nathaniel Hawthorne describes an extraction he witnessed in a western Massachusetts hamlet in 1838.

A young country fellow, twenty or thereabouts, decently dressed, pained with the toothache. A doctor passing on horseback, with his black leather saddle-bags behind him, a thin, frosty-haired man. Being asked to operate, he looks at the tooth, lances the gum, and the fellow being content to be delt with on the spot, he seats himself in a chair on the stoop with great heroism. The doctor produces a rusty pair of iron forceps; a man holds the patient's head; the doctor perceives that, it being a difficult tooth to get at, wedged between the two largest in his jaws, he must pull very hard; and the instrument is introduced. A turn of the doctor's hand; the patient begins to utter a cry, but the tooth comes out first, all bloody, with four prongs. The patient gets up, half amazed, spits out a mouthful of blood, pays the doctor ninepence, pockets the tooth, and the spectators are in glee and admiration.

Nathaniel Hawthorne
American Notebooks, 1880

Dentist with forceps gets ready to remove the tooth of an apprehensive patient.

With medicine such an inexact science, the ailing were sometimes in more danger when they called in a physician than when they suffered without his ministrations. A case in point was Dr. Benjamin Rush of Philadelphia. Dr. Rush had many ideas that were progressive far beyond his times, but he acquired the strange theory that all diseases were caused by a state of spasm in the blood vessels and that this spasm must be treated by "depletion" through bleeding and the use of violent cathartics. He first used this panacea on a wholesale basis during the great Philadelphia yellow-fever epidemic of 1793. In the following report he describes his use of murderous amounts of jalap, a vegetable drug, and calomel, a compound of mercury, in the serene faith that he was curing his patients, even though members of his own family were among his victims. Rush's faith and devotion were no substitute for knowledge.

In my attendance upon the military hospitals during the late war, I had seen it [calomel] given combined with jalap in the bilious fever by Dr. Thomas Young, a senior surgeon in the hospitals. His usual dose was ten grains of each of them. . . . It was adopted by several of the surgeons of the hospital, and was universally known, and sometimes prescribed, by the simple name of *ten* and *ten*. This mode of giving calomel occurred to me in preference to any other. The jalap appeared to be a necessary addition to it, in order to quicken its passage through the bowels; for calomel is slow in its operation, more especially when it is given in large doses. I resolved after mature deliberation, to prescribe this purge. Finding ten grains of jalap insufficient to carry the calomel through the bowels, in the rapid manner I wished, I added fifteen grains of the former, to ten of the latter; but even this dose was slow, and uncertain in its operation. I then issued three doses, each consisting of fifteen grains of jalap, and ten of calomel; one to

Country doctor making his rounds, about 1846

243

be given every six hours until they procured four or five large evacuations. The effects of this powder, not only answered, but far exceeded my expectations. It perfectly cured four out of the first five patients to whom I gave it, notwithstanding some of them were advanced several days in the disorder. . . .

After such a pledge of the safety and success of my new medicine, I gave it afterwards with confidence. . . . But I did not rely upon purging alone, to cure the disease. The theory of its proximate cause, which I had adopted, led me to use other remedies, to abstract excess of stimulus from the system. These were *blood-letting*, *cool air*, *cold drinks*, *low diet*, and *applications of cold water* to the body.

Benjamin Rush, M.D.
*An Account of the Bilious Remitting Yellow Fever as It Appeared
in the City of Philadelphia in the Year 1793*, 1794

*D*r. *Benjamin Rush bled his patients even more heroically than he purged them, sometimes taking up to four-fifths of their blood. While most other physicians looked on aghast, he dosed and bled them and continued to delude himself that he was achieving remarkable cures during the Philadelphia yellow-fever epidemics of 1793 and 1797. William Cobbett, who wrote under the name Peter Porcupine, called Rush's methods "one of the great discoveries . . . which have contributed to the depopulation of the earth." Rush sued Cobbett for libel in 1797 and was awarded five thousand dollars, but Cobbett was still attacking Rush and his methods three years later.*

RUSH called *Doctor Wistar* an *assassin*, because Wistar denied the virtue of his grand specific, the *mercurial purges*. I have this fact from *Doctor Glentworth*, a native Philadelphian, a staunch republican, in the best sense of the word, and a very candid, honest and brave man. Doctor Glentworth told me, besides (and he will tell the same to any one), that Rush attended him in the yellow fever of 1793; that he bled him till he was extremely weak, and ordered *several other bleedings* which Glentworth's knowledge made him omit, without, however, telling Rush of the omission; that he came one day, and finding his patient sitting up in the bed, ran to him, squeezed him by the hand, called him his "*dear* Glentworth," and congratulated him on the salutary effects of his bleeding system; "but," said he, "my *dear* friend, you must lose a little MORE BLOOD."— "Lose *more blood!*" replied Glentworth, "when I am so faint I can hardly support myself!"—Upon this, Rush started from the bed-side, caught up his hat, called his "*dear* friend" an *assassin*, told him he was leagued with Wistar to ruin his reputation, and ran down stairs bawling out: "you're a dead man! you're a dead man! you'll be buried before to-morrow night!"

THERE was an instance of *mildness*, *candour*, and *humanity!* Doctor Glentworth did, however, disappoint him. He recovered his health, without losing more blood, and lived to laugh very heartily at the charitable predictions of the *Pennsylvanian "Hippocrates."*

William Cobbett (pseud. Peter Porcupine)
The American Rush-Light, 1800

244

The human body's four temperaments—a medical theory of ancient times—as reflected in the countenance

Even against most of the ordinary diseases doctors could do little, and when an epidemic raged, they had no idea how to stop or slow it because they had no notion of what might have started it. A cholera epidemic was especially fearful, for it seemed to follow wherever man moved; the epidemic of 1832 spread up the St. Lawrence River, along the Erie Canal, over the Mississippi River system, and into most port cities. A news and commercial register gave eyewitness accounts of the plague in New Orleans in November, 1832.

Thursday evening, 6 o'clock.

The New Orleans *Bee*, of the 3d instant, announces the death of 177 persons on the 1st, and 170 on the 2nd November. A letter to a gentleman in Charleston, dated the 2d instant, states that they die faster than coffins can be made, and faster than they can be buried. "For the last four or five nights, there have been from 20 to 50 left unburied. A new plan has been adopted for interring the dead, viz: digging a ditch, 50 feet long, 4 feet deep and 7 feet wide; to contain from 100 to 150 bodies, where the coffins are laid two tier deep; the bottom tier across the ditch, the top tier fore and aft; the first tier are all under water; they are then covered with mud, 18 inches to two feet from the surface. There can be seen in the grave yard one or two hundred coffins at one time uncovered—as they do not cover them until completely filled. Many poor families are swept off entirely. I am aware of two families, one of 12, the other of 11, who have all died, and several composed of 5, 6 and 7 persons. . . . the artillery companies are to discharge their pieces throughout the city, to endeavor to purify the air."

. . . A letter dated Nov. 2, says—"The inhabitants are completely panic struck—bon-fires of tar and pitch are now burning in every street, and continual firing of cannon; what effect all this will have upon the atmosphere remains to be seen. Yesterday, at night, there remained nearly 150 corpse unburied in the church yard."

The New Orleans Price Current of the 3rd says—We have been informed that the epidemic has declared itself on the plantations, and already the most dreadful apprehensions are entertained, as well for the lives of the slaves as for the sugar crop, for this is the *grinding and boiling season*, when delay is irretrievable loss, perhaps pecuniary ruin—but we flatter ourselves that things may take a better turn. . . .

It is said that the bakers had closed their bakeries and the butchers ceased to furnish meat, because of the great mortality among their hands. Happy are they who have the means of obtaining food! The stock of rice was nearly exhausted, but flour was plenty. It was reported that many dead bodies had been sunk in the river, as the most convenient way of disposing of them. But in a season so appalling, great allowances must be made for exaggerated reports. The major part of those who die are slaves. . . .

The Mobile Register of the 9th inst. says:—

"The mail due from New Orleans yesterday arrived in the evening, but furnished only a single paper. The accounts of the cholera shew no abatement in the disease, and from gentlemen who came passengers in the state, we learn that it was attacking the better classes, and that several highly respectable citizens had fallen victims. . . . From the report of the sextons, for the eight days, ending on the evening of the 6th, the number of burials exceeded 1,100; and the population does not, at this time probably, exceed 35,000. This statement does not include the interments at the port, and in private lots, in the vicinity of the city, which would probably increase the whole number, to at least 1,500.

Niles' Weekly Register, November 24, 1832

Despite the ignorance and superstition that still hung over medicine, progress was being made, usually by small and gradual steps, but occasionally in a giant stride. One of the great moves forward was made by Dr. Ephraim McDowell of Danville, Kentucky, when a country woman suffering from a huge abdominal tumor came to him for help. Although any incision into the abdominal cavity was then considered almost certain to result in death, McDowell successfully removed the tumor in an operation called an ovariotomy, and went on to perform eleven similar operations, with only one death. He became the acknowledged master of abdominal surgery of his day, and performed many operations for hernia and at least thirty-two for bladder stones—one of the latter on James K. Polk, later President of the United States. All were without benefit of anesthetic. In the following letter he describes, briefly but graphically, his first operation. It is said that the patient sang hymns during the long procedure.

Sir:

At the request of your father, I take the liberty of addressing you a letter giving you a short account of the circumstances which led to the first operation for diseased ovaria; I was sent for in 1809, to deliver a Mrs. Crawford, near Greentown of twins; as the two attending physicians supposed. Upon examination . . . I soon ascertained that she was not pregnant; but had a large tumour in the Abdomen, which moved easily from side to side. I told the Lady I could do her no good and candidly stated to her her deplorable situation; Informed her that John Bell, Hunter, Hey, and A. Wood, four of the first and most eminent Surgeons in England and Scotland, had uniformly declared in their Lectures, that such was the danger of Peritoneal Inflammation, that opening the abdomen to extract the tumour was inevitable death. But, notwithstanding this, if she thought herself prepared to die, I would take the lump from her, if she could come to Danville. She came in a few days after my return home, and in six days I opened her side and extracted one of the ovaria, which from its diseased and enlarged state weighed upwards of twenty pounds. The Intestines, as soon as an opening was made, ran out upon the table, remained out about thirty minutes and, being upon Christmas day, they became so cold that I thought proper to bathe them in tepid water, previous to my replacing them; I then returned them, stitched up the wound, and she was perfectly well in twenty-five days. Since that time, I have operated eleven times and have lost but one. I now can tell at once when relief can be obtained, by an examination of the tumour; if it floats freely from side to side, or appears free from attachments, except at the lower part of the abdomen, I advise the operation, having no fear from the Inflammation that may ensue.

Ephraim McDowell, M.D.
Letter to Robert Thompson, medical student, January 2, 1829

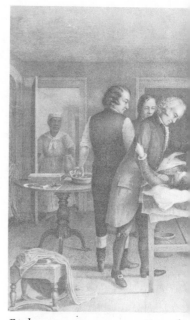

Right, a trepanning operation of 1855. Above, Dr. Ephraim McDowell performs the first ovariotomy, described at the left.

One night in 1827 Dr. John Richmond, attending a farm woman in labor in a log cabin in southwestern Ohio, came to the sobering realization that the birth was not going to be a normal one. At that time Caesarean births almost invariably proved fatal to the mother even under the best of conditions; Dr. Richmond was faced with the awesome prospect of performing one under some of the worst. He lost the baby, but before dawn he had accomplished the first successful Caesarean section west of the Alleghenies.

I had no recourse to cordials, for these could not be obtained. I was seven miles from home, and had but few medicines with me. . . . I requested advice, which, however, could not be obtained, on account of high water in the Little Miami and the darkness of the night. . . . After doing all in my power for her preservation, and feeling myself entirely in the dark as to her situation, and finding that whatever was done, must be done soon, and feeling a deep and solemn sense of my responsibility, with only a case of common pocket instruments, about one o'clock at night, I commenced the CAESAREAN SECTION. Here I must take the liberty to digress from my subject, and relate the condition of the house, which was made of logs that were green, and put together not more than a week before. The crevices were not chinked, there was no chimney, nor chamber floor. The night was stormy and windy, insomuch, that the assistants had to hold blankets to keep the candles from being blown out. Under these circumstances it is hard to conceive of the state of my feelings, when I was convinced that the patient must die, or the operation be performed. . . .

The patient never complained of pain during the whole course of the cure. She commenced work in twenty-four days from the operation, and in the fifth week walked a mile and back the same day.

John Richmond, M.D.

The Western Journal of the Medical and Physical Sciences, III, 1830

Of all medical advances, none was more revolutionary than the discovery of anesthetics; without a way of preventing pain no real advances in surgery would ever have been possible. As early as 1842 Dr. Crawford W. Long of Georgia used ether in an operation, and had used the same anesthetic in surgery seven more times by the fall of 1846. However, he failed to publish any report at the time, and credit for the discovery of anesthetics is usually given to William T. G. Morton, a Boston dentist. Morton had used ether as an anesthetic in extracting teeth, and on October 16, 1846, in Massachusetts General Hospital, he administered it while Dr. John C. Warren removed a tumor from the neck of a young man. Dr. Warren a few weeks later wrote a brief description of the operation for a circular being prepared by Morton. The dentist called his anesthetic letheon.

About five weeks since, Dr. Morton, dentist of this city, informed me that he had invented an apparatus for the inhalation of a vapor, the effect of which was to produce a state of total insensibility to pain, and that he had employed it successfully in a sufficient number of cases in his practice to justify him in a belief of its efficacy. He wished for an opportunity to test its power in surgical operations, and I agreed to give him such an opportunity as soon as practicable.

Being at that time in attendance as Surgeon of the Massachusetts General Hospital, a patient presented himself in that valuable institution a few days after my conversation with Dr. Morton, who required an operation for a tumor of the neck; and, agreeably to my promise, I requested the attendance of Dr. M.

On October [16], the patient being prepared for the operation, the apparatus was applied to his mouth by Dr. Morton for about three minutes, at the end of which time he sank into a state of insensibility. I immediately made an incision about three inches long through the skin of the neck, and began a dissection among important nerves and blood-vessels, without any expression of pain on the part of the patient. Soon after, he began to speak incoherently, and appeared to be in an agitated state during the remainder of the operation. Being asked immediately afterwards whether he had suffered much, he said that he had felt as if his neck had been scratched; but subsequently, when inquired of by me, his statement was, that he did not experience pain at the time, although aware that the operation was proceeding.

The effect of the gaseous inhalation in neutralizing the sentient faculty, was made perfectly distinct to my mind by this experiment. . . .

John C. Warren, M.D.
in *Morton's Letheon*, 1847

The realization came slowly that the insane were simply sick persons, needing help and humane treatment. They were commonly treated as brutes, penned up under conditions that were often unspeakable, until their illnesses had usually deteriorated beyond cure. Of the handful of medical men and humanitarians who worked for better treatment of the mentally ill, none was more dedicated than Dorothea Dix, a Boston schoolmistress, who by chance in 1841 had visited a house of correction where several insane persons were also locked up. Thereafter she swept across the country, looking into the care of the insane everywhere and influencing eleven states to build asylums. Below are passages from her petition to the legislature of Massachusetts, prepared after two years of investigating conditions under which the insane were kept in that state.

I come to present the strong claims of suffering humanity. I come to place before the Legislature of Massachusetts the condition of the miserable, the desolate, the outcast. I come as the advocate of helpless, forgotten, insane, and idiotic men and women; of beings sunk to a condition from which the most unconcerned would start with real horror; of beings wretched in our prisons, and more wretched in our almshouses. And I cannot suppose it needful to employ earnest persuasion, or stubborn argument, in order to arrest and fix attention upon a subject only the more strongly pressing in its claims because it is revolting and disgusting in its details. . . .

I proceed, gentlemen, briefly to call your attention to the *present* state of insane persons confined within this Commonwealth, in *cages, closets, cellars, stalls, pens! Chained, naked, beaten with rods,* and *lashed* into obedience. . . .

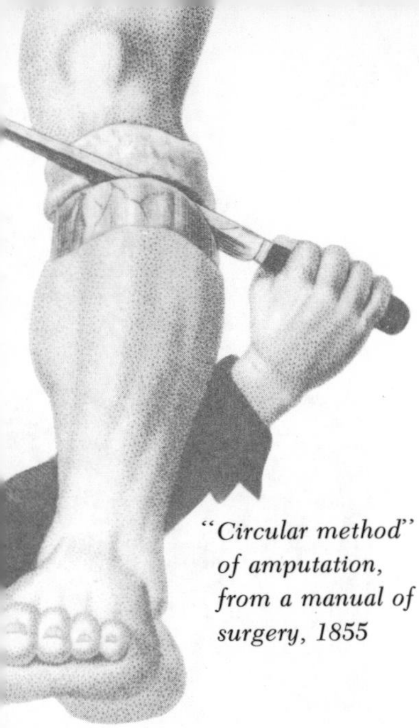

Springfield. In the jail, one lunatic woman, furiously mad, a State pauper, improperly situated, both in regard to the prisoners, the keepers, and herself. It is a case of extreme self-forgetfulness and oblivion to all the decencies of life, to describe which would be to repeat only the grossest scenes. She is much worse since leaving Worcester. In the almshouse of the same town is a woman apparently only needing judicious care, and some well-chosen employment, to make it unnecessary to confine her in solitude, in a dreary unfurnished room. Her appeals for employment and companionship are most touching, but the mistress replied "she had no time to attend to her."

. . . *Lincoln.* A woman in a cage. *Medford.* One idiotic subject chained, and one in a close stall for seventeen years. *Pepperell.* One often doubly chained, hand and foot; another violent; several peaceable now. *Brookfield.* One man caged, comfortable. *Granville.* One often closely confined; now losing the use of his limbs from want of exercise. *Charlemont.* One man caged. *Savoy.* One man caged. *Lenox.* Two in the jail, against whose unfit condition there the jailer protests.

Dedham. The insane disadvantageously placed in the jail. In the almshouse, two females in stalls, situated in the main building; lie in wooden bunks filled with straw; always shut up. One of these subjects is supposed curable. The overseers of the poor have declined giving her a trial at the hospital, as I was informed, on account of expense. . . .

Danvers. November. Visited the almshouse. A large building, much out of repair. Understand a new one is in contemplation. Here are from fifty-six to sixty inmates, one idiotic, three insane; one of the latter in close confinement at all times.

Long before reaching the house, wild shouts, snatches of rude songs, imprecations and obscene language, fell upon the ear, proceeding from the occupant of a low building, rather remote from the principal building to which my course was directed. Found the mistress, and was conducted to the place which was called "*the home*" of the *forlorn* maniac, a young woman, exhibiting a condition of neglect and misery blotting out the faintest idea of comfort, and outraging every sentiment of decency. She had been, I learnt, "a respectable person, industrious and worthy. Disappointments and trials shook her mind, and, finally, laid prostrate reason and self-control. She became a maniac for life. She had been at Worcester Hospital for a considerable time, and had been returned as incurable." The mistress told me she understood that, "while there, she was comfortable and decent." Alas, what a change was here exhibited! . . . There she stood with naked arms and dishevelled hair, the unwashed frame invested with fragments of unclean garments, the air so extremely offensive, though ventilation was afforded on all sides save one, that it was not possible to remain beyond a few moments without retreating for recovery to the outward air. . . .

Gentlemen, I commit to you this sacred cause. Your action upon this subject will affect the present and future condition of hundreds and of thousands.

In this legislation, as in all things, may you exercise that "wisdom which is the breath of the power of God."

Respectfully submitted,

Dorothea Dix

Memorial to the Legislature of Massachusetts, 1843

249

$\mathcal{M}$an's urge to promote the well-being of his fellows led him to try to free the drunkard from his bondage to the demon that lies in the bottle. One of the earliest, and certainly the best-known, works on alcoholism was by Dr. Benjamin Rush—the same who held such barbaric ideas about treating disease by purging and bleeding. Dr. Rush's description of the stages of drunkenness is classic.

I shall begin by briefly describing their [ardent spirits] prompt, or immediate effects, in a fit of drunkenness.

This odious disease (for by that name it should be called) appears with more or less of the following symptoms, and most commonly in the order in which I shall enumerate them.

1. Unusual garrulity.
2. Unusual silence.
3. Captiousness, and a disposition to quarrel.
4. Uncommon good humour, and an insipid simpering, or laugh.
5. Profane swearing, and cursing.
6. A disclosure of their own, or other people's secrets.
7. A rude disposition to tell those persons . . . whom they know, their faults.
8. Certain immodest actions. I am sorry to say, this sign of the first stage of drunkenness sometimes appears in women, who, when sober, are uniformly remarkable for chaste and decent manners.
9. A clipping of words.
10. Fighting; a black eye, or a swelled nose, often mark this [stage].
11. Certain extravagant acts which indicate a temporary fit of madness.

These are singing, hallooing, roaring, imitating the noises of brute animals, jumping, tearing off clothes, dancing naked, breaking glasses and china, and dashing other articles of household furniture upon the ground, or floor. After a while the paroxysm of drunkenness is completely formed. The face now becomes flushed, the eyes project, and are somewhat watery, winking is less frequent than is natural; the under lip is protruded,—the head inclines a little to one shoulder;—the jaw falls;—belchings and hiccup take place;—the limbs totter;—the whole body staggers;—The unfortunate subject of this history next falls on his seat,—he looks around him with a vacant countenance, and mutters inarticulate sounds to himself;—he attempts to rise and walk. In this attempt, he falls upon his side, from which he gradually turns upon his back. He now closes his eyes, and falls into a profound sleep. . . . His recovery from this fit of intoxication is marked with several peculiar appearances. He opens his eyes, and closes them again;—he gapes and stretches his limbs,—he then coughs and pukes,—his voice is hoarse,—he rises with difficulty, and staggers to a chair; his eyes resemble balls of fire,—his hands tremble,—he loathes the sight of food;—he calls for a glass of spirits to compose his stomach—now and then he emits a deep-fetched sigh, or groan, from a transient twinge of conscience, but he more frequently scolds, and curses every thing around him. In this state of languor and stupidity, he remains for two or three days, before he is able to resume his former habits of business and conversation.

Benjamin Rush, M.D.
An Inquiry into the Effects of Spiritous Liquors on the Human Mind and Body, 1784

Demons at work in a New England rum distillery—a fanciful concept aimed at encouraging temperance

A Long Island country pastor, Lyman Beecher, was so moved by Benjamin Rush's work on the effects of spirituous liquors that he preached a series of sermons against drinking in 1810, and thereby gave rise to the temperance movement. Most of the large mass of antiliquor literature that has survived has a numbing sameness: it portrays, in horrendous detail, the corrosive effects of alcohol on brain, liver, stomach, and heart; it indicts liquor as a wrecker of careers and a destroyer of families; and it makes plain that drinking can end only in the poorhouse or suicide. Occasional speakers and writers found new horrors; such a man was Jonathan Kittredge, whose speech given one winter night in the New Hampshire village of Lyme deserves to be remembered.

Out of the number of the intemperate in the United States, ten thousand die annually from the effects of ardent spirits. And what a death! To live a drunkard is enough, but to die so, and to be ushered into the presence of your angry Judge, only to hear the sentence, "Depart thou drunkard!" Ah! language fails, and I leave it to your imaginations to fill up the horrid picture.

This death happens in various ways. Some are killed instantly, some die a lingering, gradual death, some commit suicide in fits of intoxication, and some are actually burnt up. I read of an intemperate man, a few years since, whose breath caught fire by coming in contact with a lighted candle, and he was consumed. At the time, I disbelieved the story, but my reading has since furnished me with well authenticated cases of a combustion of the human body from the use of ardent spirits. Trotter mentions ten such cases, and relates them at length. They are attended with all the proof, we require to believe any event. They are attended by living witnesses, examined by learned men, and published in the journals of the day without contradiction. It would be unnecessary to relate the whole, but I will state one of them, and from this, an idea can be formed of the rest. It is the case "of a woman eighty years of age, exceedingly meagre, who had drunk nothing, but ardent spirits, for several years. She was sitting in her elbow chair, while her waiting maid went out of the room for a few moments. On her return, seeing her mistress on fire, she immediately gave an alarm, and some people coming to her assistance, one of them endeavored to extinguish the flames with his hands, *but they adhered to them, as, if they had been dipped in brandy or oil on fire.* Water was brought and thrown on the body in abundance, *yet the fire appeared more violent, and was not extinguished, till the whole body had been consumed.*—The lady was in the same place, in which she sat every day, there was no extraordinary fire, and she had not fallen." This, with nine other cases, related by the same author, was a consumption of the body produced by the use of ardent spirits. The horror of a drunkard's death beggars description. Need I point to yonder grave, just closed over the remains of one, who went from the cup of excess to almost instant death. You all know it.

Jonathan Kittredge
An Address upon the Effects of Ardent Spirits, January 8, 1827

In 1836 the teetotalers captured the temperance movement, and the moderates, who favored wines and beer, drifted away. The dry campaign gained new

Tippler and his empty source of joy

*life during the 1840's with the rise of the Washingtonians, self-proclaimed for-
mer drunkards whose emotional lectures for abstinence brought a camp-meet-
ing air to the crusade. A flood of repentant tosspots signed the pledge and gave
up drinking—at least temporarily—but by the mid-1850's temperance began to
run out of steam. However, its last years were capped by its masterpiece,* Ten
Nights in a Barroom, *a lurid account of the evils of drink. Written by journalist
Timothy Arthur in 1854, it was second only to* Uncle Tom's Cabin *in popularity,
and was soon made into a drama that may yet be playing. At one point in the
play little golden-haired Mary appears three times at the tavern where her father is far gone in drink, and in the following verses begs him to come home.*

Father, dear Father, come home with me now!
The clock in the steeple strikes one.
You said you were coming right home from the shop
As soon as your day's work was done.
Our fire has gone out, our house is all dark,
And Mother's been watching since tea,
With poor brother Benny so sick in her arms,
And no one to help her but me.

Come home! Come home! Come home!
Please father, dear father, come home!
Hear the sweet voice of the child,
Which the north winds repeat as they roam,
Oh, who could resist this most plaintive of prayers?
"Father, dear father, come home!"

Father, dear Father, come home with me now!
The clock in the steeple strikes two;
The night has grown colder, and Benny is worse—
But he has been calling for you.
Indeed he is worse, Ma says he will die—
Perhaps before morning shall dawn;
And this is the message she sent me to bring—
"Come quickly, or he will be gone."

(*Chorus*) Come home! Come home! *etc.*

Father, dear Father, come home with me now!
The clock in the steeple strikes three;
The house is so lonely! the hours are so long
For poor weeping Mother and me.
Yes, we are alone, poor Benny is dead,
And gone with the angels of light;
And these are the very last words that he said,
"I want to kiss Papa good night."

(*Chorus*) Come home! Come home! *etc.*

Henry Clay Work
"Come Home, Father," 1864

*Little Mary pleads with he[r]
besotted father to come
home in the frontispiece o[f]*
Ten Nights in a Barroom.

The early years of the republic were a time for experiments in philosophy, in economics, in religion. Communal settlements blossomed everywhere, founded on some theory of philosophy or economics, as Fruitlands or Brook Farm in New England or New Harmony in Indiana or, to make possible an isolated spiritual life, as the Shaker and Amana communities. Of the dozens of such groups, most were short-lived. Ralph Waldo Emerson felt moved to write an essay commenting with some irony on communities near his own Concord.

What a fertility of projects for the salvation of the world! One apostle thought all men should go to farming; and another, that no man should buy or sell; that the use of money was the cardinal evil; another, that the mischief was in our diet, that we eat and drink damnation. These made unleavened bread, and were foes to the death to fermentation. It was in vain urged by the housewife, that God made yeast, as well as dough, and loves fermentation just as dearly as he loves vegetation; that fermentation develops the saccharine element in the grain, and makes it more palatable and more digestible. No; they wish the pure wheat, and will die but it shall not ferment. Stop, dear nature, these incessant advances of thine: let us scotch these ever-rolling wheels! Others attacked the system of agriculture, the use of animal manures in farming; and the tyranny of man over brute nature; these abuses polluted his food. The ox must be taken from the plough, and the horse from the cart, the hundred acres of the farm must be spaded, and the man must walk wherever boats and locomotives will not carry him. Even the insect world was to be defended,—that had been too long neglected, and a society for the protection of ground-worms, slugs, and mosquitoes was to be incorporated without delay. With these appeared the adepts of homoeopathy, of hydropathy, of mesmerism, of phrenology, and their wonderful theories of the Christian miracles! Others assailed particular vocations, as that of the lawyer, that of the merchant, of the manufacturer, of the clergyman, of the scholar. Others attacked the institution of marriage, as the fountain of social evils. Others devoted themselves to the worrying of churches and meetings for public worship; and the fertile forms of antinomianism among the elder puritans seemed to have their match in the plenty of the new harvest of reform.

With this din of opinion and debate, there was a keener scrutiny of institutions and domestic life than any we had known, there was sincere protesting against existing evils, and there were changes of employment dictated by conscience. No doubt, there was plentiful vaporing, and cases of backsliding might occur. But in each of these movements emerged a good result, a tendency to the adoption of simpler methods, and an assertion of the sufficiency of the private man.

Ralph Waldo Emerson
"New England Reformers," 1844

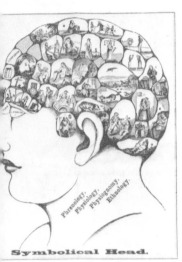

Symbolical Head.

The inner workings of the human brain as shown in an advertisement for lectures on phrenology about 1850

Among the few communities that did succeed were those of the Shakers, who combined a deep religious faith with a willingness to work for the common good. From 1787 through the first quarter of the nineteenth century, eighteen Shaker communities were established from New England as far west as Indiana.

The account below describes the Shaker worship. It does not tell that they were consummate craftsmen who influenced contemporary design, especially in furniture. Nor does it explain that the Shakers were doomed to extinction unless they continually recruited new members: they were pledged to celibacy and there was no such thing as a baby Shaker.

The worship of the Shakers consists principally of singing and dancing, and is performed in this manner: The men are arranged in pairs, and march round the room, or place of worship, followed by the women in the same order. A number of singers are stationed in the middle of the room, and centre of the circle, whose duty it is to sing lively airs for the purpose of keeping time in marching, dancing, &c. After having marched in running time for a few moments, they form a line, and begin dancing to the air of some lively tune. As the singing and dancing progress the worshippers become more zealous, then frantic with excitement, until nothing but what the "world" would call disorder and confusion reigns. As the excitement increases, all order is forgotten, all unison of parts repudiated, each sings his own tune, each dances his own dance, or leaps, shouts, and exults with exceeding great joy. The more gifted of the females engage in a kind of whirling motion, which they perform with seemingly incredible velocity, their arms being extended horizontally, and their dresses blown out like a balloon all around their persons, by the centrifugal force occasioned by the rapidity of their motion. After performing from fifty to one thousand revolutions each, they either swoon away, and fall into the arms of their friends, or suddenly come to a stand, with apparently little or no dizziness having been produced. Sometimes the worshippers engage in a race round the room with a sweeping motion of the hands and arms, intended to represent the act of sweeping the devil out of the room. In addition to singing, dancing, running, whirling, sweeping, jumping, &c. &c., they frequently have a word of exhortation from the more elderly worshippers. The Shakers believe in the efficacy of prayer, and, unlike the Quakers, have morning and evening devotions. Before partaking of their meals they reverently kneel around the table, and crave a blessing on the repast.

Rev. P. Douglass Gorrie
The Churches and Sects of the United States, 1850

In spite of changing philosophies and new approaches to salvation, the old-time religion still held its own pretty well. In fact, it began making a much more fervent appeal in 1800, when—it is generally agreed—the first camp meeting was held in Kentucky. Thereafter the three- or four-day camp meeting, where worship became a highly charged emotional experience, was a regular part of the American scene. Captain Frederick Marryat, the English traveler, visited a camp meeting near Cincinnati in 1835.

When I first examined the area I saw a very large tent at one corner of it, probably fifty feet long, by twenty wide. It was open at the end and, being full of straw, I concluded it was used as a sleeping-place for those who had not provided themselves with separate accommodation. About an hour after the service

Shakers' symb

ee of Light

was over, perceiving many people directing their steps towards it, I followed them. On one side of the tent were about twenty females, mostly young, squatted down on the straw; on the other a few men; in the centre was a long form, against which were some other men kneeling, with their faces covered with their hands, as if occupied in prayer. Gradually the numbers increased, girl after girl dropped down upon the straw on the one side, and men on the other. At last an elderly man gave out a hymn, which was sung with peculiar energy; then another knelt down in the centre, and commenced a prayer, shutting his eyes (as I have observed most clergymen in the United States do when they pray) and raising his hands above his head; then another burst out into a prayer, and another followed him; then their voices became all confused together; and then were heard the more silvery tones of woman's supplication. As the din increased so did their enthusiasm; handkerchiefs were raised to bright eyes, and sobs were intermingled with prayers and ejaculations. It became a scene of Babel; more than twenty men and women were crying out at the highest pitch of their voices, and trying apparently to be heard above the others. Every minute the excitement increased; some wrung their hands and called for mercy; some tore their hair; boys laid down crying bitterly, with their heads buried in the straw; there was sobbing almost to suffocation, and hysterics and deep agony. One young man clung to the form, crying: "Satan tears at me, but I will hold fast. Help—help, he drags me down!" It was a scene of horrible agony and despair; and, when it was at its height, one of the preachers came in, and, raising his voice high above the tumult, entreated the Lord to receive into his fold those who now repented and would fain return. Another of the ministers knelt down by some young men, whose faces were covered up and who appeared to be almost in a state of phrenzy; and putting his hands upon them, poured forth an energetic prayer, well calculated to work upon their over excited feelings. Groans, ejaculations, broken sobs, frantic motions and convulsions succeeded; some fell on their backs with their eyes closed, waving their hands with a slow motion, and crying out—"Glory, glory, glory!" I quitted the spot, and hastened away into the forest, for the sight was too painful, too melancholy. Its sincerity could not be doubted, but it was the effect of over-excitement, not of sober reasoning. Could such violence of feeling have been produced had each party retired to commune alone?—most surely not. It was a fever created by collision and contact, of the same nature as that which stimulates a mob to deeds of blood and horror. . . .

I was told that the scene would be much more interesting and exciting after the lamps were lighted; but I had seen quite enough of it. It was too serious to laugh at, and I felt that it was not for me to condemn. "Cry aloud, and spare not" was the exhortation of the preacher; and certainly, if heaven is only to be taken by storm, he was a proper leader for his congregation.

. . . it is not uncommon for the settlers in Indiana and Illinois to travel one hundred miles in their wagons to attend one of these meetings—meetings which are now too often sullied by fanaticism on the one hand, and on the other by the levity and infidelity of those who go not to pray, but to scoff; or to indulge in the licentiousness which, it is said, but too often follows, when night has thrown her veil over the scene.

Frederick Marryat
A Diary in America, 1839

PICTURE CREDITS. PAGE 241: LIBRARY OF CONGRESS; PAGES 242–43: AMERICAN ANTIQUARIAN SOCIETY; PAGE 243: M. AND M. KAROLIK COLLECTION, MUSEUM OF FINE ARTS, BOSTON; PAGES 244–45: *Columbian Magazine,* 1789, NEW-YORK HISTORICAL SOCIETY; PAGES 246–47: LIBRARY OF CONGRESS; PAGES 247 AND 249: C. BERNARD AND C. HUETTE, *Illustrated Manual of Operative Surgery and Surgical Anatomy,* 1855, NEW YORK ACADEMY OF MEDICINE; PAGES 250–51: AMERICAN ANTIQUARIAN SOCIETY; PAGE 251: METROPOLITAN MUSEUM OF ART, GIFT OF JAMES C. MC GUIRE, 1926; PAGE 252: T.S. ARTHUR, *Ten Nights in a Barroom,* 1854; PAGE 253: CINCINNATI HISTORICAL SOCIETY; PAGES 254–55: ANDREWS COLLECTION, HANCOCK SHAKER COMMUNITY, HANCOCK, MASSACHUSETTS

The Mexican War

Polk has always been a vague figure in his country's history, a drab one-term President, lank-haired, shy, hesitant of speech. Yet, although suspicious and without humor or charm, he was, beneath his negligible exterior, a tough-minded man, the strongest President between Jackson and Lincoln.

As a partisan Democrat he could see nothing good in the Whigs, noting in his diary with surprise of one acquaintance that "although a Whig he seems a gentleman." Coming to the Presidency as a dark horse, he had the good fortune to enter the White House unencumbered by pledges to any faction. He dominated his mediocre Cabinet, of which the most conspicuous member—at least in the light of succession—was the Secretary of State, that calculating side-stepper of controversial issues, the smoothly charming James Buchanan. Polk's campaign nickname, Young Hickory, indicated basically what he was: a New Jacksonian; equally against disunionists and abolitionists; opposed to Clay's American System with its internal improvements at federal expense, protective tariff, national bank, and national debt. Such a system, of benefit to the wealthy, would in Polk's opinion create "a rich and splendid government at the expense of the taxed and impoverished people," an empire rather than a union. Like Benton, he supported graduation of public-land prices and pre-emption, making his belief explicit in his first message to Congress, in which he announced that the policy of the government would be to help ordinary Americans "to become the owners of small portions of our vast public domain at low and moderate rates." Further in his Jacksonian concern for the common people he would not go, for it was not, he felt, the function of government to provide for the poor, nor was it the business of Congress to give away public property.

At the beginning of his term Polk announced publicly that he would not seek a second one. Shortly after his inauguration he told his Secretary of the Navy, the Massachusetts historian George Bancroft, that he had four great objectives. Striking his thigh for emphasis, he said that he intended to reduce the tariff, to re-establish the independent treasury, to settle the Oregon boundary, and to acquire California.

Under the title "The Land of Liberty," this cartoon of the prototype American bemused by thoughts of the war with Mexico, the lynching of slaves, the slave trade, and rowdyism in Congress appeared in the British magazine Punch *in 1847. Many Americans saw justification in* Punch's *criticism.*

The admission of Texas was so foregone a conclusion that Polk did not even mention it to Bancroft. After passage of the joint congressional resolution for annexation, England and France had tried to keep the Texans from accepting by urging Mexico to recognize the Lone-Star Republic as an independent nation. But in spite of certain lingering doubts in Houston's mind, sentiment in Texas was overwhelmingly for annexation, a sentiment reinforced by Polk's tempting promises of internal improvements and fortifications. The Texas legislature accepted the federal offer, a state convention wrote a constitution, which was approved by the national government in December, 1845, and the Lone-Star State became the twenty-eighth star in the flag.

First to demand Polk's attention was the problem of Oregon. Ever since Secretary of State John Quincy Adams had negotiated with Britain the 1818 agreement for joint occupation, Monroe, and subsequent Presidents, had been willing to offer the British the 49th parallel as the dividing line between the United States and Canada. To Easterners and Southerners, Oregon seemed a faraway and useless stretch of territory. Senator George McDuffie of South Carolina felt he would not give a pinch of snuff for crops that could be grown there. "What do we want with this vast, worthless area?" Webster asked from the ordered meadows of his Marshfield, Massachusetts, home. "This region of savages and wild beasts, of deserts, of shifting sands and whirlpools of dust, of cactus and prairie dogs?" The swarming settlers saw it otherwise as they clamored for "Fifty-four forty or fight!"

Polk in his inaugural had declared the title of the United States to the Oregon country as far north as Alaska "clear and unquestionable," but later—with a Mexican crisis shadowing him—he was willing to drop "Fifty-four forty" for the 49th parallel. The British turned down his offer, reluctant to give up the boundary of the Columbia River and the lower third of Vancouver Island. Reacting with belligerence, Polk demanded all of Oregon, and in his annual message called for the termination of the joint occupancy. American rights, he told Congress, could not be abandoned without abandoning national honor and national interest. He told a congressman that the only way to treat John Bull was to look him straight in the eye.

Such eye-to-eye confrontation was so distasteful to Southern Democrats that they were ready to side with the Whigs in preserving good relations with England.

Polk's intransigent resolution ending joint occupancy had to be modified in the Senate to a more conciliatory form before it was finally passed. Yet, for all Polk's readiness to stare down John Bull, he never let his emotion master his reason. He knew that the region above the 49th parallel was not worth fighting about so long as American ships had freedom of passage through the Vancouver straits. When reports came to him that Britain, though anxious for peace with the United States, was preparing for war, he let it be known in London through Secretary Buchanan that any new British offer would "in all probability" be submitted to the Senate for careful consideration.

The British now had sufficient reasons of their own for wanting to compromise. American settlers in Oregon outnumbered them 8 or 9 to 1. The fur trade was dying out. Pushed by the newcomers, the Hudson's Bay Company had moved its chief trading post from the Columbia River to Vancouver Island. Giving up all thought of a Columbia River boundary, the British Foreign Secretary Lord Aberdeen proposed to extend the 49th parallel to the coast, then bend the boundary south to retain all of Vancouver Island for Britain. By this time the United States was already at war with Mexico. Polk acted quickly, submitting the British offer to the Senate. Sir Richard Pakenham, the British ambassador in Washington, signed the treaty five days later, after which it was ratified by the Senate 41 to 14. This balanced and reasonable compromise brought a lasting peace between the two English-speaking countries and left the United States free to face its Mexican difficulties.

The unstable, debt-ridden twenty-one-year-old Republic of Mexico could scarcely be considered to have a functioning government, verging as it did on anarchy, with widespread unrest in its northern provinces. Yet the passage by the American Congress of the joint resolution offering annexation to Texas had roused a furious protest that united Mexicans of all shades of opinion in demanding vengeance for what they considered an act of robbery. Two days after Polk's inauguration, General Almonte, the Mexican minister to the United States, broke off diplomatic relations.

War sentiment swelled on both sides. Beyond the frontier contempt that Westerners felt for the Mexicans, there had been bitter grievances over the years that added to their belligerence: American citizens in Mexico insulted, imprisoned, robbed, murdered; American goods seized. Nor had Texans forgotten Santa Anna's

Though agreed on as the boundary in 1846, the Western
part of the 49th parallel was not surveyed until 1859.
This Washington scene is by a member of the survey crew.

wiping out of the Alamo garrison, where the bodies of the defenders had afterward been stacked like cordwood, soaked with oil, and burned. On June 15, 1845, Brigadier General Zachary Taylor, commander of the Louisiana-based First Department of the Army, was sent by Polk to Texas. At Corpus Christi on the Nueces River Taylor set up a poorly disciplined camp, formed an Army of Occupation, and prepared on short notice to move south into the disputed region between the Nueces and the Rio Grande. By November his fifteen hundred men had become almost four thousand. Like the commanding general, Winfield Scott, Taylor was a Whig, and Polk's reaction was instinctively partisan. "He is, I have no doubt, a good subordinate officer," Polk said, "but from all the evidence before me I think him unfit for command. Though this is so, I know of no one whom I can substitute in his place."

At sixty-one Taylor owed whatever reputation he had to his generalship in Florida's Second Seminole War, which had begun in 1835, the longest, costliest, bloodiest Indian war in the country's history. Without much

knowledge of military science, he was a stubborn, aggressive campaigner with a capacity for practical leadership, which he had demonstrated first as a junior officer in the War of 1812. In the four-month Black Hawk War he had seen action only in the closing stages, leading his troops against fleeing Indians. Then he had stayed on in the Army as commander of a frontier fort until he was transferred to Florida in 1837 after the outbreak of the Seminole War.

For propaganda purposes Taylor could say that he had been born in a log cabin, although he could make the claim only because his birth had taken place while his father—a Revolutionary colonel—was traveling with his mother from their home in Virginia to inspect some new holdings in Kentucky. A cousin of Madison's, Taylor was related to most of the old Virginia planter families, but he had been brought up in the more primitive region of Kentucky, where his father had settled in a brick mansion that he had built near Louisville. The son, after limited schooling, joined the Army as a lieutenant in 1808, when war threatened with England and

259

Spain, and as a captain in the War of 1812 he made a name for himself locally by successfully defending Fort Harrison on the Wabash—the first American victory in that war. Occasionally he thought of giving up the Army to cultivate his Kentucky acres, but—except for a short interval or two—he remained as a career officer while buying a plantation and from time to time picking up additional acres in Louisiana. Against his will, his daughter Sarah married the young Mississippi lieutenant Jefferson Davis, and then died three months later from malaria.

A heavy-featured man with a large nose, half-closed eyes and faulty vision, and a wide mouth that turned down at the corners, Taylor disliked the military pomp that so delighted his commanding general, Scott. Most of the time when on duty he wore untidy and badly fitting civilian clothes with only the star on his cap to mark his rank. Old Rough and Ready, his men called him. Often he rode his solid, slow-gaited horse, Old Whitey, with both legs on one side. His mind jogged along as slowly as his horse.

In addition to ordering Taylor to Texas, Polk dispatched naval detachments to the Mexican coast. Yet at the same time he still hoped to avert war. "We shall not be the aggressors upon Mexico," he said in August, 1845. As proof of this, in November he sent the Spanish-speaking states' rights Democrat John Slidell as envoy extraordinary and minister plenipotentiary to Mexico to try to arrange a peaceful settlement. Polk was willing to pay the Mexicans as much as forty million dollars for an over-all agreement that would include the signing over to the United States of New Mexico and California along with the confirmation of Texas' Rio Grande boundary. At a minimum he was prepared to settle merely for the river boundary and the satisfaction of private American claims—running to some six million dollars—against Mexico.

Slidell's arrival stirred the Mexican population and brought forth a rash of wall posters denouncing any dealings with him as treason. The tottering government, not daring to receive him, appealed vainly for help to England and France. Then a general, Mariano Paredes, swept the civilian government aside. Paredes believed in no concessions at all to the United States and let Slidell cool his heels. When word of this reached Washington, Polk sent orders to General Taylor to move his Army of Occupation from Corpus Christi southward to the banks of the Rio Grande.

Taylor, his army already reduced by fever and desertion, established a supply base at strategic Point Isabel on the Gulf of Mexico and constructed the almost indefensible Fort Texas across the river from Matamoros. Mexican reinforcements began to arrive at Matamoros with a musical-chairs switching of generals until the last, Mariano Arista, commanded eight thousand Mexican soldiers there. The day after he took command he sent a sizable cavalry force across the river, against which Taylor dispatched a small squadron of dragoons. In the ensuing engagement the dragoons were soon overwhelmed by Arista's cavalry, and after several of them had been killed, the rest were forced to surrender. Taylor grimly informed the President that "hostilities may now be considered as commenced." Arista boasted that he had "the pleasure of being the first to start the war."

Polk, on receiving the news, sent a war message to a Congress engaged in debating the abolishing of West Point because it was looked upon as a creator of a military caste. Even without Arista's challenge, he had been pondering such a message. But with this bloody provocation he needed to ponder no further. "The cup of forbearance," he told Congress, "had been exhausted. . . . But now, after reiterated menaces, Mexico has passed the boundary of the United States, has invaded our territory and shed American blood upon the American soil. . . . As war exists, and, notwithstanding all our efforts to avoid it, exists by the act of Mexico herself . . . I invoke the prompt action of Congress to recognize the existence of the war."

Within half an hour of hearing the war message, the House of Representatives voted ten million dollars for defense and authorized the President to raise an army of fifty thousand volunteers. The more cantankerous Senate took another day of debate and discussion before it approved. Polk issued his proclamation of war, then reluctantly appointed General Winfield Scott to command the new Army, admitting in his diary that he had no other choice. "Scientific and visionary in his views" was Polk's final verdict on the professional.

Like Taylor, Scott was of an old Virginia family, and like Taylor, he had joined the Army in Jefferson's administration. But there the resemblance ceased. For Scott, in spite of his vain, pompous, and domineering manner, had real military talents and a solid scholarly understanding of the science of war. As a general he had reshaped the United States Army into something resembling a modern military force.

In a day when few men reached six feet, Scott was a giant—six feet four inches tall, weighing two hundred and fifty pounds—with a broad face and gray side whiskers. He loved all the pomp and glitter of military life, wearing his full accouterments of gold braid and epaulets and insisting that his staff do likewise. At parades and inspections he was a martinet. Old Fuss and Feathers, his soldiers called him. He fancied himself urbane, spoke bad French, told bad jokes, paraded his knowledge of food, wine, and women. With his superiors and inferiors he was equally quarrelsome. He was keenly aware of his own abilities.

For all his imperious nature, Scott had a capacity for tactful diplomacy, which he demonstrated in dealing with Canadian border tensions during Van Buren's administration. In 1841, at the age of fifty-five, his country's most outstanding military leader, he was made general in chief of the Army. He recommended that Taylor remain in command of the Army of Occupation.

To Arista, Taylor at Fort Texas, with his supplies and most of his ammunition at Point Isabel, looked temptingly vulnerable. The Mexican general crossed the river with his army, investing the fort and its garrison and driving Taylor back to Point Isabel. For six days Arista bombarded the fort, the defenders lacking even the powder to return the fire vigorously. However, American losses were light. The commanding officer, Major Jacob Brown, mortally wounded, was among the casualties, and the fort was renamed Fort Brown in his honor. Taylor, emerging at last with his army, met the pageantry of the Mexicans near the watering hole of Palo Alto. But gold braid, bright tunics, shakos, and sashes proved ineffective against the superior American artillery, which was taking the lives of eight Mexicans for every American loss. Lieutenant Ulysses Simpson Grant, gravely watching the slaughter, grasped and never forgot the principle of massed firepower. For all the Mexicans suffered at the Battle of Palo Alto, the peon-soldiers held, and not until the next day in the Battle of Resaca de la Palma, after hand-to-hand combat among the thorn bushes, did they finally break, overwhelmed by their casualties. In spite of the pleas of his West Point officers, Taylor did not follow up Arista's smashed army. Not until nine days later did he cross the river for an unimpeded occupation of Matamoros, where he rested for the next six weeks, weeks in which a sudden thrust against a demoralized enemy might have won the war.

Such a quick victory against a despised enemy was

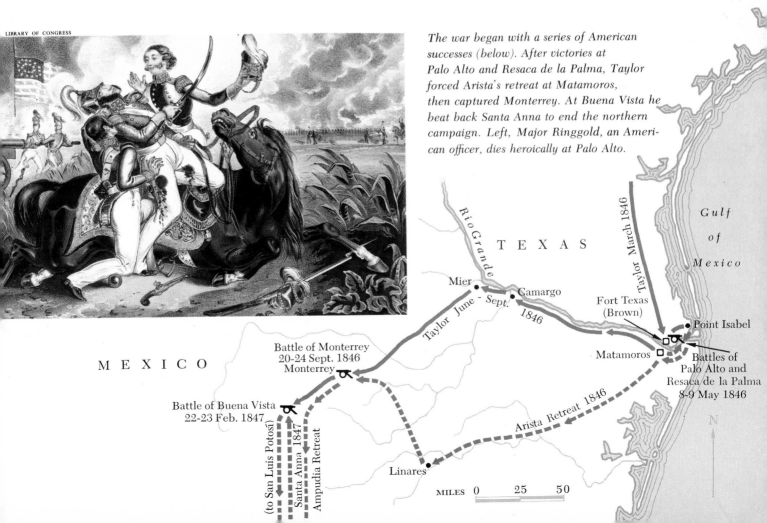

LIBRARY OF CONGRESS

The war began with a series of American successes (below). After victories at Palo Alto and Resaca de la Palma, Taylor forced Arista's retreat at Matamoros, then captured Monterrey. At Buena Vista he beat back Santa Anna to end the northern campaign. Left, Major Ringgold, an American officer, dies heroically at Palo Alto.

Gulf of Mexico

Rio Grande

T E X A S

Taylor March 1846

Mier

Camargo

Taylor June - Sept. 1846

Fort Texas (Brown)

Point Isabel

Matamoros

Battles of Palo Alto and Resaca de la Palma 8-9 May 1846

M E X I C O

Battle of Monterrey 20-24 Sept. 1846
Monterrey

Arista Retreat 1846

Battle of Buena Vista 22-23 Feb. 1847

(to San Luis Potosí)

Santa Anna 1847

Ampudia Retreat

Linares

MILES 0 25 50

N

*The landing of American troops at Vera Cruz
was much less orderly than portrayed here by an artist
of the time. The Mexican failure to attack while
the force approached in surfboats was a costly blunder.*

what Americans expected. As usual on entering a war, the country was vastly overconfident and badly underprepared. The small Regular Army, one-third of its soldiers foreign-born, was unused to anything more martial than chasing Indians. Military planners in Washington, who talked of a quick war, failed to consider the problems of supply and of distance on the rough, inaccessible Mexican terrain, with its deserts and mountains. The Mexicans in their turn were equally unrealistic about the course of hostilities. They did not believe that the United States, divided politically and with such a small Army, would really fight. Also, they overvalued their own colorful army, accepting the uniform for the deed, trusting in the skill of their artillery, the deftness of their cavalry and their European-trained engineers. That Mexico had no industrial base to sustain a military effort was minimized in the light of the aid expected from France and England.

Even as Taylor was belatedly preparing to move deeper into Mexico, Polk was writing to Paredes to propose peace negotiations. Nothing was heard from his proposals, but the President was visited by an elegantly uniformed Colonel Atocha, an emissary from the exiled former general and dictator Santa Anna. Atocha suggested that on the return of a certain person to power and the payment of thirty million dollars to Mexico plus half a million to meet "present purposes," and after an American token show of force, an accommodation could be reached between the two governments. Polk sent an envoy to Santa Anna—then in Cuba with his young and beautiful wife, passing his days in intrigue and cockfighting—to agree to help the ex-dictator to return to power. The double-dealing general, who had directed the Alamo slaughter and at Goliad had shot over three hundred American prisoners, was a strange confidant for any peace effort. Nevertheless Polk ordered him to be allowed to "pass freely" through the United States naval blockade of the Mexican coast. Once Santa Anna had returned to his country in triumph, Paredes was soon overthrown. Of course Santa Anna had merely used Polk to take over the Mexican government, and as soon as he set foot on Mexican soil he repudiated his agreement. Yet, scoundrel that he was, he was also the most competent general that Mexico had, and the folly of allowing his return would soon be paid for in American blood.

Taylor's two small victories had already made him a hero, and there were whispers—of which he was not unaware—of presidential possibilities in 1848. With an influx of volunteers his Army of Occupation had grown to twelve thousand men. At Camargo, near the junction of the San Juan River and the Rio Grande, he camped for six weeks while gathering supplies. Careless of sanitation, he soon found his army so swept by disease that in one soldier's words the camp became "a Yawning Graveyard." In mid-August of 1846 the first of his troops began to advance toward Monterrey, the key city of northern Mexico. The force included two divisions of regulars, a body of Texas Rangers, and a division of volunteers. With Taylor marched a group of young officers whose names would become famous. Besides Lieutenant Grant there were Lieutenants James Longstreet, George Gordon Meade, John F. Reynolds, and George H. Thomas, and Captain Braxton Bragg.

Not until the third week in September did he reach the outskirts of the hill city one hundred and twenty-five miles west of his base camp. Monterrey was a formidable fortress, dominated by the huge bastions of its Citadel and protected by outlying forts. Behind the Cit-

POLK HOME, COLUMBIA, TENNESSEE

James K. Polk and his wife, Sarah, were very probably the first presidential couple to have their likenesses recorded by the daguerreotype process, which had been discovered in the year 1839. The color was later added by hand.

adel's walls General Ampudia, Arista's predecessor at Matamoros, sheltered confidently with a force of ten thousand and artillery double the strength of Taylor's. The American commander sent General William Jenkins Worth, known as the Murat of the American Army because of his dashing style of dress, with two thousand men in a flanking movement to the west while he led his main body in a frontal assault. Attacking in a drenching rain, Taylor's forward troops penetrated the city within a few hours but were thrown back. A second attack failed, and by the day's end Taylor thought he had lost the battle. But even as the Americans were withdrawing from their first assault, a Captain Backus, whose force had failed to receive the order to retreat, rallied his countrymen when they found themselves in a position whence they could fire into the enemy rear until supporting troops were able to capture the bastion. The next day under a heavy bombardment Worth's men seized the western approaches. On the following morning the Americans attacked the city on two sides, charging up the steep slope and then fighting their way street by street, square by square, burrowing through adobe walls until they reached the great plaza of the city. Ampudia, fearful of an explosion in his powder magazine and with the best of his soldiers in flight, sent an aide under a flag of truce to ask for terms.

Taylor was generous. In exchange for the immediate surrender of the town and the handing over of all public property, he allowed the Mexican Army to march out retaining its arms and agreed to an eight weeks' armistice. The capture of Monterrey cost some five hundred American casualties. Military men recognized Worth as the brilliant tactician who made the victory possible, but to the public Taylor was the hero responsible for the "three glorious days."

Scott, occupied in Washington with problems of supply, harbored the dark suspicion that he was being kept from field command because he was a Whig. Polk, jealous of Taylor's rising popularity and angry at him for allowing the Mexicans to leave Monterrey with honors of war, determined that from then on Taylor would play only a minor role in the war. "He had the enemy in his grasp and should have taken them prisoners," the President wrote. In November, 1846, he ordered his general to terminate the armistice. Two months later he further instructed him to refrain from any future offensive operations. Since the enemy still stubbornly refused to consider peace terms, the President decided to open a second front by landing an invasion army at Vera Cruz in order to strike at the heartland and capture Mexico City. Reluctantly he named Old Fuss and Feathers to command the sea-borne expedition. In collecting troops for his invasion, Scott commandeered most of Taylor's regulars. After that, the two Whig generals were never again cordial.

Meanwhile Santa Anna, learning through a captured letter of Taylor's depleted force, determined to surprise and then annihilate him with an army of twenty-five thousand men, which he was then training. Napoleon of the West, Santa Anna styled himself. Marching his troops across the desert in winter, enduring lack of food and water, plagued by sickness and desertions, he nevertheless held his army relatively intact until he encountered Taylor near Buena Vista Ranch. At their approach, the Mexican sent the American a letter under a flag of truce, pointing out that Taylor was greatly outnumbered and giving him the choice of surrendering his small army or being cut to pieces. When Taylor refused to consider terms, two days of bloody hand-to-hand fighting followed. It was a nip-and-tuck battle with Taylor's army at one point facing disaster until tidily reinforced by a fresh regiment in red flannel shirts, the Mississippi Rifles, under the command of Colonel Jefferson Davis. Taylor in nerveless equanimity sat on Old Whitey while the fighting surged round him. Once when he thought he saw signs of the enemy wavering, he urged Whitey over to Braxton Bragg's battery. "Give them a little more of the grape, Captain," he told him with imperturbable coolness.

In the end the Battle of Buena Vista was a draw, with Mexican casualties double the American, and Mexican offensive morale shattered. Personally undaunted, the Western Napoleon retreated south, carrying two American flags and three cannons as evidence of his "victory."

Polk was so soured at the inconclusive outcome and so disturbed by the more than seven hundred American casualties that he refused to allow the Army to honor the battle with salutes. Taylor, snubbed and furious at the lack of regulars, who he was convinced would have given him the chance for a Mexican Waterloo, felt himself a victim of Polk's politics and asked leave to return to the United States.

In December, 1847, Old Rough and Ready at last returned home, enjoying his first taste of triumph at New Orleans. Ships in the port broke out their flags as he arrived, balconies and windows were decorated, and

massed cannon thundered a salute. In the Place d'Armes—given its present name, Jackson Square, the next year—a triumphal arch had been erected. A *Te Deum* was sung in the cathedral. As Taylor rode in procession through the streets on Old Whitey, women waved their handkerchiefs, men cheered, and the more daring onlookers dashed out to pull a souvenir hair from Old Whitey's tail. Never before had the general received such acclaim. As he entered a theater that night he heard the strains of "Taylor's March," written specially for the occasion. And in the lobby of his hotel a glowing transparency showed the general in his old brown coat with the legend underneath: "A little more grape, Captain Bragg!"

Meanwhile events far more important, though far less publicized, than Taylor's spectacular, if transitory, achievements were taking place in the Southwest. The term "manifest destiny" had for some time been applied to New Mexico and California, sparsely populated areas bordering United States territory that were in American eyes ripe for the plucking. "How long a time will elapse before *they* shine as two new stars in our mighty firmament?" the young Walt Whitman asked in Brooklyn. Polk, at the outset of a war he felt would be quick and cheap, had determined to take them.

In June, 1846, the regulars of the First Dragoons and a force of Missouri volunteers marched out of Fort Leavenworth for the conquest of New Mexico. This "Army of the West," seventeen hundred strong, was under the command of an energetic and efficient regular officer, Colonel Stephen W. Kearny. Twenty and thirty miles a day he pushed his men, instead of the regulation fifteen, moving along the dry Indian-haunted Sante Fe Trail. After advancing for two weeks into New Mexico, he was confronted by an envoy of Governor Manuel Armijo, who suggested a parley between the two leaders. Ignoring the proposal, Kearny continued on. Towns fell to him without even token resistance—Las Vegas, San Miguel. Armijo tried to set up a strategic blockade at Apache Pass with four thousand ill-trained Indians and peons, but at the approach of the Americans, Armijo fled with his soldiers behind him. Santa Fe lay open and unresisting—the mud town, Kearny's men called the adobe-built town over which the American flag now fluttered. Kearny issued a proclamation absolving the inhabitants from their tenuous loyalty to Mexico and promising them American-guaranteed protection of their persons, property, and religion. After a

Mexico City
Chapultepec 13 Sept.
Molino del Rey 8 Sept.
Churubusco 20 August
Contreras 19-20 August

Lake Texcuco

Santa Anna Retreat May

Puebla Abandoned 15 May

MILES 0 10 20

American victories in the north having failed to break Mexican resistance, the fighting was carried to a more vital area. Scott's army landed at Vera Cruz, forced the city to surrender, then set out for Mexico City. Establishing a base at Puebla after winning at Cerro Gordo, Scott moved west, beating the enemy at Contreras, Churubusco, Molino del Rey, and Chapultepec, and finally took the capital. The war was over.

number of prominent New Mexicans had taken the oath of allegiance to the United States, most of the population followed their example. In six weeks of campaigning, and without a shot being fired, Kearny's Army of the West had conquered a region of some eighty thousand inhabitants, which would become the states of New Mexico, Arizona, Nevada, Utah, the western section of Colorado, and southwest Wyoming.

After appointing a new governor, Kearny planned to move against California and to send an expedition against the Mexican state of Chihuahua. Late in September he set out with three hundred men across the deserts and mountain ranges to the Pacific. Somewhere along the way he ran into the famous scout Kit Carson, who informed him that the conquest of California had already taken place. Sending half his men back to Santa Fe, Kearny continued on his long march, with Carson acting as his guide.

In the autumn of 1845 the federal government had sent a "scientific" expedition to California under the dashing Pathfinder, John Frémont, to search out the best trade route to the Pacific. Frémont, an Army brevet captain, arrived in the northern part of the province in January, proceeded to strengthen his party of ostensible civilians by enlisting Americans living in California, then moved south near Monterey. Sensitive to such an American presence near the capital, the Californian *comandante* ordered Frémont out of the state, and after a fire-breathing pause the American captain obeyed. Frémont returned in May, however, with a band of some thirty-five freebooters—mountain men, adventurers, and settlers. On June 14 one of Frémont's lieutenants seized the adobe village of So-

noma, and after capturing a sleeping Californian general (who in any case favored annexation), ran up a homemade red-and-white-striped flag with a bear and a star in the upper corner, which became the Bear Flag of the proclaimed California Republic. Then, moving toward the coastal fort El Castillo de San Joaquin on the site of San Francisco, Frémont persuaded the captain of the American vessel *Moscow*, anchored in the bay, to assist his forces—now swollen to 130—in an amphibious assault on the fort. The attack was a brilliant success, the more because San Joaquin happened to be empty. At about this time news arrived of the outbreak of the Mexican War.

Carrying out his secret orders, the doddering and indecisive Commodore John D. Sloat, commanding the Pacific Squadron, had arrived in Monterey Harbor on July 2, and after five days of debating with himself, at last hoisted the American flag on the customhouse and seized the capital and the country in the name of the United States. Two days later the Bear Flag in Sonoma was replaced by the Stars and Stripes.

Sloat, sliding into senile disability, was relieved by Commodore Robert F. Stockton, and shortly afterward the conquering Frémont arrived in Monterey with his irregulars—now transformed into the California Battalion. The thorny question of prerogative they managed to arrange amiably, with Stockton retaining the overall command while Frémont took charge of the battalion as the two commanders prepared to move against the enemy base in Los Angeles. Stockton dispatched Frémont by sea to San Diego while proceeding with his own forces to San Pedro, in what was to be a two-pronged attack. But when Frémont delayed, Stockton

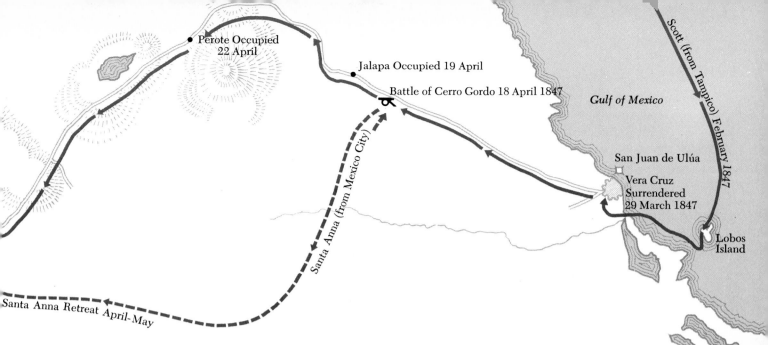

Scott (from Tampico) February 1847

Perote Occupied
22 April

Jalapa Occupied 19 April

Battle of Cerro Gordo 18 April 1847

Gulf of Mexico

Santa Anna (from Mexico City)

San Juan de Ulúa

Vera Cruz
Surrendered
29 March 1847

Lobos
Island

Santa Anna Retreat April-May

alone began to advance. The *Californios* abandoned their last stronghold at his approach and he was able to occupy Los Angeles unopposed. By summer's end the bloodless campaign was completed, with California and the Southwest in American hands.

It seemed too easy to be true, and indeed it was. Resigned at first to the inevitable, the *Californios* on second thought found their resentments exceeding their resignation. Scarcely had Stockton moved to San Francisco and Frémont gone north in search of recruits than the natives' smoldering feelings flared up in revolt. Most of the *Californios* inland either joined or at least sympathized with the insurgents. Dismayed, Stockton set out again for San Pedro while at the same time sending for Frémont. But the Pathfinder was so slow in responding that the commodore moved alone to San Diego, but lacked a sufficient force to advance farther. In this quandary he appealed to Kearny, who had just arrived in California with his travel-hardened force. Before he could reach San Diego, Kearny found himself engaged by the enemy at San Pasqual. Though short, the engagement was no comic-opera battle, for Kearny lost one-third of his men and was himself wounded.

After Kearny joined Stockton, the two managed to muster a force of five hundred soldiers, sailors, marines, and irregulars and marched against Los Angeles. They found the *Californios* drawn up on the opposite bank of the San Gabriel River. It was January 8, 1847, the thirty-second anniversary of Andrew Jackson's great victory, and in commemoration the Americans shouted the battle cry "New Orleans!" as they charged. Twice the antagonists clashed briefly, twice the *Californios* retreated, and as Stockton prepared for a general assault,

the city surrendered after the almost bloodless encounter. Meanwhile Frémont, with a force of four hundred, had arrived after the fighting but just in time for the capitulation. Coolly going over Stockton's head, the self-confident Pathfinder took it on himself to negotiate the Treaty of Cahuenga with the field forces of the enemy, even granting terms that Stockton had earlier refused.

While the California rebellion was being contained, Colonel Sterling Price, the military commander of New Mexico, uncovered a Mexican plot there to rise up and kill all the intruding Americans. In spite of stiff countermeasures, Governor Charles Bent and several of his subordinates were assassinated a month later and their bodies mutilated. Price, in a slashing two-week campaign, pursued the rebels to their stronghold of Taos and smashed all resistance. Neither in New Mexico nor California would there be any further challenge to the authority of the United States.

Farther to the south the Mexicans still showed no appreciation of the hopelessness of their position, impervious both to American arms and to Polk's attempts at bribery. With Scott's massive preparations for his Vera Cruz expedition under way, it was becoming clear that the war would be neither short nor cheap. The problems of equipping and maintaining a fleet adequate for the invasion task and for transporting and supplying an army for such a distance soon strained the country's financial and industrial capacities. But for Scott's skill and abilities such a mobilization would not have gotten off the ground.

In the first flush of war enthusiasm, Whigs and Democrats had marched off together. Whig politicians-turned-officers had appeared in uniform in the halls of

Congress. Webster had sent his son into the Army, and the son would die. At the beginning of the war the overwhelming majority of Americans supported it. But a small intellectual minority dissented; and as the war prolonged itself and grew in cost and in lives, so the dissent grew. John Quincy Adams in the House of Representatives had seen Taylor's march to the Rio Grande as "an act of flagrant War," an unconstitutional act, for Congress had not declared war. Adams, opposed from the outset, was one of the fourteen antislavery Conscience Whigs who had voted against the "most unrighteous war." Calhoun, that complex man, had abstained from voting on the war resolution for fear that public opinion toward slavery would be hurt if the South was tied to an act of aggression. In his somber, subtle view the war had "closed the first volume of our political history under the Constitution and opened the second and . . . no mortal could tell what would be written on it." In Massachusetts Charles Sumner, just burgeoning into oratory, called "Blood! Blood!" on the hands of the New Englanders who had voted for the war, and Boston's Reverend Theodore Parker maintained that the war was a sin, "a denial of Christianity and of God." Emerson in Concord indignantly traced the cotton threads binding together expansion, the agricultural South, and the industrial North in commercial bondage. Henry Thoreau, trudging from his cabin at Walden Pond to the cobbler's shop at Concord, having come to the conclusion that he did not want to belong to a nation engaged in an unjust war and holding one-sixth of its population in slavery, refused to pay his poll tax. He was lodged in Concord's jail but was freed the next morning when an aunt paid his fine. James Russell Lowell was denouncing the war through the Yankee voice of his fictional Hosea Biglow. The intellectual revolt spread. More and more Northerners were coming to feel with Hosea Biglow that the war was "jest to lug more slave states in." Mr. Polk's War they began to call it, and latent Whig opposition turned active when the Democrats lost the House of Representatives in the mid-term elections. The Whig *National Intelligencer* praised the Mexicans for their bravery and fortitude, while Horace Greeley's *Tribune* denounced the war as "unjust and rapacious" and urged Americans to take warning from the fate of Napoleon's armies in Spain. "The United States will con-

quer Mexico," Emerson predicted, "but it will be as he man swallows arsenic which brings him down in urn. Mexico will poison us."

Polk waited hopefully as his unloved general prepared for the invasion that was to win the war. Scott picked Lobos Island, seven miles off the Mexican coast, as his staging area. There he methodically organized a force of ten thousand men, coordinating his plans for what would be the largest amphibious assault undertaken to that time by an American army.

There was only the most negligible Mexican opposition from the Vera Cruz garrison as the specially constructed surfboats with the first wave of assault troops, under the command of the irascible and impeccably dressed General William Worth, headed for the beach. Once in the shallows, the men left the boats and waded through the surf unhindered, their rifles held over their heads. By the end of the week Scott had built up a supply depot on the beach and was eyeing the steep walls of Vera Cruz and its fortress of San Juan de Ulúa.

The weather turned foul, and Scott knew that yellow fever lurked in the coastal lowlands. Bypassing San Juan de Ulúa, he invested Vera Cruz, surrounding it with batteries and cutting off the water supply. On the fourth day of seige, March 26, 1847, the Mexicans began negotiating for surrender, and three days later United States troops formally occupied the city. Scott allowed the surrendered garrison to march out with honors of war. The sick and wounded were permitted to remain in the city; the other Mexican troops were paroled. Scott installed himself in the Governor's Palace and named his old friend Worth governor of the Military Department of Vera Cruz. At a cost of less than a hundred casualties Scott had acquired a firm base for his operations against the interior.

Santa Anna had been recuperating at San Luis Potosí from the Battle of Buena Vista when he had learned that a revolt was building up against him in the capital. At once he had hurried to Mexico City with his patched army, and in a swirl of energy had put down the opposition, stabilized the government, and replenished the treasury. While he was engaged in raising new troops, word came to him of the fall of Vera Cruz. Scott had already begun to move down the National Highway on the two-hundred-and-fifty-mile march to the capital. Among the engineers Scott had brought with him was

Part of the naval campaign in the war took place in the Gulf of California. A gunner on the American sloop Dale, *William Meyers, made this water color of the bombardment of a Mexican base in Lower California preceding an assault by American seamen and marines.*
FRANKLIN D. ROOSEVELT LIBRARY

OVERLEAF: *This dramatic version of the storming of the castle of Chapultepec by Scott's army appeared in a New York magazine in 1848. The valor of the young cadets—Los Niños, "the boys"—who died defending the castle gave Mexicans a proud military tradition.*
Brother Jonathan, JULY 4, 1848, NEW-YORK HISTORICAL SOCIETY

Robert E. Lee, who for all practical purposes acted as his chief of staff; and his junior officers included U. S. Grant, T. J. (later "Stonewall") Jackson, Beauregard, McClellan, Longstreet, Johnston, and Meade.

His mercurial confidence restored, Santa Anna marched his forces out of Mexico City to meet the invaders. Just below the pass at Cerro Gordo he skillfully blocked off the highway. Facing the blockade, Scott sent the division of General David Twiggs—outrageously profane but a first-rate commander—to the Mexican left flank. A skillful reconnaissance by Lee brought the troops undetected to the enemy's rear. The Battle of Cerro Gordo, though briefly imperiled by the bungling of General Gideon J. Pillow, Polk's former law partner, shattered Santa Anna's army and almost resulted in his capture. The American advance continued unimpeded. Jalapa and Perote, with its large stores of guns and ammunition, were taken without resistance. Scott's problem now lay with his twelve-month volunteers, whose time was up and who insisted they had done their duty and were going home. Neither bounty offers nor Scott's patriotic appeals could induce them to stay longer. The commanding general had never had the troops he needed, and now in the midst of enemy country he found his fighting force cut by seven regiments—one-third of his army.

On May 15, 1847, Puebla, seventy-five miles from Mexico City, fell after a half-hearted defense by Santa Anna. Worth paraded his victorious troops through the city and Scott moved his headquarters there while waiting for reinforcements. A dreary summer followed in the midst of a hostile population, the soldiers stricken with dysentery, isolated, the regulars and the volunteers squaring off against each other as they had been doing since the outbreak of the war. Scott—a sterner disciplinarian than Taylor—kept the unruly volunteers under control through the mindless repetitions of daily drill. Reinforcements finally arrived, among them a brigade led by another political general, Franklin Pierce.

Early in August Scott broke camp, abandoning his base and his line of communications to live off the country in his final thrust. Up the army climbed in the thin air, through passes ten thousand feet high, mountain crest succeeding crest toward the blue horizon until finally the men could look down on the green and ordered central valley of Mexico. Overseas the duke of Wellington followed the American advance with professional interest and concern. "Scott is lost," he con-

cluded. "He cannot capture the city and he cannot fall back on his base."

Wellington's conclusion seemed cruelly correct, for Mexico City, surrounded by wide marshland, was an island that could be entered only along heavily protected stone causeways. Santa Anna, under the slogan "War without pity unto death," had raised a force of twenty-five thousand men, which he now divided into Armies of the East, the South, and the North.

The Mexican Army of the North, under General Gabriel Valencia, was the first to clash with the Americans, at the Battle of Contreras. Scott's men, moving through a lava field, outflanked the enemy during the night. In a skillful short engagement at dawn, the Americans broke the Army of the North and opened a road into the capital. Santa Anna, on hearing the news, ordered Valencia shot on sight. The Battle of Churubusco, fought the same day, was a larger and more savage engagement, the Mexican defenders being bolstered by the San Pa-

Pictures of some of his victories in the War of 1812 and the Mexican War surround politically oriented General Winfield Scott in this lithograph of what was probably a banner for the 1852 presidential campaign.

ricio Battalion of American deserters. Santa Anna, in command, did not give up the field until the Americans pressed home the attack with bayonets. Several times when the disheartened Mexicans tried to surrender, the San Patricios tore down the white flag. The Mexicans lost one-third of their men by casualties or desertions in the two battles of the day.

After this victory Scott halted three miles from Mexico City. He deployed troops and set up artillery, then demanded the surrender of the capital. Santa Anna responded with vague peace feelers, whereupon Scott suggested an armistice as a prelude to negotiations and sent a message to Santa Anna regretting that so much blood had already been shed in "this unnatural war between the two great republics." Santa Anna, with no serious thought of negotiating, welcomed the armistice as a breathing spell, then by his defiant actions broke it off after two weeks.

Scott, after realizing that Santa Anna had outwitted him, put away any thought of peace talks and prepared to attack the city. He chose the southwest approach, dominated by a group of buildings called Molino del Rey (the King's Mill) and, directly before the city, the immense stone palace of Chapultepec, which had once been the residence of the Spanish viceroys and was now occupied by the cadets of the Mexican Military College. The Battle of Molino del Rey, one of the bloodiest of the war, was also one of the most pointless. Scott, after capturing the King's Mill—erroneously supposed to contain a cannon foundry—found himself no closer to success and with seven hundred additional casualties. One American officer remarked that a few more such victories would destroy the army. Chapultepec remained the key to the city, and Scott reconnoitered carefully for three days before resuming his advance.

Under cover of darkness, after a day of ineffective bombardment, Scott moved the divisions of Worth, Pillow, and Brigadier General John A. Quitman forward to prepare for a direct assault on the palace. At dawn a bombardment lasting two and a half hours was followed by an assault that faltered when the scaling ladders were delayed. But the ladders arrived, and Scott's men clambered up the sheer cliff under withering fire. The Mexican cadets, with the idealistic bravery of the young, held their ranks until they were overrun and cut down in the Americans' final bayonet charge. By midmorning Chapultepec had fallen. The gates were captured, the city lay open, and desperate house-to-house and street-to-street fighting followed. By evening Scott had suffered another nine hundred casualties, and if Santa Anna had been able to rally his soldiers, he might have turned the tables on the invaders. But the Mexican troops were too demoralized to fight further, and Santa Anna led them in retreat, abandoning the capital.

The next morning, with Worth's guns trained on the heart of the city and Quitman preparing for a final assault, a Mexican delegation appeared under a flag of truce to make a formal capitulation. Quitman's division proceeded to occupy the Grand Plaza, and as Scott and his staff rode into the square the American flag was already flying over it.

Scott's campaign, culminating in the capture of Mexico City, was a tremendous accomplishment, the most brilliantly conceived and achieved feat of American arms of the century. Generals had and would ride to the Presidency on far lesser triumphs. Outnumbered, on unfamiliar terrain, with only lukewarm backing from Washington, Old Fuss and Feathers had shown himself to be the ablest American general since the Revolution.

Scott, as the proconsul of a conquered country, was so successful that in the end a number of responsible Mexicans begged him to stay on as dictator. Among his Army subordinates he was less popular. He quarreled with Twiggs, and his old friendship with Worth dissolved when the latter felt he had been slighted in the official report of the Battle of Cerro Gordo. Worth and Pillow leaked reports to American newspapers puffing up their own accomplishments and belittling Scott. When the commanding general issued an order that forbade such unauthorized communications, Worth wrote a protesting letter to Polk. On learning of this, Scott had his former friend placed under arrest for insubordination and later made similar charges against Pillow. Polk, biding his time, finally removed Scott from command and instituted a court of inquiry against him.

While the generals and staff officers quarreled and intrigued among themselves, the enlisted men in the conquered city brawled and drank and gambled and abused civilians. Scott, though a strict disciplinarian, found the volunteers so hard to control that finally he was forced to move many of them, including the Texas Rangers, outside the city. Following the election of the tractable Pedro Anaya as President, the new Mexican government seemed ready at last to talk peace. Polk had sent the Spanish-speaking Nicholas Trist, chief clerk in the Department of State, to accompany Scott and had given him authority to negotiate a peace treaty. At first Scott had very much resented the civilian's presence and his independence of the military, but later the two became friends.

In the light of the Mexican defeat, Polk had laid down harsh peace terms. By October, 1847, he decided Trist needed new instructions and recalled him. News of his recall reached Trist in mid-November, just as prospects for a settlement were growing brighter. Fearing a collapse of the Mexican government if negotiations were then broken off, he disregarded the recall order on Scott's advice and met with the Mexican commissioners at Guadalupe Hidalgo, three miles from Mexico City. After a month of sticky negotiations, which Trist once threatened to break off, he and the Mexicans at last concluded a treaty by which the United States agreed to pay the Mexican government $15,000,000 and to assume the $3,250,000 American claims against Mexico, while receiving in return Upper California and New Mexico and the confirmation of Texan claims as far as the Rio Grande. Stimulated by Scott's victories, popular—if not intellectual—sentiment was rising for the annexation of all Mexico, for the supposed good of the Mexicans and the benefit of the United States. Trist's insubordination may well have preserved Mexico as a nation.

Since the Guadalupe Hidalgo Treaty had become an established fact, Polk was not ready to repudiate it even though he felt it had been negotiated by an "impudent and unqualified scoundrel," whom he would later put under arrest. The treaty was ratified by the Senate 38 to 14, most of the Whigs voting for it out of fear that the alternative might be to take over Mexico altogether. By the end of June, 1848, the last of the American Army of Occupation had left Mexico City.

In foreign affairs Polk had been successful in his objectives, as he had defined them to his Secretary of the Navy, Bancroft. Domestically he had been equally successful. In his 1845 message he had asked for a reduced tariff for revenue only, and the following year his diminutive Secretary of the Treasury, Robert Walker, piloted such a bill through Congress, in which the protectionist features of the 1842 tariff were eliminated and the country's trend toward free trade resumed. The President had also called for the reinstitution of the independent treasury, and an act to this effect passed the House and Senate in 1848. Polk still stood adamantly against internal improvements, although the demand

for them increased as the country expanded. When in 1848 Buchanan proposed a survey for a railroad or canal across the Isthmus of Panama, the President announced that this would be unconstitutional, that the government had no more right to make external than internal improvements, and that if any Panama bill were presented to him, he would veto it.

The Mexican War added half a million square miles of territory to the United States at a cost of almost one hundred million dollars and thirteen thousand dead. It made the Union a continental empire, giving it a geographical continuity from sea to sea. Yet the new unity also served to underline the dichotomy of a nation of free men in which men were slaves. Politically the war was abrasive, wearing away the party structure of both the Whigs and the Democrats. The inherent conflict within the Union—partly moral, partly economic and sectional—was symbolized in the Wilmot Proviso.

When in 1846 Polk had asked Congress for funds to "facilitate negotiations" with Mexico, and the House of

*Drawings from a book on the perils of gold mining depict,
left, a greenhorn asking a grizzled old-timer for
advice and, above, a worn-out miner voicing his plaint.*

Representatives was debating such a bill, Democratic Congressman David Wilmot of Pennsylvania tacked on an amendment prohibiting slavery in any territory that might be acquired from Mexico. The House passed the funding measure with the Wilmot Proviso, but the Senate declined to act. Again and again the proviso was brought forward in the House, only to be sidetracked by the Senate. It was supported by Van Buren antislavery Democrats, New York's so-called Barnburners, so nicknamed by their "Hunker" opponents—named thus because they were "hunkering" for office—from the story of the Dutch farmer who burned down his barn to get rid of the rats. Western Whigs and Democrats, resentful of Southern antagonism to protection and internal improvements, also backed the proviso, as did the Democrats from the Northwest, who felt the South had betrayed them in the Fifty-four forty fight. These dissenting Democrats sensed that Polk was moving closer to the orbit of the South. Northern alarm grew as Calhoun offered resolution after resolution to the effect that

Congress did not have the right to exclude slavery from any territory. After their 1846 mid-term election victory the Whigs tended to oppose further territorial gains for fear that contention over slavery would endanger both their party and the Union.

Congress was faced not only with a disintegration of party cohesiveness but with a deterioration in the quality of its members. The rise of the common man to suffrage had brought in some singularly common congressmen. Earlier there had been the Spitting Lyon from Vermont and Randolph of Roanoke strolling down the aisles with his dogs, his insolence touching the edge of madness; but there had been nothing like Ohio's "Sausage" Sawyer, who just before the Mexican War sat at the Speaker's rostrum munching sausages as he denounced West Point. The perquisites of office grew lush. So much champagne had come to be consumed in the Senate cloakroom that the Senate's acting president sardonically shuffled its cost from the stationery fund to the fuel account. Fist fights on the floor of the House were common, and one actual shooting occurred there. "Mileage-elongators" presented padded claims for travel expenses. Lobbyists with easy money found easy takers. Venality went uncurbed in the legislative halls.

The end of the Mexican War coincided with the beginning of the California Gold Rush, the turbulent, hectic swarming of forty-niners and Argonauts to the West after the discovery of nuggets in the tailrace of Captain Sutter's new sawmill on the American River. Polk set the presidential seal on this discovery and impelled the stampede when he announced in his message of December 5, 1848, that gold had been found in California.

Small amounts of gold had been gathered there earlier, but no one had paid much attention until word came of the treasure-trove on the American River. In the nine years Sutter had lived in the valley, he had expanded his holding to 160 square miles. A man of effusive charm, he got on equally well with Indians, *Californios*, and American settlers. At the fort he had built, the passing traveler was welcome, and from this strong point Sutter sent out rescue teams whenever he heard of any emigrant group like the Donner party stranded in the Sierras. Lacking lumber for his expanding needs, he hired an eccentric carpenter from New Jersey, John Marshall, to build him a sawmill above the fort on the American River. Marshall, with his work crew of about seventeen Mormons and a number of Indians, had not finished the mill before the crew discovered gold. Sutter's talkative storekeeper spread the news—to the captain's dismay, for he correctly foresaw the surge of uncontrollable adventurers to his valley.

News of the new El Dorado swept the country like a fever. Adventurers of all types from all countries made their way to California, by sailing ship round Cape Horn, or by the shorter, more perilous route across the Isthmus of Panama, or overland. Unlike the pioneer settlers, the forty-niners had no intention of settling anywhere. Theirs was the bright mirage of sudden fortune, the yellow glitter among the brook pebbles, the golden seam in the rock face. San Francisco, the chief entry port, expanded overnight like a frowzy mushroom—a brutal, brawling fly-by-night city of tents and shacks, with its prospectors and its derelicts, its sailors, gamblers, and whores. Americans came from the East, free Negroes as well as whites of all varieties; Britons, Frenchmen, Germans, Chinese, Malays, Hawaiians, Turks, wandered the muddy streets. Life, often brief, was a game of chance played with gilded dice.

"Seeing the elephant" became the bandied phrase of the Argonauts who landed at San Francisco or Monterey on their way to the gold fields. The phrase came from the story of a farmer who had never seen an elephant. When the circus came to town, he loaded his wagon with produce, hitched up his horse, and set out to view this strange beast. But at the first glimpse of the traveling menagerie his horse bolted, overturning and smashing the wagon and bruising the farmer. Even so, the farmer had seen the elephant!

The phrase was more apt than its users realized. Most of the fifty to seventy-five thousand gold seekers who arrived in California to see the elephant would have done better to have stayed at home. The average miner in the end earned less than six hundred dollars for what he had endured. Sutter's own worst fears were realized. After a brief period of gold-boom prosperity, he found his valley inundated by newcomers he could not control. He would lose both his land and his fortune.

In the end, only the legend remained, to become part of America's folklore. California, and perhaps the country, would never be the same.

Even as the flakes of gold sparkled in the tailrace at Sutter's mill, the political waters of the presidential election year seethed and bubbled—old issues were dying, new and more divisive ones looming up. Both Whig and Democratic parties were split by the slavery issue, cracks appearing in their fabric that could no longer be plastered over. The campaign had opened almost with the outbreak of the war, and it was never far from the minds of generals and politicians.

With Polk unwilling to succeed himself, the choice of the Northern radical Democrats fell on Van Buren. Calhoun and his Southern followers were determined to have no more of the Red Fox of Kinderhook and his Barnburners. Both Northern and Southern moderate Democrats felt that what the party needed was a middle-of-the-road candidate, one untouched by the Wilmot Proviso, who could take a neutral stand on the extension of slavery into the new Western territories. They found their man in Lewis Cass, the sixty-five-year-old senator from Michigan. A vintage Jacksonian, the severe, plain-mannered Cass had much to recommend him. He was moderate, an Anglophobe, a temperance man, an annexationist, and an opponent of the Wilmot Proviso. But he was also old, his military reputation had been won as a general in the War of 1812, and the energy that he had once displayed as governor of Michigan Territory and as Jackson's Secretary of War had given way to sluggishness. Nevertheless he was nominated over the ambitious Buchanan and Jackson's Secretary of the Navy, Levi Woodbury, on the fourth ballot, with the antislavery General William O. Butler of Kentucky chosen as his running mate to placate the Northerners. In his acceptance speech Cass announced ambiguously that he stood for the Constitution and brotherly love.

Zachary Taylor, as a Whig, might have said the same thing if he had thought of it. Ever since his victories at Palo Alto and Resaca de la Palma, he had been talked about as the Whig presidential candidate, and after his return to New Orleans as a persecuted hero, the talk grew to a cry. Never had he taken any interest in politics, never had he even voted, but the idea of himself as the savior of his country became more agreeable to him as his differences with Polk and Scott grew. By 1847 he was prepared to "undergo political martyrdom rather than see Scott or Cass elected." He announced that he would not declare his views on the tariff, internal improvements, the Bank, and so on, and indeed he would not because he had none. When he tried to express himself, words had a way of running away from him. "It is melancholy," one New York politician wrote, "to see how the General's *English* is suffering down there in that Spanish country. At the rate he goes on he will lose the use of his native dialect." Despite such criticism "Old Zack," in the public's estimation, seemed the people's man. A group of "Young Indians" in Congress, among them Abraham Lincoln, declared for him. That he was much less of a general than Scott, very much less of a statesman than Clay, was hardly considered in the rush of enthusiasm.

At seventy-one Clay still dreamed of the Presidency. Envious of Taylor's easy laurels, he remarked wistfully that he wished he could have killed a Mexican. A campaign on the old issues would have suited him—internal improvements, the tariff, presidential vetoes. In 1847 he had attacked Polk for having brought on the war, and he had demanded the disavowal of any intention "to acquire any foreign territory whatever, for the purpose of propagating slavery, or of introducing slaves from the United States into such foreign territory." However, in 1848 he was not prepared to come out completely for the Wilmot Proviso. If he had, the country might have been faced with a paradox of a slaveholder heading a Northern and Western antislavery

Whig party—a precursor of the Republican party.

Clay's convention chances dimmed when he failed to carry the delegates of his own state, and Taylor won the nomination on the fourth ballot. There was no party platform, the majority of Whigs being content to let the old issues die without anticipating the new. "A slaughter house of Whig principles," Horace Greeley announced bitterly, while Webster felt that Taylor's nomination was "not fit to be made." Webster refused the offer of the vice-presidential candidacy, which went to Millard Fillmore, a Buffalo politician and a friend of Clay's, though no friend of New York political leaders Thurlow Weed and William Henry Seward.

Both parties having hedged on the slavery question, dissidents in the Northwest and the East were left simmering in discontent. Taylor was pilloried as a slaveholder while Cass was labeled a Doughface—the term in vogue for a Northern man with Southern slavery views. The Barnburners had never forgiven Cass, whom they held responsible for the 1844 convention's failure to renominate Van Buren. In Ohio, with its New England roots, the antislavery Free-Soilers called a People's Convention with the idea of launching a third party. Almost at the same time the disgruntled Barnburners, refusing to support Cass, met in Utica, and after nominating the reluctant Van Buren, called for a national convention of all antislavery men to meet in Buffalo. A like-minded group of Whigs who had walked out of their own convention also agreed to go to Buffalo, as did the leaders of the diminished Liberty party. There in August the dissidents combined forces; ten thousand Free-Soilers, Liberty party men, Conscience Whigs, Clay Whigs, Barnburners, "Working Men of New York," and various splinter groups advocating free land, internal improvements, cheaper postage, "no more slave states and no more slave territory."

The Conscience and Clay Whigs joined with the others in nominating Van Buren. In turn the Whigs were granted their vice-presidential candidate, the flinty Charles Francis Adams, whose father, John Quincy Adams, had been stricken at his desk in the House of Representatives a few months before as he was preparing to oppose a congressional vote of thanks to the generals in what he termed the recent "most unrighteous war." With a high sense of morality, the party platform—written by Van Buren's former Attorney General, Benjamin F. Butler, and Salmon P. Chase of the Liberty party—denounced the "aggression of slave power" and

This 1848 anti-Taylor political cartoon capitalizes on the general's alleged carelessness with the lives of his troops during the Mexican War.

ncluded a ringing call to "fight on and fight ever" for "free soil, free speech, free labor and free men."

As far as the Whigs and the Democrats were concerned, there were no longer any consuming issues between them. The Bank controversy was dead, as was that over the distribution of land-sale funds. The tariff had become a local matter, and the question of veto power, mostly talk. Both parties contained protectionists and free traders, both had their Conscience and Cotton groupings, both preferred to turn a blind eye to slavery. The campaign was fought on personalities, with the Democrats trying to dim the luster of the Mexican War hero by means of Cass's faded general's epaulets from the War of 1812. Remembering Tippecanoe, the Whigs were confident they could repeat the performance with the inarticulate Taylor. They were strong in the Democratic South as well as in the Middle Atlantic States, whose businessmen and workers were still sulking over the 1846 tariff, which was designed for revenue rather than protection, but the Free-Soilers had eroded much of the party's strength in the Northwest. It was a close election and a light one, with fewer than three million votes cast. Taylor won with 163 electoral votes to Cass's 127 and a popular majority of not quite 140,000. But for Van Buren's candidacy, New York's 36 electoral votes would have gone to Cass instead of Taylor, exactly reversing the electoral figures and giving him the Presidency.

To the more acute observers the election marked a shift in the political wind. Greeley, who had reluctantly voted for Taylor as the only alternative to the "fat-bellied, mutton-headed, cucumber-soled Cass," sensed that a new party was in the offing. Van Buren hoped that the Northern Democrats might combine with the Free-Soilers. Others equally astute looked for the Whigs to take that step. The new Vice President saw his party as holding the solid middle ground between the Northern abolitionists and the Southern fire-eaters. Chase felt that the election results had "severed the last link that bound a large number of Democrats . . . to the Slave Power."

Taylor left his home in Baton Rouge for Washington in late January for a triumphal tour northward, but the weather turned so cold that he found himself icebound on the Ohio River on the steamer *Telegraph No. 2* some miles below Wheeling. Rescued by carriage, he finally arrived in the Capital by train. For all their private opinions of each other, the outgoing and incoming Presidents managed to preserve a surface cordiality. Polk was the second man to shake Taylor's hand after the inaugural ceremonies. The inaugural ball ran until four in the morning, but only Buchanan was present from the old regime.

Access to the White House was easy and casual in the few months that Taylor occupied it. In many of the rooms straw mats had to be put down to protect the carpets from the tobacco juice of expectorating sight-seers. Old Whitey accompanied his master to Washington. On summer evenings Taylor liked to stroll about the open grounds of the White House while the Marine Band played in the garden, and anybody who wished could walk up and shake hands.

Like all weak Presidents, the purblind Taylor preferred to leave the initiative with Congress, and the Senate was willing enough to assume it. The giants were all there—Clay, Webster, Calhoun, Benton—as well as the younger or at least somewhat younger Cass, William Seward, Stephen A. Douglas, Salmon Chase, and Jefferson Davis.

Taylor's one positive action was to send an agent to California to urge the inhabitants to form a constitution and apply at once for statehood while deciding the question of slavery among themselves. Californians quickly responded, electing a governor and drawing up a constitution in which—to the dismay of the South—slavery was prohibited.

Fearful of the growing strength of the North, Southerners determined to keep the political balance from swinging away from them. Senator Henry Foote of Mississippi proposed to leave the territories of California, New Mexico, and Utah open to slavery. The Mormons petitioned that Deseret be admitted with slavery excluded, while the radicals wanted to organize New Mexico and Utah under the Wilmot Proviso. Southern congressmen attacked Taylor for the antislavery results achieved by his agent in California. And out of all these turbulent crosscurrents, voices were becoming articulate in demanding the dissolution of the Union itself. North Carolina's Congressman Thomas L. Clingman asserted that the passage of the Wilmot Proviso or the abolition of slavery in the District of Columbia would be grounds for the South's secession and that the South would be better off without the North and its tariffs. Northern radicals were equally willing to agree to the separation. Even a moderate man like Harvard's president, Edward Everett, former Massachusetts governor

The strong features of Daniel Webster—a useful complement to his deep voice in oratory—are captured in this daguerreotype of about 1850. By supporting the Fugitive Slave Law in his zeal to preserve the Union, Webster won the enmity of New England abolitionists.

279

and minister to Great Britain, approved of the breakup if done in a friendly spirit "like reasonable men."

Henry Clay, emerging from retirement, his time almost run out, used his most persuasive manner to work out a compromise that would preserve the country and the Union that he loved. In January, 1850, he proposed that California come in as a free state; that the other territories be organized and admitted to statehood without restrictions, it being unlikely in any case that they were suitable for slavery; that New Mexico be separated from Texas, and Texas compensated for the loss; that the auctioning-off and exporting of slaves in the District of Columbia be forbidden. To the South, Clay offered the continuation of slavery in the District, a Fugitive Slave Law with teeth in it, and Congress' pledge of no interference with the interstate slave trade. Bald and fading, he held up a piece of Washington's coffin for emphasis as he warned the senators against adopting measures that might destroy the Union cemented by Washington's "exertions and example."

In subsequent speeches of the great debate that followed, in a Senate Chamber with balconies so crowded that the doors had to be closed, Clay defended his compromise, begging the two sides to be magnanimous and telling the South that secession would mean ruin. He himself felt that slavery was a "social and political evil," and he favored gradual emancipation. But "I am directly opposed to any purpose of secession," Harry of the West declaimed in the ringing tones that had so often held the balconies spellbound. "The Constitution . . . was made, not merely for the generation which then existed, but for posterity, undefined, unlimited, permanent, and perpetual . . . and for every subsequent state which might come into the Union, binding themselves by that indissoluble bond."

The glowing words sank deep, rallying to the Union all but the extremists on both sides. A congressional committee proposed the Omnibus Bill, embodying Clay's proposals. Such a bill still had to face the opposition of the "Sentinel" of the embattled South, Calhoun. Mortally ill, his leonine shock of hair turned almost white, his cheeks sunken, he still kept the flash of fire in his dark eyes. As he entered the chamber wrapped in a cloak and supported by two friends, everyone sensed that it would be his last active appearance. He sank into his seat and greeted his friends who came over to him. Then, with his clawlike hands, he pulled himself erect. Stern and unbending, his voice still crystal-clear, he

begged the chair that his speech might be read by his friend Senator James M. Mason of Virginia.

Through Mason's mouth, Calhoun elaborated upon the relentless sequence of the South's grievances: the dominance of Northern influence in the federal government, the sweeping away of states' rights, the exclusion of the South from the new territories that Southern arms had won, attacks on the character of Southern leaders. As Mason continued, Calhoun sat bundled in his cloak, "his eyes glowing with meteor-like brilliancy as he glanced at Senators upon whom he desired to have certain passages make an impression." Unless, Mason's voice went on, the North was willing to grant the South equal rights, cease the "agitation of the slave question," and restore the original equilibrium between the two sections, then North and South should part in peace— or if not in peace, *we shall know what to do.*

Only one giant of the North remained who could answer Calhoun's searing eloquence, and that was Daniel Webster. Webster himself was ailing, and at first he hesitated—for compromise was becoming as evil a word in Boston as it was in Charleston. But he agreed to take up the challenge, willing to sacrifice much for the Union he loved, even the good will of New England. Three days after Calhoun's address, he spoke.

His imposing presence as he took the floor reduced the Senate Chamber to silence. "I wish to speak today," he began his Seventh of March Speech, "not as a Massachusetts man, nor as a Northern man but as an American. . . . The imprisoned winds are let loose, the East, the North, and the stormy South, combine to throw the whole sea into commotion, to toss its billows to the skies, and disclose its profoundest depths. . . . I speak today for the preservation of the Union—Hear me for my cause!"

As he spoke, a cadaverous old man tottered down the aisle. And as Webster glimpsed Calhoun, his friend in spite of all divergences of opinion, he remained silent until the dying senator found his seat. Then, for three hours, the New Englander pleaded for compromise, for Union. Let the territories decide about slavery for themselves, he begged the antislavery members. The law of nature, of physical geography, would bar slavery from the new lands. He conceded that the South had reasonable grievances. And abolitionist agitation had merely succeeded in hardening Southern opinion. But secession was another matter.

"What am I to be?—an American no longer?" Web-

The Fugitive Slave Law had results other than those intended: the flight of many escaped slaves from free states into Canada, more Underground Railroad aid to fleeing slaves, and the writing of Uncle Tom's Cabin. *This detail from a Thomas Moran painting shows slaves being pursued through a swamp by bloodhounds.*

ster asked. "I would rather hear," he concluded, his great organ voice sounding through the chamber, "of natural blasts and mildews, war, pestilence, and famine, than to hear gentlemen talk of secession. . . . No, Sir! No, Sir! There can be no secession!"

Southerners would have been willing to agree to California's admission as a free state in exchange for slavery in New Mexico, or they might even have settled for the extension of the 36° 30′ line of the Missouri Compromise to the Pacific. But Taylor, slaveholder though he was, did not believe in extending the peculiar institution beyond its present boundaries. His 1849 plan had been to admit California as a free state and to ignore the matter of slavery in New Mexico and Utah, and so stubbornly did he cling to this "no action" plan that he threatened to veto Clay's Omnibus Bill if it was passed. Meanwhile, New Mexico applied for statehood with boundaries enclosing territory already claimed by Texas. Taylor modified his "no action" stand and called for the admission of New Mexico as a free state. Intransigent Texans and their Southern supporters at once prepared to seize the disputed area. Taylor ordered government troops in New Mexico to resist any invasion and for a time a small civil war seemed in prospect. When Southern Whig spokesmen, favorable to both the President and the Union, visited Taylor in search of a compromise, they found him immovable, threatening to hang the Texas rebels and their Southern supporters and unwilling to consider any plan but his own.

The deadlock was broken when Taylor died suddenly in July, 1850—according to legend after a surfeit of iced milk and cherries following festivities on a hot Fourth of July. Old Whitey, reversed boots in his stirrups, made his last appearance in his master's funeral parade.

With Millard Fillmore, a friend of Clay's and Webster's, in the White House, prospects for compromise became suddenly brighter. The tall, portly man with the shrewd gray eyes who succeeded Taylor, gave little indication of his humble origins. But he had been a poor farmer's son in upper New York State, friendless, undernourished, a mill apprentice who had taught himself literary English with the help of a cheap dictionary. His wife is said to have taught him to write. Later, in the nineteenth-century tradition of the clerk reading Blackstone by candlelight, he had studied law in a kindly lawyer's office. Politics had drawn him, as it did most young lawyers. Eight years he had served in Congress, where he had been dully conscientious, limited, but

liked and trusted. Though not a decisive man, he had, as Vice President, decided to favor Clay's compromise.

With the new President's encouragement, Webster and Clay once more took up the defense of the Omnibus Bill. They were opposed by an incongruous alliance of Northern and Southern radicals, followers of Seward and of Calhoun, who for all their mutual dislike were willing to unite to prevent any compromise at all. The bill, though favored by majority and apparently headed for passage, was killed through a deft parliamentary maneuver by its enemies. Clay appeared stunned, as "melancholy as Caius Marius over the ruins of Carthage." But even though the bill had been scuttled as a whole, it could still be passed piecemeal; and the "Little Giant" of Illinois, Stephen Douglas, as chairman of the Committee on Territories, took up Clay's battle. Precocious, massive of body and vibrant of voice, Douglas had been called a "steam-engine in britches." With his short legs, thick hair, pugnacious chin, pug nose, and eyes of a singularly deep blue, he was of the new mid-century generation of leaders, having been elected to Congress at the age of thirty and to the Senate four years later.

Backed by the weight of the administration, with the prestige and skill of Clay and Webster, and guided by the astute Little Giant, the bills passed one by one with resounding House and Senate majorities—the admission of California, the Texas-New Mexico boundary, the admission of Utah as a territory, the Fugitive Slave Bill, the banning of the slave trade in the District of Columbia. Clay's work, the Compromise of 1850, had become a fact, and the threat to the Union seemed over. The popular acceptance of the Compromise was overwhelming; even those who had been hesitant welcomed the easing of the crisis. Relieved Americans celebrated with bonfires, parades, speeches, cannon salutes, banquets, and illuminations. On the night following the passage of the California and Utah bills, word was passed round Washington that it was the duty of every good patriot to get drunk! Webster and Douglas found themselves visited at their homes by celebrators and spoke to jubilant crowds before their doors. Clay was cheered wherever he went in the North—Baltimore, Philadelphia, New York. "I can now sleep of nights," Webster wrote to a friend. "We have now gone through the most important crisis that has occurred since the foundation of this government, and whatever party may prevail, hereafter, the Union stands firm."

Mill Town and Factory

American industrial growth between 1789 and 1860—
slow to start but building rapidly by the 1840's—
was a result of many factors. These included natural
resources, such as water power, fuel, and iron; Yankee
ingenuity and enterprise; immigration; foreign relations; the temperament of workers. After the American Revolution—when native manufacture was almost entirely limited to handicraft operations—British
trade restrictions forced Northeast shipping merchants to look far afield for markets. The new contacts
infused the nation with vitality and furnished capital
for investment in manufacture—whose development
nationalism demanded. Water power ran the mills
that sprang up in New England to spin cotton imported from a busy South. The labor-shortage problem of an economy primarily agricultural was solved
first by the employment of farm girls and children,
later by the hiring of European immigrants. Although
America trailed Europe in industry in 1820, labor-
saving inventions—eagerly adopted by workers—soon
increased the abundance and variety of products. Expansion in the West created a constant demand.
European trade expanded. By 1860 only Great Britain
surpassed the United States in industrial might.

OVERLEAF: *In the early nineteenth century, before the
era of mass production, American craftsmen were proud
of their skill. Here a wheelwright works at his trade.*

Wind and water were the prime sources of power in American milling and manufacturing until they were largely superseded by steam. Above, an American windmill of the 1830's; right, a Maryland water wheel

n Morning Bell Winslow Homer painted a factory girl on her way to work in a bucolic setting.

The development of machinery, which allowed inexperienced operators to make cloth cheaply, stimulated textile manu-
facturing in New England. Above, a female worker attends a cotton loom; left, a male worker runs a calico-printing machine.

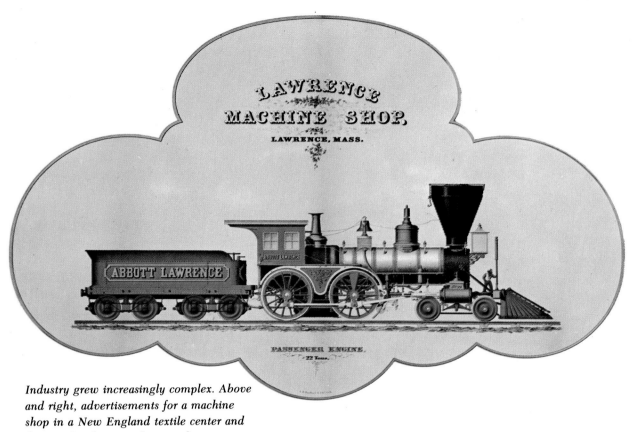

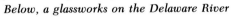

Industry grew increasingly complex. Above
and right, advertisements for a machine
shop in a New England textile center and
for an Ohio farm-implements factory.
Below, a glassworks on the Delaware River

Industrial progress was hailed at New York's Crystal Palace (above) in 1853. But progress could lead to violence (left).

OVERLEAF: *The North's advance in heavy industry is typified by this painting of a Cold Springs, New York, iron foundry.*

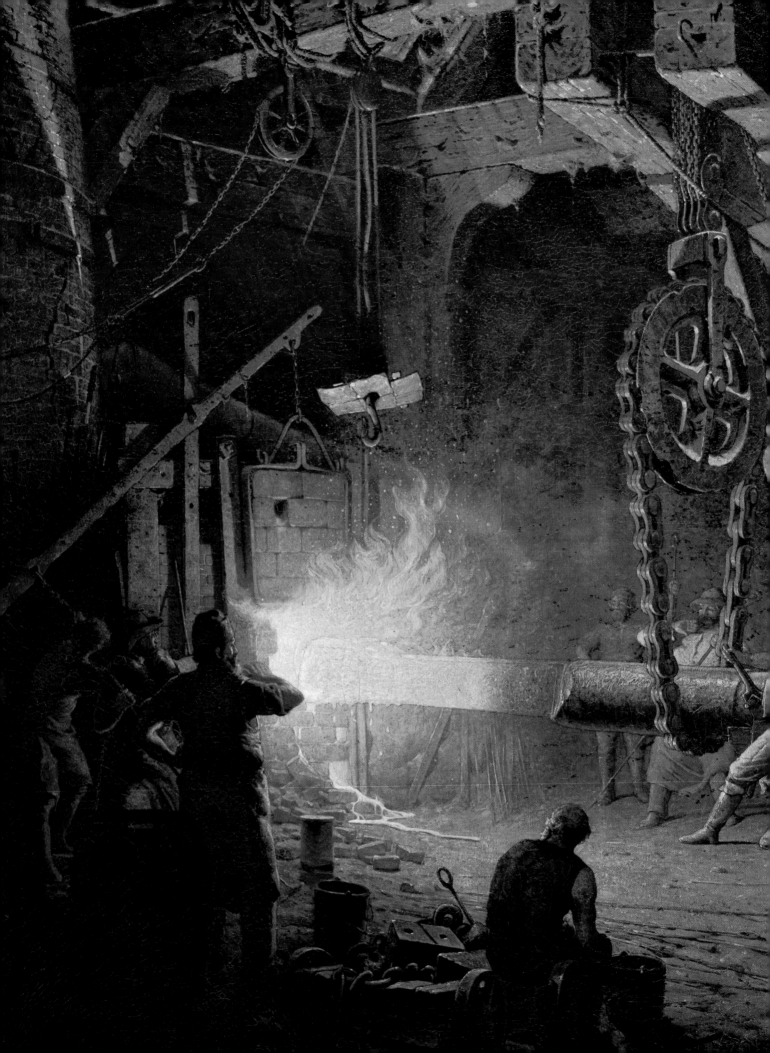

Trends and People

*I*n spite of the Union sentiment that swept the country in the wake of the Compromise of 1850, slavery would continue as the gravest social and political problem confronting the nation. What had been so casually thrust aside by the delegates to the 1787 Philadelphia Convention developed within two generations into the issue that underlay all other issues. From a matter of discussion, slavery became a matter of polemic. North and South grew adamant. Northern fanaticism bred Southern intransigency; there no longer remained any middle position.

As late as 1817 it was possible for men of good will, slaveholders and nonslaveholders, to find common ground in the American Colonization Society. Even in the thirties Northerners like the pacifist William Ellery Channing (he would become more extreme later), while insisting that the evil of slavery must be abolished, nevertheless realized that this would not happen overnight, and were willing to give priority to improving the bondsman's current lot. The American Anti-Slavery Society, founded in 1833 in New York by two wealthy philanthropists, Arthur and Lewis Tappan, had been inspired by the success of the British abolitionists in bringing an orderly end to slavery in the West Indies. The Tappans were joined by the poor minister's son Theodore D. Weld and the former Alabama slaveowner James Birney, both of whom had lost faith in the effectiveness and even the good will of the Colonization Society. The new society advocated a modification of the British formula: a qualified emancipation into peonage and apprenticeship until by degrees the ex-slave would be prepared to assume civil and political rights. Its aim was to set up antislavery organizations in every city, town, and village; to appeal to press and pulpit; to boycott the products of slave labor; and to distribute antislavery tracts "unsparingly and extensively." Under the astute guidance of Weld and Birney, the society soon became a great force in American life, with branches spreading north and west and with a weekly paper, the *Emancipationist,* whose circulation reached 217,000. Resentment of the society's activities became widespread: hostile mobs gathered before the branch meeting halls, meetings were broken up, speakers were threatened, presses were destroyed and

The wild beauty of the New York landscape on the Genesee is captured by Thomas Cole, one of the pioneer members of the Hudson River School, a group of artists who portrayed vistas of the American Northeast in a romanticized way.

297

pamphlets confiscated. Subject repeatedly to such attacks, the society turned political to protect itself.

Abolitionists in the pattern of William Lloyd Garrison rejected the more temperate approach of the New York society. Morally implacable, they could see slavery only as an obscene fact, not as an inherited problem related to its time and place. They would be satisfied with nothing less than immediate, unqualified freedom for the slave, regardless of social consequences. The eclipse of gradualism is symbolized in the person of Garrison, the founder of the *Liberator*, whose name has come down to us almost as a synonym for abolition. Violent in language, intemperate in actions, magnetic yet tactless in personal relationships, less concerned with large-scale organizational activities and with ameliorative efforts than with propaganda, Garrison was the prototype of the fanatic abolitionist. Weld and Birney, more practical in their methods, held themselves loyal to the Constitution while deploring what they considered its misconstructions. Garrison cared nothing for his inheritance. "If the Republic must be blotted out from the roll of nations," he wrote, "by proclaiming liberty to the captives, then let the Republic sink beneath the waves of oblivion."

Garrison was a New Englander whose pious Baptist mother had been abandoned by his sailor father in Newburyport, Massachusetts, when the boy was three years old. Before he had reached his teens the fatherless family had completely broken up. William became a printer's apprentice in Newburyport, serving the traditional seven years as he learned the trade. Industrious, religious, presentable if somewhat nearsighted, he was thought well enough of so that at the end of his apprenticeship he received encouragement to start a small newspaper, the *Free Press*. Although it ran but a few months, it did print the first verses of a cobbler's helper, John Greenleaf Whittier.

The young Garrison had dreams of glory—of joining the Greeks in their struggle against Turkey, of going to West Point—but put his dreams aside to work on a newspaper in Boston. Later, while working at his trade in Baltimore, he was convicted of libeling a slave trans-

Slavery advocates not only attacked abolitionist printing presses, as in this 1839 woodcut, but even raided post offices to burn antislavery tracts.
American Anti-Slavery Almanac, 1839

porter from Newburyport and for this he went to jail. While behind bars he conceived of the abolitionist paper that he would establish when he was released.

On January 1, 1831, the twenty-five-year-old Garrison published in Boston the first number of his *Liberator*. For all its small beginnings it became a gadfly. Much of it brilliantly written, it was enraging to the South. Georgia offered five thousand dollars for Garrison's apprehension. The ascetic publicist, living in his grubby, ink-spattered bedroom-office-print shop, was a person to excite both homage and rage. His intemperate zeal was especially infuriating to the respectable members of the community, many of whom did business with the South and most of whom—like their counterparts in other cities—resented and feared abolitionist agitation, seeing it as a threat to the foundations of the Union and as a prelude to war. In 1835 a Boston mob seized the defiant Garrison and led him through the streets with a rope around his body before they finally turned him loose, roughed up but unharmed.

A year after founding the *Liberator*, Garrison created his own uncompromising New-England Anti-Slavery Society with its dogma of immediate abolition. Egotistically he broke with the New England church leaders, refused to consider any kind of political action, and finally declined even to vote. The Constitution he considered "a covenant with death and an agreement with hell," and he demanded a breakup of the Union. The violence of his approach ruined the efforts of the gradual emancipationists. In the end the more temperate work of Birney and Weld and the New York society was far more influential than his. But as the personification of abolitionism Garrison, with his bald domed head and eyes glittering behind metal-rimmed spectacles, remains unequaled. Whatever his accomplishments, he made his mark even as he carried in his uncompromising wake such men as Wendell Phillips, Whittier, and Charles Sumner.

Others were not so fortunate in their encounters with a hostile public as merely to be led by a rope. Prudence Crandall, a reader of the *Liberator*, who, with Garrison's support, had opened a school for Negro girls in Canterbury, Connecticut, was forced to give it up after the building had been ransacked by enraged townspeople. In Cincinnati a mob destroyed the press on which Birney's *Philanthropist* was printed, while in Philadelphia another mob burned to the ground a hall used for abolitionist meetings. The abolitionists acquired their first

martyr in 1837, when Elijah Lovejoy was killed gun in hand while facing a mob in Alton, Illinois, across the river from St. Louis. Lovejoy, a talented but bigoted young man from Maine, had come to St. Louis to edit the nominally Presbyterian St. Louis *Observer*, which he transformed into a journal as opposed to Catholics as it was to slavery. After his office in St. Louis had been sacked, he moved to Alton, where mobs three times destroyed his presses. Lovejoy and his supporters armed and prepared to defend a warehouse that held a newly arrived fourth press. A hostile crowd set the building afire, and when Lovejoy was forced outside, he was shot down. The account of his death as edited by the abolitionist press stirred the free states. John Quincy Adams wrote that it sent "a shock as of an earthquake throughout this continent." At a protest meeting in Boston's Faneuil Hall the patrician Wendell Phillips proclaimed his own allegiance to abolitionism.

Northern reaction to slavery was at first more an antagonism to the South than any concrete feeling for the black man. The abolitionists alone, on a combination of religious and humanitarian grounds, emphasized the Negro's rights as a person. Indiana in 1851 and Illinois in 1853 passed laws excluding free Negroes, and only four Northern states refrained from restricting Negro voting. In New York City Jim Crow was in effect on all public transportation. Greeley declared bitterly that ex-slaves had no future in America. The average man in the North accepted the Compromise of 1850, but he tended to dislike or be indifferent to the free Negro who was living in his midst.

The Northern intellectuals, on the other hand, condemned the Compromise. For them slavery had come to be equated with original sin. Vociferous in their indignation, they did not have the practical man's instinct to smooth over sectional differences for the sake of the Union. They stood apart, contemptuous of the businessman's stake in the status quo, the politician's stake in the government. Opposition to slavery became a shibboleth of intellectuals, even though—as Southern critics were unkind enough to point out—Northern abolitionists showed more interest in the fate of the distant Southern bondslave than they did in the wage slave of their own factories. Webster, after his role in the Compromise, was looked on as a villain in intellectual New England. Theodore Parker compared him to Benedict Arnold. "Fallen, fallen, fallen from his high estate," Longfellow wrote reproachfully.

Wendell Phillips thought him another fallen Lucifer, and Whittier excoriated him in *Ichabod:*

> Then, pay the reverence of old days
>   To his dead fame;
> Walk backward, with averted gaze
>   And hide the shame!

What the Compromise could not conceal was the growing rift between the two sections, each becoming more acutely conscious of its regional identity. Men who fifteen years earlier had thought of themselves as Americans now thought of themselves as Southerners. There were the economic and political antagonisms: Northern objections to the three-fifths representation clause in the Constitution, Southern fears of being outvoted and overwhelmed by the growing strength of the North, the challenge of free soil versus states' rights. Beyond the economic-political factors was the moral alienation, demonstrated by the split of the Methodists and the Baptists into Northern and Southern branches. Southerners maintained that the Negro was an irresponsible child, lazy and untrustworthy while at the same time cheerful and gay—Sambo, in fact. Northern

abolitionists insisted that Negroes differed only in the color of their skin, that no preparation was needed for instant freedom. More significant than all arguments and counterarguments was the fact that the South was out of step with the times. As the nineteenth century advanced, Western civilization, despite its pockets of resistance, had come to reject slavery. The Southerners in their redoubt—sheltered against progress by their defenses—were sustaining an anachronism.

In the South of the age of reason, Washington, Patrick Henry, Jefferson, and Madison had found slavery repugnant and had looked to its gradual extinction. Slavery could not then have been defended even as being very profitable. But the cotton gin and the cheap fertile lands of the Southwest gave the "peculiar institution" a new lease on life. Cotton became king. To cultivate it without slaves seemed to Southerners impossible. As the world demand for cotton grew, so did the number of slaves—from a million and a half in 1820 to more than three million in three decades. The price of a prime Negro went from about seven hundred dollars in 1830 to fifteen hundred dollars in 1856. Virginia and the older states, where slavery had come to be unprofit-

300

Only occasionally were the swarms of European immigrants who came to America in the 1840's and 1850's granted deck privileges on the crowded vessels that carried them. Most often they were jammed into airless holds, prey to extreme discomfort and disease. The fortunate passengers at left are aboard the Cornelius Grinnell *en route from Liverpool to New York in 1851. At right, a New York City bootblack mockingly salutes an arriving Irish family. Below, two Irishmen, recently landed, engage in a lively political discussion.*

able, now flourished as centers of slave breeding.

With the growing number of slaves came the growing number of slavery's advocates. By the thirties the institution's classical apologists had given way to its romantic defenders. Slavery in its most intransigent form was hailed as a positive good. "We of the South will not, cannot surrender our institutions," Calhoun wrote. "To maintain the existing relations between the two races, inhabiting that section of the Union, is indispensable to the peace and happiness of both. It cannot be subverted without drenching the country in blood, and extirpating one or the other of the races. Be it good or bad, it has grown up with our society and institutions, and is so interwoven with them, that to destroy it would be to destroy us as a people." Southern clergymen combed the Scriptures for texts to defend slavery, viewing it as an act of God that savages had been brought from the darkness of Africa to the light of Christianity. Southern thinkers compared the lot of the happy bondsman under paternalistic protection to that of the exploited millworker of the North, for whom no industrialist felt responsible outside the factory. Much of Southern criticism of Northern capitalism was definitely socialistic in

301

its overtones. George Fitzhugh, a noted defender of slavery—who carried his arguments to the logical point of justifying enslavement of whites by whites—wrote in his *Sociology for the South:* "Until the last fifteen years, our great error was to imitate Northern habits, customs and institutions. Our circumstances are so opposite to theirs, that whatever suits them is almost sure not to suit us. Until that time, in truth, we distrusted our social system. We thought slavery morally wrong, we thought it would not last, we thought it unprofitable. The Abolitionists assailed us; we looked more closely into our circumstances; became satisfied that slavery was morally right, that it would continue ever to exist, that it was as profitable as it was humane."

To the abolitionists' grim picture of the cowering black man oppressed by the whip-wielding overseer, of wives and husbands sold apart and children torn from their mothers' arms, of the branding iron, the coffle, and the auction block, the Southerners presented a contrasting rustic idyl, in which happy Sambo and frolicsome Mandy lived out their days in peaceful security in the shadow of the columned mansion. At least some of this myth of the South had substance. There *were* slaveholders who treated their slaves with kindness and consideration and even love. Andrew Jackson went to much trouble and expense to keep his slaves happy, and when he died the spontaneous wailing from the slave quarters spread across the fields. Yet, the American bondsman,

unprotected by an established church and by law, was dependent on the caprices of his master for his well-being. And, as has been pointed out, there were no refugees from the North escaping the shackles of the industrial wage-system for the gentler bondage of the slaveholding South.

The full-blown myth of the South found its way into the verse of William Grayson, who wrote in heroic couplets of his native South Carolina under slavery's beneficent sway:

No mobs of factious workmen gather here,
No strikes we dread, no lawless riots fear;
Nuns, from their convent driven, at midnight fly,
Churches, in flames, ask vengeance from the sky,
Seditious schemes in bloody tumults end,
Parsons incite, and senators defend,
But not where slaves their easy labors ply,
Safe from the snare, beneath a master's eye;
In useful tasks engaged, employed their time,
Untempted by the demagogue to crime,
Secure they toil, uncursed their peaceful life
With labor's hungry broils and wasteful strife.
No want to goad, no faction to deplore,
The slave escapes the perils of the poor.

Of course the great majority of Southerners owned no slaves, and most of those who did owned only a few or—like Miss Watson in *Huckleberry Finn*—just one. A very small group of slaveholders possessed the great

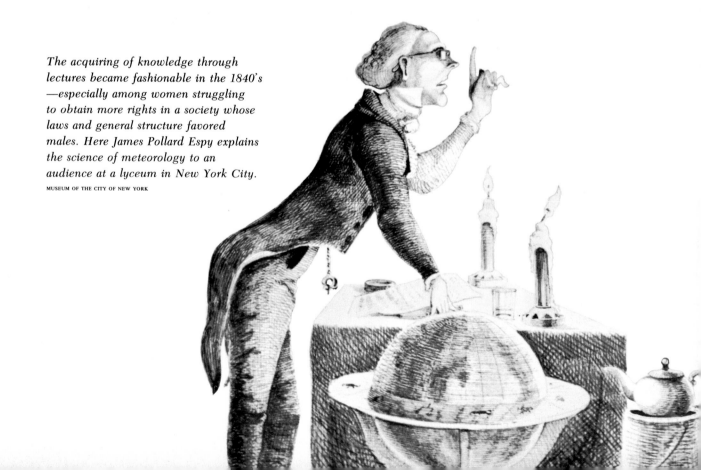

The acquiring of knowledge through lectures became fashionable in the 1840's —especially among women struggling to obtain more rights in a society whose laws and general structure favored males. Here James Pollard Espy explains the science of meteorology to an audience at a lyceum in New York City.

plantations where the gangs of field hands labored. Yet this planter ascendancy set the tone, and the rest of the South rallied to them with little practical to gain—out of a sense of regionalism, of ethnic loyalty and racial pride, and finally out of fear. For with two of every five men in the South black, what would happen if they were suddenly free? This Southern nightmare had taken on a brief reality in the 1822 conspiracy of Denmark Vesey, a free Negro of Charleston who had plotted a large-scale slave insurrection only to have it betrayed at the last moment. Nine years later the threat became a fact when the fanatic Virginia slave-preacher Nat Turner, swept by religious passion, organized a rebellion and with a band of seventy followers slaughtered fifty-five whites in two days.

After Turner there were no more slave revolts, but the fear of them haunted the South—the shadowed uncertainty, the whispered rumor of another conspiracy, more widespread, more violent, and only waiting for the right moment. Always the thought persisted that behind Sambo's disarming grin there lurked Turner with his whetted knife.

As great a problem to the North, as portentous as slavery had been for the South, was the tidal wave of immigration ushered in by the failure of the Irish potato crops from 1845 through 1849. Immigrants until then had come to America for religious, political, or personal reasons, but those of the famine years swarmed across

the ocean because they had no other refuge. Defeated and hopeless, they fled a ruined country, where by 1851 one person in eight had died of hunger or disease and where in a few years the population would be reduced from eight million to less than four million.

"This is every man's country," the French immigrant Michel de Crèvecoeur had written of America, and the new and unique republic had become the cherished dream of many a European. Ever since the Irish Sir William Johnson had established his feudal domain in upper New York State, Celts—Irish, Scotch-Irish, Scots, and Welsh—had been flocking to the United States. The Irish in particular came after the United Irishmen Revolt of 1798 and the industry-destroying Act of Union with Great Britain. French refugees from the Revolution were followed by Napoleonic exiles. Scandinavians, driven like the English yeomen from their common lands by the new enclosures, turned to the overseas republic where Western land could be had almost for the asking. Second only to the English-speaking immigrants were the Germans, who by 1840 were arriving in America at the rate of sixty thousand a year. Displaced farmers they were for the most part, hungry for land and personal freedom. Generally they came from Bavaria and the Upper Rhine. Sometimes whole villages, headed by their pastor, would make their way to the seaports and the chance for a new life. In the revolutionary year 1848 these people—mainly peas-

ants—were joined by the defeated liberal intellectuals from all over Europe.

As their numbers grew, the new immigrants were met with rising hostility. In particular the ingrained Catholicism of the Irish stirred the unreasoned American reaction against papism, which lingered from colonial times. Grayson's verses on nuns fleeing their convents in the midnight glow of burning churches were doubtless a reference to the burning of Charlestown's Ursuline Convent by a Boston mob in 1834. But it should be pointed out that at the same time many of Boston's best families sent daughters to the Ursuline school. After the famine such intermingling between Catholics and Protestants would no longer be possible.

Time, as it had before, would have settled most differences between the new immigrants and their neighbors if it had not been for the unassimilable hordes that arrived in the wake of Ireland's great disaster. America was unprepared for this unique and devastating invasion, which overwhelmed the Northeastern seaport cities. Often these Irish peasants had given the last of what they possessed to pay their passage over. Many were assisted by various charitable organizations or by relatives who had already emigrated. A large portion were illiterate and most had no trade. They came like cattle, packed in the ships whose stench a harbor master could identify three miles away. Five per cent died on the voyage. The newly arrived Paddies clustered in the fetid back alleys of the seaports, swarming in their squalor. Most of the famine survivors came to Boston because that city, as the European ship terminus, cost the immigrants the lowest fare to reach. Soon the brick peninsular town, self-contained and still quietly English in aspect and attitudes, was transformed by these ragged, pugnacious newcomers into a class-riven metropolis. Within a few years Boston's population had doubled and the Yankees had withdrawn to their Beacon Hill redoubt, reacting to the Celtic swarm by creating the self-defensive legend of the Boston Brahmin. The Irish, though a prime source of cheap, exploitable labor, were feared and mistrusted; "a race," in Mayor Theodore Lyman's opinion, "that will never be infused with our own, but on the contrary will always remain distinct and hostile."

Other masses of desperate immigrants would follow in the course of the century, fleeing the slums of Naples, the Russian pogroms, repression following the 1848 revolution in Germany. But the Irish, as the first wave,

were the most notable, destined to alter the history of their adopted country. United politically, they would put down the haughty from their seats, they would organize urban corruption out of ethnic revenge, and in the end they would move beyond corruption to respectability until finally—and in spite of Mayor Lyman's prediction—their descendants in the next century would see one of their own blood and background become President of the United States.

The ending of the Napoleonic Wars had been like the opening of an American door to European immigration. From 1820 to 1830 one hundred and fifty thousand im-

HARRIET

nigrants arrived, a number that would be quadrupled in the next decade. Between 1840 and 1850 the number rose to one and three-quarter millions. Their arrival bred the inevitable reaction, a compound of fear and dislike, among native Americans. Since most of the Germans, and almost all the Irish, were Catholics, existing anti-Catholicism was reinforced. As early as 1831 the first anti-Catholic body, the New York Protestant Association, had been founded, to be followed by similar organizations in other cities. For years Samuel F. B. Morse, inventor of the telegraph, wrote diatribes against Catholicism and immigration, calling them

Horace Greeley—reformer, newspaperman, political candidate—is caricatured at left by Adalbert Volck. Above, an evicted mother and her freezing children, tugging at the hearts of compassionate readers, appear on an 1858 winter cover of Harper's Weekly.

threats to American democracy. Later he became president of the American Protestant Union. Anti-Catholic papers sprang up, as did books that beneath a thin veneer of piety contained salacious and wholly fictional accounts of orgies between priests and nuns. In 1836 the *Awful Disclosures of Maria Monk* purported to expose the immorality of Montreal's Hotel Dieu Nunnery, and although Maria's account represented nothing more than lewd imaginings of a woman of dubious reputation, the book was still being circulated a hundred years later.

The nativistic American Republican party—founded in 1843 and not to be confused with the later Republican party of 1854—called for a twenty-one-year residence requirement for naturalization, even as its members pledged never to vote for a foreign-born candidate. Despite Catholic objections, nativists insisted on the use of the King James Version for reading of the Bible in the public schools. Germans were often resented as much as the Irish, because of their foreign speech and habits and their supposed political radicalism. In what they considered self-protection, native Americans formed the Order of United Americans, the Order of United American Mechanics, the Order of the Star-Spangled Banner, and similar antiforeign societies. The Order of the Star-Spangled Banner required its members to have been born in the United States of Protestant parents and, if married, to have non-Catholic wives. Founded in New York, it expanded rapidly on an anti-Catholic, anti-Jewish, anti-Negro platform to become in a few years the American party—known popularly as the Know-Nothings because its members took an oath to answer all questions concerning the society with "I know nothing about it." Expanding nativism brought violence with it—brawls in the cities, the damaging and occasional burning of Catholic churches, riots on election days. Anti-Catholic speakers, guarded by toughs known as Wide-Awakes, took to challenging the Irish newcomers, who did not need to be challenged twice. The Know-Nothings, accepting their nickname, published a *Know-Nothing Almanac.*

Later generations would come to regard mass immigration as a progressive force, and even at the time there were reflective Americans who so saw it. President Nathan Lord of Dartmouth in his *Tract for the Times: National Hospitality* maintained that "we should open . . . the vast, rich and productive country stretching from sea to sea, and almost wholly lying waste, which the bounty of Providence has conferred on us. Freely we have received, and freely we should give." Progress as a continuing force, though a concept novel to history, was a national assumption, singularly acceptable to a new society with a constantly expanding frontier. This easy trust in progress gave to the United States, on the threshold of the industrial era, a reforming impulse, a faith in perfectibility however imperfect the vista, a peculiar and persistent confidence that the crooked could be set straight by passing a law.

Beguiled by this belief, businessman and mayor-to-be of Portland Neal Dow succeeded in 1846 in inducing the Maine legislature to pass America's first prohibition law. The earlier temperance movement, for all its fervor, had not seemed to cut down the gross consumption of liquor—rum in New England, whiskey in the South and the West. Drink was cheaper than food, and Dow, having observed the ruin that alcohol had brought to so many families, concluded that total abstinence rather than temperance was the answer. Traveling up and down his state with a team of reformed drunkards, he tried to persuade men onto the path of abstinence, at the same time urging them to unite for political action. His 1846 law proving too difficult to enforce, he drew up a new one five years later, the famous Maine Liquor Law, which prohibited the manufacture and sale of intoxicating liquors except for medicinal purposes. By 1855 a dozen states and two territories had banned the sale of liquor within their borders, an aridity somewhat mitigated in rural areas by the fact that no state undertook to interfere with the farmer's production of hard cider. In the South the moral impulse was less in evidence. Only one Southern state adopted prohibition, whereas only four in the North and the West failed to pass a dry law.

With the advance of prohibition came the expansion of the woman's rights movement. Although by the forties there were women of note—like Maria Mitchell the astronomer, Lucretia Mott the preacher, the abolitionist Grimké sisters from the South, and the physician Harriot Hunt, to say nothing of New England's own transcendentalist bluestocking Margaret Fuller—most women existed on chivalric sufferance, with no political rights, limited educational opportunities, and severe legal restrictions if they were married. Even the female lecturers, the female contributors to *Godey's Lady's Book*, and the scores of sentimental novelists led by Susan Warner, who wrote *The Wide, Wide World*—"a

d——d mob of scribbling women," Hawthorne called them—seemed to emphasize feminine frailty rather than freedom. Yet if most men still liked to maintain that woman's place was in the home, women leaders were appearing who thought emphatically otherwise. In 1848 Lucretia Mott and Elizabeth Cady Stanton called a women's convention at Seneca Falls, New York. There in a flutter of ruffles and furbelows Mrs. Stanton read a Declaration of Sentiments, modeled on the Declaration of Independence, which declared that "all men *and women* are created equal." The history of mankind they saw as one of repeated injuries and usurpations by men against women. Women had been denied their "inalienable right" to vote, had been compelled to submit to laws that they had had no voice in making, had found themselves "civilly dead" through marriage, had been barred from higher education and profitable employment while being subject to a moral code that men could break with impunity. With the Seneca Falls Convention, the practical struggle for woman suffrage began. That struggle would last for seventy years, though other barriers would fall more easily.

In 1833 Oberlin College had become the first coeducational college in the United States and would remain the only one for seventeen years until it was followed by the University of Utah in 1850 and then by Antioch in 1853, under its first president, Horace Mann. Today Mann is remembered more for his work in the public schools of Massachusetts and for his primary part in the mid-century educational awakening all over the United States than in his role as a college president. As secretary for eleven years of the newly created Massachusetts Board of Education, he established state-wide standards of education, started the country's first state normal school for the proper training of teachers, did the preliminary work for compulsory school attendance, extended the school year from a number of weeks to six months, secularized and modernized the old Calvinist-oriented curriculum, and by inspections and persuasion and at times compulsion raised the almost brutish standard of rural education. Since the more well-to-do patronized private schools, the public schools in the 1830's had tended to become charity schools—and not always free, at that. Mann was much opposed to any system for creating an elite. Class conflicts, he felt, could be solved by good public schools alone since only "universal education can counterwork this tendency to the domination of capital and the servility of labor.

The editors of a revitalized New York Mirror—*Nathaniel P. Willis and George P. Morris*—*were cartooned in the rival* Broadway Journal *in 1845. New York by this time was the country's communications center.*

Broadway Journal, JANUARY 25, 1845, NEW-YORK HISTORICAL SOCIETY

. . . Education . . . is a great equalizer of the conditions of men—the balance wheel of the social machinery." The influence of this Yankee lawyer and legislator-turned-educator was pervasive in the movement to bring a modern systematized education to every child. It is in recognition of this that so many public schools across the country still preserve his name carved in the stone above their portals.

Reform in the mid-century, linked with the expansive belief in progress, took multiple forms: noble, quixotic, useful, futile, dogmatic, ridiculous, and yet inevitable. Extending from the agitation for the ten-hour day to the perfectionism of religious cults—utopian colonies, such as New England's transcendentalist Brook Farm and John H. Noyes's socialistic-sexual experiment

in Oneida, New York, and strange dabblings in phrenology, mesmerism, and spiritualism—reform in all its manifestations was nurtured by the easy availability of print. New techniques had made newsprint much cheaper, and this, coupled with Richard Hoe's invention of the double-cylinder steam-driven press in the mid-1830's and of his rotary press in 1847, would blanket the United States with newspapers. By 1833 there were three times as many papers in America as in England. That same year marked the most spectacular journalistic phenomenon of the period, the advent of the penny paper, in itself a reaction to the great mercantile papers that sold for six cents. With the penny press, newspapers found an audience in Jackson's common man and editors were enabled to reach—and sometimes even to influence—the masses with their ideas.

The first such paper, the New York *Sun*, was a venture of the young Benjamin Day, who had come to New York at the age of twenty from the Springfield *Republican*. Day started out with more ideas than cash, but in four months he had built up a circulation of five thousand, to lead the whole New York field. His paper was brash, lively, innovative, flippant in covering crime, explicit in its sensationalism. Until then most newspapers had been sold by subscription, but Day sent newsboys out on the streets to hawk the single copies that would soon make his paper's circulation the largest in the country.

Two years later James Gordon Bennett, a Scottish-born reporter and journalist with only five hundred dollars to his name, founded the New York *Morning Herald*, the *Sun*'s great rival. Under Bennett the newspaper showed itself wittier than the *Sun*, with more extensive foreign news and with the most candid Wall Street reports that had ever appeared. Each paper tried to outdo the other in reports of mayhem, murder, rape, and robbery; both exploited crime and sex. The pungent, saucy *Herald* crept up on the *Sun*'s circulation, and Bennett soon felt sure enough of his paper to raise the price to two cents. By 1850 he was selling over thirty thousand copies daily in spite of the "moral war" the more sedate papers had earlier waged against his sensationalism.

Designed to compete with the Democratic *Sun* and the *Herald* was Horace Greeley's Whig *Tribune* of 1841. As a tow-haired, nasal-voiced boy from Vermont, Greeley had looked the bumpkin when he had arrived in New York. For a time he worked for the New York *Evening Post,* under its editor William Cullen Bryant, the poet turned newspaperman. With a thousand dollars he had saved up and a thousand he had borrowed he launched his own newspaper. The *Tribune*'s circulation reached eleven thousand in two months, and within two years Greeley raised the price to two cents. It never reached the circulation of the daily *Sun* or the *Herald,* but with his *Weekly Tribune,* which just before the Civil War attained a record-breaking circulation of two hundred thousand, Greeley made his mark in the land, the mark of a social reformer with antislavery his greatest cause. In that period, during which the struggle against slavery reached its climax, the *Weekly Tribune* became the country's most influential journal of opinion.

By mid-century, with New York's population reaching half a million, three young men, headed by the journalist Henry J. Raymond, decided that there was room for still another penny paper in New York and in 1851 founded the *Daily Times,* a Whig paper that soon turned to the Free-Soilers. By avoiding Greeley's

Many American architects abandoned Georgian styles after 1820 to turn to the more soaring Gothic. This drawing of a Gothic house is probably an architect's exercise in geometric projection.

eccentricities and Bennett's sensationalism while covering all the news, by its objective appraisal of events, its extensive foreign coverage, the *Times* managed to become the most balanced and respected paper in the United States.

The expansion of the newspaper, centered in New York but spreading to every city, was paralleled by the rise of the popular magazine, beginning with the *Knickerbocker,* which appeared in 1833. Its chief rival was Philadelphia's *Graham's Magazine,* which published contributions by Longfellow, Bryant, Lowell, and Cooper and of which Edgar Allan Poe was literary editor in 1841-42. Poe had earlier been editor of the *Southern Literary Messenger* of Richmond, which, with *De Bow's Review,* became the literary spokesman of the ante-bellum South. Hawthorne, Bryant, Longfellow, Whittier, Lowell, and Whitman appeared in the pages of the *United States Magazine and Democratic Review,* a journal that survived only from 1837 until 1859. *Godey's Lady's Book,* the most important of the early women's magazines, appeared in 1830 under the joint editorship of Louis A. Godey and the authoress of "Mary Had a Little Lamb." The *Dial,* the literary quarterly of the New England transcendentalists, took its place alongside the much older *North American Review* as a highbrow literary journal, lasting only from 1840 to 1844 under the editorship first of Margaret Fuller, then of Emerson. In 1827 was founded the most enduring magazine for young people, the *Youth's Companion.* *Harper's Monthly,* which still survives, was established in 1850 by the publishing house of the same name and found the sure-fire formula for success by offering twice as many pages as its rivals, by profuse use of wood engravings, and above all by serializing the novels of Dickens, Charles Reade, and Wilkie Collins, for which the American appetite seemed insatiable. Not until 1857 did the Boston-edited *Atlantic Monthly*—still being published today— appear, under the editorship of James Russell Lowell.

"Who reads an American book?" Sydney Smith's supercilious question of 1820 was more than answered thirty years later. American authors of the third generation since the Revolution were becoming as well known in England as in their own country. American books held forward positions on the shelves of British booksellers. Longfellow was read more in England than Tennyson; his volumes were in every drawing room.

Later generations might find his rhythms as strummingly repetitive as a player piano, but as a young man he had brought back Europe with him to Cambridge and Harvard and transformed it into verse. Whitman called him a poet of the mellow twilight of the past in Italy, Spain, and northern Europe. His first volume of poems, *Voices of the Night,* published in 1839, when he was thirty-two, contained "A Psalm of Life," which would be memorized by generations of reluctant school children. Other volumes followed in mechanical sequence. Yet, whatever Longfellow's deficiencies as a poet, he moved beyond literature to embed himself in the national consciousness with such poems as "The Wreck of the Hesperus," "The Village Blacksmith," "Paul Revere's Ride," *The Song of Hiawatha,* and *The Courtship of Miles Standish.*

Longfellow—with the more homespun Whittier, the more narrowly regional Dr. Oliver Wendell Holmes and James Russell Lowell, and the lesser lights of Boston and Cambridge—formed what has been called the New England Renaissance. In Salem, Hawthorne the solitary was probing his way back to New England's Gothic past. To the south Edgar Allan Poe —born out of his time, whose death-haunted supernatural tales would endure in spite of their artificiality, the inventor of the detective story—died in wretchedness in 1849. Still an obscure journalist in Brooklyn, Walt Whitman—crossing over to New York on the ferry, wandering through the Manhattan streets—was storing up and cataloguing the impressions he would shortly use in *Leaves of Grass.* Singing of himself in a new American manner of his own conceiving, he strove to be to poetry what Jackson had been to politics, a democratic voice of every man.

Already America had produced its first seer in Concord's Ralph Waldo Emerson, who lived both bodily and mentally beyond reach of Boston and Cambridge in the white and gracious colonial village where the minutemen had made their stand that opened the American Revolution. To that ever-occurring enigmatic question of what a man must do to be saved, Emerson found no easy answer in expansion and material progress. Rooted in a section of the country with more than two hundred years of history, formed by the German romantics, the sacred books of the East, Plato, and the Neoplatonists, finding even the mild yoke of Unitarianism too restraining, Emerson created his answer in transcendentalism, the creed that he himself expounded in his lectures as the idealism of 1842. Mankind he divided into materialists and idealists. "The senses give us representations of things, but what are the things themselves, they cannot tell. The materialist insists on facts, on history, on the force of circumstances and the animal wants of man; the idealist on the power of Thought and of Will, on inspiration, on miracle, on individual culture."

In his 1837 address "The American Scholar," given before Harvard's Phi Beta Kappa Society, Emerson proclaimed the freedom of American scholarship from the European past. Dr. Holmes called the address "our intellectual Declaration of Independence." Emerson taught that the universe was in its essence beneficent and that the individual who relied on his deepest instincts could achieve a kind of unity with the Divine. Neither tradition nor financial success mattered. The duty of the individual was to himself. These were fiery thoughts to young men and women out of harmony with the commercialism of the expanding country. Concord became the center of the new philosophy, and Emerson its representative man.

The quiet village became home for Hawthorne; Bronson Alcott, that Yankee Don Quixote; and lesser figures, like the poetaster William Ellery Channing, nephew of the founder of Unitarianism. Henry David Thoreau, the most inconspicuous and the most enduring of the Concord figures, lived there. For it was left to him to practice what the others preached, staying for two years in the hut he had built with his own hands on the edge of Walden Pond "to live deliberately, to front only the essential facts of life."

Concord was a magnet that drew the famous and the obscure, the native and the foreign, the crackpots and the scholars—for Emerson's door swung open easily. Whitman the unknown sent one of his first copies of *Leaves of Grass* to Emerson, who greeted him "at the beginning of a great career." Margaret Fuller visited him; as did Westerners, like John Brown and Bret Harte; and the Boston literati; and eccentrics, like Theodore Parker, who had solved the problem of money by dispensing with it, and Jones Very, who believed he had risen from the dead.

The two volumes of Emerson's essays that would make his name almost as familiar in England as Longfellow's were printed in 1841 and 1844; his first volume of poems appeared three years later. In 1850 Hawthorne's *The Scarlet Letter* was published. The decade that followed was a period of unique literary production. Melville's *Moby Dick* and Parkman's *His-*

tory of the Conspiracy of Pontiac appeared in 1851, and *Uncle Tom's Cabin* began appearing in serial form the same year. *Walden* was published in 1854, and in 1855 came *Hiawatha* and *Leaves of Grass*. Oliver Wendell Holmes collected the pieces of *The Autocrat of the Breakfast Table* in 1858, and Whittier, as the ballad singer of abolition, ushered in 1860 with his *Home Ballads*. It was a remarkably prolific period in New England literature.

To the generation after West and Copley and Stuart, Boston's Washington Allston seemed the greatest artist in the United States even though he had produced little. He had studied in England under West and had lived for several years in Rome, a cosmopolitan figure, the friend of Irving and Wordsworth, of Thorvaldsen, of Longfellow and Coleridge. Returning to Boston, he spent the next twenty years working on the enormous canvas of his *Belshazzar's Feast*, which was to be his masterpiece. But when he died in 1843, his gift to his country was discovered to be only half finished and poorly conceived. With him the period of classicism in American painting came to an end and the school of romantic idealism was born.

Thomas Cole fared better with the grand theme on his five canvases of the rise and fall of a civilization, *The Course of Empire*, which he painted during the 1830's. But he remains more lastingly known as the founder of the first group of American painters, the Hudson River School, artists who in their vast canvases succeeded in making the course of the Hudson appear as romantic as that of the Rhine. But while the Hudson River group painted in the genteel atmosphere and ordered landscape of a Sunday afternoon excursion, other artists, like George Catlin, abandoned the genteel to go west and record in unforgettable canvases the ways and pursuits of the Indians. Albert Bierstadt, the German émigré, whose greatest work came after the Civil War, brought the technique of the German romantics to make himself an unequaled recorder of the Indians, the buffalo, the wild life, the wagon trains, and the towering mountains of the West.

The most distinctive artistic achievement of the period lay elsewhere, evolving obscurely in the person of John James Audubon as he wandered through the woods and swamps of the lower Mississippi Valley, obsessed with the idea of recording with his painter's brush the birds—and later the animals—of his adopted country. Born in Haiti, the illegitimate son of a French

Louis Agassiz, below, a Swiss naturalist who taught in America, drew this flying fish.

ognized for the master he was, for the uniqueness of his accomplishment. His paintings, engraved over the years and issued as 435 life-sized, hand-colored plates in four double-elephant folios, have remained among the masterpieces of American art.

Horatio Greenough was the leader of that group of young American sculptors who left for Italy in the twenties to study the pseudoclassic style of Canova. In 1832 Greenough was commissioned by Congress to carve a statue of Washington for the rotunda of the Capitol. The huge marble figure that he produced ten years later showed the Father of his Country seated in a curule chair and naked to the waist but still wearing his wig. Even at the time the overblown classicism was too much for the unclassical eyes of a number of congressmen, and the masterpiece was relegated for fifty years to a place on the Capitol grounds protected by a canopy; it is now in the Smithsonian Institution. Greenough's fellow classicist Hiram Powers had better luck with his universally admired and quite naked *Greek Slave*. Sheltered by the sanctions of classicism, Powers was able to break the taboos of the period in presenting this enticing nubile figure to the public. His full-breasted slave girl became the most popular, the most ogled, American statue of its time.

Realism of an uncompromising exactness appeared quietly at the end of the 1850's with the small genre group figures of John Rogers. A Massachusetts machinist, Rogers was a self-taught sculptor in clay. His figures, two feet or less in height and contrived with a meticulous, almost microscopic realism, seem human beings in miniature. Because each of his groups, such as *Coming to the Parson* or *Checkers Up at the Farm*, tells a sentimental tale, because the plaster reproductions proliferated in middle-class parlors to the point that they became unendurable for later generations, one tends to overlook the extent of his accomplishment. Yet in originality he far outshone the Greenoughs and the Powerses. Owing nothing to Europe, using a native American idiom, he managed to capture, far more than words could have, his age's manners, fashions, and gestures. Rogers' art, for all its coyness and overabundance, is in fact a segment of time molded in clay.

Architecture, too, was shifting with the times, the columns and pediments of the Greek Revival giving way to the elaborations of the revived Gothic. Spreading from England, the style, with its furbelows, soon captured the American small house. Even the previ-

sea captain, Audubon had been brought up by his father in France but had left Europe for America in 1804 at the age of nineteen to avoid the Napoleonic conscription. He married an American girl, moved to Kentucky, and became a merchant, crowning his career with failure when he went bankrupt in the Panic of 1819 and was sent to jail for debt. Once freed from jail and a dead-end occupation, penniless, middle-aged, he turned his avocation of bird painting into his life work, living from hand to mouth far from his family, subsisting as best he could by making pastel portraits and by teaching drawing, dancing, and hair-braid jewelry making. Every moment he could spare he devoted to studying and sketching and painting birds. Before Audubon, birds had been drawn with wooden exactitude even by so great a naturalist as Alexander Wilson. Audubon painted them in the free air, caught up in the present moment, alive, vital. When he, as an unknown artist, took his paintings to Europe in 1826, he was at once rec-

311

ous century's colonial was given a Gothic trim. In the cities stone Gothic churches sprang up, while in the country pointed arches, wooden finials, and garish stained glass replaced the familiar meetinghouse proportions. With the fading of the Georgian and the eclipse of the Greek Revival there was no longer a commanding tradition. Gothic cottages, Italian villas, and Swiss chalets found themselves contemporaries of Egyptian banks and Oriental mental institutions. Orson Fowler, the celebrated phrenologist, even proposed an octagonal house, which he believed was not only functional but also had certain mystical qualities. Such houses can still be seen here and there not only in upper New York State and New England but also in the Middle West.

Science, in both its practical and theoretical aspects, turned from the brilliant amateurs of the age of reason, like Franklin and Jefferson, to dedicated professionals. In 1846 Jean Louis Agassiz, the Swiss-born geologist and zoologist, arrived in the United States, where he would become the father of American natural history. As a professor at Harvard College, he brought to the classical-based curriculum an unprecedented emphasis on original research. Through his efforts the college began to transform itself into a university, and other American colleges followed the Harvard pattern. At Princeton Joseph Henry—pioneer experimenter in magnetic fields, developer of the principles of the electric motor—showed himself as distinguished in his field as was Agassiz in his, although as a teacher and theorist his name has remained relatively unknown.

Scientific discovery was in the air, and practical men were ready to gain some immediate advantage from it. In May, 1844, Samuel Finley Breese Morse, from the Supreme Court chambers in Washington, sent to Baltimore, forty miles away, the first long-distance telegraph message: "What hath God wrought!" Morse, a New Englander, had first become interested in electricity through various elementary experiments he had observed as a Yale undergraduate of the class of 1810. However, his first goal was to be a painter, and after graduation he spent four years in Europe with Washington Allston. Only in later years did he renew his interest in electricity, an interest that soon became an obsession as he observed the apparently instantaneous velocity with which electric current passed through wire. By 1837 he had evolved his first telegraphic apparatus, but the panic-depression of that year delayed until 1843 a congressional appropriation for running the necessary wires to Baltimore. With that first message the modern age of communication began.

The advent of the telegraph was followed in the spring of 1854 by the preliminary planning for the first Atlantic cable by Cyrus W. Field and a group of wealthy backers. After several breaks and other setbacks the cable was finally completed from Newfoundland to Ireland in the summer of 1858, and Queen Victoria and President Buchanan exchanged messages of good will. A few weeks later the cable broke again and was not restored until 1866.

The telegraph and the rotary press still needed the typewriter to form a trinity of communication media. William Burt had made a typewriter as early as 1829, and Alfred Ely Beach devised a model in 1847. Ten years later another inventor solved the problem of inking the type—through a saturated ribbon. But these models still seemed toys, and not until after the Civil War was a practical machine developed.

Basic to the age that was to come was the development of the use of rubber, and this resulted from the indefatigable labors of one man, New Haven-born Charles Goodyear. Rubber had been a curiosity ever since Columbus had discovered natives bouncing balls made from a substance they called caoutchouc, which they obtained by curing and hardening a milky tree-gum over fire. It became known as rubber only in the eighteenth century when someone discovered that it could be used as an eraser. In the early nineteenth century Yankee traders learned from the Indians that the gum elastic could be carved into waterproof, if clumsy, shoes. Attempts to make cloth out of it failed, for it stiffened in cold weather and in warm weather it grew tacky and ran.

In 1834 Goodyear, examining a rubber life preserver, was told by the store manager that the great need was for some way to keep rubber firm but pliable at all temperatures. He was then thirty-four years old, an unsuccessful hardware merchant, in and out of debtors' prison. At this point he became obsessed with the idea of making gum rubber into a durable material. For the next five years, through all degrees of poverty, with his family sharing his wretchedness, he devoted himself with single-minded stubbornness to making rubber usable, even to clothing himself in his experimental materials. A friend described him: "If you meet a man who has on an India rubber cap, stock, coat, vest and shoes, with an India rubber money purse without a cent of money in it, that is he." Yet his clothing still grew stiff in winter, dissolved odorously in summer. For all his self-denial and his experimenting, he had not been able to change the basic nature of rubber.

One day he accidentally dropped a blob of rubber and sulphur mixture on his wife's hot kitchen stove. The mixture instantly hardened. Goodyear had discovered the secret of vulcanization! The secret did not help him at first. For five years he wandered through Boston and the neighboring towns trying to interest others in his discovery. Recognition finally came to him in the form of pirating and of infringements of his rights. Daniel Webster, in his last great case, finally established that

his client, Goodyear, was the sole inventor of vulcanized rubber. Goodyear died in 1860, still deep in debt but leaving behind him sixty patents to enrich his heirs.

Equally tenacious of an idea was Elias Howe, the inventor of the sewing machine. Others abroad had designed rudimentary sewing machines, but Howe knew nothing of this nor of experiments by Walter Hunt in New York, who had become more interested in exploiting his invention of the safety pin. Watching the motions of his wife's hands as she sewed, trying vainly to duplicate them mechanically, Howe finally found the answer in glancing at the shuttle movement of a loom. Then in 1844, at the age of twenty-five, he quit his job to devote all his energies to this idea. In one winter he

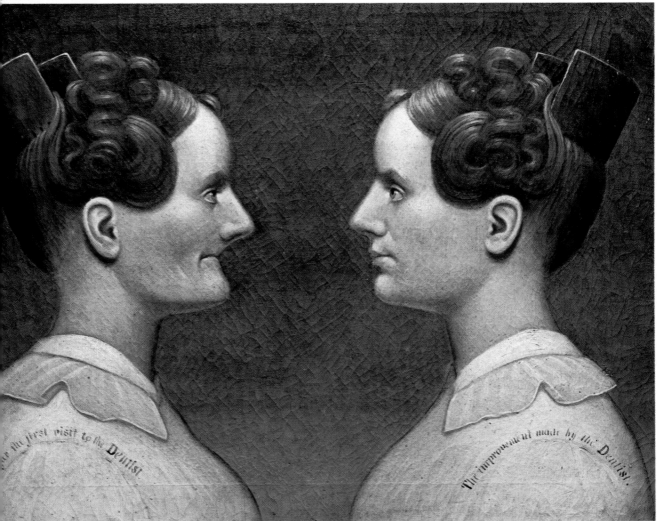

This advertisement shows how improved dentures—still somewhat a novelty—could add to one's appearance.

OVERLEAF: *The sinking of the American ship* Arctic, *after it collided with a French vessel off Newfoundland in 1854, was a severe blow to the popular Collins Line.*

perfected the principle of his sewing machine. But with success he found others exploiting his invention. Isaac Singer, with his later improvements, made his name almost synonymous with sewing machines. But after a long legal battle Howe had his patents recognized as fundamental to all subsequent sewing machines. The accruing royalties made him rich almost overnight. At the expiration of his patents, however, he refused to renew them, saying he had made enough money and did not want more from the labor of others.

Samuel Colt, born in Hartford, was another ingenious Yankee, his interest running to explosives and firearms. In 1836 he patented a revolving-cylinder pistol. Like Howe, he was not the first to light on his besetting idea, but he was the first to develop it in simple and workable form. Even so it roused no great interest until the Mexican War. Then the government suddenly ordered a thousand of his revolvers. Colt arranged with the plant founded by Eli Whitney to make the first models until he could open his own plant in Hartford in 1847. In the Colt factory firearms were manufactured on the principle of interchangeable parts, an inheritance from Whitney, and it was in this arms factory—soon to become the world's largest—that the modern assembly line developed.

In raising the money to develop his revolving pistol, Colt, in the dignified guise of "Dr. Coult," had gone round the country giving popular scientific lec-

The Blacksmith Shop *by Eastman Johnson; blacksmiths were among the artisans who formed unions in the 1840's, but the movement hardly reached into the village smithy.*

ures, during which he had used volunteers from the audience to demonstrate the effects of the newly discovered laughing gas. Laughing-gas and ether-sniffing parties had become popular forms of parlor entertainment. A Hartford dentist, Horace Wells, observing that those who had inhaled laughing gas seemed immune to pain, began to use it when extracting teeth. His success in Hartford was marred, however, by an unsuccessful demonstration before a Harvard medical class, and in his chagrin he gave up his experiments. His former partner, William T. G. Morton, after observing the Harvard fiasco, determined to find a more reliable pain-killing agent than laughing gas.

Morton, a Massachusetts boy and a dentist, had then studied medicine for a year at Harvard, but when his money ran out, he returned to practicing dentistry. In his search for a pain reliever he turned to the Boston doctor, scientist, and Harvard professor Charles T. Jackson. Jackson mentioned sulphuric ether, the substance used for parlor games, which—unbeknown to them—had already been used by Dr. Crawford W. Long of Georgia in removing a tumor. Morton, after practicing ether inhalation on himself and others, came to the realization that it might be used to banish pain in surgical operations. After designing a glass inhaler, he approached Dr. John C. Warren, one of the founders and the senior surgeon of the Massachusetts General Hospital, explaining what he had accomplished and requesting that he be allowed to try out his discovery on one of Warren's patients.

On October 16, 1846, the first documented surgical operation performed under an anesthetic (Dr. Oliver Wendell Holmes would coin that word a month later) took place in the operating theater of the General Hospital under the eyes of Boston's leading surgeons. A young man was brought in with a vascular tumor on his neck. Morton first administered the ether from his inhaler. The senior surgeon then made an incision and removed the tumor while the patient lay on the table motionless. On concluding the operation, Warren called out excitedly to his colleagues: "Gentlemen, this is no humbug!" It was, in fact, the conquest of pain, one of the greatest blessings and the most momentous medical event of the century.

In Morton's time dentists were looked down on by the medical profession as mere mechanics. Yet dentistry had progressed immeasurably since John Greenwood had made Washington the spring-controlled dentures with the ivory teeth that had given the Father of his Country such a look of unwonted sternness in his later portraits. Americans were early notorious for their bad teeth, and American dentists developed ingenious techniques of repair and replacement. Morton himself evolved a new method for cementing gold caps. Although improved artificial teeth were developed in Europe, it was Goodyear's vulcanized rubber that permitted the first close-fitting dental plates.

Scientific discovery was only a segment of the forward impulse that carried over into every section of American life. In transportation a national and even an international system was beginning to emerge. In the brief era of the clipper ships, one of naval architect Donald McKay's graceful vessels crossed the Atlantic in two weeks, but most of them were used on the longer runs around Cape Horn to California and the Orient. Steam was taking over in the Atlantic, however. In 1851 the side-wheeler *Baltic*, of the Collins Line, crossed from New York to Liverpool in not quite ten days.

On land in the United States, the Overland Mail took over where the railroad lines ended, its coach covering the twenty-eight hundred miles from St. Louis to San Francisco in twenty-five days. The railroads themselves were consolidating. Seven or eight local lines in New York State formed the New York Central system in 1853. Familiar names were emerging elsewhere: the Grand Trunk, the Michigan Central, the Rock Island and Chicago, the Erie. The Appalachian barrier had long since been broken, and steadily the rail lines extended west. During the 1850's, aided by lavish government land grants, railroad mileage tripled to thirty thousand miles. With state and federal subsidies, by the sale of stock, often with crass corruption, the railroads expanded with giant strides and thrust aside the older forms of transportation. Canals stagnated as freight moved across the country at a dozen miles an hour and travelers more than twice as fast. Locomotives had switched from wood to coal, roadbeds had improved, and a standard gauge had been introduced. One could travel from Boston to Cincinnati in forty hours. Sleeping cars of a primitive sort made their appearance in the early 1860's. By 1860 Chicago had fifteen lines running into it. Cleveland, Cincinnati, St. Louis, the whole upper Mississippi Valley, were being linked economically to the East. Chicago, as a railroad terminus, became the wonder city of the West. New towns sprang up everywhere along the lines of track

*Male clothing fashions of mid-century—men in dark uni-
formlike apparel, youngsters in more imaginative
garb—are revealed in New York's Astor House ballroom.*

stretching across the prairies. Main lines linked the Atlantic and the West, and there was talk of a transcontinental line, an iron road from sea to sea.

As the farm products of the West sped east, great
changes were taking place in agriculture. The wheat
states were now along the Mississippi and beyond,
while Illinois and eastern Iowa and Missouri were developing into the corn country. In 1847, the year of
famine in Europe, the price of wheat had risen to $1.25
a bushel, and the later gradual decline was reversed by
the demands of the Crimean War in 1854.

Settlers soon discovered that the cast-iron plows of
the East had difficulty in cutting the stickier clay soil of
the prairies. John Deere, a New England blacksmith
who had taken his tools and his trade to Illinois,
contrived a steel plow with improved contours and

smoother surfaces. It did its work so well that Deere
established a factory in Moline, which in a few years
was producing thirteen thousand plows annually.

The law of simultaneous invention—that sense of
things in the air—makes it uncertain as to just who originated the harvester, the thresher, and the grain binder,
but whatever the claims and the counterclaims, it was
Cyrus McCormick who made his name synonymous
with farm implements. At the age of twenty-two
McCormick had invented a hillside plow for his father's
Virginia farm. The elder McCormick had spent twenty
years trying to construct a reaping machine, but finally
it took the son's ingenuity to develop one. Although he
constructed several crude models as early as 1832, he
did not go into the manufacture of reapers seriously
until some time after the Panic of 1837, when he

318

started his own factory in Chicago. Not only did he soon produce four thousand reapers annually but he set up a network of local sales agents who also made repairs and supplied spare parts. His machines became indispensable to the West. In 1860 an observer standing on a hillock in northern Illinois counted 146 reapers at work within range of his spyglass.

A mowing machine was invented by McCormick's rival Obed Hussey, reducing the cost of cutting an acre of hay by two-thirds. Horse rakes, tedders, and balers developed in the same period. At harvest time portable threshers made their appearance in the fields. At the Paris exposition of 1855 an American threshing machine won the prize over all others.

America still remained an agricultural country, but as industries grew, the total value of manufactured goods inexorably crept up on that of farm products. Even the products themselves were changing. By 1820 preserved sea foods were already on the market, and after 1840 vegetables and fruits were being put up in cans or glass jars. In the fifties Gail Borden developed his method of evaporating milk. Everywhere shop and handicraft industries were giving way to the factory system. The whole textile industry was becoming completely mechanized. Before 1845 carpet weaving had been a hand industry; fifteen years after that date it had been largely taken over by power looms. Furniture, carriages and wagons, hats and shoes, all were being mass-produced. In the basic industries, blast furnaces and rolling mills proliferated. Coal replaced charcoal in smelting, and coal smoke begrimed the industrial towns.

319

Advances in industry were marked by no comparable advances in labor; in fact, the wretched living and working conditions of the unskilled worker in the North were not exaggerated by the Southern apologists for slavery. During the Panic of 1837 the whole structure of the trade unions had been destroyed. Only in the forties did weak local associations of the more skilled workers begin to emerge again—bookbinders, blacksmiths, tailors, stonecutters, and carpenters. The principal agitation was for the ten-hour day, and this was particularly strong in New England. A ten-hour-day convention in Boston in 1844 drew delegates from many parts of New England, but even though workers brought pressure to bear on state legislatures and a few half measures were passed, the twelve- or fourteen-hour day in the textile mills still held. By the fifties the trade-union revival had become brisk, although of the eight important national unions only the National Typographical Union, the Hat Finishers' National Association, and the Journeyman Stone Cutters Association were strong enough to survive the Panic of 1857.

The unskilled workers remained unorganized and disregarded. Many, if not most, of the mass workers in industry were foreigners or women and children tending looms; most casual laborers of the big cities were foreigners. Horace Greeley in 1851 published data that showed that the minimum budget for a worker's family of five came to $10.37 a week. Only skilled workers received that much, and not all of them. Factory hands received $5 to $6, women $3 to $4. Most of the female needleworkers earned only 14 to 24 cents a day.

Whittier had called the New England mill girls of the thirties the "fair unveiled Nuns of Industry." By the late 1840's mass immigration had replaced them with shanty Irish, the pallid and beaten refugees of the famine. With an overabundance of docile labor, the iron law of wages took effect. Lowell's neat boardinghouses disintegrated. Whole families inhabited a single room. Festering slums, warrens of crime—such as Europe had known, but had not been known in the United States— grew up in American cities. Each city had its own depraved area, with its terrorist gangs, of which New York's Five Points was the prototype. Hordes of unemployed existed even in times of prosperity. Oscar Handlin in his study of Boston's Irish immigrants describes the slum dwellings of the period:

"Built entirely beneath the street level, they enjoyed no light or air save that which dribbled in through the door leading down, by rickety steps, from the sidewalk above. Innocent of the most rudimentary plumbing, some normally held two or three feet of water, and all were subject to periodic floods and frequent inundations by the backwater of drains at high tide. Above all, there was little space. Some windowless vaults no more than eighteen feet square and five feet high held fourteen humans."

In that prewelfare period the ordinary well-to-do city dweller felt little personal responsibility for the misery he might see about him—and indeed he did not need to see it. For in the fifties a city like New York, America's first metropolis, seemed to ooze prosperity. To an American who had reached three score and ten by mid-century, the world of his boyhood had changed beyond recognition, almost beyond comprehension, and with each decade the rate of change accelerated. A man born into the age of reason would reach his allotted Biblical three score years and ten with the oncoming of the industrial age. Rarely had one lifetime encompassed such tremendous—indeed, revolutionary—changes.

The men of the seventeenth century had thought that the human body could not withstand a velocity of fifteen miles an hour. During the 1850's the prosperous New Yorker could travel north, west, or south at thirty miles an hour while eating his lunch. Standing on Broadway as the horse-drawn omnibuses passed, he could see before him the St. Nicholas Hotel, with its six hundred rooms, one of the largest hotels in the world. He could buy his penny paper for the latest Wall Street reports, and if it was evening, he could read it by the city's gaslight. Probably he had gaslight in his own home, and certainly running water and—since he could afford it—a bath and an inside toilet. The great stores and banks lining Broadway, with its opulence, he had come to take for granted, although policemen in uniform were still a novelty. An even more pleasing novelty was the occasional young lady who tripped by with a daring flash of ankle in the new bloomer costume, which here and there was replacing the "streetsweeper" dress. The New Yorker himself wore a far soberer costume than had his grandfather and his father—a machine-made stovepipe hat, a dark suit stitched by machine, factory-stitched boots. Soberly optimistic he appeared, looking down a vista of American prosperity, which seemed to stretch into a rosy infinity—as such vistas always do—and which would come to an abrupt end in the Panic of 1857.

320

RAFFLE

Mr. Joseph Jennings respectfully informs his friends and the public that, at the request of many acquaintances, he has been induced to purchase from Mr. Osborne, of Missouri, the celebrated

DARK BAY HORSE, "STAR,"

Aged five years, square trotter and warranted sound; with a new light Trotting Buggy and Harness; also, the dark, stout

MULATTO GIRL, "SARAH,"

Aged about twenty years, general house servant, valued at *nine hundred dollars*, and guaranteed, and

Will be Raffled for

At 4 o'clock P. M., February first, at the selection hotel of the subscribers. The above is as represented, and those persons who may wish to engage in the usual practice of raffling, will, I assure them, be perfectly satisfied with their destiny in this affair.

The whole is valued at its just worth, fifteen hundred dollars; fifteen hundred

CHANCES AT ONE DOLLAR EACH.

The Raffle will be conducted by gentlemen selected by the interested subscribers present. Five nights will be allowed to complete the Raffle. BOTH OF THE ABOVE DESCRIBED CAN BE SEEN AT MY STORE, No. 78 Common St., second door from Camp, at from 9 o'clock A. M. to 2 P. M.

Highest throw to take the first choice; the lowest throw the remaining prize, and the fortunate winners will pay twenty dollars each for the refreshments furnished on the occasion.

N. B. No chances recognized unless paid for previous to the commencement.

JOSEPH JENNINGS.

The Peculiar Institution

The South defended slavery long, vehemently, and elaborately, yet, for all its bravado, it tended to be a little embarrassed. Slavery was often referred to by circumlocutions, one of the favorites being the South's "peculiar institution." However, no number of euphemisms could hide the truth from a visitor to the South. He did not even have to see slaves at work; the first newspaper he picked up reminded him that black human beings were beasts of burden: there were advertisements for slave sales, for the services of bloodhounds for catching runaway slaves, for goods for the slave trade. The following are from an early South Carolina newspaper.

January 14, 1804.

Public Auction. On Tuesday, the 17th instant, will be sold before my store, 7 prime African Negroes, just landed, *viz*. Five Boys, about 14 years of age, two Girls, from 15 to 16 years of Age. Conditions Cash. JAMES SCOT.

February 8, 1804.

Public Auction. On Tuesday, the 14th inst. will be sold by the Subscribers, before their Vendue Store, precisely at 11 o'clock, 70 grown African Negroes. Terms will be declared at the time of Sale. VERREE and BLAIR.

July 12, 1804.

This Day, the 12th inst. will be sold before the subscribers Vendue Store, suitable for the African trade: 20 Collars, 6 Deck Chains, 143 Pair Shackles, 6—without bolts. HENRY SMERDON.

April 8, 1807.

A Jury of Inquest was held on Monday last, on the body of a Negro Man, found floating by Benjamin Johnson's new wharf; supposed to be an African, and thrown overboard from some slave ship in the harbour, to save the expense of burial. The jury brought in a verdict, that he came to his death by the visitation of God.

A Jury of Inquest was held yesterday, on the body of an African Negro, found floating in Pritchard's dock. It appeared to be one thrown overboard from one of the slave ships from Africa, now in the harbour. A practice too prevalent among the captains, and disgraceful to humanity. The jury brought in a verdict, that he came to his death by the visitation of God.

April 21, 1807.

A Jury of Inquest was held on Sunday afternoon, on the body of an African negro woman, found floating near the Market dock—it appeared to the jurors, from its having on the usual dress, of a blue flannel frock, to have belonged to one of the slave ships in the harbour, and thrown into the river, to save the expense of burial; a custom too prevalent in this port with the officers of slave ships, and in itself shocking to humanity. The jury brought in a verdict, that she came to her death by the visitation of God. And the coroner begs leave to remind the seamen and petty officers of those ships, that the City Council have passed an Ordinance, prohibiting so inhuman and brutal a custom, and have offered a reward of One Hundred Dollars, to any person or persons, who will give information, so that the offender or offenders, may be prosecuted to conviction, and their names exposed to the good citizens of this state. The Coroner has received information that there are at this time, the bodies of three or more of these poor wretches floating about Hog-Island, and the marshes opposite the city—the effluvia arising from which, must be very prejudicial to the health of passengers in boats, passing and repassing them daily.

Charleston (S.C.) *Courier*

Scores of descriptions of life in the South were written, and except for those produced by Southerners, they seldom had much good to say about the slave system. Isaac Weld, Jr., an English visitor to America in 1795–97, was about as favorable as any observer had been—but he was seeing Virginia before the cotton gin and other developments had made a slave's lot much harsher.

The principal planters in Virginia have nearly every thing they can want on their own estates. Amongst their slaves are found tailors, shoemakers, carpenters, smiths, turners, wheelwrights, weavers, tanners, &c. I have seen patterns of excellent coarse woollen cloth made in the country by slaves, and a variety of cotton manufactures, amongst the rest good nankeen. Cotton grows here extremely well; the plants are often killed by frost in winter, but they always produce abundantly the first year in which they are sown. The cotton from which nankeen is made is of a particular kind, naturally of a yellowish colour.

The large estates are managed by stewards and overseers, the proprietors just amusing themselves with seeing what is going forward. The work is done wholly by slaves, whose numbers are in this part of the country more than double that of white persons. The slaves on the large plantations are in general very well provided for, and treated with mildness. During three months nearly, that I was in Virginia, but two or three instances of ill treatment towards them came under my observation. Their quarters, the name whereby their habitations are called, are usually situated one or two hundred yards from the dwelling house, which gives the appearance of a village to the residence of every planter in Virginia; when the estate, however, is so large as to be divided into several farms, then separate quarters are attached to the house of the overseer on each farm. Adjoining their little habitations, the slaves commonly have small gardens and yards for poultry, which are all their own property; they have ample time to attend to their own concerns, and their gardens are generally found well stocked, and their flocks of poultry numerous. Besides the food they raise for themselves, they are allowed liberal rations of salted pork and Indian corn. Many of their little huts are comfortably furnished, and they are themselves, in general, extremely well clothed. In short, their condition is by no means so wretched as might be imagined. They are forced to work certain hours in the day; but in return they are clothed, dieted, and lodged comfortably, and saved all anxiety about provision for their offspring. Still, however, let the condition of a slave be made ever so comfortable, as long as he is conscious of being the property of another man, who has it in his power to dispose of him according to the dictates of caprice; as long as he hears people around him talking of the blessings of liberty, and con-

African captives on the deck of an 1860 American slave ship

siders that he is in a state of bondage, it is not to be supposed that he can feel equally happy with the freeman. It is immaterial under what form slavery presents itself, whenever it appears there is ample cause for humanity to weep at the sight, and to lament that men can be found so forgetful of their own situations, as to live regardless of the feelings of their fellow creatures.

Isaac Weld, Jr.
Travels Through the States of North America, 1799

James Henry Hammond of South Carolina was a leading spokesman for slavery, and presented quite skillfully the picture the South wanted the world to accept: the Negro slave was a carefree and irresponsible creature, required to do only a moderate amount of work, certain of security in old age, his needs taken care of by a kindly master. Hammond was a governor of his state, a United States senator, and a supporter of secession. In 1845 he wrote a defense of slavery, of which the following are selected passages.

You seem well aware, however, that laws have been recently passed in all these States, making it penal to teach slaves to read. Do you know what occasioned their passage, and renders their stringent enforcement necessary? I can tell you. It was the abolition agitation. If the slave is not allowed to read his bible, the sin rests upon the abolitionists; for they stand prepared to furnish him with a key to it, which would make it, not a book of hope, and love, and peace, but of despair, hatred and blood; which would convert the reader, not into a christian, but a demon. To preserve him from such a horrid destiny, it is a sacred duty which we owe to our slaves, not less than to ourselves, to interpose the most decisive means. If the Catholics deem it wrong to trust the bible to the hands of ignorance, shall we be excommunicated because we will not give it, and with it the corrupt and fatal commentaries of the abolitionists, to our slaves? Allow our slaves to read your writings, stimulating them to cut our throats! Can you believe us to be such unspeakable fools? . . .

The research and ingenuity of the abolitionists, aided by the invention of runaway slaves—in which faculty, so far as improvizing falsehood goes, the African race is without a rival—have succeeded in shocking the world with a small number of pretended instances of our barbarity. The only wonder is, that considering the extent of our country, the variety of our population, its fluctuating character, and the publicity of all our transactions, the number of cases is so small. It speaks well for us. Yet of these, many are false, all highly colored, some occurring half a century, most of them many years ago; and no doubt a large proportion of them perpetrated by foreigners. With a few rare exceptions, the emigrant Scotch and English are the worst masters among us, and next to them our Northern fellow-citizens. Slaveholders born and bred here are always more humane to slaves, and those who have grown up to a large inheritance of them, the most so —showing clearly that the effect of the system is to foster kindly feelings. . . .

If a man steals a pig in England, he is transported—torn from wife, children, parents, and sent to the antipodes, infamous, and an outcast forever, though probably he took from the superabundance of his neighbor to save the lives of his famishing little ones. If one of our well fed negroes, merely for the sake of fresh meat, steals a pig, he gets perhaps forty stripes. If one of your cottagers breaks into another's house, he is hung for burglary. If a slave does the same here, a few lashes, or it may be, a few hours in the stocks, settles the matter. Are our courts or yours the most humane? If Slavery were not in question, you would doubtless say ours is mistaken lenity. . . .

With regard to the separation of husbands and wives, parents and children, nothing can be more untrue than the inferences drawn from what is so constantly harped on by abolitionists. Some painful instances perhaps may occur. Very few that can be prevented. It is, and it always has been, an object of prime consideration with our slaveholders, to keep families together. Negroes are themselves both perverse and comparatively indifferent about this matter. It is a singular trait, that they almost invariably prefer forming connexions with slaves belonging to other masters, and at some distance. It is, therefore, impossible to prevent separations sometimes, by the removal of one owner, his death, or failure, and dispersion of his property. In all such cases, however, every reasonable effort is made to keep the parties together, if they desire it. And the negroes forming these connexions, knowing the chances of their premature dissolution, rarely complain more than we all do of the inevitable strokes of fate. Sometimes it happens that a negro prefers to give up his family rather than separate from his master. I have known such instances. As to wilfully selling off a husband, or wife, or child, I believe it is rarely, very rarely done, except when some offence has been committed demanding "transportation."

James Henry Hammond
Letter to Thomas Clarkson, Esq., January 28, 1845

Slavery in its worst possible aspects was publicized by the abolitionists; their picture, in its way, was as distorted as that presented by Southerners. The passage below is from a book by Theodore Weld, an extremely effective abolitionist agitator. While he could probably have found an instance of every type of abuse he mentions, slaveowners did not habitually indulge in cruelty for pleasure. A slave was too valuable a piece of property to be damaged for mere sport.

Are slaveholders dunces, or do they take all the rest of the world to be, that they think to bandage our eyes with such thin gauzes? Protesting their kind regard for those whom they hourly plunder of all they have and all they get! What! when they have seized their victims, and annihilated all their *rights*, still claim to be the special guardians of their *happiness*! . . .

We will prove that slaves in the United States are treated with barbarous inhumanity; that they are overworked, underfed, wretchedly clad and lodged, and have insufficient sleep; that they are often made to wear round their necks iron collars armed with prongs, to drag heavy chains and weights at their feet while working in the field, and to wear yokes, and bells, and iron horns; that they are often kept confined in the stocks day and night for weeks together, made to wear gags in their mouths for hours or days, have some of their front teeth torn out or broken off, that they may be easily detected when they run away; that they are

Above, slaves around their cabin on a Southern plantation. Left, slaves in a musical mood —from a proslavery book

frequently flogged with terrible severity, have red pepper rubbed into their lacerated flesh, and hot brine, spirits of turpentine, &c., poured over the gashes to increase the torture; that they are often stripped naked, their backs and limbs cut with knives, bruised and mangled by scores and hundreds of blows with the paddle, and terribly torn by the claws of cats, drawn over them by their tormentors; that they are often hunted with blood hounds and shot down like beasts, or torn in pieces by dogs; that they are often suspended by the arms and whipped and beaten till they faint, and when revived by restoratives, beaten again till they faint, and sometimes till they die; that their ears are often cut off, their eyes knocked out, their bones broken, their flesh branded with red hot irons; that they are maimed, mutilated and burned to death over slow fires. All these things, and more, and worse, we shall *prove*. Reader, we know whereof we affirm, we have weighed it well; *more and worse* WE WILL PROVE. Mark these words, and read on; we will establish all these facts by the testimony of scores and hundreds of eye witnesses, by the testimony of *slaveholders* in all parts of the slave states, by slaveholding members of Congress and of state legislatures, by ambassadors to foreign courts, by judges, by doctors of divinity, and clergymen of all denominations, by merchants, mechanics, lawyers and physicians, by presidents and professors in colleges and *professional* seminaries, by planters, overseers and drivers. We shall show, not merely that such deeds are committed, but that they are frequent; not done in corners, but before the sun; not in one of the slave states, but in all of them; not perpetrated by brutal overseers and drivers merely, but by magistrates, by legislators, by professors of religion, by preachers of the gospel, by governors of states, by "gentlemen of property and standing," and by delicate females moving in the "highest circles of society."

Theodore Dwight Weld
American Slavery As It Is: Testimony of a Thousand Witnesses, 1839

Barbarous treatment of an allegedly free Negro—a detail from an engraving in an antislavery book of 1817

English-born actress Frances "Fanny" Kemble married plantation owner Pierce Butler in 1834 and later went to live with her husband in Georgia. The experience was deeply distressing to her; she was so repelled not only by her close contact with slavery but by the sight of her husband as a slave master that she left after a winter and eventually obtained a divorce. The following is from a book she published in 1863 to help turn British sentiment against the South.

The Infirmary is a large two-story building, terminating the broad orange-planted space between the two rows of houses which form the first settlement; it is built of whitewashed wood, and contains four large-sized rooms. But how shall I describe to you the spectacle which was presented to me on entering the first of these? But half the casements, of which there were six, were glazed, and these were obscured with dirt, almost as much as the other windowless ones were darkened by the dingy shutters, which the shivering inmates had fastened to in order to protect themselves from the cold. In the enormous chimney glimmered the powerless embers of a few sticks of wood, round which, however, as many of the sick women as could approach were cowering, some on wooden settles, most of them on the ground, excluding those who were too ill to rise; and these last poor wretches lay prostrate on the floor, without bed, mattress, or pillow, buried in tattered and filthy blankets, which, huddled round them as they lay strewed about, left hardly space to move upon the floor. . . . Here lay women expecting every hour the terrors and agonies of childbirth, others who had just brought their doomed offspring into the world, others who were groaning over the anguish and bitter disappointment of miscarriages—here lay some burning with fever, others chilled with cold and aching with rheumatism, upon the hard cold ground, the draughts and dampness of the atmosphere increasing their sufferings, and dirt, noise, and stench, and every aggravation of which sickness is capable, combined in their condition—here they lay like brute beasts, absorbed in physical suffering. . . . Now pray take notice that this is the hospital of an estate where the owners are supposed to be humane, the overseer efficient and kind, and the negroes remarkably well cared for and comfortable.

Frances Anne Kemble
Journal of a Residence on a Georgian Plantation in 1838–1839, 1863

The slave in the South was principally a field hand; he supplied the man power for plantation agriculture. But slaves were put to other work besides picking cotton, and as the following two excerpts show, the gap between the field hand and the house slave was an enormous one. Josiah Henson, who wrote of field-hand life, was a slave until 1830, when, at the age of forty-one, he escaped to Canada and thereafter helped other slaves to get away. Frederick Douglass, author of the second item, made his way to freedom in 1838, educated himself, became an abolitionist, and even founded a newspaper.

The principal food of those upon my master's plantation consisted of corn-meal, and salt herrings; to which was added in summer a little buttermilk, and the few vegetables which each might raise for himself and his family, on the little piece of ground which was assigned to him for the purpose, called a truck patch.

In ordinary times we had two regular meals in a day:—breakfast at twelve o'clock, after laboring from daylight, and supper when the work of the remainder of the day was over. In harvest season we had three. Our dress was of tow-cloth; for the children nothing but a shirt; for the older ones a pair of pantaloons or a gown in addition, according to the sex. Besides these, in the winter a round jacket or overcoat, a wool hat once in two or three years, for the males, and a pair of coarse shoes once a year.

We lodged in log huts, and on the bare ground. Wooden floors were an unknown luxury. In a single room were huddled, like cattle, ten or a dozen persons, men, women and children. All ideas of refinement and decency were, of course, out of the question. There were neither bedsteads, nor furniture of any description. Our beds were collections of straw and old rags, thrown down in the corners and boxed in with boards; a single blanket the only covering. Our favorite way of sleeping, however, was on a plank, our heads raised on an old jacket and our feet toasting before the smouldering fire. The wind whistled and the rain and snow blew in through the cracks, and the damp earth soaked in the moisture till the floor was miry as a pig-sty. Such were our houses. In these wretched hovels were we penned at night, and fed by day; here were the children born and the sick—neglected.

Josiah Henson
Truth Stranger than Fiction, 1858

Behind the tall-backed and elaborately wrought chairs stood the servants, fifteen in number, carefully selected, not only with a view to their capacity and adeptness, but with especial regard to their personal appearance, their graceful agility, and pleasing address. Some of these servants, armed with fans, wafted reviving breezes to the over-heated brows of the alabaster ladies, whilst others watched with eager eye and fawn-like step, anticipating and supplying wants before they were sufficiently formed to be announced by word or sign.

These servants constituted a sort of black aristocracy. They resembled the field hands in nothing except their color, and in this they held the advantage of a velvet-like glossiness, rich and beautiful. The hair, too, showed the same advantage. The delicately-formed colored maid rustled in the scarcely-worn silk of her young mistress, while the servant men were equally well attired from the overflowing wardrobe of their young masters, so that in dress, as well as in form and feature, in manner and speech, in tastes and habits, the distance between these favored few and the sorrow and hunger-smitten multitudes of the quarter and the field was immense.

Frederick Douglass
Life and Times of Frederick Douglass, 1892

A decisive event in the history of American slavery was the rebellion in 1831 of a small group of Virginia slaves led by Nat Turner, a man with some slight education and a messianic complex. The short but bloody uprising collapsed at the first sign of armed resistance but left fifty-five dead. Turner was hanged, but more important, the rebellion frightened the South into greatly increasing the severity of the slave codes, and the strong Southern emancipation movement collapsed completely. Below are brief portions from Turner's own account of the rising, which he related to one Thomas R. Gray while in prison.

Sir,—You have asked me to give a history of the motives which induced me to undertake the late insurrection, as you call it—To do so I must go back to the days of my infancy, and even before I was born. I was thirty-one years of age the 2d of October last, and born the property of Benj. Turner, of this county. In my childhood a circumstance occurred which made an indelible impression on my mind, and laid the ground work of that enthusiasm, which has terminated so fatally to many both white and black, and for which I am about to atone at the gallows. . . . Being at play with other children, when three or four years old, I was telling them something, which my mother overhearing, said it had happened before I was born—I stuck to my story, however, and related some things which went in her opinion to confirm it—others being called on were greatly astonished, knowing that these things had happened, and caused them to say in my hearing, I surely would be a prophet, as the Lord had shewn me things that had

House and field slaves: above, two brothers, members of a Virginia family, and their Negro nurse; below, slaves in the cotton fields of Alabama

happened before my birth. And my father and mother strengthened me in this my first impression, saying . . . I was intended for some great purpose, which they had always thought from certain marks on my head and breast. . . .

Since the commencement of 1830, I had been living with Mr. Joseph Travis, who was to me a kind master, and placed the greatest confidence in me; in fact, I had no cause to complain of his treatment to me.

. . . it was quickly agreed we should commence at home (Mr. J. Travis') on that night, and until we had armed and equipped ourselves, and gathered sufficient force, neither age nor sex was to be spared, (which was invariably adhered to.) . . . Hark got a ladder and set it against the chimney, on which I ascended, and hoisting a window, entered and came down stairs, unbarred the door, and removed the guns from their places. It was then observed that I must spill the first blood. On which armed with a hatchet, and accompanied by Will, I entered my master's chamber; it being dark, I could not give a death blow, the hatchet glanced from his head, he sprang from the bed and called his wife, it was his last word. Will laid him dead, with a blow of his axe, and Mrs. Travis shared the same fate, as she lay in bed. The murder of this family five in number, was the work of a moment, not one of them awoke; there was a little infant sleeping in a cradle, that was forgotten, until we had left the house and gone some distance, when Henry and Will returned and killed it; we got here, four guns that would shoot, and several old muskets, with a pound or two of powder.

. . . as we approached, the family discovered us, and shut the door. Vain hope! Will, with one stroke of his axe, opened it, and we entered and found Mrs. Turner and Mrs. Newsome in the middle of a room almost frightened to death. Will immediately killed Mrs. Turner, with one blow of his axe. I took Mrs. Newsome by the hand, and with the sword I had when I was apprehended, I struck her several blows over the head, but not being able to kill her, as the sword was dull. Will turning around and discovering it, dispatched her also. A general destruction of property and search for money and ammunition, always succeeded the murders. By this time my company amounted to fifteen, and nine men mounted. . . . I proceeded to Mr. Levi Waller's, two or three miles distant. I took my station in the rear, and as it was my object to carry terror and devastation wherever we went, I placed fifteen or twenty of the best armed and most to be relied on, in front, who generally approached the houses as fast as their horses could run; this was for two purposes, to prevent their escape and strike terror to the inhabitants—on this account I never got to the houses, after leaving Mrs. Whitehead's until the murders were committed, except in one case. I sometimes got in sight in time to see the work of death completed, viewed the mangled bodies as they lay, in silent satisfaction, and immediately started in quest of other victims—Having murdered Mrs. Waller and ten children, we started for Mr. William Williams'—having killed him and two little boys that were there; while engaged in this, Mrs. Williams fled and got some distance from the house, but she was pursued, overtaken, and compelled to get up behind one of the company, who brought her back, and after showing her the mangled body of her lifeless husband, she was told to get down and lay by his side, where she was shot dead.

. . . the white men pursued and fired on us several times. Hark had his horse shot under him, and I caught another for him as it was running by me; five or six of my men were wounded, but none left on the field; finding myself defeated here I instantly determined to go through a private way, and cross the Nottoway river at the Cypress Bridge, three miles below Jerusalem, and attack that place in the rear, as I expected they would look for me on the other road, and I had a great desire to get there to procure arms and ammunition. After going a short distance in this private way, accompanied by about twenty men, I overtook two or three who told me the others were dispersed in every direction. . . .

On this I gave up all hope for the present; and on Thursday night, after having supplied myself with provisions from Mr. Travis's, I scratched a hole under a pile of fence rails in a field, where I concealed myself for six weeks, never leaving my hiding place but for a few minutes in the dead of night to get water, which was very near; thinking by this time I could venture out, I began to go about in the night and eaves drop the houses in the neighborhood; pursuing this course for about a fortnight and gathering little or no intelligence, afraid of speaking to any human being, and returning every morning to my cave before the dawn of day. I know not how long I might have led this life, if accident had not betrayed me. . . . During the time I was pursued, I had many hair breadth escapes, which your time will not permit you to relate. I am here loaded with chains, and willing to suffer the fate that awaits me.

Nat Turner, as related to Thomas R. Gray
The Confessions of Nat Turner, 1832

The Underground Railroad was one answer of the antislavery forces to the Fugitive Slave Law, which required that all escaped slaves found in the North be returned to the South and to their owners. Along intricate and changing routes, daring and selfless slavery haters spirited bondsmen to the safety of Canada. The Reverend John Rankin, who lived on the Ohio (and free) side of the Ohio River and helped many slaves to escape, was the prototype of the man who aided the fleeing Eliza and her child in Uncle Tom's Cabin.

I kept a depot on what was called the underground railway. It was so called because they who took passage on it disappeared from public view as really as if they had gone into the ground. After the fugitive slaves entered a depot on that road, no trace of them could be found. They were secretly passed from one depot to another until they arrived in Canada. This road extended its branches through all the free states. These were formed without any general concert. There was no secret society organized. There were no secret oaths taken, nor promises of secrecy extorted. And yet there were no betrayals. Anti-slavery persons were actuated by a sense of humanity and right, and, of course, were true to one another. It may seem incredible that lines over so extensive a region as that of the free states could have been formed without some general council having been held, but it is true that there was no such council. These lines were formed in the following manner. There were anti-slavery men living at various points on the border of the free states. With them fugitives would stop, and this made it necessary for safety to find some anti-slavery men on the way to whom these fugitives could be taken. I will give my own case as an instance. I lived on the top of a high hill at Ripley. My house was in full view of Kentucky. The slaves by some means discovered that I was an abolitionist, and consequently, when any of them ran away, they came to my house, and I knew that there were anti-slavery men on Red Oak, at Decatur, and Sardinia, and hence I could send them to any one of these places, and I had sons to convey them to such places as I chose to send them. And then they could be sent to Hillsborough, and then to Greenfield, and on from point to point until they arrived in Canada. In this way the various branches of the underground railway were formed. . . .

Seven valuable slaves started for Canada, and designed coming to my house but made [a] mistake and came to the house of my neighbor. He . . . had laborers whom he felt it was not safe to let know that he had fugitive slaves at his house. Consequently, he brought them to my house. . . . In the morning the slave-hunters came to town in pursuit. The fugitives saw their horses in the streets, and knew them. My neighbor went to town, and one of the slave-hunters having met him, said to him, "I know it is not popular in Ohio for a gentleman to take up slaves, but if you will tell me where those slaves are, I will give you one thousand dollars, and no one shall ever know it." He could have pointed at my house and said, they are in yonder house, and would have received one thousand dollars, and I would never have known that he did it. But he could not be bribed to do such a deed of wickedness. The fugitives were forwarded by night, to another state, and so to Canada.

Rev. John Rankin
Reprinted in *Make Free*, William Breyfogle, 1958

In 1852 the bible of antislavery burst on the American scene—and "burst" is hardly too strong a word. Uncle Tom's Cabin *was melodramatic and its author knew little of slavery firsthand, but she wrote from her heart, and the North was eager for anything that would bring the slavery controversy alive by putting it in terms of human beings and human suffering. Mrs. Stowe's book did exactly that. In the following selection, unalloyed good confronts utter evil as Uncle Tom defies Simon Legree.*

Slowly the weary, dispirited creatures, wound their way into the room, and, with crouching reluctance, presented their baskets to be weighed.

Legree noted on a slate, on the side of which was pasted a list of names, the amount.

Tom's basket was weighed and approved; and he looked, with an anxious glance, for the success of the woman he had befriended.

Tottering with weakness, she came forward, and delivered her basket. It was of full weight, as Legree well perceived; but, affecting anger, he said,

"What, you lazy beast! short again! stand aside, you'll catch it, pretty soon!"

The woman gave a groan of utter despair, and sat down on a board. . . .

"And now," said Legree, "come here, you Tom. You see, I told ye I didn't buy ye jest for the common work; I mean to promote ye, and make a driver of ye; and to-night ye may jest as well begin to get yer hand in. Now, ye jest take this yer gal and flog her; ye've seen enough on't to know how."

Drawing for a newspaper announcement calling attention to the Underground Railway

"I beg Mas'r's pardon," said Tom; "hopes Mas'r won't set me at that. It's what I an't used to,—never did,—and can't do, no way possible."

"Ye'll larn a pretty smart chance of things ye never did know, before I've done with ye!" said Legree, taking up a cow-hide, and striking Tom a heavy blow across the cheek, and following up the infliction by a shower of blows.

"There!" he said, as he stopped to rest; "now, will ye tell me ye can't do it?"

"Yes, Mas'r," said Tom, putting up his hand, to wipe the blood, that trickled down his face. "I'm willin' to work, night and day, and work while there's life and breath in me; but this yer thing I can't feel it right to do;—and, Mas'r, I *never* shall do it,—*never*!"

Tom had a remarkably smooth, soft voice, and a habitually respectful manner, that had given Legree an idea that he would be cowardly, and easily subdued. When he spoke these last words, a thrill of amazement went through every one; the poor woman clasped her hands, and said, "O Lord!" and every one involuntarily looked at each other and drew in their breath, as if to prepare for the storm that was about to burst.

Legree looked stupefied and confounded; but at last burst forth,—

"What! ye blasted black beast! tell *me* ye don't think it *right* to do what I tell ye! What have any of you cussed cattle to do with thinking what's right? I'll put a stop to it! Why, what do ye think ye are? May be ye think ye'r a gentleman, master Tom, to be telling your master what's right, and what an't! So you pretend it's wrong to flog the gal!"

"I think so, Mas'r," said Tom; "the poor crittur's sick and feeble; 'twould be downright cruel, and it's what I never will do, nor begin to. Mas'r, if you mean to kill me, kill me; but, as to my raising my hand agin any one here, I never shall,—I'll die first!"

Tom spoke in a mild voice, but with a decision that could not be mistaken. Legree shook with anger; his greenish eyes glared fiercely, and his very whiskers seemed to curl with passion; but, like some ferocious beast, that plays with its victim before he devours it, he kept back his strong impulse to proceed to immediate violence, and broke out into bitter raillery.

"Well, here's a pious dog, at last, let down among us sinners!—a saint, a gentleman, and no less, to talk to us sinners about our sins! Powerful holy crittur, he must be! Here, you rascal, you make believe to be so pious,—didn't you never hear, out of yer Bible, 'Servants, obey yer masters'? An't I yer master? Didn't I pay down twelve hundred dollars, cash, for all there is inside yer old cussed black shell? An't yer mine, now, body and soul?" he said, giving Tom a violent kick with his heavy boot; "tell me!"

In the very depth of physical suffering, bowed by brutal oppression, this question shot a gleam of joy and triumph through Tom's soul. He suddenly stretched himself up, and, looking earnestly to heaven, while the tears and blood that flowed down his face mingled, he exclaimed,

"No! no! no! my soul an't yours, Mas'r! You haven't bought it,—ye can't buy it! It's been bought and paid for, by one that is able to keep it;—no matter, no matter, you can't harm me!"

"I can't!" said Legree, with a sneer; "we'll see,—we'll see! Here, Sambo, Quimbo, give this dog such a breakin' in as he won't get over, this month!"

The two gigantic negroes that now laid hold of Tom, with fiendish exultation in their faces, might have formed no unapt personification of powers of darkness. The poor woman screamed with apprehension, and all rose, as by a general impulse, while they dragged him unresisting from the place.

Harriet Beecher Stowe
Uncle Tom's Cabin, 1852

On March 6, 1857, the Supreme Court ruled that a Negro named Dred Scott did not have the right to sue in a federal court because he was not a citizen and, moreover, that no Negro slave nor his descendants could be citizens. In a related opinion the Court ruled the Missouri Compromise illegal and denied to Congress the right to exclude slavery from any territory. The angry outcry in the North greatly hastened the split between North and South. Below is the petition that Dred Scott had filed, unnoticed, ten years earlier and that, after its long journey through the courts, led to the famous decision.

Left, the cover of a children's version of Uncle Tom's Cabin, *1853. Above, Uncle Tom as he frequently appeared on programs for theaters*

Dred Scott
vs.
Alex. Sandford,
Saml. Russell, and
Irene Emerson
} To the Honorable, the Circuit Court within and for the County of St. Louis.

Your petitioner, Dred Scott, a man of color, respectfully represents that sometime in the year 1835 your petitioner was purchased as a slave by one John Emerson, since deceased, who afterwards, to-wit; about the year 1836 or 1837, conveyed your petitioner from the State of Missouri to Fort Snelling, a fort then occupied by the troops of the United States and under the jurisdiction of the United States, situated in the territory ceded by France to the United States under the name of Louisiana, lying north of 36 degrees and 30′ North latitude, now included in the State of Missouri, and resided and continued to reside at Fort Snelling upwards of one year, and held your petitioner in slavery at such Fort during all that time in violation of the Act of Congress of 1806 and 1820, entitled An Act to Authorize the People of Missouri Territory to form a Constitution and State Government, and for the admission of such State into the Union on an equal footing with the original states, and to Prohibit Slavery in Certain Territories.

Your petitioner avers that said Emerson has since departed this life, leaving his widow Irene Emerson and an infant child whose name is unknown to your petitioner; and that one Alexander Sandford administered upon the estate of said Emerson and that your petitioner is now unlawfully held in slavery by said Sandford and by said administrator and said Irene Emerson claims your petitioner as part of the estate of said Emerson and by one Samuel Russell.

Your petitioner therefore prays your Honorable Court to grant him leave to sue as a poor person, in order to establish his right to freedom, and that the necessary orders may be made in the premises.

Dred Scott.
Petition filed on July 1, 1847

The issue of freeing the slaves carried along with it the problem of granting them equality, which posed a dilemma for politicians attempting to remain true to their conscience without at the same time frightening away voters who were not prepared for equality with blacks. Lincoln had to face up to this challenge. After stating that he adhered to the Declaration of Independence, which says that all men are created equal, he was accused by Stephen Douglas of wanting to make Negroes equal. Lincoln, speaking in Springfield, Illinois, on July 17, 1858, then enlarged upon his statement.

My declarations upon this subject of negro slavery may be misrepresented, but cannot be misunderstood. I have said that I do not understand the Declaration to mean that all men were created equal in all respects. They are not our equal in colour; but I suppose that it does mean to declare that all men are equal in some respects; they are equal in their right to "life, liberty, and the pursuit of happiness." Certainly the negro is not our equal in colour—perhaps not in many other respects; still, in the right to put into his mouth the bread that his own hands have earned, he is the equal of every other man, white or black. In pointing out that more has been given you, you cannot be justified in taking away the little which has been given him. All I ask for the negro is that if you do not like him, let him alone. If God gave him but little, that little let him enjoy.

When our government was established, we had the institution of slavery among us. We were in a certain sense compelled to tolerate its existence. It was a sort of necessity. We had gone through our struggle, and secured our own independence. The framers of the Constitution found the institution of slavery amongst their other institutions at the time. They found that by an effort to eradicate it, they might lose much of what they had already gained. They were obliged to bow to the necessity. They gave power to Congress to abolish the slave-trade at the end of twenty years. They also prohibited slavery in the Territories where it did not exist. They did what they could and yielded to necessity for the rest. I also yield to all which follows from that necessity. What I would most desire would be the separation of the white and black races.

Abraham Lincoln
Speech at Springfield, Illinois, July 17, 1858

As 1860 neared, the nation was so delicately balanced on the edge of chaos that almost every movement pushed it closer to the brink, and panic was created by the act of a madman who thought that with a corporal's guard he could set free the slaves of the South. The first account, a distorted one, of John Brown's 1859 raid, relayed to the outside world through Baltimore, was the nation's initial word of an event that would shake the Union to its roots.

INSURRECTION AT HARPER'S FERRY!

To the Associated Press:

Baltimore, *Monday, Oct. 17, 1859.*

A dispatch just received here from Frederick, and dated this morning, states that an insurrection has broken out at Harper's Ferry, where an armed band of

His coffin waiting, John Brown ascends the scaffold in Charlestown, Virginia.

334

Abolitionists have full possession of the Government Arsenal. The express train going east was twice fired into, and one of the railroad hands and a negro killed, while they were endeavoring to get the train through the town. The insurrectionists stopped and arrested two men, who had come to town with a load of wheat, and, seizing their wagon, loaded it with rifles, and sent them into Maryland. The insurrectionists number about 250 whites, and are aided by a gang of negroes. At last accounts, fighting was going on.

The above is given just as it was received here. It seems very improbable, and should be received with great caution, until affirmed by further advices. A later dispatch, received at the railroad office, says the affair has been greatly exaggerated. The reports had their foundation in a difficulty at the Armory, with which negroes had nothing to do.

Baltimore, *Monday, Oct.* 17—2 P.M.

Another account, received by train, says the bridge across the Potomac was filled with insurgents, all armed. Every light in the town was extinguished, and the hotels closed. All the streets were in the possession of the mob, and every road and lane leading thereto barricaded and guarded. Men were seen in every quarter with muskets and bayonets, who arrested the citizens, and impressed them into the service, including many negroes. This done, the United States Arsenal and Government Pay-house, in which was said to be a large amount of money, and all other public works, were seized by the mob. Some were of the opinion that the object was entirely plunder, and to rob the Government of the funds deposited on Saturday at the Pay-house. During the night, the mob made a demand on the Wager Hotel for provisions, and enforced the claim by a body of armed men. The citizens were in a terrible state of alarm, and the insurgents have threatened to burn the town.

The following has just been received from Monocacy, this side of Harper's Ferry:

"The Mail Agent on the western-bound train has returned, and reports that the train was unable to get through. The town is in possession of the negroes, who arrest every one they can catch and imprison. The train due here at 3 P.M., could not get through, and the Agent came down on an empty engine."

Reprinted in Horace Greeley
The American Conflict, 1864

*O*n the morning of his execution John Brown handed a message to one of his prison guards. It contained a prediction that would begin to be fulfilled only two years later.

Charlestown, Va, 2d, December, 1859.
I John Brown am now quite *certain* that the crimes of this *guilty, land: will* never be purged *away*; but with Blood. I had *as I now think: vainly* flattered myself that without *verry much* bloodshed; it might be done.

John Brown
Handwritten note

The Gathering Storm

Speaking in Charleston in August, 1848, Calhoun, after enumerating the so often enumerated grievances of the South, had called for the formation of a "great Southern republican party" to demand a recognition of Southern rights. This would be followed, if necessary, by Southern withdrawal. The next January, in response to a proposal to restrict slavery in the District of Columbia, he had issued his "Address of the Southern Delegates in Congress," a warning—and a dismayingly accurate prophecy—of the results of emancipation. Then, after Mississippi Whigs and Democrats had met to enunciate their point of view that Congress lacked the power to prohibit or restrict slavery in the territories, Calhoun persuaded them to summon a convention in Nashville of all the slave states to debate and even decide the issue of secession.

Acceptance of the Compromise of 1850, almost as general in the South as in the North, took the wind out of secessionist sails. Though the Nashville Convention was still held—over Calhoun's dead body, for he had died several months before—the rallying eloquence of Clay and Webster made the gathering seem more a redundancy than a threat. Only nine states bothered to send delegates, and of the delegates a number appeared with "very dubious credentials." In spite of the extremists—the nullifiers of the 1830's and the fiery young followers of Calhoun—in spite of an inflammatory manifesto by South Carolina's Robert Barnwell Rhett, the delegates put secessionist sentiments on the shelf and contented themselves with resolving that as a "concession" the South would be willing to see the new territories divided by an extension of the Missouri Compromise line to the Pacific.

By Southerners the 1850 Compromise was viewed as a bargain struck. They had yielded on the autonomy Calhoun had demanded, they had yielded on California, New Mexico, and Utah, and they had yielded on slave trading in the District of Columbia. In return they had been compensated with the Fugitive Slave Act of 1850, and they demanded its strict enforcement as part of the bargain. In accordance with that act, a Negro fugitive in the North—even if he had lived there fifteen or twenty years—could be seized on the presentation of the affidavit of a Southern slaveholder.

Eyre Crowe of England, who accompanied William Makepeace Thackeray to America as his secretary in 1852, made the original sketch for this engraving of a Charleston, South Carolina, slave auction, which appeared, with Crowe's text, in an English periodical in 1856. Like most Europeans, Crowe heartily disapproved of the institution of slavery.

The fugitive could not testify or summon witnesses or have a jury trial. His fate would be decided by a federal commissioner from whom there was no appeal. Enforcement lay in the hands of federal marshals. They and their deputies were subject to a one-thousand-dollar fine if they refused to apprehend a fugitive on service of the commissioner's writ. Anyone who concealed or rescued a fugitive was subject to a similar fine plus civil damages plus a possible jail sentence of six months.

Intellectual opinion in both North and West grew increasingly outraged by the act. Emerson lectured publicly against it. Privately he noted in his journal that it was a "filthy enactment." "I will not obey it, by God," he added. One result of the act was the expansion of the Underground Railroad, which had been formed in Ohio at least as early as 1817 to smuggle escaping slaves across the border to Canada. By 1850 a network of lines with their way stations ran north, and the fugitives—never as many as the abolitionists made out—were hustled across the border with efficient dispatch. Many ex-slaves served as "conductors" on the road north, the most celebrated being Harriet Tubman, who had escaped from Maryland in 1849 after almost thirty years of bondage and who, from 1850 on, returned secretly to the South nineteen times to aid in the escape of others.

Most runaways, like Harriet Tubman, were from the border states and were often considered good riddance by their masters. Their numbers were not large, and a reasonable attitude for Southerners would have been to forget about legal rights and to write off the fugitives. But the South, accepting the challenge, became as emotionally committed to the Fugitive Slave Law as the North was opposed to it. Whenever a fugitive was seized by the federal marshals, uproar and demonstrations followed. In February, 1851, a colored waiter, an ex-slave named Shadrach, was arrested in Boston and lodged in the courthouse. Before he could be returned to the South, two Negroes made their way into the courthouse and spirited him away beyond the reach of any law officer. When several months later a Negro boy, Thomas Sims, was apprehended in Boston, the marshals were careful to have the courthouse guarded and fenced off with chains. Under the custody of United States Marshal Charles Devens, Sims was led down State Street to Long Wharf and shipped to Savannah, where on arrival he was publicly whipped. The law had taken its due course, but the experience was so unnerving to Devens that he later paid eighteen hundred dollars to buy Sims's freedom.

In the same month that Shadrach's rescuers had snatched him to safety, the small dowdy wife of an obscure Bowdoin professor was sitting in her house in Brunswick, Maine, beginning the novel destined to be the most momentous American book of the century. The thirty-nine-year-old mother of six writing away on a Sunday afternoon was Harriet Beecher Stowe, and the chapter that she was creating was "The Death of Uncle Tom," for her as yet only vaguely conceived *Uncle Tom's Cabin, or Life Among the Lowly.*

Mrs. Stowe was starting her book at the end, with the climactic death of Uncle Tom. The whole scene had come to her that day, she later claimed, with the vividness of actuality as she sat in the wooden college-church during a communion service. Moved to tears, she went home and wrote out her vision, using scraps of brown grocer's wrapping paper when she ran out of sta-

tionery. "God wrote it," she was to say later, though what had immediately impelled her was the Fugitive Slave Act. Building toward that tearful scene of Uncle Tom's death, she began a serial for a Washington abolitionist newspaper, the *National Era*. Originally scheduled to run for three issues, *Uncle Tom's Cabin* appeared in forty under Mrs. Stowe's creative urge. In March, 1852, the Boston firm Jewett published it as a book—even though the young publisher felt hesitant about a two-volume book by a woman on such a controversial subject. It was, however, an immediate success, selling ten thousand copies in a few days. Within weeks, eight power presses were running night and day to keep up with the demand, and within a year more than three hundred thousand copies had been sold.

More than a book, it was a phenomenon, not to be measured by literary standards. *Uncle Tom's Cabin* was like a burning glass, focusing and bringing to white heat the whole emotional issue of slavery. The abstrac-

tions became embodied in Mrs. Stowe's pages—Uncle Tom, Simon Legree, Eliza crossing the ice. What matter that her blacks were of the burned-cork variety. What matter that her actual experience of slavery was limited to one visit to a Kentucky plantation plus the talk she had heard while living in Cincinnati on the free side of the Ohio River. What matter the tear-streaked sentimentality, the crudities of style, the lurid melodrama. Her woman's passion carried conviction and gave the book a folk reality that went beyond literature. Topsy, Eva, Uncle Tom, came to seem more real than their creator. *Uncle Tom's Cabin* polarized the emotions of the North and the South in the few years before the Civil War, and the middle way faded. No Northern mob would ever again lead a trussed Garrison through the streets. No Southern moderate would come out for gradual emancipation.

Mrs. Stowe's book would be translated into half the languages in the world. Only *Pilgrim's Progress* or *Rob-*

Harriet Beecher Stowe, left, fashioned the character Uncle Tom partly after Josiah Henson, an escaped slave whose autobiography she had read. Above, Eliza, fleeing slavery, crosses the Ohio River to freedom with her child. The lithograph, from about 1852, was probably based on an early stage version of the novel.

339

*Charles Nahl's painting of California gold seekers pass-
ing a wrecked boat in the Chagres River in Panama
helps explain why both Britain and America wanted a
canal for readier passage across the Isthmus. The
Clayton-Bulwer Treaty eased the rivalry, and in time the
Panama Canal would follow this same Chagres River.*

inson Crusoe* could compare with it in pervasive popularity. In England it became the first best seller—
more than a million and a half copies. In czarist
Russia it was the most popular foreign book translated to that time. And so on, in all European countries. For all its literary flaws, *Uncle Tom's Cabin*
became one of the three or four books besides the
Bible that have helped determine the destinies of
mankind. Charles Sumner thought that Lincoln would
never have reached the White House without its im-
petus. Lincoln himself, when he met Mrs. Stowe for
the first time during the Civil War, held out his huge

knobby hand, exclaiming: "So you're the little woman
who made the book that made this great war!"

The Mexican War, with its resulting prosperity, had
left the country in a bombastically expansive mood, a
mood enhanced by the European uprisings of 1848 and
1849. From the far side of the Atlantic the revolutionary
impulse of 1848 seemed a surge of the democratic spirit
that had nurtured the American Union. With the Hungarian revolt against the Hapsburg monarchy, Webster
thought to see the American model on the lower Dan-
ube. When that revolt was crushed by Austria with Russian assistance, its leader, Lajos Kossuth, came to the

340

United States seeking support from the New World republic. Americans gave a tremendous reception to the picturesquely bearded Hungarian freedom fighter. President Fillmore received him at the White House. For a time he was the vogue. Only gradually would he discover that this transient sympathy was not going to be translated into the practical assistance that would enable him to resume his liberating war.

With the discovery of gold in California swarms of immigrants had disembarked in Panama and Nicaragua on the quick route to the Pacific coast. To any such impatient traveler the idea of ship passage across the Isthmus was both obvious and appealing, and Americans soon began to drum up sentiment for an exclusively American Isthmian canal—a project that seemed far easier in prospect than it turned out to be in fact half a century later. Meanwhile the British, controlling the Mosquito Coast—eastern Honduras and Nicaragua—from their colony British Honduras, were considering their own plans for an Isthmian canal. Each country feared possible Central American annexations by the other; neither was willing to tolerate the other's having the exclusive control of a canal.

To ease the developing tension the English, late in 1849, sent a negotiator to the United States, Sir Henry Lytton Bulwer. Just a few months before President Taylor died, Bulwer and the American Secretary of State, the bibulous but realistic John M. Clayton, agreed on a treaty. By the terms of the treaty either nation was free to construct a canal, but neither was to fortify it or exercise exclusive control over it. They also agreed that neither nation would "occupy, or fortify, or colonize" any part of Central America.

Given the weakness of the United States as a maritime power, the Clayton-Bulwer Treaty was an advantageous one, which could have ended British-American rivalry in Central America. But expansionists did not see it that way, and the treaty became one of the most resented documents in American diplomatic history. Americans assumed that the British would not fortify the Mosquito Coast; the British interpreted the treaty as applying only to regions not already under their control. By 1852 the controversy grew sharp.

Americans had for some time been casting a covetous eye on Cuba. Polk had even offered Spain one hundred million dollars for the island. Taylor showed himself less eager to incorporate a territory with a million and a half slaves. But Southerners, disillusioned by the negligible advantages they had drawn from the Mexican War, were all in favor of this overseas expansion. Narciso López, a Venezuelan adventurer living in New Orleans, had several times made preparations for an expedition against Cuba, with the support of many Southerners and in spite of President Fillmore's objections. Fillmore did not want Cuba, even though he refused to tie his hands by pledging that the United States would never acquire it under any circumstances.

López, with five hundred adventurers, landed on Cuba in August, 1851, convinced that a restive population was only waiting to rise against Spanish misrule. Instead he found dull apathy. His small force was overwhelmed by Spanish regulars and he was forced to surrender. López was garroted. Fifty-one of his recruits—a number of them American—were slain, and many others were sentenced to penal servitude. The news brought indignant reactions throughout the South, and in New Orleans a raging mob sacked the Spanish consulate. For a time the "gallant fifty-one" were hailed as heroes, but in the end the United States government felt obliged to proffer apologies to Spain and to make restitution for the New Orleans damage, and the Cuban crisis quickly subsided.

Gambling on the country's expansionist mood, William Walker—physician, lawyer, journalist, and adventurer avid for fame—organized a small filibustering expedition to Lower California in October, 1853, and briefly proclaimed a republic there until he ran out of food and followers. Hardly noticed among these brash, publicized ephemeral events was Fillmore's dispatch of Commodore Matthew Perry in 1852 to secure a treaty with the hermit kingdom of Japan. The Japanese, roused at cannon's mouth from their isolation by Perry's arrival, were so impressed by the little American fleet that the Shogun—the nation's military and civil ruler—agreed to a treaty for the opening of trade between the two countries. At the time Perry's voyage seemed a minor matter, but this forced awakening of Japan would prove of vast import not only to America but to world history.

As the 1852 presidential election approached, it was obvious that the half century marked an end of an era. The old leaders, the young War Hawks of 1812, had vanished. Calhoun, the Voice of the South, had died in March, 1850, a few weeks after Webster's Seventh of March Speech. Webster and Clay were among his pallbearers. Clay died in June, 1852, eulogized by Illinois

Congressman Abraham Lincoln, who took the occasion to assail both Northern abolitionists and Southern firebrands. Webster's rolling voice would be stilled four months later. Thomas "Old Bullion" Benton, because of his opposition to slavery and to the Compromise, was refused re-election to the Senate in 1850 by indignant and thoroughly proslavery Missourians.

The kaleidoscope of history, relentlessly changing, was creating new patterns out of the old forms, filling the Capital with new faces. There were the younger men, like Stephen Douglas and Salmon Chase and Jefferson Davis. From New York to the Senate had come the state's former governor, an Antimason turned Whig, William H. Seward. Although a cautious politician, Seward had made a name for himself as an antislavery governor by refusing to extradite sailors who had helped in the escape of a slave from Virginia. Favoring the gradual abolition of slavery through compensation, he had denounced the 1850 Compromise and appealed to a "higher law" than the Constitution—a phrase that ticketed him inaccurately as a radical. An outstanding orator, he would come to embody the growing antislavery sentiment of the North. Radicalism would be personified in the disdainful, handsome six-foot-four Massachusetts senator, abolitionist Charles Sumner, leader of the Conscience Whigs. In 1845, at the age of thirty-four, Sumner had first made his name known by an Independence Day oration in Boston, when to the outrage of conservatives he had attacked the Mexican War, asking rhetorically: "Can there be in our age any peace that is not honorable, any war that is not dishonorable?" Intense, pedantic, corrosively eloquent, with a God-given sense of his own righteousness and rightness, he had been elected to the Senate following the political overturn in Massachusetts brought about by the Compromise of 1850. Many of those who knew him well distrusted his egotism. Although loathing slavery, he remained a Constitutionalist. To the ab-

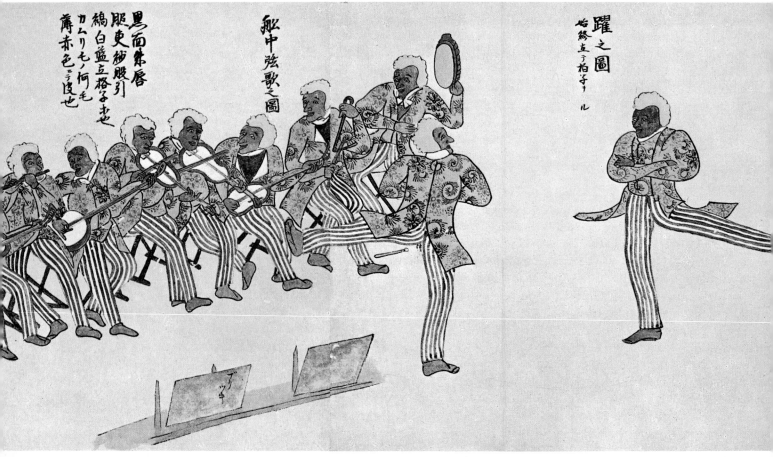

342

The two visits of Commodore Perry to Japan moved many native artists to set down their impressions of the bizarre foreigners and their smoke-belching ships. Above, a rendition of a minstrel show Perry's men staged for Japanese officials. Right, a fanciful portrait of the clean-shaven Perry. Far right is the U.S.S. Powhatan.

olitionists he was a hero, but to State Street the venom-tongued Harvard scholar who had denounced "the lords of the lash and the lords of the loom" seemed much less heroic.

Prosperity and the Compromise of 1850 made the 1852 election more a matter of personalities than issues. Both parties had their deep divisions; both hoped to smooth them over in order to elect a President. The colorless Fillmore, the accidental President, had inspired little love and little loyalty, and most Whigs were prepared to thrust him aside. Among the Democrats, the free-soil Northerners and the states' rights Southerners viewed each other darkly; but party leaders hoped by running a compromise Northerner for President and a moderate Southern-rights man for Vice President to unite the party and recapture the House and the Senate as well as the Presidency.

The four leading Democratic contenders were Cass, Buchanan, Douglas, and Polk's Secretary of War, Wil-liam L. Marcy. Cass, still sluggishly ambitious to avenge his 1848 defeat, held his chief strength in the West. The dignified white-haired Buchanan was averse to action, but a vision of the White House danced in his head as it had since the days when he was briefly considered as a favorite-son candidate in 1844. Marcy of New York was so obsessed by his own White House vision that he was even willing to bury his differences with his old enemies the Barnburners. Opposing these party elders, all veterans of the War of 1812, was the dynamic, challenging Stephen Douglas, the representative of Young America, that section of the party ready to shelve the slavery issue and concentrate on national power and national expansion. "Douglas and Cuba" was to be the campaign slogan. Younger men flocked to the Little Giant, as did the German and Irish immigrant groups, the cotton planters, the astute Northern merchants, and the railroad-bond holders, as well as the lobbyists and privilege seekers who caught the scent

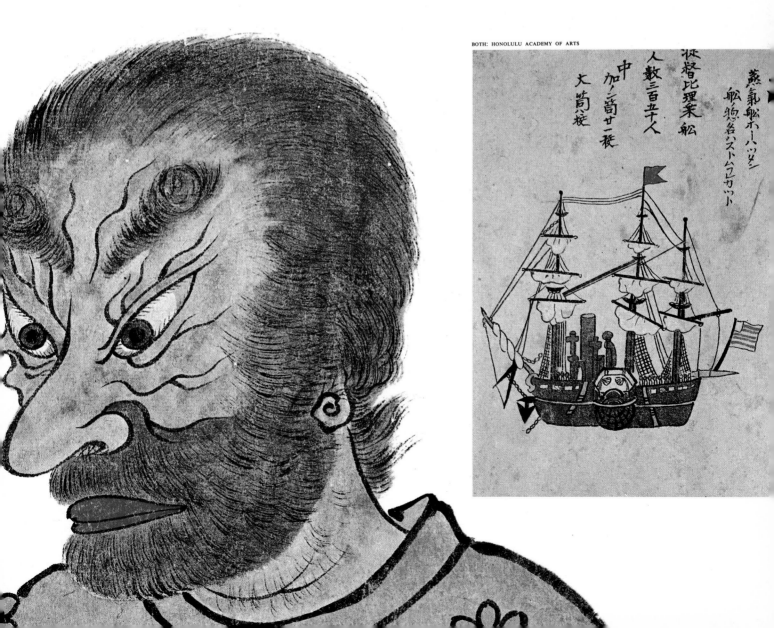

*A city sportsman and his country cousin discuss the 1852
election in this painting by William S. Mount.
The artist may have wished to symbolize improved city-
country relations by the lowered bars on the fence.*

of money in Douglas' expansionist views.

To the acute political observers behind the Democratic scene it seemed apparent that none of the chief rivals would be strong enough to carry the convention. After the leaders had worn themselves out, a compromise candidate, a dark horse, would have to be chosen. New England Democrats thought they had found their man in that inconspicuous Mexican War general Franklin Pierce, a harmonizer, a younger man, handsome enough to please everybody and mild enough to offend no one. Pierce's chief virtue was that he had so few enemies. His role in the Mexican War had been too small, too brief, to antagonize other generals. In the nine years he had spent representing New Hampshire in the House and the Senate he had shown himself a faithful committeeman, an inconspicuous Jacksonian Democrat, a superficial good fellow. Born and bred in New England—he had graduated from Bowdoin College the year before Longfellow and Hawthorne—he nevertheless stood by the Compromise of 1850, and the enforcement of the Fugitive Slave Law, even though he personally disliked it. His person attractive, his manner gracious, his talk easy, he was fatally flawed by indecision, which negated other qualities of leadership.

It was the strategy of Pierce's supporters not to submit his name to the convention at the beginning but to scatter his delegate votes among other leaders. Cass led on the first ballot with Buchanan second and Douglas third, the Little Giant's followers making up in vociferous belligerence for what they lacked in votes. Thirty-three ballots followed during the next two days, with Cass still in the lead but Douglas now in second place and a number of votes having drifted to Marcy. With the convention in near deadlock, the name of the dark horse Pierce was introduced. Buchanan's managers decided to give Pierce nominal support on the forty-seventh ballot just to demonstrate the impossibility of his commanding the necessary two-thirds of the delegates. Then, as they saw it, Buchanan would be nominated. The strategy backfired when, in one of those inexplicable emotional outbreaks that affect public gatherings, the delegates stampeded in favor of the obscure Pierce, all but 6 of the 286 voting for him. Faced with candidate Pierce, most Democrats found themselves rather pleased with the result. Southerners saw a respectable, conservative gentleman apparently impervious to Northern abolitionist intemperance, and they looked forward to friendly associations with him. Northern free-soilers and moderates were content with a New Englander. The Democratic platform pledged to execute the Fugitive Slave Law faithfully while resisting all attempts in or out of Congress to renew the agitation for the extension of slavery.

The balloting at the Whig convention was even more prolonged than it had been with the Democrats. Webster, in a last pathetic burst of ambition, had hoped, on the strength of his Seventh of March Speech, to head his party. But time had passed him by. The contest lay between President Fillmore and Old Fuss and Feathers Scott. Fillmore, persuaded to try for vindication and with the weight of federal patronage behind him, had decided to run despite the hostility of Seward and Greeley and the radicals. The party that had never won a presidential election without a general eyed Scott. Beyond his record as a soldier he seemed a satisfactorily neutral candidate, one who would have an appeal to both North and South.

On the first ballot Fillmore and Scott were almost even, with 133 and 131 votes respectively, while Webster trailed them with a humiliating 29. On the fifty-third ballot the Pennsylvania delegates broke to Scott and the nomination was made. Hedging as much as possible, the party platform "deprecated" further agitation over the slavery question while endorsing the Compromise "until time and experience shall demonstrate the necessity of further legislation." Henry J. Raymond, editor of *The New York Times*, disgustedly labeled the platform a bargain with the South.

Webster, ailing and disgruntled, returned to his Marshfield farm, advising his acquaintances to vote for his long-time friend Pierce. Fillmore remained rigidly aloof from the contest, as did his "Silver Gray" faction of conservative Whigs. The Free-Soilers—among them Chase, Sumner, and Horace Mann—spurned Scott to nominate Senator John P. Hale of New Hampshire on a platform proclaiming, "Slavery is a sin against God, and a crime against man." At the other end of the political spectrum a group of Southern Whigs, enraged by Scott's refusal to comment on the Compromise, bolted the party to form their Southern Rights party, which nominated George M. Troup of Georgia—and on Election Day would draw only thirty-five hundred voters.

The election was a lackluster one, enlivened only by personal abuse. The Whigs, recalling Pierce's senatorial drinking exploits, dubbed him the hero of many a well-fought bottle and a coward in the Mexican War. The Democrats made much of Old Fuss and Feathers' pompous mannerisms and occasional gaffes. They, at least, were able to present a united front, with Douglas, Cass, Buchanan, and Marcy stumping the country for Pierce. Clay and Webster had died before the election, and there was a feeling that the Whig party was dying too, a feeling shared even by the divided Whigs themselves, who had lost confidence in victory despite the glitter of Scott's epaulets. In the electoral college Pierce's victory was overwhelming: 254 votes to 42 for Scott, who carried only Kentucky, Massachusetts, Tennessee, and Vermont. In the popular balloting Pierce received 1,601,474 votes to 1,386,580 for Scott and a mere 156,667 for the Free-Soiler, Hale.

Pierce was inaugurated on a raw and blustery March day laced with flurries of snow. Any joy he might have had in winning the Presidency was blotted out by private grief, for a few weeks earlier his only surviving child, a boy of eleven, had been killed before his eyes in a railroad accident. At his inauguration he spoke with-

Pierce and his running mate, William R. King, are displayed on a campaign poster of 1852. King, who had tuberculosis, was allowed to take his oath of office in Havana and died before ever serving as Vice President.

345

out notes or manuscript, the first and only time that an American President would deliver an extemporaneous inaugural address. "I fervently hope that the question is at rest," he said, speaking of slavery, "and that no sectional or ambitious or fanatical excitement may again threaten the durability of our institutions or obscure the light of our prosperity."

It was the vain hope of a weak man. At the outset of his administration Pierce could have taken a strong line, asserting the permanence of the Compromise of 1850 against the free-soil Democrats of the North and the Southern-rights fire-eaters. But such strength would have been foreign to his character. Instead, he tried hard to please everyone; and as is usually the case in such attempts, he ended by pleasing no one. For his Secretary of State he chose the Unionist William Marcy. Jefferson Davis, inheritor of Calhoun's secessionist mantle, he made Secretary of War. The brilliant, unprincipled Caleb Cushing—a Massachusetts Democrat whose views were not dissimilar to those of Davis—became Attorney General. James Guthrie, an able Louisville lawyer, took charge of the Treasury Department. Among his diplomatic appointments Pierce made Buchanan minister to England and he sent the reckless expansionist senator from Louisiana, Pierre Soulé, to Spain. The administration was, in Benton's jaundiced summing up, one "in which he [Pierce] was inoperative, and in which nullifiers, disunionists, and renegades used his name and his power for their own audacious and criminal purposes."

In foreign affairs Pierce continued the Democratic tradition of expansionism. In order to secure a possible route for a Southern railroad, the American minister to Mexico, James Gadsden, approached Santa Anna—back in power and short of money—with an offer to buy a huge area below the Gila River boundary. By the year's end Santa Anna had signed the Gadsden Treaty, ceding a much smaller area than Gadsden had wanted for fifteen million dollars, which the Senate reduced to ten million dollars. There were those, among them Benton, who held the land worthless, a gift to railroad speculators seeking a Southern route to the Pacific. Gadsden himself was disappointed at failing to secure a port—a Southern Trieste, as he saw it—to provide an outlet on the Gulf of California.

Cuba, so ardently desired by Southerners and by Northern speculators, was no such easy matter, even though Spanish colonial officialdom was sunk in a

lethargy of corruption and the conditions of the slaves on the great Cuban plantations were such as to make *Uncle Tom's Cabin* seem an idyl. Any American humanitarian motives for annexation were subordinate to the Southern hopes of acquiring a slave-breeding and slave-trading area and to Southern fears of a British-inspired emancipation of the island. Northerners like Edward Everett, Webster's successor as Secretary of State, considered Cuba a natural extension of the United States, its incorporation into the Union strategically necessary. Whether Spain would ever have considered parting with Cuba is doubtful, but the diplomatic ineptness of the minister to Spain, Pierre Soulé, and his boorishness at court made anything even approaching reasonable negotiations impossible.

This scene of an Indian ruin near the Gila River—part of the Mexican-United States boundary after the war with Mexico—was made in 1852 by John R. Bartlett, a naturalist and artist appointed to survey the 2,000-mile-long border. One year later the Gadsden Purchase set the western part of the boundary farther south.

The 1850's were a period of great rail expansion, and the clamor grew for a transcontinental line or lines to the Pacific. The various promoters and politicians and speculators vociferously proclaimed the advantages of their favored route. Four routes were being considered; of these all but the southernmost crossed the Nebraska country—that huge northern remnant of the Louisiana Purchase, a still-empty Indian region, which included what would one day be the states of Kansas, Nebraska, the western Dakotas, the eastern parts of Colorado, Wyoming, and Montana.

Douglas, eager for the expansion of settlements beyond the Mississippi and not unmindful of his own land and railroad speculations, was an earnest advocate of a railroad to the Pacific. Early in 1854 he introduced a bill in Congress providing for a Northern, a Central, and a Southern route, a proposal fair to all sections. To finance this undertaking he proposed that the railroads be granted belts of public land twenty miles wide through the states and forty wide through the territories. But before any route across the central plains could become a practical possibility, the Indian-held Nebraska country would have to be defined as a territory, with its own functioning government.

While chairman first of the House, and then of the Senate, Committee on Territories, Douglas had helped create four territories and had supported the admission of Florida, Iowa, Wisconsin, and California into the Union. As settlers pushed closer to Nebraska, he had repeatedly proposed a territorial government for the region, and—as the land lay north of the Missouri Compromise line—he had prepared, as a matter of course, to organize it as a free territory. He had found the usually easy task of setting up a territorial government hindered not only by the indigenous Indian tribes but by stubborn Southern insistence that the Missouri Compromise was unconstitutional and that slaveholders had the right to take their "species of property" into any new territories, specifically Nebraska. Missouri slaveholders were particularly hostile, fearing to see their

When Douglas returned to the United States in November, 1853, after an extended European tour, the aspect of the country was encouragingly calm. The Union was prosperous, there was an almost embarrassing surplus in the treasury, foreign relations remained peaceful, and the majority of the people of the North and the South still supported the 1850 Compromise. Yet the calm to which Douglas returned was superficial, and he above all others was destined to be the one to shatter it. President Pierce might have lacked any policy except to drift, but the administration's Democratic majority decisively controlled both the House and the Senate. Even before the new President's first year was up, it was clear that the inept Pierce would not succeed himself and that Douglas was already eyeing the Presidency.

347

state hemmed in on three sides by free-soil boundaries and by antislavery neighbors.

In the summer of 1853, Pierce's commissioner of Indian affairs concluded negotiations with eighteen Indian nations of the Nebraska country by which thirteen million acres were opened for settlement. Territorial organization became more urgent than ever in the constant push westward, with settlers so eager to enter the region that many were making their way there illegally. And with the urgency, the South grew more adamant. That harsh-voiced apologist for slavery Senator David Atchison of Missouri announced that he would see Nebraska "sink in hell" before he would see it organized on a free-soil basis.

Douglas, lacking any strong feelings one way or the other on the slavery issue, realized that any plan of his to organize the territory and to extend a railroad line through it would require Southern support. After consulting with his colleagues on the Committee on Terri-

tories, he produced the Kansas-Nebraska Bill, in which, reversing his earlier position, he advocated organizing the territory on the same terms as Utah and New Mexico—"with or without slavery," according to its constitution on admission to statehood. This principle of popular choice, or "squatter sovereignty," north of the Missouri Compromise line was an effective, if equivocal, repudiation of the Compromise. But Atchison insisted on an explicit declaration in the bill that "all questions pertaining to slavery in the Territories . . . are to be left to the people residing therein." But still the South was not satisfied. What would be the prospects for bringing slaves into the territory before the people had made their decision? The restrictions of the Missouri Compromise would still remain in force, effectively blocking slaveholders from the nascent territory. To change this, Senator Archibald Dixon of Kentucky demanded an amendment stating that the Missouri Compromise did not apply to the proposed Nebraska

Below, free-soilers and proslavery forces fight at Hickory Point in Kansas Territory. Left, a cartoon of 1858 pokes fun at congressional passion over the issue.

ANNE S. K. BROWN MILITARY COLLECTION, BROWN UNIVERSITY LIBRARY; LEFT: *Harper's Weekly*, APRIL 10, 1858

Territory or to any territory. In brief, the amendment would repeal the Southern-hated Missouri Compromise. Douglas hesitated at such a step—perhaps remembering how five years earlier he had eulogized the Compromise as "a sacred thing"—but finally gave in, observing, "I know it will raise a hell of a storm." Once resolved, he, with a delegation of members of Congress, visited the President to persuade the amenable Pierce that it was necessary to give the amended bill the administration's backing.

In its final form Douglas' bill divided the Nebraska country into two parts. Kansas Territory included the present state of Kansas, but its western boundary extended to the Rockies, taking in what is now eastern Colorado. Nebraska Territory to the north included the vast remaining part of the region and extended to the Canadian border. Politicians more or less tacitly assumed that Nebraska would become free soil while Kansas would admit slavery. With such large Democratic majorities in Congress, the Little Giant was certain of the passage of his bill in spite of the opposition of many of the Northern Democrats. But in the tense months before the Kansas-Nebraska Bill passed, the rising attacks against him roused all the combative instincts of his nature. At the beginning of debate Chase penned an "Appeal of the Independent Democrats in Congress to the People of the United States," in which he branded Douglas a liar and a cheat, willing to sell his honor for the sake of the Presidency. Chase, Seward, and Sumner took the lead against the bill, speaking with eloquent bitterness in the Senate to the country at large. Douglas maintained that the Compromise of 1850—by exempting Utah, New Mexico, and the part of California north of the 36° 30' parallel from the restrictions of the Missouri Compromise—had in effect repudiated the earlier Compromise. By contrast, the self-determination offered in his bill "would avoid the slavery agitation for all time to come."

Though Douglas had predicted a storm, he had not foreseen its full force and consequences. As soon as the text of his bill became known, Northerners reacted with fury. The diffuse emotions aroused by *Uncle Tom's Cabin* now found a specific outlet. Conservative merchants, clergymen, lawyers, and professional men, who had gone along with the Compromise of 1850 with its hateful Fugitive Slave Law, who had voted for Pierce and condemned the radicals, found themselves in the same company and often on the same platform as the abolitionists. Mass meetings were held throughout the North. For once even the clergy were united. Democratic newspapers vied with the Whigs in denouncing Douglas. In contrast Southerners greeted the bill with indifferent approval, although some of the more astute felt the measure would do the South no practical good and would merely unleash antagonisms that could not be restrained again.

While the debate on the Kansas-Nebraska Bill was still going on in the Congress, the case of the third fugitive slave seized in Boston, Anthony Burns, a stowaway on a vessel bound from Alexandria, gave a grim indication of the North's hardened mood. The author-turned-lawyer Richard Henry Dana, Jr., who had written so vividly of his voyage as a deck hand to California in *Two Years Before the Mast,* and who had volunteered to act as Burns's counsel, described the fugitive as "a piteous object, rather weak in mind and body, with a large scar on his cheek, which looks much like a brand, a broken hand from which a large piece of bone projects, and another scar on his other hand."

In the seething reaction to Burns's capture it became clear at once that radical opinion had become general opinion. A huge protest meeting was held at Faneuil Hall, "the Cradle of Liberty," with fiery speeches by Theodore Parker and Wendell Phillips. People from surrounding towns thronged to Boston during the four days Burns's hearing lasted. In one attempt by the crowd to rush the courthouse a special deputy was shot and killed. Two militia companies, a company of regulars, and a company of marines had to be dispatched to Boston to keep order. The area around the courthouse was cordoned off, and the courtroom itself filled with plug-uglies, who had been specially chosen to serve as the marshal's guard.

When Burns, according to the letter of the law indisputably a fugitive, was returned to the South, many of Boston's buildings were draped in black. Police and soldiers stood by with shotted guns as the chained and trembling Negro was led past. It took a thousand soldiers to keep the crowd in order. Hundreds jammed the streets from the courthouse to the water front. Church bells tolled, and at the sight of Burns, men roared their indignation; there were curses and shouts of "Kidnapper! Kidnapper!" After that turbulent day the Fugitive Slave Law became a dead letter.

At the close of the Nebraska debate, Chase, defiant and refusing to accept defeat, announced that a new party would rise to combat the act. "Raise your black flag; call up your forces; preach your war on the Constitution," Douglas replied with equal defiance. Chase's gesture was one both of challenge and hope. The old two-party system was dying. The majority Democratic party was hopelessly split, while the leaderless Whigs were disintegrating as had the Federalists a generation before them. William Cullen Bryant abandoned his thirty-year adherence to the party of Jefferson and Jackson and urged free-soil Democrats to form a new party. Horace Greeley made the same appeal to the free-soil Whigs, calling his party "a thing of the past." Everywhere there were movements of fusion, drawing disparate free-soil Democrats, Northern Whigs, Free-Soilers, temperance men, and the rising Know-Nothings into an anti-Nebraska party, a party by merger that soon assumed the Jeffersonian label Republican. Many were to claim credit for christening the new Republican party, but however the name originated, it rapidly came into general use. In the mid-term elections following the vote on the Kansas-Nebraska Bill, the Democrats, while still keeping control of the Senate, lost half their seats in the House of Representatives. Drawing on the ruins of the Whigs, the nativistic Know-Nothings elected governors in nine states—Massachusetts was one of them—and boasted that they controlled 104 of the 234 members of the House. The actual membership of the new House consisted of 108 Republicans, 83 Democrats, and 43 Know-Nothings.

While the old parties were dissolving and new political alignments beginning to emerge, the struggle moved from words to deeds beyond the Missouri. Kansas, that undulating land of "smoky waters," lay open and inviting, eighty thousand square miles empty except for wandering buffalo herds, Indians, and a few eager settlers from Missouri. Missouri slaveholders resolved to see those fertile acres flourish with tobacco and hemp. Small farmers from the Old Northwest were equally determined to move in and grow their mixed crops on their own free land. With the passage of the Kansas-Nebraska Act it became clear that those who got there first would win the prize. In the spring of 1854 the Massachusetts educator and politician Eli Thayer formed the Massachusetts—later New England—Emigrant Aid Society and undertook, without success, to raise five million dollars to send groups of free-soil settlers to Kansas. Much publicized by journalists like Greeley and Bryant, the society turned out to be more a

moral force than a practical one. New England was too remote to contribute any large number of settlers. Before the year's end the society did manage to dispatch five zealous companies into Kansas, one of which arrived with a brass band. And Whittier even wrote a hymn for the new settlers:

> We cross the prairie as of old
>   The Pilgrims crossed the sea,
> To make the West, as they the East,
>   The homestead of the Free!

But most of the free-soil newcomers pressing into the new territory were from the Ohio Valley and the Middle Atlantic States. Land-hungry rather than doctrinaire, practical farmers with scant concern either for abolition or the Negro, they opposed slavery primarily as a threat to their acres.

In opposition to Thayer, Senator Atchison in Missouri formed the bellicose Platte County Self-Defensive Association, whose members were prepared, when called on, to enter Kansas "to assist in removing any and all emigrants who go there under the auspices of the Northern Emigrant Aid Societies." Thousands of Missourians—most of them sober-minded settlers—were eager to stake their claims for Kansas land, but relatively few slaveholders were prepared to take their human property there. Why risk the large capital investment of a slave in uncertain Kansas in preference to the certain alternative of Texas and New Mexico? Supporters of slavery in Kansas far outnumbered the actual slaves. The flotsam of the Missouri River frontier counties, the swaggering, eye-gouging Border Ruffians, for whom violence was a way of life, were ready to swarm across the Missouri to defend their Southern principles with fist and bowie knife and pistol against the Northern vermin. Egged on by aggressive slaveholders, bullies who would never own a slave formed their vigilance committees.

At first, as Missouri and Ohio settlers, preoccupied with the practical problems of survival, met on Kansas soil there was less conflict than had been anticipated; but the uneasy potential remained. Pierce, aiming in his desultory way to strike a balance, appointed a Southerner governor of Nebraska Territory while naming a plump obscure lawyer from Pennsylvania, Andrew H. Reeder, governor of Kansas Territory. By November, 1854, the first Kansas election was held to name a delegate to Congress; almost two thousand adult males

TEXT CONTINUED ON PAGE 354

The American Negro in Art

While many Southerners, and even some Northerners, regarded Negro slaves as property rather than as thinking, feeling individuals and considered black people generally—slave or free—as a race inferior to whites, a number of American artists in the decades preceding the Civil War evinced compassion and insight in their portrayals of Negroes. This was in contrast to colonial painters, who seldom bothered to strip the mask of servility from their Negro subjects, the proslavery artists of the 1800's, who showed slaves happy in their poverty, and some genre artists, who placed Negroes marginally in their pictures as mindless props.

An example of the sensitive handling of the Negro subject is the oil sketch above by Thomas S. Noble for his painting *John Brown's Blessing*. Works by three other artists who imbue the Negro with grace and dignity are on the following two pages.

Left, a detail from Kitchen Ball at White Sulphur Springs *by Christian Mayr, who came to America from Germany in about 1834. Top, William Sidney Mount's* The Power of Music. *A resident of Long Island, New York, Mount was noted for his sympathetic portraits of Negro subjects. At right is a pencil study by English-born James Clonney for a painting entitled* In the Cornfield.

TEXT CONTINUED FROM PAGE 350

were then in the new territory. Border Ruffians doubled that figure for Election Day, crossing over in armed droves to stuff the ballot boxes and pad the voting lists. They carried the election overwhelmingly, although, ironically enough, they might at that early date have won honestly. Spurred by this success, the slavery men determined to make an equal sweep of the election for a territorial legislature, to be held in March, 1855. By this time Kansas had a total population of 8,500, of which 242 were slaves.

Rumors circulated throughout Missouri that the Emigrant Aid Society planned to send twenty thousand Easterners to Kansas in time to vote. Proslavery Missourians were convinced that to maintain the peculiar institution in their state they must extend it to Kansas. Border Missourians formed the Sons of the South vigilance committee, identifiable by the hemp badge they wore. At least five thousand Border Ruffians crossed into Kansas in companies for the election of the legislature, some with flags flying, fifes shrilling, and drums beating. The dogged Atchison led his own body of some eighty armed men, spurring them on with whiskey and the glad tidings that "there are eleven hundred coming over from Platte County to vote, and if that ain't enough we can send five thousand—enough to kill every God-damned abolitionist in the Territory!" By force, threats, ballot stuffing, and illegal vote counts, the Missouri intruders were able to elect all but one of their candidates, gaining 5,427 votes against a free-soil vote of only 791.

Later it was shown that 4,908 votes had been cast illegally. Pressed by the proslavery settlers, Governor Reeder had certified most of the results, but when he became aware of the extent of the fraud, he protested, declaring openly during a trip east that "Kansas has been invaded, conquered, subjugated by an armed force from beyond her borders, led on by a fanatical spirit." In Washington he begged Pierce to take action. The President at first seemed sympathetically indignant, saying that Kansas had caused him more sorrow than anything since the death of his son. But instead of moving, Pierce took static counsel with his Southern advisers. Soon after Reeder's return to Kansas, the "Bogus Legislature," which he had called to meet at inland Pawnee City, met instead at Shawnee Mission a few miles from the Missouri line and proceeded to pass law after law designed to perpetuate its hold on office and slavery in Kansas. It ruled that public office in Kansas

354

This wood figure, abolitionist Henry Ward Beecher praying, was probably made during his pastorate in Indianapolis, before he came to Brooklyn in 1847.

must be restricted to those believing in slavery, that anyone who asserted slavery did not legally exist in the territory would be subject to a minimum of two years' hard labor, that there would be a ten-year penalty for aiding a runaway slave, that to connive in a slave's escape or to circulate papers inciting slaves to revolt was punishable by death. Reeder vetoed all such bills as fast as they were passed, and the legislature with equal speed passed them over his veto. The administration in Washington seemed immobile. Then suddenly Reeder found himself removed from office by the President on the grounds of his being implicated in land speculations. He was succeeded by a blustering former governor of Ohio, Wilson Shannon, who could be counted on to side with the slavery element. Shannon announced that the Bogus Legislature—which shifted its capital to proslavery Lecompton late in 1855—was the legitimate law-making body for the territory and that he personally was "for slavery in Kansas."

At the opening of the territory the antislavery settlers, though soon to be in the majority, lacked unity and leaders. Before long they were to find both in the former congressman from Indiana James H. Lane and the New Englander Dr. Charles Robinson, who had arrived in Kansas with Thayer's first emigrant party. Lane was an adventurer, tall, swarthy, magnetic—a demagogue more concerned with power than principles. But whatever his reasons for joining the free-soil settlers, he turned into one of their most dynamic and militant leaders. Dr. Robinson, a milder man, had helped found Lawrence, the town destined to become the free-soil center of the territory. Lane, with Reeder, was the leading light of a preliminary Free State convention held in the log-cabin settlement of Big Springs near Lawrence in September to organize anti-Missouri sentiment into a Free State party.

Several weeks later a second Free State convention of thirty-four delegates, held at Topeka with Lane presiding, drew up a constitution prohibiting slavery in Kansas after July, 1857, and naming Topeka the temporary capital. The constitution was approved by popular vote, and in January Robinson, a moderate on the slavery issue, was chosen "governor." Faced with the solidifying opposition of the Free Staters, the slavery men gathered at Leavenworth, and with Governor Shannon present, organized the Law and Order party. Two parties, two governments in two capitals, faced each other with growing belligerence. Slavery men

grew convinced that their opponents had a secret military organization throughout the territory. A young free-soil settler was murdered. Civil war seemed imminent as twelve hundred Missouri volunteers swarmed over the border and the Free Staters turned Lawrence into a strong point, forming drill companies and fortifying the Free-State Hotel.

When Congress met, two rival Kansas delegations presented their credentials. The spineless Pierce, falling back on Attorney General Cushing for advice, finally produced a much-delayed message in which he upheld the Bogus Legislature and its laws and urged that the Shawnee Mission legislators organize the territory for statehood. To the President the Free State movement appeared of "revolutionary character," and he warned the free-soilers that any sign of resistance would be considered "treasonable insurrection." A few weeks later he issued a proclamation ordering both sides to refrain from the violence that he himself had done so much to make inevitable.

Well into the spring of 1856 the House and Senate chambers echoed to the Kansas debate. Douglas in the Senate defended the President, denounced the Topeka Convention, and branded the emigrant aid societies alien intruders. Seward in his turn demanded that Kansas be admitted at once as a free state under the Topeka constitution. South Carolina's Representative Preston S. Brooks wrote in the Atchison, Kansas, *Squatter Sovereign* that "the admission of Kansas into the Union as a slave state is now a point of honor with the South."

North and South took up the Kansas challenge, while one of the most bitter winters in memory swept the plains. Ex-Senator Atchison appealed to the slave states to send settlers to Kansas and "let them come well armed." All over the South young men stepped forward to volunteer, both as fighters and farmers. Businessmen and planters subscribed money and weapons for the Southern settlers, Southern women gave their jewelry, and railroads offered free passage.

No Southern effort, however, could equal the press of settlers from the Northwest, supported by the North with an equally fervid crusading spirit. Henry Ward Beecher—Mrs. Stowe's clergyman brother—in a sensational sermon in his Plymouth Church in Brooklyn, called on the "friends of freedom" to furnish the free-soil settlers with Sharps rifles, adding that "one Sharps rifle will have more moral influence upon slaveholders than a hundred Bibles." He was taken at his word. Beecher's Bibles, the rifles became known as when they arrived in Kansas in boxes labeled "Books," "Revised Statutes," "Hardware," and even "Bibles." "Every day's experience convinces me that matters are approaching a crisis in this country on the subject of slavery," Edward Everett, the clergyman-statesman-educator, wrote in his diary. "The differences, not of interest but of opinion and feeling are irreconcilable."

Spring, 1856, brought new threats of violence. The *Squatter Sovereign* called for "Blood for Blood!" A congressional investigating committee arrived in Kansas and met in the frontier towns of Leavenworth, Lawrence, and Lecompton, the latter named after Judge Samuel D. Lecompte, the guzzling proslavery Marylander whom Pierce had appointed to serve as chief justice of the territory.

To distract attention from the committee's disclosures, Lecompte, in an unforeseen countermove, charged the grand jury to indict all the Free State leaders, "men who are dubbed governors . . . men who are dubbed all the various other dubs," for high treason. Lane was arrested, Robinson seized on a Missouri River steamboat as he was starting for the East, and Reeder escaped only by claiming the protection of the investigating committee. Following the indictment, Federal Marshal J. B. Donaldson claimed that attempts by his deputy to serve process in Lawrence had been met with violence, and he called on law-abiding citizens to rally to Lecompton and form a posse. The law abiders appeared in swaggering bands—the Lecompton Guards, the Doniphan Tigers, the Platte County Rifles commanded by Atchison—a ragtag array of six or seven hundred Southerners well primed with liquor and armed with four brass six-pounders.

Led by Donaldson and Atchison, the posse occupied Lawrence on May 21, 1856, the inhabitants offering no resistance to a federal marshal. Hoisting a red flag with a white star in the center inscribed "Southern Rights" on one side and "South Carolina" on the other over the premises of the *Herald of Freedom*, the invaders occupied the paper's offices as well as those of the *Kansas Free State*. After sacking the two establishments on the grounds that the grand jury had ordered them to be "abated as nuisances," the raiders threw the presses into the river and then moved on to Robinson's house, which they destroyed along with his library. Although Atchison and Donaldson had dined at the Free-State

Hotel on the invitation of the proprietor, they were unable to prevent their supporters from burning the building to the ground. Before the posse left Lawrence, one volunteer was killed when a wall fell on him. Yet, for all its paucity of casualties, the "Sack of Lawrence" was seen in the North and the South as a declaration of war.

The day before the events in Lawrence, Senator Charles Sumner had delivered a carefully rehearsed speech in the Senate, which he later called "The Crime Against Kansas." The brilliant but pedantic senator from Massachusetts, considering himself the Demosthenes and the Cicero of his day, had planned his speech as a "most thorough philippic." His corrosive name-calling had long since made him the best-hated man in the Senate, and many Southern members refused to speak to him. In his philippic, a ranting pseudoclassic diatribe, he singled out Douglas and the elderly Senator Andrew Butler of South Carolina for specific attack.

Events in Kansas he described as "the rape of a virgin territory, compelling it to the hateful embrace of Slavery; and it may be clearly traced to a depraved longing for a new slave State, the hideous offspring of such a crime." Douglas he ridiculed as a Sancho Panza, then in rebuttal as a "noisome, squat and nameless animal." Butler, a mild and chivalrous gentleman, universally popular among both his Northern and Southern colleagues, a scholar and a former judge, a moderate opposed to secession, had stirred Sumner's vitriolic tongue by a measured defense of the Lecompton regime. With malicious implications of sexuality, Sumner accused him of having chosen "a mistress to whom he has made his vows, and who, though ugly to others, is always lovely to him. . . . I mean the harlot, Slavery."

Preston Brooks, Butler's nephew, who represented Calhoun's old district in the House, brooded on the insult to his kinsman and his state. Brooks determined to extract an apology from Sumner or else chastise him. Two days later, after the Senate had adjourned, the congressman, carrying a gutta-percha cane, stalked into the almost empty Senate Chamber, where the senator from Massachusetts was at his desk writing a letter. Standing directly over Sumner, Brooks called out the senator's name. Brooks had intended to humiliate rather than hurt, but the Southerner's temper flared and he lashed out with his cane, raining half a dozen full-force blows on the other's head until the cane broke. Bleeding and half-blinded, Sumner struggled to his feet, wrenching his desk free of its floor fastenings, then staggered forward ten feet until he fell. Several Southerners present made no effort to help him.

Brooks's violent act made him a hero in the South, and Sumner a martyr in the North. Southern papers extolled the congressman as a knight-errant. Southern sympathizers—among them students of the University of Virginia—presented him with handsome commemorative canes. Even a number of slaves contributed to buy a present for the man who, according to the Columbia *South Carolinian*, had made "the first *practical* issue for their preservation and protection in their rights and enjoyments as the happiest laborers on the face of the globe." Brooks was censured by the House; he resigned and was promptly re-elected.

In the North and the West tens of thousands of pamphlets of Sumner's Crime Against Kansas Speech were sold. Within a week of the beating two mass protest meetings were held in Boston, one in Faneuil Hall, presided over by the new Know-Nothing governor, Henry J. Gardner. Wendell Phillips and Theodore Parker were among the speakers at the other meeting. The Massachusetts legislature condemned the Sumner assault as "a gross breach of Parliamentary privilege—a ruthless attack upon the liberty of speech—an outrage upon the decencies of civilized life, and an indignity to the Commonwealth of Massachusetts." In New York a huge and simmering meeting at the Tabernacle was addressed by William Cullen Bryant, Henry Ward Beecher, and the president of Columbia. Similar meetings proliferated throughout the North and the West. Bryant felt that the violence of Kansas had found its way into the Capitol, that violence was becoming "the order of the day."

Not for three and a half years would Sumner return to the Senate. "My brain and whole nervous system are jangled and subject to relapse," he wrote the autumn after the attack. Southerners maintained that Brooks had inflicted only superficial injuries and that Sumner was playing on popular sympathy. Sumner's scalp

The North's point of view is expressed in this political cartoon of the assault on Senator Sumner by South Carolina's Representative Preston Brooks. Brooks was saved by the two-thirds rule from expulsion from the House.

wounds may have been minor, and much of his illness may have been psychosomatic, a reaction of his over-wrought temperament, but the symptoms were real enough—insomnia, lassitude, paralyzing headaches. He grew fiercely indignant at suggestions that he was feigning. Although he could no longer take his place in the Senate, the Massachusetts legislature re-elected him almost unanimously. For three years his Senate seat would remain empty, more eloquent in its silence than his oratory could have been.

When Douglas returned to Illinois in August, 1854, after Congress had adjourned following the passage of his Kansas-Nebraska Bill, he found the Northwest turned hostile toward him. As he himself said, he could have traveled from Boston to Chicago by the light of his burning effigies. In Philadelphia he had denounced the Know-Nothings by name, urging all Democrats to stand firm against the "allied forces of Abolitionism, Whiggism, Nativism"—and in Chicago the Know-Nothings were waiting for him. His most uncritical and devoted supporters were the Irish in the city—newly minted citizens, solidly Democratic and as hostile to the Negro as any Southerners.

As the first step in defending his record in his home state, Douglas arranged to speak in North Market Hall in the Chicago Irish district. On the day of his speech much of the city went into mourning. On the hot September afternoon the ships of the port lowered their flags to half-mast, and just after six o'clock all the church bells tolled. Since the hall was small and the crowd huge, the Little Giant spoke in the open on a raised platform facing Market House Square. Ten thousand of his friends and enemies were packed in the space in front of him in the heat of that clear evening. He began by declaring that he wished to explain the Kansas-Nebraska Act, since he was satisfied that no-body there understood it. Three hearty groans greeted him. Interrupted by continual salvos of catcalls, hisses, and jeering laughter, his own temper rising, he told the voluble doubters before him that the Kansas-Nebraska Act was right and just, based as it was on the great American principle of popular sovereignty. After three-quarters of an hour of heckling, Douglas lost his temper altogether. He tossed aside his manuscript to bandy insults with his audience until finally, his face distorted with rage, he stalked off the platform, shaking his fist and shouting: "It is now Sunday morning; I'll go to church and you may go to hell!"

Wearing an old linen suit, Lincoln was reluctant to have his picture taken, but the photographer persuaded him. The sitting took place in 1858, on the day Lincoln won an acquittal for a client on a murder charge.
COLLECTION OF LLOYD OSTENDORF

Flaming effigies and insulting signs confronted the Little Giant throughout Illinois. Audiences responded coldly, but never again did Douglas lose his temper in public, although epithets still shot out of his mouth like bullets: "Abolitionists!" "Black Republicans!" "Know-Nothings!" "Nigger-lovers!" Announced by handbills in English and German, heralded by brass bands, he toured the towns and cities of his state, repeating the standard speech with its by now fine-honed arguments. There were, he told his audiences, two rival principles in conflict: one, that of the Missouri Compromise, sectional; the other, popular sovereignty, national in scope. Popular sovereignty, embodied in the Compromise of 1850, had replaced a geographical line with the will of the people. That principle he, in good faith, had extended to the Nebraska country, even though he himself was convinced that the climate and soil would never sustain a slave-based economy there.

Backed by the full force of the Democratic regulars, more eloquent, more dynamic, and more convincing than he had ever been, the Little Giant was beginning to regain many of his old Illinois supporters. A number of the state's newspapers had fallen into line. As he progressed, his audiences grew larger and more friendly. On October 3, 1854, at the opening of the state fair in Springfield, he delivered his set speech, this time, because of rain, in the packed House of Representatives hall in the state capitol. Until then he had not been opposed by anyone of consequence. But when he finished speaking, a colleague of his state legislative days, the tall and ungainly Abraham Lincoln, took his stand on the landing and announced that he would reply to Senator Douglas the following day.

Most of the legislators and lawyers present recognized the looming, awkward figure in the ill-fitting black tail coat as a former Illinois political leader and one of Springfield's more successful lawyers. But they were puzzled as to what had brought this old-line Whig out of retirement to the hustings. In 1849, after having served a term in Congress, he had failed to obtain a hoped-for appointment as commissioner of the General Land Office and had returned to his Springfield law practice at the age of forty, letting it be known that he was putting politics behind him.

As a prospering lawyer, he had found no practical objection to Clay's Compromise of 1850. Not until the passage of the Kansas-Nebraska Bill did he find himself pushed to the point of thinking beyond practical considerations. During the congressional debates over the bill his acquaintances had noticed that he had grown more silent and withdrawn. Later he was to write in his third-person autobiography: "His profession had almost superseded the thought of politics in his mind, when the repeal of the Missouri Compromise aroused him as he had never been before."

Myths would later obscure the actuality of this unkempt prairie lawyer with the large ears, the dark leathery complexion, and the unexpectedly gentle mouth, but in that transient moment of history, as he stood on the landing to announce his speech, there seemed nothing particularly out of the ordinary about him. He had been born in a log cabin; that was commonplace so close to the frontier. He was self-made, self-educated, had taught himself law; but most of his colleagues had also read Blackstone and Chitty's *Pleadings* by can-dlelight. Most of them were equally unsure of their ancestors more than a generation or two past.

Abraham Lincoln could trace his ancestry back as far as his namesake grandfather, but no further. Thomas Lincoln, the father, was a man who had made his way down in the world, starting out with some property and ending in a shack in a pioneer's clearing—the frontier story of poor land, thin cultivation, law suits, and moving on. The son was born in Kentucky and his first memories were of his second home at Knob Creek on the Cumberland Trail. When Abraham was seven, Thomas trekked with his family to the new lands of Indiana, where they spent the winter living in an open-faced shelter and subsisted mostly on game. Within two years Abraham's mother, Nancy Hanks Lincoln, was dead. Thomas married again, and though the son came to love his stepmother as a real mother, he never had much affection for his lackluster father.

The intervals the boy spent at the backwoods schools never added up to more than a year. He read the few books available in his primitive community: Parson Weems's *Life of Washington*, *Robinson Crusoe*, *Pilgrim's Progress*, *Aesop's Fables*, and inevitably the Bible. Although he was not a religious boy, he would absorb the stately rhythms of the Old Testament, to echo them in his later prose.

The boy had a zeal for learning without the single-minded bent of the scholar. When hired out by his father, he performed farm duties conscientiously rather than enthusiastically. By seventeen he had grown to a lean, tall, hard-muscled giant, grotesquely awkward in appearance, but the best athlete in the neighborhood as well as a mimic and a jester, with a fund of jokes and smokehouse stories. At nineteen he saw his first city when he and a friend floated on a flatboat loaded with farm produce down the Ohio and the Mississippi to opulent New Orleans. In the Indiana settlement he cleared acres, split rails, swung his partner in square dances, took part in house-raisings, wolf hunts, corn-huskings, and shooting contests. No doubt he attended a few revival meetings.

In 1830 Thomas Lincoln again sold out and moved with his family to Illinois, building still another cabin in a clearing near the Sangamon River. But when, after a bad winter, he moved on once more, the boy Abraham—now of age—struck off on his own. After a second voyage to New Orleans, Lincoln found his way to New Salem, a village perched on a bluff above the Sangamon. A frontier boy with country ways and skills, homespun in aspect and with a homespun twang to his speech, he seemed at the age of twenty-two—in his later words—"a piece of floating driftwood." His first job was as a clerk in Denton Offutt's store at fifteen dollars a month plus sleeping quarters in the back. At first the newcomer was eyed belligerently by the tough neighborhood boys of Clary's Grove to the west until he demonstrated his superiority in wrestling. Then he was accepted. He was also accepted into the New Salem Debating Society, whose president admitted after the first meeting that Abe was a fine speaker and all he lacked was culture.

By 1832 Lincoln, a supporter of Henry Clay's, considered himself popular enough to announce his candidacy for the legislature. But between his announcement and the election itself the Black Hawk War intervened. At the governor's call for militia volunteers, Lincoln, with most of the Clary's Grove boys, joined up for thirty days, the Clary's Grovers' votes electing him captain. His war service consisted of that month plus two re-enlistments for an additional fifty days in other units as a private. Floundering in the swamps of southern Wisconsin with his fellow volunteers, he saw neither action nor Indians. In later years he poked fun at his military service, admitting that he had once borne a musket and had had "a good many bloody struggles with the musquitoes." He was mustered out just before the election, in which he ran eighth among thirteen candidates for the seat in the legislature.

Offutt having given up his store, Lincoln found himself jobless. For a time he thought of becoming a blacksmith, but finally joined William F. Berry to buy one of New Salem's three general stores. It turned out to be an unlucky venture, with the heavy-drinking Berry taking them deep into debt before his death in 1835. From 1833 to 1836 Lincoln earned fifty dollars a year as the village postmaster, picking up extra money as a rail splitter, a farm hand, and for a time the deputy county surveyor.

In 1834, as the Whig and Democratic parties were beginning to take form, he again ran for the legislature. This time the young surveyor was better known, campaigned harder, and easily won one of the two places in his district. Spurred on by his election, he spent the interval before the legislative session—in the time he could snatch from odd jobs—reading law. Then, after borrowing two hundred dollars and buying his first tailor-made suit for sixty dollars, he set off on the two-day trip to Vandalia, at that time the capital.

The history of his next decade is a common enough Western chronicle of its era. He was admitted to the bar while in the legislature, and as a Whig, became the minority floor leader in his second term. At the end of the term it was clear that he had outgrown the declining New Salem, and he moved on to Springfield, which in 1839 would supplant Vandalia as the capital. In all, he would serve four terms in the legislature, to become the most outstanding Whig in the House. He did much to foster an internal improvements program, although it became a ghost project with the Panic of 1837. Countrified and careless in appearance, he had the ability and the magnetism to form an advantageous law partnership in Springfield, but entered an unfortunate betrothal, which he was able to get out of. Through his law partnership and his Whig connections he was taken up in the social life of the small city. An acquaintance described him at about this time as "very tall, awkward, homely, and badly dressed. . . . Although he then had considerable ambition to rise in the world, he had, or seemed to have, done very little to improve his manners, or appearance, or conversation. He generally wore an old rusty hat; his pantaloons were often too short and his coat and vest too loose. His features were rugged, his hair coarse and rebellious, and he was, when in repose, by nature and habit a man of sad countenance."

In those rising years he met and married Mary Todd, a young lady of high social standing from Kentucky, plump, willful, sometimes witty, pretty with a fugitive charm. "A very creature of excitement," he described her during their courtship. They were married in 1842. It is probable that she did not make him happy. It is doubtful if, with her hidden mad streak, she could have made any man happy.

After several law partnerships, in 1844 he entered into his last one—with William H. Herndon, a lawyer nine years his junior and just licensed to practice. Lincoln's legislative years had given him a taste for politics, a sense of his ability to lead, a feeling that he was entitled to advance to a seat in Congress. Not until 1846, however, less than two weeks before the outbreak of the Mexican War, did he finally receive his party's congressional nomination. Certain inner doubts about the war troubled him, but he voiced no public opposition to it and was later even among the speakers urging young men to volunteer. Against the fife-and-drum back-

In his Chicago studio Leonard Volk works on a bust of Lincoln, with a completed bust of Stephen Douglas in the rear. Volk made his studies for the sculptures as he followed the Lincoln-Douglas debates of 1858.

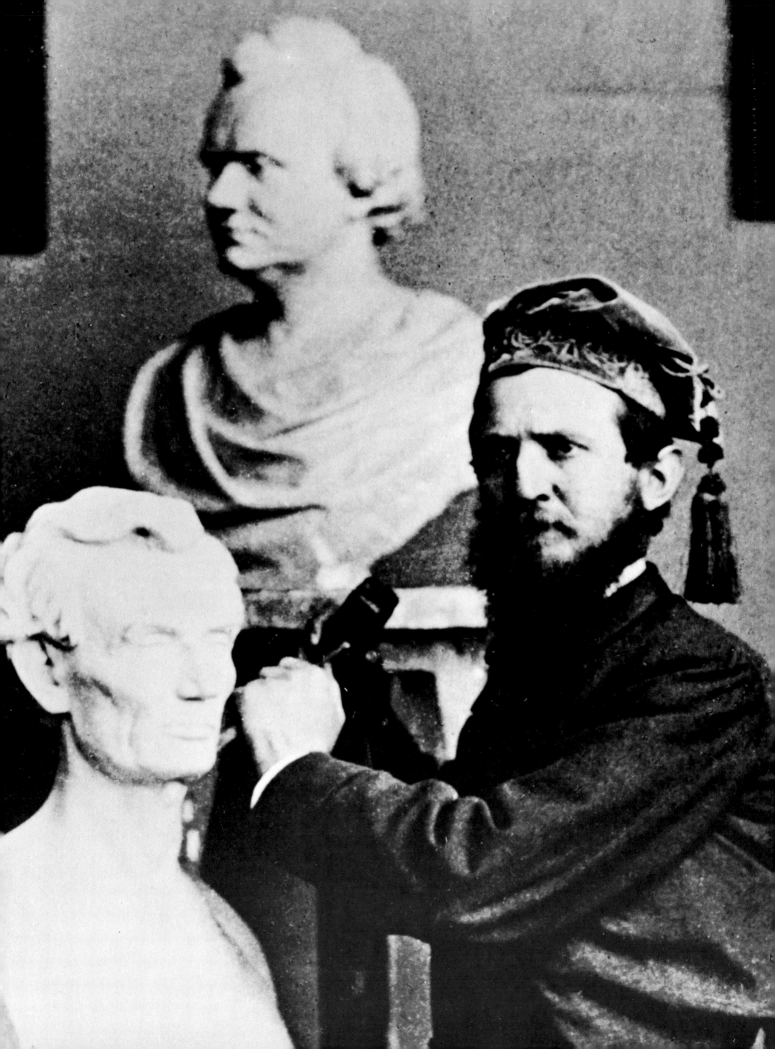

ground of the war, the congressional campaign lacked excitement, and Lincoln won easily over an uninspiring opponent to become the sole Whig congressman from Illinois. Congressman-elect Lincoln, conservative Whig and follower of Henry Clay's, did not seem a crusading type. The divisive agitation of abolitionism he avoided. His own personal dislike of slavery did not prevent him from representing a slaveowner who was suing to recover his Negro family that had slipped across to the free state of Illinois. Except for a few brief speeches on temperance, he did not concern himself with the contemporary reform movements. He had no strong feelings about the annexation of Texas.

Not until seventeen months after Lincoln's election did Congress convene, and by that time General Scott had occupied Mexico City and the war had come to an end. In the interval before the signing of the actual peace treaty, Lincoln joined with his fellow Whigs in blaming Polk for the "infamous and wicked" war. The congressman's speeches and votes for antiwar resolutions did not sit well with the prowar expansionists in Illinois whom he represented in Washington.

In his single congressional term Lincoln showed himself conscientious, inconspicuous except for his height, an average Westerner by all appearances. In line with party policy he was succeeded by another Whig at the next nomination. Resuming his law practice in Springfield, he brought to it the experience and the prestige of an ex-congressman. As a well-known leading citizen of the state capital, he could contemplate life's path stretching ahead in a regular, even, and prosperous line, which would be terminated only by a marble tombstone. Yet there was a quality of the unpredictable in this grave-faced man that did not quite fit the conventional Springfield success pattern, an introspective melancholy in which—many noticed it—Lincoln seemed to stand alone and apart.

He re-entered politics peripherally in 1854 to aid a Whig candidate, an opponent of the Kansas-Nebraska Bill, who was up for re-election to the congressional seat that had once been his. From the time of the bill's passage he had brooded about it, poring over books, following the congressional debates, turning the slavery question over and over in his mind. From his deliberations had come a quickening power of expression, which men soon sensed in his speeches and which finally led him to challenge the dialectics of the Little Giant. When, on the day following Douglas' speech, Lin-

coln mounted the rostrum in the representatives' hall, the rain had given way to overpowering heat. Discarding his coat and necktie, he stood in a collarless white shirt and galluses. Soon his shirt was soaked with sweat, his tousled hair dank and matted. He began with some hesitancy, his voice uneasily shrill until his earnestness overcame his nervousness. His speech, delivered again twelve days later in Peoria and known as his Peoria Speech, opened with a historical explanation of the Missouri Compromise and a denial that the organization of Nebraska had required its repeal. The Founding Fathers, in his view, had intended the gradual extinction of slavery. As America had expanded, various compromises had been adopted to keep as much territory as possible free while sustaining the Union. The Kansas-Nebraska Act was a direct violation of one of those hallowed compacts, and as such was wrong, "wrong in . . . letting slavery into Kansas and Nebraska—and wrong in . . . allowing it to spread to every other part of the wide world, where men can be found inclined to take it." Douglas' "sacred right of self-government" was for Lincoln the right of a fugitive minority in a territory to overrule majority opinion in the United States. The Negro, he declared, was a man and not property. He did not himself know what he would do with the problem of slavery, for all his hatred of it. He did not hold the Southerners responsible for it, nor did he deny their constitutional right to own slaves. What he called for at this moment was the restoration of the Missouri Compromise and the support of the Fugitive Slave Law in order to stand on the middle ground of Union between the extremes of the abolitionists and the Southern fireeaters. "To desert such ground because of any company, is to be less than a Whig—less than a man—less than an American." He concluded: "Near eighty years ago we began by declaring that all men are created equal; but now from that beginning we have run down to the other declaration, that for some men to enslave others is a 'sacred right of self-government.' These principles cannot stand together."

The steamy hall echoed repeatedly with applause during his speech. Here at last was a fresh voice from the prairies, a Union voice, with articulate logic and restrained passion, exposing Douglas' brilliant sophistries, raising the arguments brought about by the repeal of the Missouri Compromise from political considerations to the weighing of those moral precedents on which the republic had been founded.

Growth of the Cities

American cities, especially those in the North, grew phenomenally between 1830 and 1860. Farmers—no longer needed to raise food—flocked to urban centers seeking work. Multitudes were immigrating from Europe, and most settled in the cities. As canals, roads, and railroads were extended, towns sprang up along their routes and were nurtured by them. A textile mill in New England or an ore deposit in the West could be the nucleus of a growing city. The older cities maintained their historical characteristics: Quaker-founded Philadelphia remained the cleanest and most public-spirited; Boston in many ways kept the look of a provincial English town; New York was still the most aggressively commercial and, with New Orleans, the most cosmopolitan. Cincinnati, featured on the following pages, exemplifies the Western cities that throve due to location or other advantage. Cities faced myriad problems: slums, fires, crime, traffic confusion, sewage disposal. But despite their faults, they gave opportunity to the ambitious, and provided intellectual stimulation with their cultural life and constant contact with many diverse personalities.

OVERLEAF: *Some early settlements grew into large cities; others, after flourishing for a while, languished or even disappeared entirely. Still others—such as Montpelier, the capital of Vermont—maintained a village-like tranquillity, as can be seen in this water color of 1841.*

Originally called Losantiville, Cincinnati was founded in 1788; a membership certificate of the Pioneer Association, above, bears a vignette of the early village. Right, the bustling Cincinnati river front as it looked at the end of the Civil War

*Its position on the Ohio enabled Cincinnati (called Porkopolis) to become the nation's chief pork-packing center
—a distinction not without disadvantages. Above, swarms of pigs on their way to the slaughterhouse jam the city streets.*

A major scourge of the cities was fire. Above, Cincinnati
fire fighters try to control the burning of a tinderbox theater.

OVERLEAF: Henry Mosler, Jr., painted Cincinnati's Canal
Market in 1860. Many cities used pigs as street scavengers.

A very early city slum area was New York's Five Points section, above, a breeding ground for violent crime and vice.

Recreation for the more fortunate of society included ice skating, below, on the frozen Delaware, near Philadelphia.

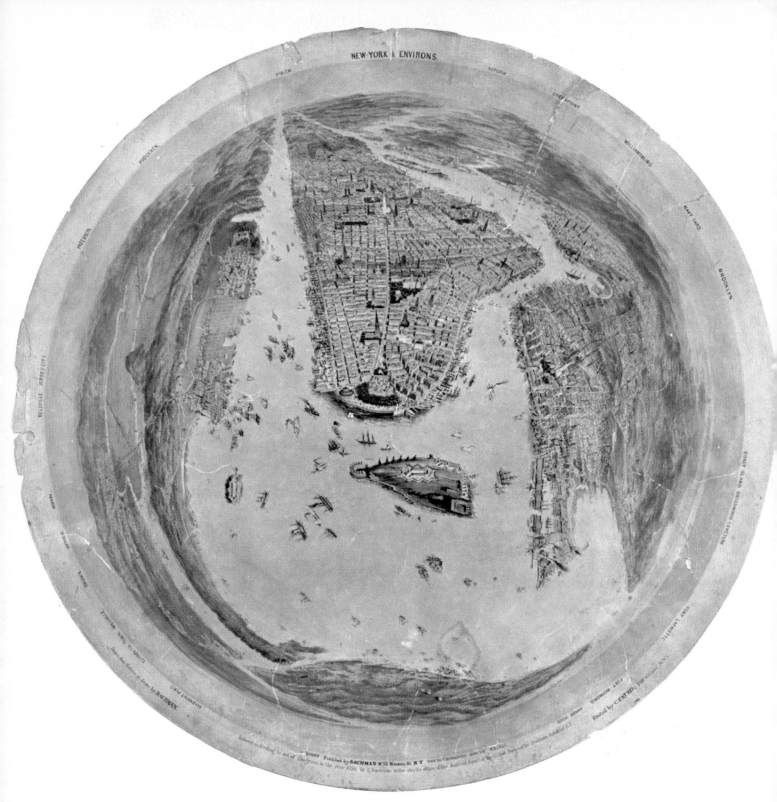

In the 1850's the growth—and congestion—of the larger cities accelerated, adding to urban problems. New York and its environs appear in unusual perspective in the circular bird's-eye view above, made in 1859. New Jersey lies to the left of Manhattan Island and Staten Island is in the foreground. River commerce swelled the population of St. Louis, shown in part at right in a detail from an 1854 engraving.

The Nation Divided

*I*n the North wild reports of the sack of Lawrence had pictured the "Athens of Free-State Kansas" as laid waste and burned to ashes. Among the Kansas Free Staters who reacted with violence to the news was the middle-aged John Brown, a Yankee settler near the free-soil village Osawatomie. Brown was that most dangerous and at times most earth-shaking of men, one who is convinced that his inner voice is the voice of God.

This man, who would become a legend, was in 1856 a gaunt, bearded failure. His father, a seedy itinerant handy man, had wandered to Ohio from Connecticut. The son, disliking lessons, grew up with scarcely enough schooling to read the Bible. When grown, he enjoyed the grimmer sections of the Old Testament, one of his favorite passages being, "Without the shedding of blood there is no remission of sins." Unsettled, with no liking or aptitude for work, he tried his hand at many trades—farming, tanning, sheepherding, small land speculations—without ever earning a decent living. Successful only in begetting children, he had had twenty by two wives. Like his father he was a fanatic abolitionist. He was early a believer in violence.

In the summer of 1855 five of his sons had emigrated to Kansas and he had followed in a wagon full of rifles, ammunition, and supplies, which he had purchased with money raised at antislavery meetings. Among his weapons were a number of short sabers, razor-sharp. A day too late Brown, as a member of a local defense company, reported for service in the relief of Lawrence. Three days after the sack of Lawrence he took his personal vengeance on the handful of proslavery settlers at Dutch Henry's Crossing on Pottawatomie Creek.

The crossing was named for a German, Henry Sherman, who had been living there for a decade. Two neighboring cabins were occupied by a lawyer, Allen Wilkinson, and by William Doyle, with his wife, Mahala, and their children. Though the crossing was Southern in sympathy, none of the three cabins had ever sheltered a slave.

On the night of May 24, 1856, Brown, four of his sons, and two or three other men, armed with rifles and sabers, groped their way along Pottawatomie Creek to the

A Northern belle consecrates the sword her beloved will carry
into battle against the Confederacy. The majority of
Northern women, aroused by antislavery tracts, Uncle Tom's Cabin,
lectures and political orations, were convinced that
the North's cause was just and supported the war to defend it.

crossing. Brown's impulse may not have been purely ideological, since Sherman was then attempting to prosecute him for the theft of two horses and twenty-four head of cattle. The raiders knocked at Doyle's door, and when he opened it, seized him and two sons. Not till morning did Mahala find her husband, shot dead, and her boys, butchered by saber blows. Wilkinson, next in line, was taken outside and hacked to death. Dutch Henry, whom Brown feared as well as hated, was away, but the killers dragged his brother William into the bushes, where he was found the next day with his skull split open and one hand cut off.

News of the Pottawatomie massacre spread through Kansas from settlement to settlement and beyond with the malignant glow of a prairie fire. For all the casual killings that had occurred, this was the first deliberate

atrocity by either side. "WAR! WAR!" the headlines of the Westport, Missouri, *Border Times* proclaimed. Proslavery men were quick to retaliate. Freebooters and fanatics, men of violence, flocked to both sides in the spreading guerrilla warfare. Settlers were shot from ambush or at the doors of their cabins. From Missouri, bands of raiders moved rapidly across the border. North and South gathered men, money, and supplies to be added like kindling to the flames. James Lane took charge of the free-soil newcomers in his "Northern Army." Eastern newspapers reported daily on the "progress of the civil war," while Kansas settlers of both persuasions began to flee the territory. Proslavery raiders pillaged Osawatomie twice; the second time John Brown lost one of his sons in the fighting. Obscure settlements with frontier names, like Fort Titus, Osawkee, Hickory

With a whoop and a roar, a wagonload of armed toughs—violent members of the ultranationalist, anti-Catholic, anti-immigration American, or Know-Nothing, party—invade Baltimore, Maryland, to pick up votes for their mayoral candidate, Thomas Swann.
MARYLAND HISTORICAL SOCIETY

Point, became symbols of carnage.

The civil war in Kansas was the lurid background to the presidential election of 1856. A week after the Pottawatomie massacre the Democratic convention met in Cincinnati with Pierce, Douglas, Buchanan, and—at least in his own opinion—Cass as the leading candidates. From the tatters of his administration Pierce, like Fillmore before him, hoped to salvage a vindicating second term, assured at least of support from a grateful South. Douglas' strength lay in the West, but many Democratic leaders felt that he was young enough to wait another four years. Then, too, many ordinary Democrats, though ready to accept popular sovereignty, were repelled by the Little Giant's bellicose and abusive manner and also felt, as one critic remarked, that too much of the smoke of the Kansas conflict clung to his garments. The suave Buchanan had the bland appeal of a compromise candidate. He called himself a conservative, meaning in his case that he was prudent and politically calculating. It was certainly true in 1848 and 1852, when he had stood in the wings waiting for the cue that had never come. During the Kansas-Nebraska discord, he had had the good fortune to be minister to England, where he could remain neutral. As the adroit Democratic leader of the crucial state of Pennsylvania, as United States senator, and later as Polk's Secretary of State, he had built up a solid political following. Any Democrat could win in the South, but Buchanan was the least divisive Democratic figure in the North.

The convention opened in the carnival atmosphere of bands and speeches. The first ballot gave Buchanan 135½ votes, Pierce 122½, Douglas 33, and Cass 5. Because New York sent two sets of delegates, each man from that state was given half a vote. At the end of the day, at the fourteenth ballot, Buchanan had reached 152½ votes—still 46 short of the two-thirds majority required—with Pierce at 75 and Douglas at 63. Although the Douglas managers extended themselves during the night to capture wavering Pierce delegates, the next morning Buchanan led by 168½ votes to only 118 for Douglas. The latter then withdrew for the sake of party harmony, and Buchanan was chosen by acclamation, with the Douglasite John C. Breckinridge of Kentucky as his vice-presidential running mate.

The Republicans met for their first presidential convention in the Musical Fund Hall in Philadelphia. No Southern states sent delegates and only a handful came from the border states. Old-line Whigs, dissident Democrats, Free-Soilers, Know-Nothings, and abolitionists gathered together in a crusading spirit, the chief element of which was a determination to stop the further extension of slavery. Among the prospective candidates the name Frémont led all the rest. A new party required a dashing young figure, and whatever his faults and his lack of experience, the Pathfinder with his romantic beard—unique among presidential candidates—was undeniably young and superficially dashing. Also he was a moderate, a former Democrat, and a free-soiler who at the same time had never said anything to alarm the South. Seward and Chase were considered to be too tarred by the brush of radicalism.

Since his Springfield speech Lincoln had spoken again several times, and his fairness and moderation had made him by 1855 an obvious choice for the United States Senate. Once more entering politics as a Whig, he canvassed the anti-Nebraska legislature, only to be nosed out by the anti-Nebraska Democrat Lyman Trumbull. But this time he would not retire to his law office. At an anti-Nebraska state convention held in Bloomington in May, 1856—the assorted delegates still balked at the name Republican, with its connotations of radicalism and abolition—Lincoln spoke so earnestly that engrossed reporters forgot to take notes. With his speech, the new party was born in Illinois.

In their platform the emerging Republicans at Philadelphia called for "the saving of Cuba" for the United States, a railroad to the Pacific by "the most central and practical route," and their most important plank—the barring in the territories of "those twin relics of barbarism—Polygamy and Slavery." Frémont was nominated on the first formal ballot, although Lincoln and other Whigs would have preferred the more conservative John McLean, an associate justice of the Supreme Court from Ohio. Lincoln himself received 110 votes for Vice President on the first ballot, but faded out on the second because he was not well enough known.

The Know-Nothings—already beginning to decline —chose ex-President Fillmore even though he was not a party member. The party split on the Kansas-Nebraska issue, and the Northern faction walked out of the convention to nominate its own candidate, who, by prearrangement, soon resigned in favor of Frémont. In September, long after the campaign had started, a remnant of the fading Whigs gathered in Baltimore to give their endorsement to Millard Fillmore.

It was the most vociferous campaign since Harrison's hard cider and log cabins started the ball rolling. Republican Wide-Awakes marched through the streets with fifes and drum corps. Parades, fireworks, illuminations, huge torchlight processions, all the ballyhoo of politics, carried the campaign surging into the autumn. Everywhere the Republicans displayed their slogan: "Free soil, free speech, and Frémont." "Bleeding Kansas" became their issue, even though Kansas troubles had subsided to a degree under the energetic command of a new governor, John White Geary of Pennsylvania.

The Democrats, campaigning under the banner of squatter sovereignty and with the slogan "Buchanan, Breckinridge, and Free Kansas," frightened conservatives into joining them by predicting the dissolution of the Union if Frémont was elected. Wall Street brokers and bankers, fearful that such a breakup would upset their financial world, opened their purses for Buchanan. Whigs in the North drifted hesitantly to the Republicans, while in the South they joined the Democrats or the Know-Nothings. Bryant, Longfellow, Whittier, Emerson, and other Northern intellectuals campaigned for Frémont.

Democrats called attention to Frémont's illegitimacy and to his Army court-martial, and hinted that he had been baptized a Catholic. Republicans recalled the nickname Ten Cent Jimmy given Buchanan for having once suggested that American wages be lowered to those of Europe to keep the tariff down. Yet beneath all the billingsgate and ballyhoo there was this time a rift that would not be healed by any conventional gestures of good will after the election. Republicans might parade with squealing fifes and flaring torches, but they would also espouse the sober argument that Lincoln would develop over the next two years: the Founding Fathers had intended an ultimate end to slavery, the Missouri Compromise was an expression of this intent, the best hope for saving the Union was to keep slavery within its present bounds until its gradual abolition.

On the relatively calm Election Day—broken only by riots between Democrats and Know-Nothings in New Orleans and Baltimore—Buchanan carried the country, with 174 electoral votes to 114 for Frémont and 8 (Maryland) for Fillmore. In popular votes Buchanan emerged a minority President with 1,838,169 votes to Frémont's 1,341,364, while Fillmore dragged the Know-Nothings toward oblivion with 874,534. Conservative Whig voters, fearful of disunion, by drifting to

Buchanan and Fillmore had done most to carry the day for the Democrats. Yet the Republicans, ill organized and lacking resources as substantial as those of the Democrats, sensed victory in their defeat. With a few thousand more votes in Pennsylvania and Indiana, they would have carried the electoral college.

The thick, wavy blond hair of the sixty-five-year-old bachelor President-elect had long since thinned and turned white. To emphasize his stature and dignity, he always wore a high collar and a white cravat. A defect in vision made him seem at times to be winking, and to conceal this he adopted the mannerism of keeping his head cocked to one side. In his long Pennsylvania political career this distinguished-looking man had made many reversals of position. After four terms in Congress as a Federalist, he had come out in 1828 as a Jacksonian Democrat against John Quincy Adams. In 1831 Old Hickory, who never wholly trusted him, shipped him out of the country as minister to Russia. In faction-ridden Pennsylvania he eventually became the acknowledged leader of the Democrats. Returning to Congress, he served three terms in the Senate. Yet, in twenty-three years as a legislator, he had never had his name attached to any important bill nor had he taken a significant part in any important debate.

He had early seen slavery as the weak point in American institutions. "Touch the question of slavery seriously," he had written, "and the Union is from that moment dissolved." As President he did not intend to touch it. He had favored the extension of the Missouri Compromise line to the Pacific and had taken a somewhat dim view of the Compromise of 1850. Writing to a friend at that time, he had predicted that in four years "the union will not be in existence as it now exists. There will be two Republics . . . there will be no civil war." Only through consideration for the South, he was convinced, could the Democratic party and the Union be held together.

Buchanan, the President-to-be, considered himself conservative, but his conservatism was nearer timidity. He saw himself as a defender of the Constitution and of states' rights, but he was more a reed bending to the South. Southerners would have nothing to fear from this Northerner in the White House, and Northerners would have little to gain.

His inauguration was one of the most elaborate on record. The courtly bachelor had long had a taste for ceremony. Taking the oath from Chief Justice Taney,

Buchanan wore his "Lancaster suit" of homespun, made for him by a Lancaster, Pennsylvania, tailor, with stars stitched on the coat lining to represent the thirty-one states, the Keystone State being in the center. His uninspired inaugural address was relieved only by his promise to serve a single term. But the ball that followed in the evening was of an expansive elegance limited only by the hard fact that gentlemen's tickets cost ten dollars. Ladies were admitted free, and they preponderated. The ball was held in a building specially erected on Judiciary Square, crude on the outside but sumptuous within. The white ceiling was studded with gold stars, and the walls were hung with red, white, and blue cambric. Three thousand dollars' worth of wine is said to have been consumed, as well as five hundred gallons of oysters and huge quantities of chicken, venison, beef, turkey, pheasant, ham, and lobster. Some congressmen "got so over-excited with wine that they had to be locked up in the upper rooms." Dancing lasted

Because of his fear that a too powerful federal government dominated by Northerners would stifle the South, Chief Justice Roger B. Taney, in the Dred Scott decision, denied to Negroes all basic constitutional rights.

until four in the morning. Brilliant receptions would continue to be a feature of Buchanan's White House sojourn, in contrast to the semimourning of the Pierces.

Buchanan, lacking both courage and executive experience, would for the next four years defer to his Cabinet. Four of the seven offices were occupied by Southerners, with the old and failing Northerner Cass the figurehead Secretary of State. The three dominant Cabinet members were Secretary of the Treasury Howell Cobb, Secretary of the Interior Jacob Thompson, and Attorney General Jeremiah S. Black. The three, with the shrewd and unscrupulous John Slidell of Louisiana as administration leader in the Senate, formed a Directory that would determine administration policy. Cobb, efficient and keen-minded, became the President's chief personal adviser. Cobb was a lawyer, a former Speaker of the House of Representatives, a Georgian aristocrat who, with a thousand slaves on his plantation, disapproved of slavery in principle; the aim of his political life was peace and security for the South. Thompson, a ruthlessly ambitious Southern rights man, was a parvenu, who had started out in North Carolina as a poor boy. He had turned the black earth of Mississippi to gold, becoming the owner of three large plantations. From 1839 to 1851 he had served in Congress. In his opinion slaves were property and should be treated as such. By contrast Attorney General Black was a Northerner, Buchanan's old Pennsylvania friend, self-taught, a self-made lawyer, with a cutting wit, learned, upright, but grim and prejudiced. In the ultimate crisis he would show himself a Unionist.

The Dred Scott decision, which followed only two days after Buchanan had crossed the White House threshold, had been long in the making. Dred, born in Virginia about 1795, had been taken by his master, a St. Louis Army surgeon, to Illinois and to Wisconsin Territory between 1834 and 1838. After returning to Missouri, Dred, ailing and inefficient, grew increasingly burdensome to his owner, who would have been glad to get rid of him. Then in 1846, perhaps at the instigation of a lawyer, Dred and his wife brought suit in circuit court to obtain their freedom.

Had residence on free soil made Dred a free man, or were slaves private property? That was the question tossed from court to court, from the circuit court to the state supreme court and then back again, to the federal district court, and finally, in 1854, to the Supreme Court of the United States. After still more delays, the final argument before the Supreme Court opened in December, 1856. By then it was clear that the case far transcended the fate of a slave whom nobody wanted. The ultimate question that would be decided by the Court was the one that had been so bitterly debated in Congress. Did any legislative body have the power to exclude slavery from the territories? It was a confrontation of North and South on the highest level. As a measure of the case's importance, both sides were represented by several of the country's leading legal lights. Appearing for Dred Scott were Montgomery Blair, of the noted border family and Lincoln's future Postmaster General, and one of the leaders of the American bar, George Ticknor Curtis. On the owner's side were ranged a former Attorney General of the United States, Reverdy Johnson of Maryland; and Senator Henry S. Geyer, the most eminent lawyer in St. Louis.

By early 1857 rumors about the Court's decision were seeping through Washington. Buchanan was informed of the verdict before his inauguration. The Court still met in the small dark basement room in the Capitol where Marshall had pronounced his *McCulloch v. Maryland* decision. On the morning of March 6, the nine black-robed justices, led by shrunken, tremulous Chief Justice Taney, entered the room. Five of the justices in this solemn procession were Southerners by birth and temperament, a sixth was Southern by temperament only. After the crier had opened the session with the tradition-hallowed triple "Oyez," Taney, gathering his papers together in front of him, began to read.

Thirty-one years on the bench had given the Chief Justice the withered aspect of a mummy. His heavily crosshatched face, with its parchment skin and high forehead brushed by straggling hair, seemed dead; only the flashing eyes showed life. The years had also given him the dignity of an institution. Nobody questioned his intellectual ability, his unblemished character, his conscientiousness, his sincerity. A Southerner he remained, but a Southerner who personally found slavery repugnant and who long ago had freed all his own slaves.

For two and a half hours, in a thin reedy voice that trailed away to indistinctness, the Chief Justice read his Court's decision. Two lesser questions were followed by the overshadowing major question: Could a Negro be a citizen, entitled to sue in the federal courts? The Court, with four justices abstaining and two dissenting, ruled that he could not be a citizen. Did Dred's residence on

free soil entitle him to freedom after he had returned to a slave state? The Court held that it did not. As to the wider question of whether Congress had a right to exclude slavery from any territory, Taney and five other justices held that Congress did not have the power and that hence the Missouri Compromise was unconstitutional. The implications of the decision were overwhelming. Outside the free states, slavery had broken its bonds and could advance with the flag. Neither geographical boundaries nor the popular will could stand against it. Squatter sovereignty was as dead as were the great compromises.

Although Scott and his family were freed a few weeks after the Court had ruled against him, the decision set the North into a turmoil of denunciation. Southerners moved from the position that slavery could not be kept *out* of the territories to the assertion that it must be protected *in* them. Northerners and Westerners saw the decision as a Southern ruling, political rather than legal,

and accused Taney of conspiring with Buchanan "to undermine . . . the liberties of the people." Thomas Hart Benton, dying of cancer, wrote that it was "the heaviest political blow that ever fell upon my heart." Lincoln appealed to the Declaration of Independence and the intentions of the Founding Fathers. He would, he said, refuse to obey the judgment "as a political vote." In the end the Dred Scott decision would shatter the authority of the Court for a generation.

What Buchanan as incoming President feared most, what he would most try to avoid while in office, was the secession of the South; and the unsolved Kansas issue troubled his dreams. Governor Geary, who had restored peace to the territory, had shown himself too upright as he attempted to merge the rival Topeka and Lecompton regimes. Lecompton leaders would have none of it or of him. Knowing that they were in the minority, that each month the free-soil settlers and land speculators were moving on Kansas by covered wag-

on, on horseback, and afoot, the Lecomptonites determined to strike for a slave state before it was too late. Southerners regarded Kansas as a symbol. Already there were sixteen free states to fifteen slave, with free Minnesota and Oregon on the threshold of statehood. Kansas seemed necessary, however ill adapted for slavery, to hold the balance, to prove that there could be another slave state.

The Kansas Bogus Legislature passed a bill that rigged the register of voters sufficiently in favor of the proslavery party to insure them a proslavery constitutional convention. Geary vetoed the bill, and it was immediately passed over his veto. The governor's integrity having by this time become galling to Washington, Pierce refused to give him either support or military assistance, and the day Buchanan took office Geary resigned. Buchanan then appointed the Pennsylvania-born Mississippian Robert J. Walker governor. Though a fussy little man, Walker turned out to be both able and honest. Even before his arrival, he realized that climate, cultivation, and the swarms of new settlers would make slavery in Kansas impossible. The great migration of free-soilers had begun, such a preponderance that the Border Ruffians had given up trying to interfere with the newcomers. Even the *Squatter Sovereign* now had a free-soil editor. Walker's aim was to create a free-soil Democratic state.

Undismayed by the rising tide against them, the Lecomptonites continued on their relentless proslavery course, using every chicanery to bar the newer settlers from the voting lists and stopping at no fraud to insure their own victory at the polls. There were 20,000 or so adult males in the territory, but only 9,251 were registered voters, many of them fraudulent. Of these a mere 2,200 appeared at the polls to vote for delegates to the constitutional convention. Antislavery men boycotted the election, calling it a swindle, and refused to put up Free State candidates. Thus unimpeded, the Lecomptonites swept the slate, electing all sixty delegates.

When the convention opened in Lecompton in the autumn, even Buchanan's observers were taken aback by the pugnacious crudity, the complete cynicism, of most

383

of the delegates, three-quarters of whom came from the slave states. The *Kanzas News* correspondent saw them as a set of "broken-down political hacks, demagogues, fire-eaters, perjurers, ruffians, ballot-box stuffers, and loafers." Yet, though the delegates might have been boozy louts, their leaders were shrewd. They and everyone else in Kansas knew that an overwhelming majority of residents wanted a free state. The best counterapproach, they felt, would be to assume slavery—with two hundred slaves already in the territory—as an accomplished fact. One group wanted to adopt a proslavery constitution to be sent directly to Congress. But more subtle minds felt the need for at least a token submission of such a constitution to the people. From Washington Secretary Cobb advised them to submit it to those voters who recognized the Lecompton regime. Finally the delegate leaders agreed to allow selected voters to decide one issue only: whether the constitution should be accepted "with slavery" or "without slavery." If the restricted voters chose slavery, then Kansas would be admitted as a slave state. But even if the people decided in such an election on a constitution without slavery, this would in no way affect the slaves already in Kansas, their status as property being guaranteed in the new constitution. Whatever the public will, there would be no possibility of excluding slavery entirely from the new state.

Northern Democrats were as outraged as Republicans at this blatant repudiation of popular sovereignty. Nineteen of the twenty Kansas editors came out in opposition. The Great Swindle, the Emporia *Kanzas News* called it. Governor Walker hurried east to persuade Buchanan to take a stand against the Lecompton Constitution as being a clear violation of popular sovereignty, the principle to which the Democrats were pledged.

In the South the Lecompton Constitution was hailed as promising the end of abolitionist schemes to cheat the South out of Kansas. Alabama, Mississippi, and South Carolina leaders threatened to secede if the new constitution was not accepted by Congress. Buchanan had promised Walker and others that Kansas would have an opportunity of a fair vote on their constitution. But the aging and irresolute President soon found himself faced with the overbearing persuasions of the Cobb-Thompson-Black Directory in his Cabinet. Finally, in his December, 1857, message to Congress Buchanan, while deploring the country's preoccupation with the Kansas question, upheld the validity of the Lecompton Constitution and urged the voters to make the nonchoice between "with" and "without."

While political clouds swirled over Kansas, an economic storm was brewing that would bring the increasingly feverish prosperity of the decade to a chilling halt. After the years of expanding railroads and mines and factories, of pyramiding values and easy wealth, the North seemed an invincible industrial giant. Suddenly the smoke was gone from factory chimneys, the blast furnaces grew cold, and the streams of hopeful immigrants dried up as swarms of sullen jobless tramped the streets past dead factories and deserted docks.

The Panic of 1857 had its roots in a wider European crisis, but its precipitating factor was the failure of the huge New York branch of the Ohio Life Insurance and Trust Company in August. That initial collapse, compounded by embezzlement, set off a wave of bank failures across the country, marking an end to the speculative fervor of the fifties. Railroads had extended themselves with corrupt extravagance, the land boom had reached its speculative peak in the West, and not only businessmen but merchants and lawyers and doctors were gambling on Wall Street while everyone who could scrape a few dollars together was gambling in land. A conspicuous opulence flourished from Boston

A Negro fruit seller rests on cotton bales piled on a New Orleans levee. The demand for its cotton led the South to consider itself economically invulnerable.

and New York to Charleston and New Orleans. Names like Tiffany took on overtones of luxury, Newport and Saratoga struck new-rich notes of fashion.

Then the bubbles burst—the railroad bubble, the land bubble, the shimmering bubble of eternal prosperity. Compared to that of 1837 and other collapses, the Panic of 1857 was a relatively transitory one. The South with its cotton crop was least affected, Southern banks remaining the most stable in the country. Southerners were quick to see this immunity as a demonstration of the economic superiority of their way of life. Northern industrialism had shown itself a weak-kneed giant after all. Without cotton, Europe and the North could not flourish. One result of the bad times of 1857 and 1858 was to strengthen Southern tendencies to intransigency.

At first Douglas had made no public comment on the Lecompton Constitution, but privately he let it be known that he would stand unalterably on his popular sovereignty principle, that he would never accept less than a fair vote in Kansas, that he held his personal honor and integrity at stake with his principle. "I will show you that I will do what I promised," he told a visitor. "By God, sir, I made Mr. James Buchanan, and by God, sir, I will unmake him!"

Arriving in Washington a few days before the President was to deliver his December address, Douglas had at once called at the White House. The meeting of the two men, neither of whom had ever liked the other, was a historic confrontation: the angry, aggressive Little Giant, smarting from his suspected betrayal; the elderly President, regarding him with stubborn petulance. Douglas advised Buchanan not to recommend the Lecompton Constitution to Congress. When Buchanan—his message in his desk drawer—replied huffily that he had already decided to recommend it, Douglas announced that he would attack it "the moment your message is read." Glaring down at his scowling adversary, Buchanan warned him: "Mr. Douglas, I desire you to remember that no Democrat ever yet differed from an Administration of his own choice without being crushed." And he recalled the fate of two politicians whom President Jackson had driven from the party. "Mr. President," said Douglas, just before turning on his heel, "I wish you to remember that General Jackson is dead."

For the Buchanan Directory the Lecompton Constitution became a shibboleth of party loyalty, and they were confident that they could muster enough Demo-cratic votes to force acceptance by both houses of Congress. Douglas, taking up the challenge, was willing even to enter into a temporary alliance with Seward and the Republicans. The day after the President's message, he took the Senate floor for one of his greatest speeches. With a cold politeness unusual to him, he denounced the Lecompton Constitution and the forthcoming Kansas vote. "If this constitution is to be forced down our throats," he concluded, "in violation of the fundamental principle of free government, under a mode of submission that is a mockery and an insult, I will resist it to the last." As he sat down, the packed galleries rang with applause.

Douglas felt he could best defeat the administration by delaying a House vote on Lecompton until late spring or summer, when he would have succeeded in mobilizing public opinion. Meanwhile the struggle in Kansas continued unabated. On December 21 the Lecompton referendum was held on the new constitution. It was so blatantly fraudulent that most Free State supporters boycotted it completely. By the familiar tactics of false registrations, ballot-box stuffing, and intimidation, the Lecompton regime achieved an apparent vote of 6,226 for the constitution with slavery to 569 votes for the constitution without it. Anticipating a fraudulent election, the acting governor had arranged for a second plebiscite to be held on January 4, in which the Lecompton Constitution might be approved with or without slavery or might be rejected altogether. At this relatively honest election, held without incident, 10,266 free-soilers flocked to the polls to vote against the imposed constitution. Only 138 voters were willing to accept it without slavery, and only 24 with.

Southerners held the December vote to be legal and final. Northerners felt that the January election vindicated them completely. Buchanan, guided by his Directory, accepted the December election. On February 2, 1858, he sent the Lecompton Constitution to Congress with a message urging the immediate admission of Kansas as the sixteenth slave state, "at this moment as much a slave state as Georgia or South Carolina." The bill passed the Senate 33–25, although when the Little Giant made his final speech against it on March 22, possibly the greatest crowd in the Capitol's history flocked to hear him.

To defeat the measure in the House, Douglas needed the votes of only about 20 of the 131 Democratic congressmen to add to those of the Republican opposition—assuming he could also pick up half of the dozen-odd Know-Nothing votes. On these pivotal representatives he used all his dramatic powers of persuasion. The administration in turn used every ounce of political pressure it could muster to hold the waverers in line, employing promises of patronage, threats of retaliation, and even outright bribery. Cobb and Thompson circulated affably among the legislators. Dozens of congressmen were invited to share White House hospitality. So tense did the feeling grow during the debates that one midnight session broke up in fisticuffs. By April, as Republican strength continued to grow, it became increasingly clear to Northern Democratic congressmen that a vote for Lecompton would be a vote for their own political extinction. Senator John J. Crittenden of Kentucky offered an amendment to admit Kansas on condition that the Lecompton Constitution be submitted to the voters for approval or rejection. Twenty-two Democrats supported the measure, and with a wild shout from the galleries it was passed 120 to 112. Lecompton was dead! "This Crittenden substitute carries out those principles to which I have given my life," said Douglas with satisfaction. To the South it was an unacceptable affront. Buchanan and his Directory evolved a face-saving substitute, the English Bill, by which, if Kansans rejected the Lecompton Constitution, the territory could not enter the Union until it had attained the population of a congressional district—about ninety thousand—a level not expected for several years. Although the measure passed both houses and Buchanan signed it, Douglas refused to have any part of it. In the fair and orderly election that followed, Kansas voters rejected the constitution by 11,812 to 1,926.

Though the Lecompton controversy split the Democratic party, it left Douglas the undisputed leader of the Northern Democrats, the potential leader of the free-soilers, and the possible presidential fusion candidate of Northern Democrats and Republicans in 1860. Men like Greeley praised him, urging Eastern Republicans to forget the past. When in July, 1858, the Little Giant arrived back in Chicago, where four years before he had been booed and hissed, he found the streets packed with admirers, while women's handkerchiefs fluttered from every window. Douglas saw his re-election to the Senate that year as a step that would lead him to the White House two years later.

Illinois Republicans were not so ready to forget the past. For them Douglas, despite his stand against the Lecompton Constitution, was still the Southern-applauded champion of popular sovereignty, still the renegade leader who had defended the Dred Scott decision. Since Lincoln's re-entry into politics, the Springfield lawyer had come to be recognized as the leader of the Illinois Republicans. When the Republican state convention met at Springfield in June, the delegates unanimously endorsed Lincoln as "the first and only choice of the Republicans of Illinois for the United States Senate as the successor of Stephen A. Douglas." "I shall have my hands full," Douglas commented when he heard the news in Washington. ". . . if I beat him my victory will be hardly won."

The night following his nomination, in the same Statehouse hall where he had answered Douglas in 1854, Lincoln delivered the address that would become known as his House Divided Speech and that, with its Biblical overtones, would echo across the country. Its basic theme was contained in its opening sentences.

We are now far into the fifth year, since a policy was initiated, with the avowed object, and confident promise, of putting an end to slavery agitation. Under the operation of that policy, that agitation has not only not ceased, but has constantly augmented. In my opinion, it will not cease, until a crisis shall have been reached, and passed. "A house divided against itself cannot stand." I believe this government cannot endure permanently half slave and half free. I do not expect the Union to be dissolved—I do not expect the house to fall—but I do expect it will cease to be divided. It will become all one thing, or all the other. Either the opponents of slavery, will arrest the further spread of it, and place it where the public mind shall rest in the belief that it is in course of ultimate extinction; or its advocates will push it forward, till it shall become alike lawful in all the states, old as well as new, north as well as south.

The rest of the speech fell off from its sonorous beginning. It was unjust in accusing Douglas of conspiring with Pierce, Buchanan, and Taney to extend slavery, and it failed to suggest any practical solution for the slavery enigma. Nevertheless it was a speech of power, establishing Lincoln as a potential national leader. Just before the convention Lincoln had read it to a dozen friends. All were critical, with the exception of Lincoln's law partner, who gave a dissenting verdict. "Deliver that speech as read," Herndon told him, "and it will make you President!"

Douglas was quick to respond. The "house divided" doctrine, he maintained, would mean war between the North and the South. He accused Lincoln of standing for Negro equality and asserted that the American government was "made by the white man, for the white man, to be administered by the white man." Lincoln in his reply took the moral tone of his Peoria Speech. "Let us then," he urged his listeners, "turn this government back into the channel in which the framers of the Constitution originally placed it. Let us discard all this quibbling about this man and the other man—this race and that race and the other race being inferior . . . and unite as one people throughout this land, until we shall once more stand up declaring that all men are created equal."

These speeches by the two rivals marked the opening of the campaign. For the rest of the summer and into the fall they moved across Illinois, speaking almost every day, in remote hamlets as well as cities, journeying by rail, steamboat, horse and buggy, enduring heat, dust, rain, mud, bad food, fly-specked lodgings. Douglas traveled with his secretaries and his beautiful second wife in the relative comfort of his private railroad car when possible, the car festooned with flags and bunting and followed by a flatcar with a brass cannon, which two uniformed men fired off at the Little Giant's approach to each prairie town. Lincoln dogged his trail by day coach—often on the same train—and was on hand to answer the country's foremost orator whenever he spoke, finally challenging him to a series of debates, to which Douglas reluctantly consented.

The Lincoln-Douglas debates, held at a central point in seven congressional districts, were word battles of giants; and politics was still the great American diversion. Crowds converged from the surrounding countryside at each town where the two men spoke. Farmers and their families drove up in carts and hay wagons. Bands and glee clubs took up the echo of the Douglas cannon. In spite of dust and heat, Douglas usually managed to appear dapper, and his wife fresh and charming. Lincoln, for all his success as a lawyer, still looked misfit and ill at ease wearing stiff black clothes and carrying an old carpetbag. Though both men respected each other, tempers frayed at times in the trying weather, Douglas letting slip epithets like "slanderer" and "sneak," while Lincoln spoke of Democratic "fraud" and "forgery."

Slavery was the burning issue of the debates. Douglas expounded his principle of popular sovereignty: each political community should determine its own institutions. Lincoln reduced his argument to the elementary

An unknown wood carver made this figure of Lincoln in his folk-hero garb of top hat and frock coat. The arms and head are movable.

*Prospectors stake the first claim on the silver-rich Comstock
Lode in what is now Nevada in 1859. Henry
Comstock, after whom the lode was named, is at the left.*

premise that no man was good enough to govern another without that other's consent.

At their first debate, lasting three hours under a broiling sun in the treeless public square of Ottawa, Douglas proclaimed that peace and progress depended on the accepting of popular sovereignty and the Dred Scott decision. Endeavoring to remove any abolitionist taint from the Republicans, Lincoln denied wanting to establish "political and social equality between the black and white races." Nevertheless he insisted that the Negro had every man's right to life, liberty, and the pursuit of happiness. Whatever the black man's innate inequalities, "in the right to eat the bread, without leave of anyone else, which his own hand earns, he is my equal, and the equal of Judge Douglas, and the equal of every living man." The way out of the present crisis was to return to the course of Washington and Madison and Jefferson, to restrict the expansion of slavery with a view to eventually bringing about its complete extinction.

At Freeport, in reply to a series of questions from Douglas, Lincoln admitted that the South was entitled to the Fugitive Slave Act, that a territory had the right to admission as a slave state if the people so voted in a fair election, and that he was not pledged to abolish slavery in the District of Columbia or to prohibit the domestic slave trade. He reiterated that he wished to see slavery placed on the road to gradual extinction. In turn, he asked Douglas how he could reconcile popular sovereignty with the Dred Scott decision.

Douglas had already answered that question, but Lincoln wanted the answer plain. The Little Giant did not hesitate, whatever the effect he might have on the South. In what came to be known as the Freeport Doctrine he stated that though by the Supreme Court's decision slavery could not theoretically be barred from a territory, practically it could be prohibited if people, through local legislation, refused to grant it protection.

Under the stern discipline of the debates Lincoln

continued to grow in confidence and in vision. "The real issue in this controversy," he was able to say in his last debate, "—the one pressing upon every mind, is the sentiment on the part of one class that looks upon the institution of slavery *as a wrong*, and of another class that *does not* look upon it as a wrong. The sentiment that contemplates the institution of slavery in this country as a wrong is the sentiment of the Republican party. . . . Judge Douglas . . . contends that whatever community wants slaves has a right to have them. So they have if it is not a wrong. But if it is a wrong, he cannot say that people have a right to do a wrong."

On a raw and rainy Election Day the Republican candidates managed to poll 4,000 more votes than their opponents, but the districting so favored the Democrats that they were able to capture the legislature. In the later balloting by the state legislature for United States senator, Douglas was elected, with 54 votes to 46 for Lincoln. On election night Lincoln trudged home after he had learned the results. "The path had been worn pig-backed and was slippery," he wrote six years later. "My foot slipped from under me, knocking the other out of the way; but I recovered and said to myself, 'It's a slip and not a fall.'"

Even as the 1858 political thunderclouds became charged with electricity, the country grew, the West expanded. Already the Territories of Minnesota and Oregon were knocking on the door of statehood; they were admitted to the Union in 1858 and 1859 respectively. Gold was discovered in the Pike's Peak region and in Nevada's Comstock Lode, and even as Douglas and Lincoln debated, adventurers and the unemployed of the East flocked to Colorado and to Virginia City, Nevada, in new gold and silver rushes.

The 1858 congressional elections were a rout for Buchanan. Republicans swept New England and maintained their hold on Michigan and Wisconsin. Lecompton was the dominant issue. Republicans and Douglas Democrats triumphed in Ohio, Illinois, and New York. The administration lost 18 House seats, and with them, control of the House. With the rise of the Republicans came an increase in radical strength in the South, the shrill and passionate voices of fiery-tongued leaders, like Virginia's Edmund Ruffin and South Carolina's Robert Barnwell Rhett and Alabama's William L. Yancey, raised for secession. In the North Seward, whose tongue at times ran away with him, attacked slaveholders as well as slavery, and in one address he

spoke of the "irrepressible conflict," which must make the United States "either entirely a slaveholding nation, or entirely a free-labor nation."

Meanwhile, after a period of obscurity, in which he had lectured and raised funds in New England and New York and slipped back for further violence in Kansas and Missouri, John Brown re-emerged in May, 1858, in the small Canadian town of Chatham, in present-day Ontario. For twenty years he had nursed a bloody fantasy of launching a slave uprising. He felt the time had come to act. As he explained it to his audience of eleven whites and thirty-four colored men in the schoolhouse of Chatham, he intended to secure a mountain redoubt somewhere in the Appalachians. From there with a band of armed men he would strike into the plantation areas, liberating slaves and recruiting the ablest of them as soldiers to build up a force sufficient to withstand even the assault of federal troops. Brown proposed to establish his own state with its own government to wage war against the Southern states and their slaveholders. For, he told Emerson on a fund-raising visit to Concord, it would be better for a whole generation to die violently than for slavery to endure.

Brown planned to strike his first blow at Harpers Ferry, Virginia, a village of two gaunt streets at the edge of the Blue Ridge Mountains above the sparkling junction of the Potomac and Shenandoah rivers. Not only did this hamlet of two thousand inhabitants—including eight hundred Negroes—seem the gateway to the South but it was also the site of a small federal arsenal that included a rifle works. Brown aimed to take the arsenal in a sudden assault, then to send agents to enlist the slaves of the nearby plantations. The Negroes, he was convinced, would flock to his standard. He then intended to move his avenging army of God south along the line of the Appalachians to Tennessee and even Alabama, raiding the slave country on either side and adding to his strength in men, supplies, and hostages. "When I strike," he predicted, "the bees will swarm."

In the summer of 1859, Brown rented an isolated farmhouse five miles from Harpers Ferry. By autumn he had assembled twenty-one followers there, including three of his sons, a daughter, and a daughter-in-law. For weapons he had brought in fifteen heavy boxes of "tools," containing 198 Sharps rifles plus 950 pikes with which to arm the slaves he freed. On the night of October 16, with seventeen white men, five Negroes, and a one-horse wagon loaded with pikes, Brown set out to

seize the arsenal. There was no alert. A sleepy night watchman was effortlessly overpowered, and the walled arsenal was occupied without incident. Brown at once sent out parties to seize hostages and slaves. They returned with an indignant, bewildered planter, Colonel Lewis Washington, the great-grandnephew of the first President, and four of his slaves. The colonel's neighbor, John Allstadt, with six slaves, was also brought in, and the prisoners were assembled in the unlighted brick enginehouse, where the arsenal's fire-fighting apparatus was stored. The captured slaves were informed that they were free, but they showed no interest in their freedom, standing mute, apathetic, and fearful. When Brown was asked what he was trying to do, the grim leader replied: "Free the slaves." And when asked on what authority, he snapped back, "By the authority of God Almighty."

As the snail-paced hours moved past midnight, Brown's revolt seemed a squib lacking any spark to set it off. At 1:25 A.M. the Wheeling-Baltimore night express was flagged down short of the Harpers Ferry station by a hotel clerk, who informed the engineer that the Baltimore and Ohio bridge on the other side of the station was held by armed men. Two of the train crew who investigated were fired on. Passengers, thronging the station in bewilderment, thought it might be a railroad strike. More shots followed, and a freed Negro was brought in dying, struck down by one of the trigger-quick raiders. The local doctor who came to tend the dying man was the first to raise the alarm, tolling the bell on the Lutheran church, then riding to Charlestown to summon the militia. In the drizzling gray morning, groups of armed locals began to deploy around the arsenal. Those gunsmiths and arsenal workers who had not heard the news reported for work to find themselves prisoners. For some reason Brown, still controlling the bridge, later allowed the night express to proceed.

By noon the Jefferson Guards had arrived from Charlestown and seized the bridge, while other volunteers occupied the heights above Harpers Ferry. Brown was surrounded, and he knew that the bees were not going to swarm. Twice he attempted to negotiate a truce, but his enemies killed the first man sent out with a white flag and mortally wounded one of Brown's sons making a second attempt. Late in the afternoon a company of railroad workers broke into the arsenal yard from the rear and penned the raiders and a handful of captives in the fortresslike enginehouse. It had been a

bloody day: the town's mayor had been shot down, while Brown had lost his best men and seen two sons fatally wounded. In the Eastern cities headlines proclaimed a "Negro Insurrection at Harpers Ferry." The mayor of Washington, believing reports of seven hundred white and Negro raiders occupying the arsenal, stationed guards on every road to the Capital, and Buchanan ordered three companies of regular artillery and the ninety-odd marines of the Washington Barracks to Harpers Ferry under the command of Colonel Robert E. Lee. Lee, with Lieutenant J. E. B. Stuart, arrived at the arsenal late the second night, but to avoid injuring the eleven hostages, decided not to attack the enginehouse until morning.

At sunrise Lee sent Stuart to confer with Brown, offering to protect the raiders and hand them over to the

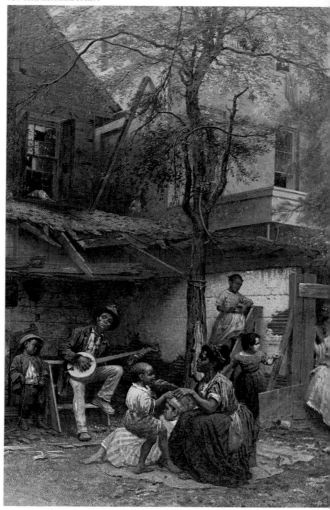

Carefree slaves are depicted in a detail from Eastman Johnson's 1859 painting Old Kentucky Home—*a version of Negro life that did not displease Southerners.*

proper legal authorities if they would surrender. Brown, through a crack in the massive door, answered that he would surrender only if he and his raiders were given a safe head start from pursuers. Cutting Brown short, Stuart signaled with his cap, and Lee's storming party attacked, battering down the door as the defenders fired through improvised loopholes. It was all over in a minute, with two marines dead and two raiders bayoneted. Colonel Washington calmly pointed out Brown, who was kneeling and firing, and an officer thrust at him vainly with a dress sword, then beat him unconscious with the hilt. Ten of Brown's party had been killed or fatally wounded, five were taken prisoner, and the rest escaped, some for good.

Brown went on trial in Charlestown a week after his capture. His one hope was to plead insanity, but this he refused to allow his lawyers to do. Still weak from his wounds, the old man was placed on a cot in the courtroom and lay wrapped in a blanket, sometimes closing his eyes but never losing his dignity. Inevitably he was found guilty. When asked if he had anything to say, he rose slowly from his cot, and speaking with great distinctness, addressed himself not so much to the court as to posterity, in a five-minute apologia, concluding:

Now, if it is deemed necessary that I should forfeit my life for the furtherance of the ends of justice, and mingle my blood further with the blood of my children and with the blood of millions in this slave country whose rights are disregarded by wicked, cruel and unjust enactments, I say, let it be done.

A month later it was done. The intervening weeks fortified Brown with the stern consolation of martyrdom. Serene and courageous, he showed neither grief for his sons nor fear of death. Many, even in the South, appealed to Virginia's Governor Henry A. Wise to commute Brown's death sentence to life imprisonment on grounds of insanity and pointed out that to execute him would be to make him an abolitionist saint. But the governor, bemused by immediate political advantages, not only refused but abetted the legend that a Northern conspiracy lay behind the Harpers Ferry raid.

At noon on his bright, warm execution day the condemned man, flanked by riflemen and seated on his coffin, his arms bound at the elbows, was hauled in a furniture wagon from the Charlestown jail to an open field where the gallows had been erected. There, against the serene background of the Blue Ridge in a hollow square of Virginia militiamen, which included the Richmond actor John Wilkes Booth, and a company of red-shirted cadets from the Virginia Military Institute with their professor, Thomas J. Jackson—later to be called Stonewall—Brown climbed down from his coffin and briskly mounted the thirteen steps to the platform. After shaking hands with the jailer and the sheriff, he stood erect and motionless as a white linen hood was slipped over his head and a noose placed round his neck. For eight interminable minutes he stood there while late-arriving troops marched into place. Then at last the sheriff's axe flashed, the rope holding the trap parted, and John Brown's body dangled at the rope's end. "So perish all such enemies of Virginia," V.M.I. Colonel J. T. L. Preston's clipped military voice rang out. "All such enemies of the Union! All foes of the human race!"

At the hour of Brown's execution, across the North bells tolled, flags were lowered to half-mast, minute guns echoed, buildings stood draped in black. Thousands flocked to memorial meetings. Seward had denounced the raid as an "act of sedition and treason." Lincoln, on a speaking tour of Kansas when he heard of Brown's death sentence, had commented: "We cannot object, even though he agreed with us in thinking slavery wrong. That cannot excuse violence, bloodshed and treason." But the voice of the moderates was drowned in the blood of the martyr as the crazy venture at Harpers Ferry became transformed into a holy cause. Emerson proclaimed Brown a "new saint," who made "the gallows glorious like a cross." Thoreau saw the dead man as an angel of light. Within weeks the legend solidified as it spread. Lithograph portraits of Brown proliferated. The intransigent South had given the abolitionists their religion, Mrs. Stowe had given them their Bible, and now John Brown had become their martyr.

However futile and insane the Harpers Ferry raid, it was profoundly disturbing to the South, rousing the never wholly suppressed fear of the bondsman, which lurked beneath the boldly proclaimed doctrine of slavery as a positive good. Brown's apotheosis was seen as an indication of the North's desire to destroy the South. More and more Southerners considered themselves as living in a beleaguered fortress, and more and more secessionist sentiment grew. Young Southern men withdrew from Northern colleges. Hatred and suspicion lumped the Republicans with the abolitionists under the label the Black Republican party.

With the dawning 1860, its tension marked by increasingly angry debates in the House and Senate, presidential hopes also dawned. Seward, demonstrating a singularly conciliatory attitude to the South, saw himself as a "moderate" Republican candidate. Douglas felt that his leadership would give the Democrats their last chance of uniting the party. Vice President Breckinridge, who lived next door to Douglas in Washington, embodied the hopes of the Southern Democrats. Lincoln, the Illinois leader, had not so much as hinted at any wish to be a candidate. "I must, in candor, say I do not think I am fit for the Presidency," he wrote to an editor friend. Then, in February, he spoke at Cooper Union in New York, sponsored by the Young Men's Central Republican Union. Ostensibly one of a series of lectures "for the general education and enlightenment of the public," it was organized by a group of Republicans—among them Horace Greeley—to prevent the nomination of Seward.

In spite of a heavy snowstorm a crowd of fifteen hundred gathered at Cooper Union to hear the man from Illinois. Lincoln, ill at ease, spoke at first with awkward shrillness until his nervousness disappeared. Then he swept his audience with him. He had prepared his speech carefully. In essence it was a plea for toleration. But would the Southerners believe that the Republican party had peaceful intentions? Lincoln was afraid that they would not, since nothing short of the admission of the rightfulness of slavery would satisfy them. "All they ask, we could readily grant if we thought slavery right," he admitted; "all we ask, they could as readily grant, if they thought it wrong. Their thinking it right, and our thinking it wrong, is the precise fact upon which depends the whole controversy. Thinking it right, as they do, they are not to blame for desiring its full recognition, as being right; but thinking it wrong, as we do, can we yield to them?"

"If our sense of duty forbids this," he concluded, "then let us stand by our duty fearlessly and effectively. . . . Let us have faith that right makes might, and in that faith let us, to the end, dare to do our duty as we understand it."

As the tall speaker finally ended, men and women sprang cheering to their feet and pushed forward to grasp his hand. From that moment Abraham Lincoln was considered a Republican candidate for President. He himself sensed and responded to the mood. When his Illinois friend Senator Lyman Trumbull asked if he really thought himself a candidate, he admitted wryly, " . . . the taste *is* in my mouth a little."

Unobtrusively Lincoln began writing letters, making contacts, lining up what delegates he could for the Republican National Convention in May. A month before the start of the convention the Democrats held their convention in Charleston, with Douglas towering above all the other candidates. If the Democratic party could remain united, with Douglas as candidate it would have every chance of winning. But the South had been alienated, and the whole weight of the Buchanan administration was directed to block the Little Giant. Seven Southern states warned that they would withdraw if the party platform did not demand a congressional code protecting slavery in the territories. Jefferson Davis told Douglas that if he wanted the nomination he must repudiate popular sovereignty and agree to a slave code. Douglas refused to budge from the principles of the Compromise of 1850.

The convention's platform committee split, bringing in two reports. One called for a slave code; the other, popular sovereignty in the territories. Yancey, the orator for Southern independence, demanded that the convention acknowledge slavery as a positive good. Senator George E. Pugh of Ohio pronounced the demand intolerable. Passions rose too high for compromise. When the convention refused to approve a slave-code resolution, delegates from nine Southern states stalked out of the hall. Douglas could not obtain the necessary two-thirds majority from the rump convention, and his followers refused to consider a compromise candidate, so the delegates adjourned, to meet again in Baltimore in June. Meanwhile the Constitutional Union party, made up largely of elderly former Whigs and of Know-Nothings, nominated John Bell of Tennessee for President and the aging Edward Everett for Vice President in the forlorn hope of occupying the middle ground between Republicans and Democrats.

A week before the Republican National Convention met in Chicago, the Illinois state convention had endorsed Lincoln's candidacy with enthusiasm so overwhelming that it collapsed a section of the canvas roof. One of Lincoln's more astute backers arranged to have Lincoln's bearded country cousin, John Hanks, and a friend march down the aisle with two weather-beaten, flag-decked fence rails and a huge banner inscribed: "Abraham Lincoln. The Rail Candidate For President in 1860. Two Rails From a Lot of 3,000 Made in 1830 by Thomas Hanks and Abe Lincoln—Whose Father Was the First Pioneer of Macon County." Though the banner was inaccurate and the rails spurious, the tableau was a publicity stroke to rival "Old Hickory," "Tippecanoe," and log cabins. From that moment the successful lawyer was transformed into the humble man of pioneer virtues, "The Rail Splitter."

Chicago, a bustling, expanding city of one hundred and ten thousand inhabitants, with its fifteen railroads, fifty-six churches, and a thousand saloons, was a happy convention choice for the buoyant, expansive Republicans. To them the very air smelled of victory. Among the contenders only Lincoln was free of scars of party strife. Seward, the favored candidate, was marked as a radical by his indiscreet phrases. Not only was he opposed by the powerful Greeley but by many a leader who felt that such a man could not carry the party to victory. Salmon Chase, for all his record in the Senate

This 1861 detail, from a larger drawing, of Lincoln cogitating in a somewhat ungainly pose is by A. J. Volck, a Baltimore caricaturist who favored the South.

and as governor of Ohio, was more radical than Seward, more stubborn, and less liked. Simon Cameron, Pennsylvania boss and Buchanan's old associate, had a murky political reputation. Supreme Court Justice John McLean was too old. Conservative Governor Edward Bates of Missouri had once associated with the Know-Nothings. Lincoln was fortunate in being less well known, in having acquired fewer enemies. He was equally fortunate in his campaign manager, the three-hundred-pound Judge David Davis, a Falstaffian man, rich, unscrupulous, and dedicated. He took charge of the Lincoln forces in Chicago, marshaling the delegates, persuading other delegations that Lincoln was the "available" candidate who "excited no hates anywhere." Davis traded political horses freely and made whatever deals he felt essential. Among his secret bargains was the promise to Cameron of a place in the Cabinet. Lincoln telegraphed from Springfield: "I authorize no bargains and will be bound by none." But Davis in the sweat of battle shrugged it off. "Lincoln ain't here," he grunted, "and don't know what we have to meet."

The convention was held in the Wigwam, a vast pine-board structure—the largest auditorium in the country, Chicagoans boasted—built for the occasion to hold ten thousand people. Davis had thousands of admission tickets forged, and when balloting began, packed the galleries with Lincoln supporters.

The convention opened on May 16. Two days were expended in routine business and in adopting a platform. Playing down the slavery issue as much as possible, the platform acknowledged the right of each state to regulate its own domestic institutions, but attacked as criminal any reopening of the slave trade, opposed popular sovereignty, and demanded the admission of Kansas as a free state. Not until the third day did the balloting begin. Two hundred and thirty-three votes were required for nomination. On the first ballot Seward led with 173½ votes, then came Lincoln with 102, Cameron with 50½, Chase with 49, and Bates with 48. On the second ballot Seward gained 11 more votes, but this time Lincoln with 181 was only 3½ behind him. Cameron had dropped out by arrangement with Davis, Chase was down to 43½, and Bates to 35. Lincoln's partisans, watching the tide turn, were confident that the third ballot would carry him through, but at the roll call's end he still lacked a vote and a half. Then, in a flurry of bobbing heads, the stuttering chairman of the

Ohio delegation announced that his state had shifted four of its votes to Lincoln.

The galleries exploded at the stammered words. A cannon on the Wigwam's roof blasted off a salute, and bells pealed all over the city as telegraphs flashed the news across the country. The nomination of the former Democrat Senator Hannibal Hamlin of Maine as the vice-presidential candidate was a scarcely heeded anti-climax. "Well," said Pennsylvania Judge W. D. Kelley afterward as he walked down Eighth Street with Carl Schurz, the German-born Republican leader from Wisconsin, "we might have done a more brilliant thing, but we could certainly not have done a better thing."

When the Democratic convention resumed in Baltimore, it at once engaged in arguments over the conditions under which the Southerners present would be accepted as qualified delegates. When the Southerners withdrew in disgust, the convention chose Douglas as its candidate. The Southern seceders also convened in Baltimore, and reinforced by a few Buchanan supporters from the North, nominated Vice President Breckinridge as their candidate on a platform of positive protection of slavery.

Beneath the ballyhoo of the campaign lay a sense of impending doom. The country was, in Douglas' opinion, "in more danger now than at any moment since I have known anything of public life." Republican Wide-Awakes marched by torchlight wearing oilcloth capes and forage caps and carrying rails. The "Bell Ringers" sounded for Bell and Everett. Douglas men called themselves Union Sentinels. But as the summer came to an end, it became more and more apparent that the split in the Democratic party had made Lincoln's election inevitable. Early elections in Maine, Vermont, Pennsylvania, and Indiana confirmed the trend. Douglas admitted to his secretary that Lincoln would be the next President, and then courageously went South to defend the Union he loved. In city after city he spoke until his body sagged and his voice grew hoarse. Southerners listened coldly as he tried to convince them that a Republican victory would be no justification for breaking up the Union.

Lincoln stayed in Springfield, neither speechmaking nor campaigning. Yet he received a higher electoral college total than his three rivals combined: 180 votes to 72 for Breckinridge, 39 for Bell, and only 12 for Douglas. Breckinridge carried the Solid South, Bell the border states, Lincoln the North and the West, leaving only Missouri and New Jersey for Douglas. In the popular voting, however, Lincoln was a minority victor, receiving 1,866,452 votes to 1,376,957 for Douglas, 849,781 for Breckinridge, and 588,879 for Bell.

In the four-month interregnum between Lincoln's election and his inauguration, the structure of the republic seemed to disintegrate. The old Congress met for the last time in December. Buchanan, torn between his sympathy for the South and his loyalty to the Union, asserted in his annual message that a state did not have the right to secede and that the federal government did not have the right to prevent it. He suggested a new constitutional convention that would frame an amendment guaranteeing the right of slavery in the states and territories where it existed.

Lincoln was ready to tolerate slavery where it did exist and to accept the Fugitive Slave Law but refused to make any concession to slavery in the territories. "Let there be no compromise on the question of extending slavery," he wrote. The President-elect spent the interregnum months in Springfield, silent on the major issues, haggard from the importunities of seekers after office and favors, who arrived on every train. In a gesture of unity he chose his Cabinet from his defeated rivals: Seward, who still considered himself the head of the Republican party, as Secretary of State; Chase as Secretary of the Treasury; Bates as Attorney General; and, against his better judgment, Cameron as Secretary of War.

Lincoln's election roused the South to a frenzy of secessionist sentiment. Southerners took to wearing the blue cockade of secession in their hats or their buttonholes. In Charleston the Stars and Stripes was replaced by the red-starred State Rights flag and the palmetto emblem. Regional pride found additional support throughout the South in the belief that secession would be bloodless. Yet Unionist sentiment persisted, particularly in the border states. North Carolina and Tennessee voted against a secessionist convention. Arkansas, Missouri, Kentucky, Maryland, and Virginia held back. Nevertheless, as often happens in times of crisis, the initiative remained with the radicals.

South Carolina was the first state to strike, the legislature calling a convention for mid-December. Already the two South Carolina senators had resigned, along with most federal judges and officials. On December 20 South Carolina seceded. Jubilant crowds thronged the streets of Charleston, cannon boomed, bands played,

396

OUR COUNTRY'S FLAG HAS BEEN INSULTED!
REBELLION HAS BEEN INAUGURATED!
INVASION OF THE CAPITAL IS THREATENED!

FREEMEN, RALLY

PATRIOTS OF MARSHALL COUNTY, are called to meet at Lacon, on Saturday the 20th inst., at 1 o'clock P. M., to organize a Volunteer Company, to be tendered to the Government to support the *Constitution* and the *Laws*, in answer to the President's call.

"To Arms, to Arms ye Braves—
Our God and our Country."

Lacon, April 18th, A. D. 1861.

and church bells rang as if in victory, and everywhere the palmetto flag appeared. THE UNION IS DISSOLVED! the Charleston *Mercury* blazoned in its largest headlines. Mississippi seceded on January 9th, Florida on the 10th, Alabama on the 11th, Georgia on the 19th, Louisiana a week later, and Texas on February 1st.

On February 4, delegates from the first six seceding states met in Montgomery to adopt a constitution for the Confederate States of America. Five days later they elected Jefferson Davis president and Alexander Stephens vice president. Davis was at his Mississippi plantation when he received the news and arrived in Montgomery on the evening of the 16th. To the cheering crowd that met him at the railroad station he announced: "Our separation from the old Union is complete. No compromise and no reconstruction can now be entertained."

Buchanan, old and weary of office, found himself faced with a divided Cabinet as well as a divided country. Cobb, Thompson, and the peculating Secretary of War, John B. Floyd, stood for the right of secession, while Attorney General Jeremiah Black broke from the Directory to join Cass and his Unionist colleagues. In October, 1860, the ancient General in Chief Winfield Scott recommended that the three defense works in Charleston Harbor—Castle Pinckney and Forts Moultrie and Sumter—be reinforced against possible attack. During November Major Robert Anderson, in charge of the forts, wrote repeatedly for additional troops and supplies. Cobb, Thompson, and Floyd insisted that reinforcement would be a provocative action. When Cass endorsed Anderson's request, Buchanan held that the interests of the country did not demand it. Cass quit, and in a surprising turnabout the President then replaced him with Black and appointed the passionate Unionist Edward M. Stanton to take Black's place in the Attorney General's office.

Fort Moultrie and Castle Pinckney being in his opinion indefensible, Major Anderson withdrew his small garrison to Fort Sumter in the middle of the harbor. At the next Cabinet meeting Floyd angrily denounced the "unfortunate move" as making war inevitable and recommended that the garrison be withdrawn completely from Charleston Harbor. While Buchanan vacillated, Floyd resigned, ostensibly as a protest but actually because his financial irregularities were catching up with him. With his going, the Unionists found themselves in control of the Cabinet where the Southern Di-

rectory had so long held sway. Bolstered by Black and Stanton, Buchanan at last faced the challenge. To South Carolina's demand that the nation's forces be removed from Charleston Harbor, he replied: "This I cannot do; this I will not do." Major Anderson would remain and Sumter would be defended "against hostile attacks from whatever quarter they may come."

On February 11, Lincoln left for Washington and his inauguration. The day before, he had stopped in at his old law office and told Herndon: "I am sick of office-holding already, and I shudder when I think of the tasks that are still ahead." Only seventy-two years had elapsed—there were still those who could remember the day as children—since Washington had left Mount Vernon in his coach for his inauguration as the first President of the republic. One could easily imagine him—in his silver-buckled shoes, knee breeches, blue coat, ceremonial sword, and powdered wig—reproduced in miniature in Meissen porcelain. Lincoln in somber black, wearing a stovepipe hat, the fine lines of his chin obscured by a sprouting beard, was of another age, a genre figure that might have been—that indeed would be—modeled in clay by John Rogers for one of his statuary groups. Several hundred of the President-elect's townsmen—among them Judge Davis in a white silk hat—had gathered in a cold morning rain at the small brick Great Western Station to see him off. Standing on the rear platform of his special train, looking at the familiar faces under the up-tilted umbrellas, his dark face creased with melancholy, he spoke at last:

My friends, no one, not in my situation, can appreciate my feeling of sadness at this parting. To this place, and the kindness of these people I owe everything. Here I have lived a quarter of a century, and have passed from a young to an old man. Here my children have been born, and one is buried. I now leave, not knowing when, or whether ever, I may return, with a task before me greater than that which rested upon Washington. Without the assistance of that Divine Being who ever attended him, I cannot succeed. With that assistance I cannot fail. Trusting in Him who can go with me, and remain with you and be everywhere for good, let us confidently hope that all will yet be well. To His care commending you, as I hope in your prayers you will commend me, I bid you an affectionate farewell.

Slowly the train pulled out of the station in the rain, carrying the sad-faced man from the sight of Springfield to his unknown and perilous destiny, the sixteenth President, perhaps the last President of the United States.

The Last Look at Peace

Like most people in most times, the majority of Americans in the 1850's were more preoccupied with their own problems than with the momentous issues of state. While politicians fulminated over the morality of slavery, while violence broke out sporadically in the territories and legislation of far-reaching import was fought through Congress, individual citizens tended their individual concerns. Farmers raised their crops, New England factories hummed, railroads were planned and built, sailors went to sea, and settlers cleared Western lands. Children did their chores and probably grumbled, countryfolk helped erect their neighbors' houses and later danced to the fiddle, swains courted their sweethearts, city dwellers attended plays—and not always *Uncle Tom's Cabin*. War was almost unthinkable.

On the next few pages are pictures of America and Americans made by daguerreotype and other photographic processes just before the Civil War.

OVERLEAF: *This scene of a rude but tranquil settlement on the Mississippi River called Skipwith's Landing—a name now vanished—was recorded by the pioneer camera.*

METROPOLITAN MUSEUM OF ART, WHITTELSEY FUND, 1955; ABOVE: GEORGE EASTMAN HOUSE, ROCHESTER

Despite the foreshadowing of armed conflict, the cycle
of life, with its personal involvements, joys, and
sorrows, continued to turn, as shown in the albumlike
pictures of a people still at peace. At extreme
right is a portrait of Caesar, the last Negro slave in New
York State, made long after he obtained his freedom.

*Left, students at their lessons in a New England girls'
school, about 1855. Above, wives of New Bedford whaling
captains. The lonely vigil, which was their traditional
lot, would soon be shared by women throughout the nation
when men of the North and South joined battle.*

OVERLEAF: *With war declared, the 52nd Illinois—called
the Lincoln—Regiment arouses home-state patriotism as it parades with its band through the town of Elgin.*

Acknowledgments & Index

The Editors appreciate the generous assistance provided by many individuals and institutions during the preparation of this book. They especially wish to thank the following:

Abby Aldrich Rockefeller Folk Art Collection, Williamsburg: Marguerite Gignilliat, Mrs. Helen Turvey

American Antiquarian Society, Worcester: Mrs. Gordon Marshall, Jr.

Dr. George M. Anderson, Baltimore

Anne S. K. Brown Military Collection, Brown University Library, Providence: Richard Harrington

Bancroft Library, University of California, Berkeley: John Barr Tompkins

Berry-Hill Galleries, Inc., New York City

Mr. and Mrs. John E. Chance, Lafayette, Louisiana

Chicago Historical Society

Cincinnati Art Museum: Betty Zimmerman

Cincinnati Historical Society: Richard Haupt, Mrs. Lee Jordan, Mrs. Jane Sikes

Corcoran Gallery of Art, Washington, D.C.: Mrs. Ralph Phillips, Mrs. Rosemary Jones

Denver Public Library: Mrs. Alys Freeze

Department for Defense Information, Washington, D.C.: Betty Sprigg

Department of the Navy, Naval History Division, Washington, D.C.: Henry Vadnais, Capt. F. Kent Loomis, Lt. Thomas Quigley

E. F. Fisher, Brighton, Michigan

Franklin D. Roosevelt Library, Hyde Park, New York: Elizabeth Drewry, James Whitehead, Mrs. Anne Morris

Frick Art Reference Library, New York City

Edgar William and Bernice Chrysler Garbisch, New York City

Mrs. Mary Noble Welleck Garretson, Scarsdale, New York

George Eastman House, Rochester, New York: Robert Bretz

Henry Francis du Pont Winterthur Museum, Wilmington: Ian Quimby, Mrs. Helen Schlatter, Mrs. Beatrice Taylor, Helen Belknap

Historical Society of Pennsylvania, Philadelphia: J. D. Kilbourne, Mrs. O. MacDonald, M. Kenin

Library of Congress, Washington, D.C.: Milton Kaplan, Virginia Daiker, Mrs. Renata Shaw, Walter W. Ristow, Richard Ladd

Mr. and Mrs. Screven Lorillard, Far Hills, New Jersey

Maryland Historical Society, Baltimore

Mercantile Library, St. Louis: Mrs. Elizabeth Kirchner

Metropolitan Museum of Art, New York City: Margaret Nolan, Mrs. Colta Ives, Harriet Cooper

Mr. and Mrs. J. William Middendorf II, New York City

Missouri Historical Society, St. Louis

Arthur N. Miyazawa, Tokyo

Museum of the City of New York: A. K. Baragwanath, Mrs. Henriette Beal

Museum of Fine Arts, Boston: Mrs. St. John Smith, Mrs. Wendy Topkins, Mrs. Wendy Goodell, Anne Parker

National Archives, Washington, D.C.: Albert Leisinger, Jr.

New-York Historical Society, New York City: Carolyn Scoon, Wilson Duprey, Martin Leifer, Thomas Dunnings

New York Public Library, New York City: Mrs. Maud D. Cole, Mrs. Philomena Houlihan, Elizabeth Roth

New York State Historical Association, Cooperstown: Sybil Frank

Beaumont and Nancy Newhall, Rochester, New York

Old Print Shop, New York City: Robert Harley

Old Sturbridge Village, Massachusetts: Etta Falkner

Rhode Island Historical Society, Providence: John Kirk, Mrs. Clifford Monahon, Clarkson Collins, Mrs. Lawrence Tilley

Smithsonian Institution, Washington, D.C.: Peter Welsh, Anne Serio

Suffolk Museum, Stony Brook, New York

Wakefield Historical Society, Massachusetts: Ruth Woodbury

Yale University Art Gallery, New Haven: Caroline Rollins, Egbert Begemann, Mrs. Ann Logan

Yale University Library, New Haven: Dale Roylance, Alexander O. Vietor, Mrs. Margit Kaye

Maps by Cal Sacks

The Editors also make grateful acknowledgment for permission to use material from the following works:

Documents Illustrative of the History of the Slave Trade to America edited by Elizabeth Donnan. Copyright © 1935 by Carnegie Institution of Washington as Publication No. 409. The news items from the Charleston *Courier* on pages 322–23 reprinted by permission of the Carnegie Institution of Washington

Military Medicine, April, 1928, issue. Official journal of the Association of Military Surgeons of the United States, Washington, D.C. The letter from Dr. Ephraim McDowell on page 246 reprinted by permission of the Association of Military Surgeons of the United States

The Papers of Thomas Jefferson edited by Julian P. Boyd. Copyright © 1952 by Princeton University Press. The letter from Thomas Jefferson on page 96 reprinted by permission of the Princeton University Press

Acknowledgment for assistance is also made to the following sources:

Chicago Historical Society. The handwritten note by John Brown on page 335 made available by the Chicago Historical Society

Slavery in the South edited by Harvey Wish. Copyright © 1964 by Farrar, Straus and Company, Inc., New York. An accurate text was provided by this source for the excerpt from *The Confessions of Nat Turner* on pages 328–30.

414